Discovering Irish Origins Using the Records of Ireland

By Dwight A. Radford

Getting Them Over the Water—An Irish Immigration Strategies Series, V.2

Published by Family Roots Publishing Co., LLC
PO Box 1682
Orting, WA 98360-1682
www.FamilyRootsPublishing.com

Library of Congress Control Number: 2021930062

Paperback ISBN: 978-1-62859-295-5;
eBook ISBN: 978-1-62859-296-2
Item# FR0152

Printed in the United States of America

Recommended Citation:
Radford, Dwight A., *Discovering Irish Origins Using the Records of Ireland.*
Orting, WA: Family Roots Publishing Co., LLC, 2021.

Other volumes currently in this series:

V.1: Radford, Dwight A., *American Scots-Irish Research—Strategies and Sources
in the Quest for Ulster-Scots Origins.* Orting, WA: Family Roots Publishing Co.,
LLC, 2020.

*Front Cover: The ruins of Hore Abbey, located in Cashel, Tipperary County,
Ireland. Photo by Olga Fradkin, licensed via ShutterStock #1299641011.*

Dedication

Once again, I dedicate this book to two of my good friends whose devoted assistance and donated time made this work possible. First, to Karen Meyn of Pennsylvania, who spent countless hours with the manuscript and questioning me so that the text would emerge as comprehensible as possible. Writing about and explaining genealogy is difficult, and she was on my left side throughout it all despite other commitments. Second, to Wade Hone of Utah, whose friendship over the last 30 years resulted in his creation of an amazing layout of graphics for the book. He was on my right side while withstanding daily interferences.

Both Karen and Wade are my inspiration for never allowing any circumstance to be a hindrance to friendship and love. They are indeed the best friends one could have. It has been my honor to be part of their lives.

Dwight Radford
West Valley City, Utah
U.S.A

Map/Image/Chart/List/Photograph Reference List

Photographs/Illustrations

Ecclesiastical/Religious Orders

Access/Reference Aids

Table of Contents

Foreword

By Tom Rice

One purpose of a book foreword is to summarize what is in the volume and why the information is valuable—and to recommend it with some enthusiasm. That is an easy assignment in this instance. *Discovering Irish Origins Using the Records of Ireland* is a happy combination of reference sources for Irish genealogy and methods for how to skillfully employ them. The strength of this book as a guide is its exceptional explanations of not only the usual Irish genealogy records but also of some that are mentioned less often in other works, such as those of Petty Court Sessions, workhouses, and prisons. For methods' instruction, its worth is twofold. It goes to some length about how to effectively search within Ireland's resources, whether online or at sites. A major aspect is its repeated discussion of further steps to research after obtaining results from each of the record types, that is, "If you find this, then look here or here next." This facet of how to successfully search and what to do with the material discovered is not often found or explained well in most other genealogy texts.

So, what is so special about this presentation of Irish genealogy research? Breadth of coverage of helpful details is provided. All the usual sources are contained: censuses and census substitutes, church records, civil registrations, cemeteries and tombstones, estates, taxes, deeds, and voters' lists. Some sources often neglected are included that are a must in any thorough Irish investigatory project because of the loss of nineteenth-century censuses and the late start of church registers for most of the Catholic Irish population: voters' lists and records of workhouses, prisons, and Petty Court Sessions. To make searching these papers more productive, Radford incorporated an exhaustive inventory of resources to explore as well as helpful directories. Included are religious denominations that might be considered minor; lists of early, often-forgotten occupations; situating Church of Ireland diocesan courts into their respective counties; examples of fair towns and fair dates in County Leitrim; and detailed lists of mills by location and types of key mines, prisons by location and type, principal destinations for prisoner transportation by date and current names, and historical terms with definitions relating to hangings, land measurements, and land records. Radford's review of Griffith's Valuation and associated manuscripts is one of the best to be found.

All the information in the abovementioned sources is useless if researchers do not know what to do with what they find. The answer to this dilemma is what clearly sets Radford's work apart. The methods' aspect of the book is extensive and its strongest point. Radford repeatedly suggests how the researcher should utilize the search results from each source for the most rewards. Time and again, he starts with "If you know …, search this way in this record type." Then he proceeds by showing "If you found …, look here next." He ends with chapters on strategies that focus in depth on how to handle the vagaries of Irish names, tying families together through name distribution surveys, how to find the ancestral homesites, and how to navigate the perplexities of online databases. This sort of guidance is seldom found in other genealogy works.

Research strategies combined with painstaking document evaluations make this an excellent teaching tool for Irish researchers of any competence. All can benefit from Radford's knowledge.

Tom Rice, PhD, CGSM
Managing editor of *The Septs*, Journal of the Irish Genealogical Society International
Mendota Heights, Minnesota, USA

Introduction

By Dwight A. Radford

For the more than thirty years I have lived in Salt Lake City. I worked as a professional genealogist. I researched almost daily in the huge Family History Library. I also pursued investigations at archives in the United States, the United Kingdom, Ireland, and Northern Ireland. Throughout my career, I have encountered almost all family history questions and the most puzzling lineages because the cases people finally present for opinions from knowledgeable researchers are often complex. Fortunately, my experi-ence from these decades of employment has given me opportunities to explore tech-niques that result in breakthroughs in tracing genealogies and those that do not.

Researching Irish ancestries can be among the most challenging in the world. They pro-vide unparalleled complications in solving family history riddles because the records started late and names can be common and inconsistent, if they can be located at all. The present book, *Discovering Irish Origins Using the Records of Ireland,* is intended to pre-sent strategies that I have found to be successful through accessing evidence generated in Ireland. The goal is not to replicate the many wonderful works already on the market that outline the sources in Ireland and Northern Ireland. Instead, it is meant to comple-ment them by offering tactics that anyone can use from an immigration perspective.

This is but the second in the series of Irish immigrant instruction and reference books I have written. The first is *American Scots-Irish Research: Strategies and Sources in the Quest for Ulster-Scots Origins* (Orting, Washington: Family Roots Publishing, 2020), and the third, being assembled, is *Irish-American Ancestors' Book: Using U.S. Strategies and Records to Identify Origins* (Orting, Washington: Family Roots Publishing Company, LLC, 2021). Additional volumes are in the process of publication.

Irish Reference Works

The current and historical guides do an excellent job of describing the documents of Ire-land and the ways to work from them. Most of the volumes are dated because of the explosion in technology and Internet databases, yet their discussions about types of rec-ords remain valid. Only the information about where the records are stored and how to access them is outdated. However, because so many researchers are mired in the "getting them over the water" stage, the books produced by genealogists in the Republic of Ireland and Northern Ireland cannot be explored, let alone appreciated, for their full worth. *Dis-covering Irish Origins Using the Records of Ireland* has a different focus. As any veteran researcher knows, going to a database for the needed answer often is not easy. Even if a solution is that simple, what is next? Have the correct persons really been found in the database? Many people simply forget to ask that foundational question.

To begin with, this work is not meant to cover every topic and, therefore, should be read in conjunction with some out-of-print and current how-to books on the market. I address immigration problems, mainly methods for solving taxing resettlement issues and how to find the ancestral homes in Ireland with Irish records. Recommended books are the following:

Blatchford, Robert and Elizabeth Blatchford. *The Irish Family and Local History Handbook.* Poppleton, UK: Robert Blatchford Pub., 2012.

Begley, Donal F. *Irish Genealogy: A Record Finder.* Dublin, Ireland: Heraldic Artists, Ltd., 1981.

Daly, Marie E. and Judith Lucey. *Genealogist's Handbook for Irish Research.* Boston, Massachusetts: New England Historic Genealogical Society, 2016.

Falley, Margaret Dickson. *Irish and Scotch-Irish Ancestral Research: A Guide to the Genealogical Records, Methods and Sources in Ireland.* 1962. 2 vols. Baltimore, Maryland: Genealogical Company, 1988, 1998.

Grenham, John. *Tracing Your Irish Ancestors.* Dublin, Ireland: Gill Books, 2019.

Maxwell, Ian. *Tracing Your Ancestors in Northern Ireland: A Guide to Ancestry Research in the Public Record Office of Northern Ireland.* Edinburgh: The Stationery Office, 1997.

Ouimette, David S., *Finding Your Irish Ancestors: A Beginner's Guide.* Provo, Utah: Ancestry, 2005.

Paton, Chris. *Tracing Your Irish Family History on the Internet: A Guide for Family Historians.* Barnsley, South Yorkshire, UK: Pen and Sword Family History, 2013.

Radford, Dwight A. *American Scots-Irish Research: Strategies and Sources in the Quest for Ulster-Scots Origins.* Orting, Washington: Family Roots Publishing, 2020.

Radford, Dwight A. and Kyle J. Betit. *A Genealogist's Guide to Discovering Your Irish Ancestors: How to Find and Record Your Unique Heritage.* Cincinnati, Ohio: Betterway Books, 2001.

Roulston, William J. *Researching Scots-Irish Ancestors: The Essential Genealogical Guide to Early Modern Ulster, 1600-1800.* Belfast, Northern Ireland: Ulster Historical Foundation, 2018.

If a county in Ireland has been identified, some handbooks that are specific to counties are available. They can usually be found online or through genealogy book dealers and are standards in libraries that focus on Irish genealogy. Flyleaf Press in Dublin publishes a series of practical guides. An example of a title is Noreen Higgins-McHugh's *A Guide to Tracing Your Tipperary Ancestors* (Dublin, Ireland: Flyleaf Press, 2018). The Ulster Historical Foundation in Belfast issues a set for Northern Ireland, one of which is Ian Maxwell's *Researching Down Ancestors: A Practical Guide for the Family and Local Historian* (Belfast, Northern Ireland: Ulster Historical Foundation, 2004). While the books written from the local viewpoints are wonderful and essential, they are most fully appreciated if counties are known. Their purposes are not to explain immigration strategies to find the counties.

Myths about Irish Records

A popular myth among novices that can damage attempts to discover immigrant origins is "All the Irish records were destroyed." There were various reasons for record destructions, most stemming from the 1922 Irish Civil War. The Public Record Office in Dublin was also burned during that event, but as ruinous as that was, remnants must still be evaluated. The primary records lost were about half of the Church of Ireland registers, the 1841 and 1851 Irish censuses, and most pre-1858 wills. The informative censuses were probably the most serious loss because they covered the entire country. (As a sidenote, the later censuses of 1861-1891 were not destroyed by the Four Courts fire in 1922, but were determined of no further use and sadly pulped for the paper long before the Irish Civil War.)

Keep in mind that because most people never left wills and only about 12 percent of the population was Anglican, the fire did not consume the records for the total population. Therefore, part of Irish immigrant inquiries through the archives and libraries of Ireland, including local studies in each county, is to become educated about how the scarcity of documents may or may not affect personal research.

The most frustrating aspect of Irish records is that most began late, often after people emigrated or were born. It has nothing to do with record destruction. Registers and civil documents simply were not created in the manner they were in other parts of Europe. The average Roman Catholic and Presbyterian registers began in the late 1820s or early 1830s. Poverty and the landlord-tenant relationships kept most people out of the Registry of Deeds because the peasantry simply did not own land. The popular Methodist Church did not evolve from the Church of Ireland and Presbyterian Churches until 1818. Because of the absence of the registers, research before the 1820s is extremely demanding but not impossible.

For most Irish lineages, the earliest time beyond which research can progress is the late 1700s or early 1800s. Although exceptions are undeniable, overall, the period is a fair assessment for the majority of the population. Some amazing collections were not deposited at the archive in 1922, and so from them, detailed histories about families can be reconstructed. The records include private genealogical collections and those for taxes, Masonic members, deeds, courts, poorhouses, and other prime sources.

Locating the homesites where ancestors lived is also not infrequent when utilizing Irish records appropriately. Doing so, by any account, makes the genealogical process especially personal. Many people from all over the world find the lands and then go to Ireland (and Northern Ireland, per modern-day references) to set their feet on the exact spots their ancestors did.

When Are You Ready for Irish Records?

One question that is important in all Irish genealogy is: Are you really ready for Irish records? Many novice researchers want to jump straight into the historical records and peruse databases. An example to help comprehend the obstacles is Mary Kelly, one of the most common names. If research in the immigrant country has not verified the names of Mary Kelly's parents, Irish records and databases have little accuracy. The name is too ordinary. Even if a date of birth is found, for instance, from a tombstone in the United States or Canada, do not expect it to be correct. The dates are usually wrong.

The names of Mary Kelly's parents likely are not enough either if her mother's maiden name is not known. If some of her siblings and their approximate birth dates are found, the outlook is better. Even so, her day of birth may not be in the indexes and databases. Discovering a county, parents' names, and some siblings would be a boon to the research but still does not assure positive results. But if the maiden name of Mary Kelly's mother is obtained, the databases can be searched with an excellent chance of success. Recognizing the correct Mary Kelly depends on how much solid information is gathered before entertaining the idea of seeking Ireland's records.

The purpose of the foregoing illustration is that enough details must be secured ahead of time to be able to determine which Mary Kelly in Ireland is the ancestor. If not prepared with adequate facts, Mary Kelly christenings within the time frame of her birth are of no shortage.

Realize that when dealing with an early immigration, regardless of the name, common or not, someone from a family of tenant farmers probably was not in a record in Ireland. The wealthy people may have been in another category but not the commoners on the farms. The latter group comprises the typical Presbyterian Scots-Irish (Ulster-Scots) tenant farmers who left in the 1700s for the American colonies. It also includes the indentured servants, usually poor Catholics in the 1600s who arrived in the American and Caribbean colonies. They remain immigrant country problems, and some moderate use of the Irish records can reveal where the surnames are found in Ireland long after the ancestors left. The answers are not confirmations but, rather, indications of where those early ancestors might have lived in Ireland. For assistance with this category of difficult research are books such as Dwight A. Radford's *American Scots-Irish Research: Strategies and Sources in the Quest for Ulster-Scots Origins* (Orting, Washington: Family Roots Publishing, 2020).

Special Strategy Chapters

At the end of this book are three "Special Strategy" chapters containing necessary, expanded information. They are presented in the style of mini-research papers.

The first "Special Strategy" concerns "Names, Nicknames, and Naming Patterns," which can be a key to sorting through families with common names. The plan also can aid in pinpointing where in Ireland an immigrant family originated.

The second "Special Strategy" chapter is "Surname Distribution Survey." It describes the use of various sources to triangulate where surnames are found in Ireland. This is a standard research tactic commonly utilized in Irish research and may be the only way to determine where a family was from in Ireland.

The third and last "Special Strategy" chapter is about documenting the old homesites in Ireland, the goal of most Irish researchers. Researchers want to see what their forebears saw and where they walked. If fortunate, the old houses or their ruins may be standing now. Documenting the old homesites is typically the journeys' ends for the Irish lines. Although the majority of lineages cannot be traced before the late 1700s or early 1800s, being in the places where the ancestors lived is as rewarding as following a line into the 1500s in other parts of Europe.

Use of Websites and Databases

Within each chapter is a listing of websites and databases. Unfortunately, one of the curses of writing in the modern age of technology is that website addresses can become obsolete the moment a book is published. To attempt to avoid the matter, the websites are mentioned in brief. For example, the assumption is that the standard ones, such as Ancestry.com, AncestryIreland.ie, Askaboutireland.ie, FamilySearch.org, Findmypast.com, IrishGenealogy.ie, and RootsIreland.ie, will remain constant as brand names, similar to book titles. They, therefore, are referenced in that format, but most other websites are by names.

In the present day, one organization cannot index everything, and various organizations are cooperating to index and share databases and indexers. Because of their collaborations, the same database may be on Ancestry.com or Findmypast.com as part of their for-profit subscription memberships, whereas it is free on FamilySearch.org, which is a non-profit organization.

Chapter Topics

The material herein is not intended to cover all sources for all times and places. The chapters have been chosen carefully to suggest how an immigration strategy can be developed from the assortment of records being discussed. Not all sources generated historically in Ireland are of value in identifying immigrant origins, but some that are less significant can be effective for approaches that often are not straightforward.

One area that is noticeably absent is a chapter on DNA. The reason for this is deliberate. Even if a DNA match is found and the residence in Ireland is specified, a paper trail con-necting to ancestors in that area needs to be established. The research of a DNA cousin in Australia may have a definite locale in Ireland where the family lived, but the fact re-mains that the documentation may not date back far enough to unite the two lines. The missing records for a link are the nature of a place in which the average church register did not start until the 1820s or 1830s. Nonetheless, the paper trail must be pursued to determine how far the lineage can be extended in the extant records. Perhaps a connec-tion can be made to that Australian DNA cousin. The only way to be certain is to conduct the required exploration.

The use of repetition in this book is for a purpose. For example, a tactic such as the sur-name distribution strategy is so important that it is repeated in several chapters. If it is overlooked in one chapter, it is restated in another.

Conclusions

I hope that the material presented in this work will help open some new research possi-bilities for documenting Irish lineages. Irish research cannot be judged by the standards of other European countries, whose parish registers can be hundreds of years old. This is hard work. However, the accompanying social history, injustices, politics, religions, and famines were all reasons for the culture of mass departure, and, therefore, Irish emigration history cannot be separated from Irish history. The two are forever conjoined, often in the most traumatizing ways.

Dwight Radford
West Valley City, Utah, USA

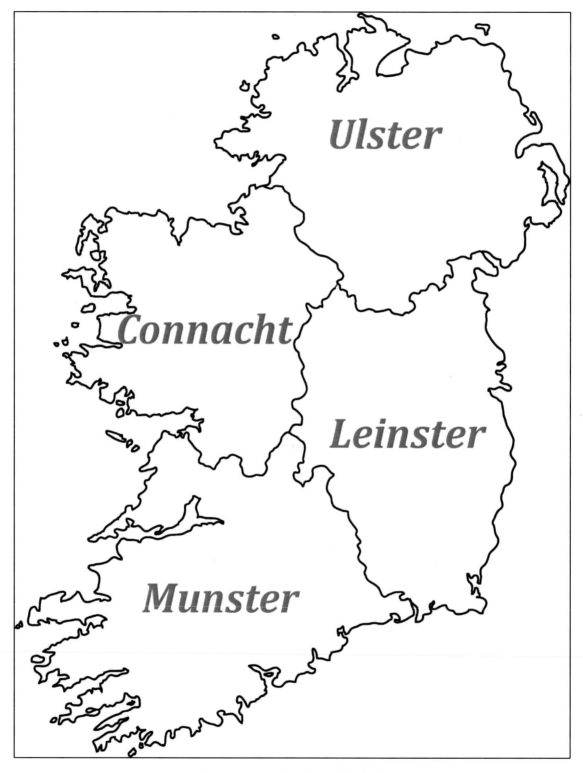

Figure 1: Province boundaries of Ireland.

Chapter One

Administrative Divisions and Place Names

Place names and administrative divisions in Ireland's history are somewhat complicated, but they are among the most fascinating and essential topics at the foundation of Irish research. The filing and cataloging of documents can be appreciated through knowledge of the manner whereby the land was divided for administrative purposes. Many of the geographical units discussed in this chapter overlap, whereas others make little sense from a modern point of view. Nevertheless, they are significant and must be understood for research to be successful.

A basic map of the counties in Ireland with their boundaries can be found in Brian Mitchell's *A New Genealogical Atlas of Ireland* 2nd edition (Baltimore, Maryland: Genealogical Publishing Co., 2009). His book is a standard, necessary reference for the larger administrative

divisions, yet it also includes the smaller units, the civil parishes, and the Catholic parish boundaries. Similar maps can be found on the website JohnGrenham.com, and more detailed ones showing the smaller units, including townland boundaries, can be accessed on Townlands.ie. The maps are essential for Irish immigrant research because the places being sought are the parishes and the townlands and not just the counties.

General Research Strategies

From an immigration perspective, documents in Ireland may state persons' origins. When the places are obvious, few issues arise because the surviving Irish documents can then be checked. At that point, the administrative units do not have to make sense. Either the ancestors were noted in the records or they were not.

Frequently, though, the places registered were either phonetically spelled or simply do not seem reasonable as current place names. Sometimes, they are not recognizable, and so finding exactly where the place names might be situated is necessary so that efforts can proceed appropriately. Perhaps the best way to examine locations listed in the immigrant records is to determine what they might have been labeled, which possibilities are:

- An official government place name, often spelled phonetically by clerks, clergy, and the family upon immigrating. The most common ones are for townlands and civil parishes. The parishes are easier to identify than are the townlands in the many Irish databases of maps displaying boundaries and place names.

- An unofficial local place name, known as "sub-denomination" or a "sub-townland." A local place name was originally in a townland and might have been the townland itself. Once the Ordnance Survey teams standardized spellings, names, and boundaries, many sub-townlands ceased to exist on official maps and in gazetteers. The Ordnance Survey teams traveled throughout the island from 1825 through 1846. Yet, regional, little known place names often continued to be used and were carried around the world wherever the Irish settled.

Because the localities of townlands and sub-townlands are the most frequent problems in the immigrant records, identifying them requires some time.

Several place name databases and websites that provide the basics of administrative units are generally used by Irish researchers. They include both official and unofficial names. For official place names, the standard published book, now available on the Internet, is the 1851 *General Alphabetical Index to the Townlands and Towns...* (1861. Reprint. Baltimore, Maryland: Genealogical Publishing Co., 2006), universally referred to as *Townland Index* in genealogy circles. The work, upon which so many of the online place name databases are built, lists the townland or town and the county,

barony, and Poor Law Union where it is located. It also has the number of surveyed acres, listed in English acres, and the Ordnance Survey map on which each townland appears for the period.

The editions for 1871 and 1901 do have an important difference from the standard 1851 one. They have a column for the electoral division (seen as ED or DED), which is helpful in accessing records, that is, where government unit records were filed. However, the 1851, 1871, and 1901 townland indexes are for officially surveyed townlands only recognized by the Ordnance Survey. They do not include sub-townlands. The 1851 version is a database on Askaboutireland.ie, Findmypast.com, JohnGrenham.com, and IreAtlas.ie, among others. The 1901 edition can be found online at Irishancestors.ie, and an especially useful one is on the website of the Irish Genealogical Research Society in London.

For unofficial place names, two websites are exceptionally helpful. The first is the website "Irish Townlands" on Townlands.ie, and although it has maps and official names (including Gaelic names), it also has a "subtownlands" section for those that have been identified. The second is Logainm.ie, which draws from historical records, such as the "John O'Donovan Name Books" and the "Irish Folklore Commission" papers. They are not books but are collections of manuscripts and typescript material. The Logainm.ie database carries the variant spellings of townlands and minor place names within the townlands. It is a fundamental research aid and can quickly locate a

CENSUS OF IRELAND, 1901.

GENERAL ALPHABETICAL INDEX

TO THE

TOWNLANDS AND TOWNS OF IRELAND.

With the Number of the Sheet of the Ordnance Survey Maps in which each will be found; the Area in Statute Acres of each Townland; the County, Barony, Parish, County District, and District Electoral Division in which each is situated; and the Index Number of its District Electoral Division in the arrangement followed in Table VII. of the Census County Books of 1901, in which Area, Houses, Population, and Valuation are given.

. The names of Towns are printed in SMALL CAPITALS, and those of ISLANDS which are not Townlands in *Italics*. County Districts with the letter "U" affixed are Urban Districts, all others are Rural. The County District is in the Poor Law Union of the same name except where noted.

No. of Sheet of the Ordnance Survey Maps.	Names of Townlands and Towns.	Area in Statute Acres. A. R. P.	County.	Barony.	Parish.	County District.	District Electoral Division. Name.	No. in Table VII. of Census County Book, 1901.
34	Abartagh	34 2 32	Waterford	Decies-within-Drum	Clashmore	Youghal No. 2	Clashmore	100
97	Abberanville	24 0 29	Galway	Athenry	Kiltullagh	Loughrea	Raford	128
93	Abbernadoorny	62 2 29	Donegal	Banagh	Killymard	Donegal	Donegal	9
58	Abbert	178 3 30	Galway	Tiaquin	Monivea	Tuam	Abbey East	187
58, 59	Abbert Demesne	1,293 2 21	Galway	Tiaquin	Monivea	Tuam	Abbey East	187
4	Abbeville	943 2 7	Tipperary, N.R.	Ormond Lower	Lorrha	Borrisokane	Lorrha East	17
118	Abbey (a)	—	Cork, W.R.	Bantry	Kilmocomoge	Bantry	Bantry Urban	23
116, 117, 125	Abbey	334 3 28	Galway	Leitrim	Ballynakill	Portumna	Tynagh	184
58	Abbey	875 3 7	Galway	Tiaquin	Abbeyknockmoy	Tuam	Abbey West	188
56	Abbey	222 3 21	Limerick	Coshlea	Kilfiyn	Kilmallock No.1	Kilfiyn	38
13	Abbeycartron (b)	—	Longford	Longford	Templemichael	Longford (U.)	Longford No. 2 Urban	55
16	Abbeycartron	32 1 3	Roscommon	Roscommon	Elphin	Strokestown	Elphin	96
18, 19, 22, 23	Abbeyderg	865 2 17	Longford	Moydow	Taghsheenod	Ballymahon No. 1	Kilcommock	9
21	ABBEYDORNEY T.	—	Kerry	Clanmaurice	O'Dorney	Tralee	Abbeydorney	129
4	Abbeydown	454 3 6	Wexford	Scarawalsh	Moyacomb	Enniscorthy	Moyacomb	25
3	Abbey East	301 1 10	Clare	Burren	Abbey	Ballyvaghan	Abbey	1
47	Abbeyfarm	55 1 12	Limerick	Kilmallock	St. Peter's and St. Paul's	Kilmallock No.1	Kilmallock	43
42, 51	Abbeyfeale East	1,330 3 23	Limerick	Glenquin	Abbeyfeale	Newcastle	Abbeyfeale	90
42	ABBEYFEALE T.	—	Limerick	Glenquin	Abbeyfeale	Newcastle	Abbeyfeale	90
42	Abbeyfeale West	718 2 4	Limerick	Glenquin	Abbeyfeale	Newcastle	Abbeyfeale	90
86	Abbeyfield	18 0 36	Galway	Kilconnell	Kilconnell	Ballinasloe No. 1	Kilconnell	8
107	Abbeygormacan	94 1 18	Galway	Longford	Abbeygormacan	Ballinasloe No. 1	Abbeygormacan	11
33	Abbeygrey or Monasternalea	503 1 14	Galway	Killian	Athleague	Mount Bellew	Killeroran	149
33	Abbeygrey or Monasternalea	157 3 37	Galway	Killian	Killeroran	Mount Bellew	Killeroran	149
20	Abbeygrove	59 0 25	Kilkenny	Gowran	Blanchvilleskill	Kilkenny	Dunbell	33
30	Abbeyhalfquarter, pt. of (c)	93 0 34	Mayo	Tireragh	Kilmoremoy	Ballina	Ardnaree South Rural	2
107	Abbey Island	17 1 33	Donegal	Tirhugh	Kilbarron	Ballyshannon No. 1	Ballyshannon Rural	3
106	*Abbey Island*	90 3 1	Kerry	Dunkerron South	Kilcrohane	Cahersiveen	Darrynane	7
20	Abbey Land (d)	—	Cavan	Loughtee Upper	Urney	Cavan (U.)	Cavan Urban	48
14	Abbeyland	68 3 19	Kildare	Clane	Clane	Naas No. 1	Clane	58
40	Abbeyland	144 1 8	Kildare	Kilkea and Moone	Castledermot	Athy No. 1	Castledermot	11
15, 20	Abbey Land	9 0 0	Longford	Ardagh	Mostrim	Granard No. 1	Edgeworthstown	34
27	Abbeyland	92 2 23	Meath	Duleek Lower	Duleek	Drogheda No. 2	Duleek	5
25	Abbeyland, pt. of (e)	302 3 38	Meath	Navan Lower	Navan	Navan	Navan Rural	57
6, 7	Abbeyland	75 1 6	Westmeath	Corkaree	Multyfarnham	Mullingar	Multyfarnham	92
11	Abbeyland & Char-							

Figure 1: General Alphabetical Index to the Townlands and Towns of Ireland. This example is for 1901, which includes electoral divisions. (Works created by an officer or employee of the Irish Government or State are copyrighted for 50 years from the end of the year in which the work is created. No permissions required.)

strange place name in an immigrant record.

It is still possible to go through the databases and not find a place name. Ways of approaching this difficulty have been successful. Among some of the strategies are:

- Looking at the list from the database and asking, without preconceptions: What sounds or looks like what is on the immigrant document? Simple ones are the interchangeable *Bally, Ballina, Ballna*. As long as the *Bal** is intact, the remainder likely can be recognized in a database listing. *Bal** is easy if the rest of the place name can be reconstructed. Conversely, the process can be complex. For example, an *Sl** and an *St** at the beginning may throw off a database search. If the county is known, merely perusing a list of all *S** place names in a database may reveal the name phonetically. An excellent approach to places begins with using IreAtlas.ie, which allows searching with only fragments of the actual place name and can constrain the search to various boundaries.

- Another approach when a county is known is entering the ancestor's name into a tax database, such as Griffith's Primary Valuation (1847-1864). This can work even if the ancestor emigrated before 1864 because the point is to discover where the surname appears in the county. Subsequently, look closely at the standardized spellings of the townlands. Do they look anything like what is on the immigrant record? The method can be effective with common and uncommon surnames since the aim is determining the townland name. A word of caution is needed. If the immigrant was using a sub-townland as a place of

origin, it will not appear in a Griffith's Valuation search. Do not let that hinder efforts.

The preceding principle does not extend to only immigrant records because the official Irish records can also be a problem. Sometimes, Irish documents, such as civil registrations, have minor place names. The clerks were not supposed to use unofficial names, but they did. Every registrar's office had a published pamphlet as a reference for names and spellings of townlands, and they are in George B. Handran's monumental work *Townlands in Poor Law Unions* (Salem, Massachusetts: Higginson Books, 1997). The pamphlets, originally issued in 1885 by the General Register Office, standardized the register information.

The advantage of using Handran's book is that it has all official place names by poor law unions, which are the same as the civil registration districts. Therefore, with the Irish birth, marriage, or death certificates in hand, that information is known. The area of the unfamiliar or misconstrued place name then can be restricted to the district within the poor law union. The poor law union is further subdivided in this work into Registrars' Districts, Electoral Divisions, Baronies, and Civil Parishes. On a civil registration certificate of birth, marriage, or death, the Civil Registration District (Poor Law Union) and Registrar's District are at the top of the page. Scan the list of approved official townland names and see if anything can pass for what is on the record itself, a proven way of limiting where a place name may be located within a county. If a place name database online allows a search to be narrowed by Poor Law Union (Registration District), the same study can be accomplished.

Phonetically spelled addresses for places such as townlands or sub-townlands are customary in the Irish Catholic registers. Naturally, the spelling is transferred to indexes of church records, for instance, those on RootsIreland.ie. The same principle applies in undertaking immigrant records or the government Irish records, such as Civil Registrations or those in the Registry of Deeds. Where is that place?

There is also a source that splits the difference between what is official and what is not, only in this case, it is a compilation of minor place names as they appeared on the original Ordnance Maps generated by the government in the mid-nineteenth century. It is the first map series produced by way of the Ordnance Survey teamwork (1825-1845), and it was updated periodically afterward. The maps show official townland boundaries, and they also can have unofficial, local place names within the townlands. The boundaries and names changed or were deleted when the maps were revised, and thus the index to the first maps is indispensable.

Called "Index of all Names on the First 6-In. Survey Maps," the manuscripts alphabetically list the minor place names and the townlands where they were located along with other identifying information, such as civil parishes and baronies. It is one of the sources from which databases extract place names, and it is on microfilm at the National Library of Ireland as well as at the Family History Library. The National Library microfilm numbers and the counties on each film, in order of appearance, are found in the table below. They can also be found on www.osi.ie, but navigating through this collection is more challenging.

Administrative Divisions that Affect Research

The following information is about each administrative division and why it is essential to immigrant research.

Provinces: Historically, Ireland was divided into the provinces of Connaught, Leinster, Munster, and Ulster. Present-day Northern Ireland encompasses six of

---

Index of all Names on the First 6 in(ch) Survey Maps
(as found on microfilm at the National Library of Ireland)

NLI#	Counties
N4633	Cork
N4635	Tipperary, Galway, Leitrim, Mayo
N4635	Sligo, Antrim, Armagh, Cavan, Donegal, Roscommon, Waterford, Limerick
N4636	Kildare, Carlow, Down, Dublin, Fermanagh, Kilkenny, Offaly, Longford, Louth, Meath, Monaghan
N4637	Laois (Queens), Tyrone, Westmeath, Wexford, Wicklow, Derry (Londonderry)

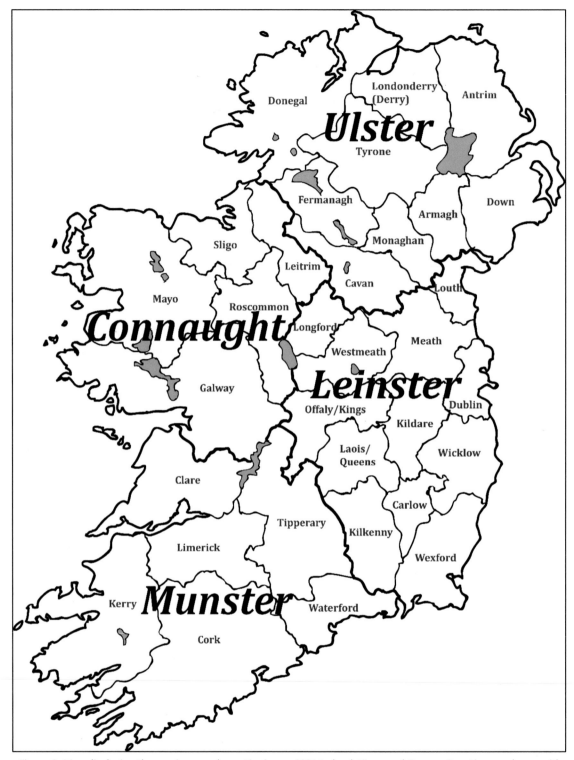

Figure 2: Map displaying the provinces and counties in pre-1921 Ireland. Kings and Queens Counties are shown with both historical and modern-day names.

the nine Ulster counties, exceptions being the counties of Cavan, Donegal, and Monaghan, which have been part of the Republic of Ireland since 1922. While provinces typically are not seen in immigrant records or on tombstones, they

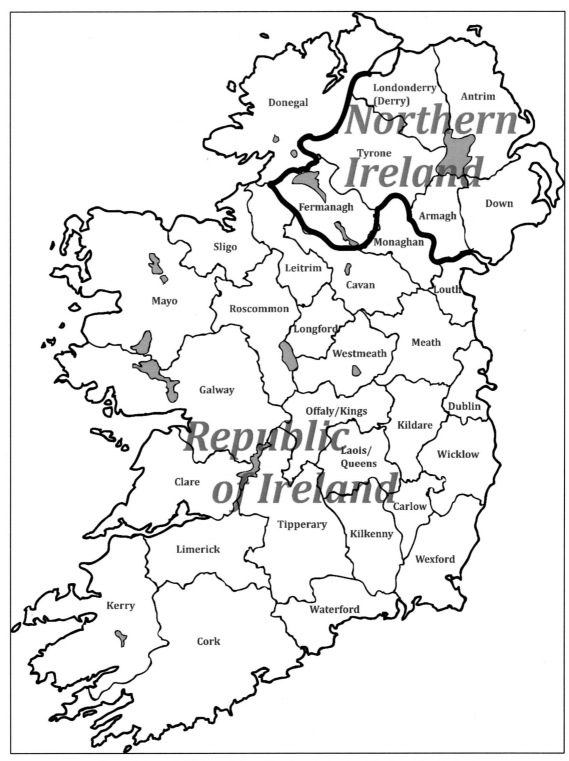

Figure 4: Present-day boundaries of Northern Ireland and the Republic of Ireland.

can be widely found in published family histories or on websites where some knowledge seems to have been passed down. The most familiar provinces in immigrant sources are Ulster and Connaught. The two have been retained in the family lore of immigrants to America more often than Leinster or Munster have.

Dioceses: Both the Church of Ireland and the Roman Catholic Church had highly organized, overlapping diocesan systems. Before 1858, wills, administrations, and marriage licenses were under the jurisdiction of Church of Ireland dioceses, regardless of the person's religion. Knowing the dioceses can be necessary when studying the records they filed, for instance, will indexes and marriage license bonds. Catholic records, such as those on the National Library of Ireland website, are grouped by Catholic dioceses. The diocesan systems for both churches do not correlate, and both do cross county lines. Whether they were Anglican or Catholic dioceses, they usually are not found in immigrant records, but they are used in modern library cataloging.

Counties: Historically, Ireland comprised thirty-two counties. All still exist, but they are now divided between Northern Ireland and the Republic of Ireland. A county is a political unit made up of several civil parishes. County names have changed. In the Republic of Ireland, after independence in 1921, Queens County became County Laois (or Leix), and Kings County became County Offaly. In Northern Ireland, Londonderry and Derry are the same county, except in this case, it is layered with political overtones. The Roman Catholics in Northern Ireland prefer Derry, but the Protestants favor Londonderry. In the immigrant records before 1921, expect Kings, Queens, and, most likely, Londonderry to have been noted.

County names are routinely found in immigrant records as the places of origin. Even if they are misspelled, like "Mao" for "Mayo," recognizing them is not difficult.

Civil Parishes: The civil parishes are important designations. Several libraries, including the Family History Library, reference the civil parishes as the locations for cataloging their holdings because in the past, they were stable government units. Civil parish names are found in such Irish records as censuses, church records, deeds, taxes, and wills—to name but a few. Technically, the civil parishes are the same as those of the Church of Ireland, which was the state religion through 1870. Yet, this also is complex. Civil parish names are found recurrently in immigrant records as well as on tombstones.

Church (Ecclesiastical) Parishes: The Church of Ireland parishes are not predictably the same as civil parishes. Following the Reformation, the Church of Ireland was the state religion from 1536 through 1870. The Protestant Church of Ireland took over the medieval Roman Catholic parishes and their buildings. While Church of Ireland parishes in theory had the same boundaries as civil parishes, the situation is more complicated. More than one Anglican parish or no Anglican church parish may be within a civil parish. Roman Catholic parishes are not the same as either the civil parishes or the local Church of Ireland parishes, but they sometimes do share the same geographical boundaries. Catholic parish names routinely are found engraved on immigrant tombstones in church cemeteries worldwide. Other denominations, such as Christian Brethren (Plymouth Brethren), Congregationalist, Methodist, Moravian, Mormon, Presbyterian, and Quaker, had other ecclesiastical systems and did not have parish systems.

Baronies: A barony is comprised of several civil parishes or parts of civil parishes. Baronies cross county boundaries. The baronies were used to a great extent in land records. For example, the Registry of Deeds arranged some deed indexes by barony and then by the townland or town within that barony. The barony for the town, townland, or parish of an ancestor's residence may be found by consulting the typical *Townland Index* online. Once in a while, and definitely the exception, an immigrant record may have a barony as the birthplace of an ancestor.

Poor Law Unions: Under the Poor Law Act of 1838, Ireland was divided into clusters or unions of townlands whose inhabitants were responsible for the care of the poor. The names of unions were derived from the towns where the workhouses for the poor were located. The union boundaries can cross county and civil parish boundaries to encompass the geographical areas around the towns. Poor Law Unions were divided into Electoral Divisions (ED or DED). In the Irish records, the Poor Law Union units of administration are used in censuses, civil registrations, and workhouse registers, among others. The units are requisite in immigration research, especially if ancestors left Ireland from poorhouses. Otherwise, if an immigrant referred to the Poor Law Union, it was to the market town in the area and was an identifying point in

discussions, not because it was a Poor Law Union. At www.workhouses.org.uk, more can be learned about the workhouse culture and poor laws along with a visit to a virtual museum.

Superintendent Registrars' Districts: Civil registrations of births, marriages, and deaths in Ireland were compiled by the Superintendent Registrars' Districts (sometimes referred to in genealogy books as the registration districts). The Superintendent Registrars' Districts in the nineteenth century were divided into local Registrars' Districts and had the same names and boundaries as the Poor Law Unions. As with the Poor Law Unions, they were the main towns where events were registered and the poorhouses were located. They were remembered upon immigrating but not because they were districts.

Electoral Divisions: An Electoral Division (ED), also called a District Electoral Division (DED) is a number of townlands joined together as a unit for the purpose of electing its representative to the Poor Law Union Board of Guardians. In essence, it is a neighborhood. EDs are key sections because they were used in arranging Griffith's Valuation revision books. The 1901 edition of the *Townland Index* as found on Irishancestors.ie on the Irish Genealogical Research Society website is an excellent aid in identifying in which ED a townland is located. Records, such as the tax revision books after Griffith's Primary Valuation (1847-1864) were filed by ED (later Rural District and Urban District) within the Poor Law Union. Also, the 1901 and 1911 Ireland censuses listed the ED.

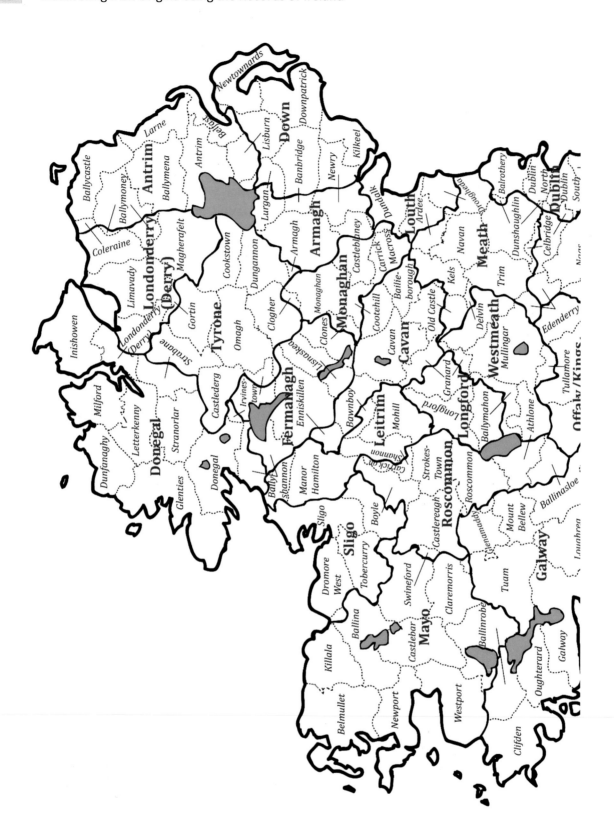

Figures 5a and 5b: Poor Law Union boundaries of Ireland, which also serve as the jurisdictions for civil registration filings, censuses, and other records.

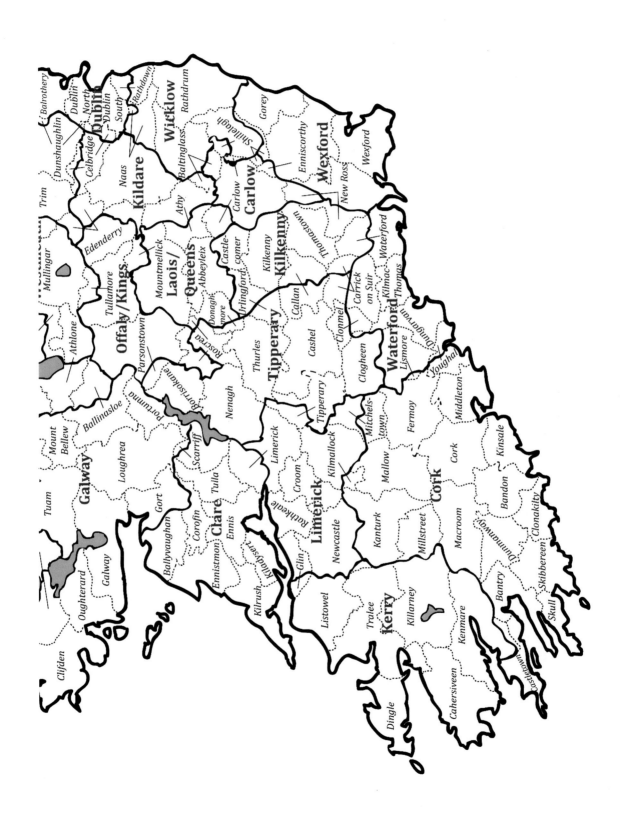

Cities and Towns: In Ireland, towns are not necessarily townlands, but towns or villages may be located *within* one or more townlands. For example, the town of Draperstown in County Londonderry (Derry) lies in three intersecting townlands: Cahore, Moykeeran, and Moyheeland. They literally join in the middle of the street in Draperstown. Small towns and villages did not have their own governments, but larger ones did. Cities, towns, and small villages are continually found as references in immigrant records as places of origin, which does not mean immigrants were from these places. They may have been from surrounding areas. Farmers normally had houses in the villages, and their countryside farmlands were within walking distances. Observed in Griffith's Valuation are both properties being taxed with one person's name attached to them as the responsible party. The town property was taxed for only a house, and the farmland, for only land.

Townlands: The townland is the smallest official geographical unit in Ireland and is central to research. A townland is not a town, nor does it have its own government. It is a surveyed piece of ground that may not have people living within its boundaries. A townland may be just a cow pasture, a bog, or a mountainside, and it frequently has a Gaelic name. Its size may vary from a few acres to several thousand acres, and its boundaries generally conform to the topography. A valley may be long and narrow but not be large. If it is on a mountainside, a townland may be quite large in acreage. Either way, on an Ordnance Survey map, it has a strange appearance, which is usually the first clue to its geography. Townland

names are commonly found in immigrant records as well as in records in Ireland. Historically, they were addresses. Today, in the rural parts of the Republic of Ireland, they can still be addresses.

Townland Sub-denominations: Smaller places within official townlands, such as names of fields, orchards, and farms, are also called sub-townlands. They are not named in the official *Townland Index* published by the government, but they often appear on Ordnance Survey maps. Many became extinct after the Ordnance Survey teams determined what would or would not be recognized. Gradually, these sub-denominations fell out of use and memory, but they consistently appear in both the Irish records and immigrant records as birthplaces or residences.

Place Name Societies and Units
The history of place names is a fascination in Ireland (including Northern Ireland). In fact, when the government in Northern Ireland abandoned the concept of townlands on maps, opting for street addresses, an outcry arose. It was not that the residents necessarily wanted townland addresses instead of street addresses. After all, ambulances need street addresses! The protest was over the histories and stories of the places. The townlands are links to the past and identities, and so they were restored by the government on maps and on signs. However, the ambulances can still reach their destinations by street addresses.

There are some exceptional place name societies and websites. They can be used for background, history, and for a contact if a place name from the old records simply cannot be identified or converted to a modern name.

For Northern Ireland, a popular website is Placenamesni.ie, which hosts the database of the Northern Ireland Place-Name Project from Queen's University, Belfast. The database, which is still growing, has information on 9,600 townlands and at least 20,000 non-administrative names, such as geographical features. It also includes previously unrecorded place names and historical documentations for them as they are discovered. Another website is the Ulsterplacename.ie, part of the Ulster Place-Name Society that promotes collecting, studying, and verifying local place names. The society publishes the bi-annual *Ainm: A Journal of Name Studies*.

For the Republic of Ireland, the main database "Placenames Database of Ireland" is on the Logainm.ie website. It is the product of collaboration between Fiontar & Scoil na Gaeilge and The Placenames Branch (Department of Culture, Heritage and the Gaeltacht) and is a government website. The Northern Ireland Place-Name Project and Logainm.ie have continuing cooperation. The Logainm.ie database currently has 61,123 townlands, 2563 civil parishes, 2320 population centers, 834 sub-townlands, and 792 towns, and it also includes thousands of geographical features, crossroads, artificial features, historical names, and hamlets in the 32 counties.

Even with marvelous websites and databases, researchers need to manipulate the data when seeking difficult place names. What does it sound like? What does it look like? Is anything close to it?

Sometimes, if a database cannot be manipulated effectively, it helps to go to a website such as Townlands.ie and examine an alphabetical list by county for anything that illuminates itself as a possible match.

Ordnance Survey Maps

When a place name is identified, the next step is to find it on a modern map as well as a historical map as produced by the Ordnance Survey. An excellent website for this is Askaboutireland.ie. It has a basic search for the official townland or town, and attached to it is not only the Griffith's Primary Valuation (1847-1864) page but also the old Ordnance Survey map displaying where the Griffith's property was located. The old Griffith's maps have amazing details of roads, property lines, houses, antiquities, and geographical features. Askaboutireland.ie also offers modern road and satellite maps. With them, it is possible to focus on a feature or area from Griffith's maps and then a modern road map and a satellite map, all by pushing a button on the screen.

Griffith's maps were not the only Ordnance Survey maps that supplemented tax lists, but they and their accompanying maps are the most widely used by researchers for locating homesites. Plots of lands or houses are on the "Map Reference Numbers" from the lots' numbers on the Griffith's Valuation pages, and those numbers were handwritten on the Ordnance Survey maps. All the mapping with its discoveries of lands contributes to rendering Irish family history, despite its many complications, one of the most remarkable studies in the world.

Figure 6: Memorial from the St. James Catholic Cemetery at Ballinameela, Aglish Catholic Parish in County Waterford, Ireland, 1856. James Condon, therefore, was alive in 1856, and at some time, he was living in California. James Condon residing in California in 1856 is not implied, but he was there when the undated marker was added to the wall. He sent money to have it made after learning his father had died on June 24th. James may never have seen the plaque, and Richard Condon may not have been buried at the foot of it. Two memorials for unrelated people are directly below Condon's. More information is in what is not engraved about the Condons than what is. (Photographs courtesy of Dwight A. Radford. Permissions received.)

Chapter Two

Cemeteries and Tombstones

In Ireland and Northern Ireland, memorials in cemeteries are often termed "monumental inscriptions" as well as "tombstones," "gravestones," and "markers," among others. Although tombstones in Ireland and Northern Ireland are similar to those almost anywhere in the world, their one distinction assists research.

Because of Ireland's traumatic emigrations, stones and plaques on cemetery walls commemorating those who left, those who stayed, or both are overly abundant. They could have been erected by people abroad or people in Ireland. In the older graveyards, inscribed on some of the memorials, along with information about those interred in the plots, are the names and locations of family members who died in other parts of Ireland or in far-off countries. The practice was customary in both Catholic and Protestant cemeteries. The supposition, although not always correct, is that someone outside the country sent funds for a stone to be set within the family plot or elsewhere in the cemetery.

An example of an emigrant presenting a memorial is in St. James Catholic Cemetery in Ballinameela, Aglish Catholic Parish, County Waterford. The plaque on the wall of the graveyard reads:

> Erected by James Condon of California in memory of his worthy Father Richard Condon of Whitechurch who died June 24, 1856 Aged 70 years.

James Condon, therefore, was alive in 1856, and at some time, he was living in California. James Condon residing in California in 1856 is not implied, but he was there when the undated marker was added to the wall. He sent money to have it made after learning his father had died on June 24th. James may never have seen the plaque, and Richard Condon may not have been buried at the foot of it. Two memorials for unrelated people are directly below Condon's.

Often on family headstones are records of where family members emigrated. Persons abroad as well as those at home in Ireland might have commissioned the memorials. Frequently seen are remote places such as Australia, Canada, England, New Zealand, and the United States, the last certainly being the most common. Other countries, such as Brazil, India, and South Africa, also are well represented. Some of the especially far-flung areas of the world may denote men in the British Army, Royal Navy, or Merchant Marines who died overseas. Ranks and regiments of the soldiers or sailors are typically in the engravings, and inscriptions for sea captains are familiar.

In Catholic research, do not overlook community cemeteries or the Church of Ireland parish graveyards. All residents had the right to be buried in the state Protestant parish churchyards because the Church of Ireland was the state religion. Catholic sections are conventional and are sometimes on one side of the walkways through the cemeteries with the Protestant ones opposite. Other graveyards in communities are classified as "mixed." The cemetery layouts and the immigrant tombstones are but some of the novelties generally found in Irish cemetery research.

Figure 7: Located at Murrisk Abbey, County Mayo, this stone illustrates several relationships. (Photograph courtesy of Bernie McCafferty. Permissions received.)

Websites, Transcripts, and Databases of Tombstones

Many websites document tombstones throughout Ireland and Northern Ireland. However, as with any transcription, understanding exactly what was and was not copied from the stones is essential. Did the indexer or team of indexers note everything on the stones or just the vital information? This can affect the search for additional place names for relatives who died overseas or for local townlands of residences, which also are ordinarily on the stones. To test whether a transcription is complete, examine other texts of grave markers, whether published or online, for place names. If they are listed, the assumption can be, within reason, that the indexer indeed did transcribe the entire engraving.

The major Internet websites are continuing projects, and so they should be consulted more than once over time to make sure all tombstones in a parish or county of interest have been addressed in their databases. One is RootsIreland.ie, which has monuments' inscriptions under its County/Gravestone Inscriptions section.

Church burial registers are a little more complicated. They are not tombstones, nor do they list what is on stones or even if the stones are present. An entry in these registers may be all that is left to indicate who is buried in the church graveyard. The burial registers do not mention relatives in foreign countries, but the tombstones often have such memorials. Collections on RootsIreland.ie include graveyard transcriptions from a wide variety of denominations as well as municipal and other cemeteries.

An interesting website is Irishgraveyards.ie, for which a team of surveyors canvass cemeteries, plotting where the graves are located. Sometimes, pictures of the deceased are included, and thus the database is more than a simple one. The website Historicgraves.com is an organized, community-based project wherein the people residing near cemeteries are trained in transcribing cemetery burials through modern technology and oral histories, consigning the project to a more holistic category. Other transcriptions, submitted by individuals, are by county and are part of the Irish Genealogy Project (IGP) website: www.igp-web.com. They include references to the deceased from all over the world who are memorialized in Ireland, their homeland, as seen in several examples in this chapter.

Findagrave.com, Interment.net, and Billiongraves.com are standard websites for cemeteries worldwide, but they do have some inadequacies. First, and perhaps foremost, is that the gravestone transcriptions and pictures are on them only if they are inserted by some person or persons from the cemeteries or organized projects. The thoroughness of the cemetery survey can be difficult to establish. A single instance of one surname from a certain cemetery is an indication of incomplete listings, which most likely suggests an individual added his or her family research to the website. Another

Figure 8: Marker from the Mt. Jerome Victorian Chapel in Dublin, although the death occurred in Burma. (Photograph courtesy of Yvonne Russell. Permissions received.)

clue, for example, is a register of 100 tombstones for a cemetery that logically has thousands, best represented by urban graveyards that should be serving a large population.

Occasionally, a cemetery corporation's burial records are on the websites. They are not tombstones or even necessarily death dates but specifically the burials in the cemetery. The advantage of the inventory is that researchers have access to everyone buried in the cemetery and not to only those who have tombstones. When evaluating websites and databases, be cognizant about whether both burials and tombstones are included.

Online databases have some limitations. For instance, to prove an immigrant connection or a migration from one parish in Ireland to some other community and country, being able to search the data by the immigrant history would be helpful. In almost all cases, though, no search allows all tombstones inscribed with "Australia," "Liverpool," or any other locale outside of Ireland to be called up and studied for more clues.

Figure 9: As found on the site Findagrave.com, this stone reveals information about the family of John Barr, including a son who was lost (cast away) on Lake Erie. Burial in Bangor, County Down, (Northern) Ireland. (Photo courtesy of Dean Alan Thomas. Permissions received.)

Some websites do not list tombstone transcripts but provide the location of each cemetery and what kind it is. If a townland where the family lived is known or, at least, suspected from the tax lists, such as Griffith's Primary Valuation or a civil registration certificate, it is valuable. From the tax reports, charting where a targeted townland's nearest cemeteries are located is possible.

One such source is "County Roscommon Cemeteries" on the Roscommoncoco.ie website. It has a map that can be enlarged, and once the townland is found on the modern road map, the nearby cemeteries can be plotted. The search can continue for any surrounding cemeteries that have been transcribed in book form or on an Internet website. Just knowing the names of the potential cemeteries and in many cases, when each one opened, which the Roscommon site provides, simplifies the search for the correct cemetery. For example, if looking in the Fairymount Catholic Parish area, the Fairymount Graveyard in Mullaghnashee Townland would be of interest—unless the burial was before 1925, the

year the graveyard was established. If seeking an older graveyard, the nearby Loughglinn Catholic graveyard in Loughglinn Townland that opened in 1841 would be a good alternative.

Even if graveyards do not have the prized immigrant information on stones, knowing who in the family did not emigrate can assist in positioning the immigrant into an area. As is the case in Irish research, names can be common, both first and last, and so make sure the correct family in Ireland has been identified. If graves of people who were thought to have emigrated but apparently did not are identified, some hypotheses need to be reevaluated.

What has been published online and what was originally published in books have crossed over. As a result of the weather in Ireland, which erodes soft stone, find an earlier transcription of an online graveyard if possible. A previously published book may have details that were once legible and that no longer were when the online version was surveyed.

An exceptional work is the series of books *Gravestone Inscriptions, County Down* that has transcriptions of everything on the tombstones for all cemeteries, listed by barony within the county. Because everything is

Figure 10: In Louth Cemetery, Louth, County Louth, Ireland, stands this stone, which leads to places such as Hull and Liverpool, England, and even provides clues to the order with which the priest, Fr. John J. McKeown, was associated, the Society of Mary (Marist Fathers). (Photo courtesy of J.P. Finn. Permissions received.)

listed, some patterns can be found. Tombstones comprise ones erected from abroad, stones placed locally by families, and those with enough particulars to provide a virtual "who went where" in families. An immigration strategy then becomes quite holistic in its method because everyone is considered and not just the direct lines. One illustration of the "who went where" approach is the Ryan family buried in Killyleagh Presbyterian Graveyard (Volume 7 Baronies of Dufferin and Lecale, p. 73):

> RYAN
> /Two weathered marble tablets broken and on the ground, in a large high-railed enclosure/. Of the Ryan's. William Villers Ryan, born 1811, died 14 Sep. 1865 AE 54. Archibald Ryan died 17th Jan. 1842. Ellen Jackson Ryan died 11th April 1845. William Ryan died 27th Jan. 1852. Ellen Ryan died 19th Oct. 1852. Edward Villers Ryan died 18th Oct. 1874. Sydney Hamilton Ryan died 4th Oct. 1877.
>
> Of their children...died at Killyleagh in 1826 AE 4 years... died at Downpatrick in 1831 AE 16 (William) was killed whilst assisting to (save) life at a fire in New Orleans in 18(38) AE (18). Archibald died at Hamiltin, U. States, in 1848 AE 33. William died at Carndonagh, Co. Donegall, in 1851 AE 32. Mildred died at Downpatrick in 1853 AE 36. Sydney died at Madeira in 1858 AE

> 31. Anne, wife of Robert Ford M.D., died at Downpatrick in 1858 AE 46. John died at Nashville, Tennessee 1862 AE 43. Sarah, wife of W.V. Ryan, born 1811, died 26th Feb. 1868 AE 57. "Prepare to meet thy God," "The wages of Sin is Death, but the gift of God is Eternal Life, through Jesus Christ our Lord."

Not only did Ryan family members die overseas but also some moved to other parts of Ireland. The foreign places include New Orleans, Hamiltin [*sic*], and Nashville in the United States, and Maderia. Two areas require some further thought to acquire the most from this entry.

The first is "Hamiltin, U. States." Is that transcribed correctly from the tombstone? The indexers already mentioned the stone was in poor condition, and so perhaps what was meant was Hamilton, Upper Canada, which is now Ontario. Upper Canada was in existence from 1791 through 1841. Therefore, within reason, Archibald Ryan lived in "Hamilton" in Canada when political changes were occurring in British North America. Ontario did not officially come into being until 1867. Did the indexers make an assumption the *U* had to be for "United States"? Until a picture of the stone can be viewed or Archibald Ryan is documented in the records of the United States or Ontario, the question should remain unanswered.

The other is Maderia, an island off the coast of Africa owned by Portugal. A quick search of the island's history reveals that the British had a connection to Maderia, occupying it in the early nineteenth century. However, in 1856, British troops recovering from cholera were stationed in Funchal, Madeira. In 1858, was Sydney Ryan part of the British Army or perhaps the Merchant Marines?

A series of four plaques on the same cemetery wall provide a history of the Moore family, including "who went where." The family story over the four plaques reads almost like a book (p. 67):

> MOORE
> /Four white marble tablets in an elaborate surrounded against the graveyard wall, with a high-railed enclosure/, A.D. 1866. Erected to the memory of William Moore, Lisnau, who died 6th September 1863 aged 71 years. Also his wife Mary who died 6th April 1867 aged 59 years. Sarah Cleland, wife of James Moore, born 13th August 1835, died 26th November 1879. Also Harry, second son of James and Sarah Moore, who died 12th January 1895 aged 29 years. Also Sarah, eldest daughter of James and Sarah Moore and wife of Harry Sloan, who died 14th September 1900 aged 37 years. Also William T., eldest son of the said James Moore who died 21st October 1906 aged 44 years. Also the said James Moore, born 13th August 1835, died 23rd April 1913.

> Continued from adjoining stone. To the memory of Lucy, second daughter of the said James Moore and wife of Robert Lawther, who died 18th October 1914 aged 46 years. Also James E. G. third son of the said James Moore, who died at Cape Town, S.A., 19th June 1918 aged 46 years. Samuel Hastings Moore who died 13th March 1942.

> In memory of James, infant son of Patrick Moore, Lisnaw, who died 22nd Feby. 1881. Also Mary wife of said Patrick Moore, who died 21st July 1885 aged 44 years. Also the said Patrick Moore, who died 22nd January 1901 aged 69 years. Also William, son of said Patrick Moore, who died 10th November 1948 aged 69 years. Interred in Canterbury Crematorium, Christchurch, New Zealand.

> In memory of Henry More, Moorhall, who died 31st January 1924 aged 82 years.

The immigrant residences of the Moores include Cape Town, South Africa, and Christchurch, New Zealand, but stones like the Ryans', cited above, have accounts about those who stayed in Ireland.

With the "who went where" approach, regardless of social statuses, the branches of the family could be researched to learn more about them, which is especially helpful if local records have not survived for the documentation process to begin. The tombstones may be the only evidence in Ireland for the families. The papers for overseas' immigrants or for members of the military in the British Army, Royal Navy, or Merchant Marines may provide additional specifics not found in Ireland. As with any tombstone or plaque, having a memorial made and how much can be placed on it depends on the funds, whether coming from abroad or locally.

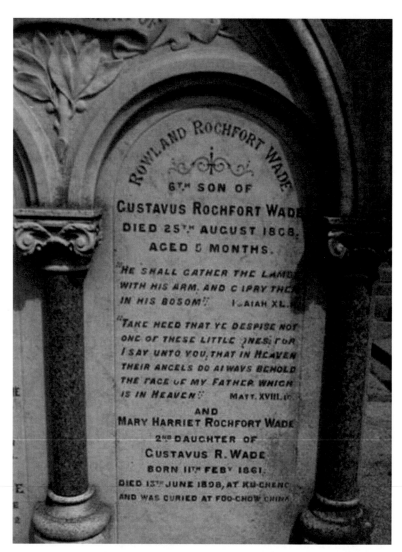

Figure 11: Another Mt. Jerome Cemetery image in Dublin discloses that Mary Harriet Rochfort Wade was buried in Foo-Chow, China. (Photograph courtesy of Yvonne Russell. Permissions received.)

Chapter Three

Censuses and Census Alternatives

The first complete censuses for the whole of Ireland were in 1901 and 1911, a setback that is significant for most researchers who are seeking ancestors who left the country in the 1700s and 1800s. To circumvent the problem, almost every Irish genealogy instruction book has a chapter on the "census substitute," a descriptive and accurate term for what is being correctly discussed in the books even though nothing can replace it. Perhaps "census alternative" is more accurate. What can substitute or furnish information for missing, lost, or destroyed records? From an immigration perspective, the value of any alternative source must be assessed.

Over the decades, researchers have identified certain sources that can document segments of the population in specific areas. Some, for instance, Griffith's

Primary Valuation (1847-1864), supply excellent reports of heads of households throughout Ireland. Several, such as the 1796 Spinning Wheel Premium Survey, were returns of occupations and only included a portion of the population involved in the weaving industry. Both are standards in the field of genealogy. Each, when used appropriately, is informative and serves its purpose, but when properly understood, they also have limitations and peculiarities. For as many research problems as the two solve, they have as many that are not addressed.

1901 and 1911 Censuses

The 1901 and 1911 censuses are amazing in their detail. They have each person's townland of residence, name, age, relationship to head of household, occupation, county of birth, religion, and his or her ability to read, write, and speak English or Irish or both. Both schedules are widely available in the frequently used indexes on the National Archives of Ireland website, which also has the digitized images. The same index is available on Ancestry.com, FamilySearch.org, and Findmypast.com, and all have additional fields from which to search for the correct entry. If a match is not found on the National Archives of Ireland website, which has the basic search, exploring one of the other sites would be prudent.

Both censuses once were considered too recent to help with immigrant research, but that attitude is now changing with the advent of indexes. Applying the principle that not all family members emigrated, the two enumerations may be perfect for locating those who stayed. Typically, if someone was still living in

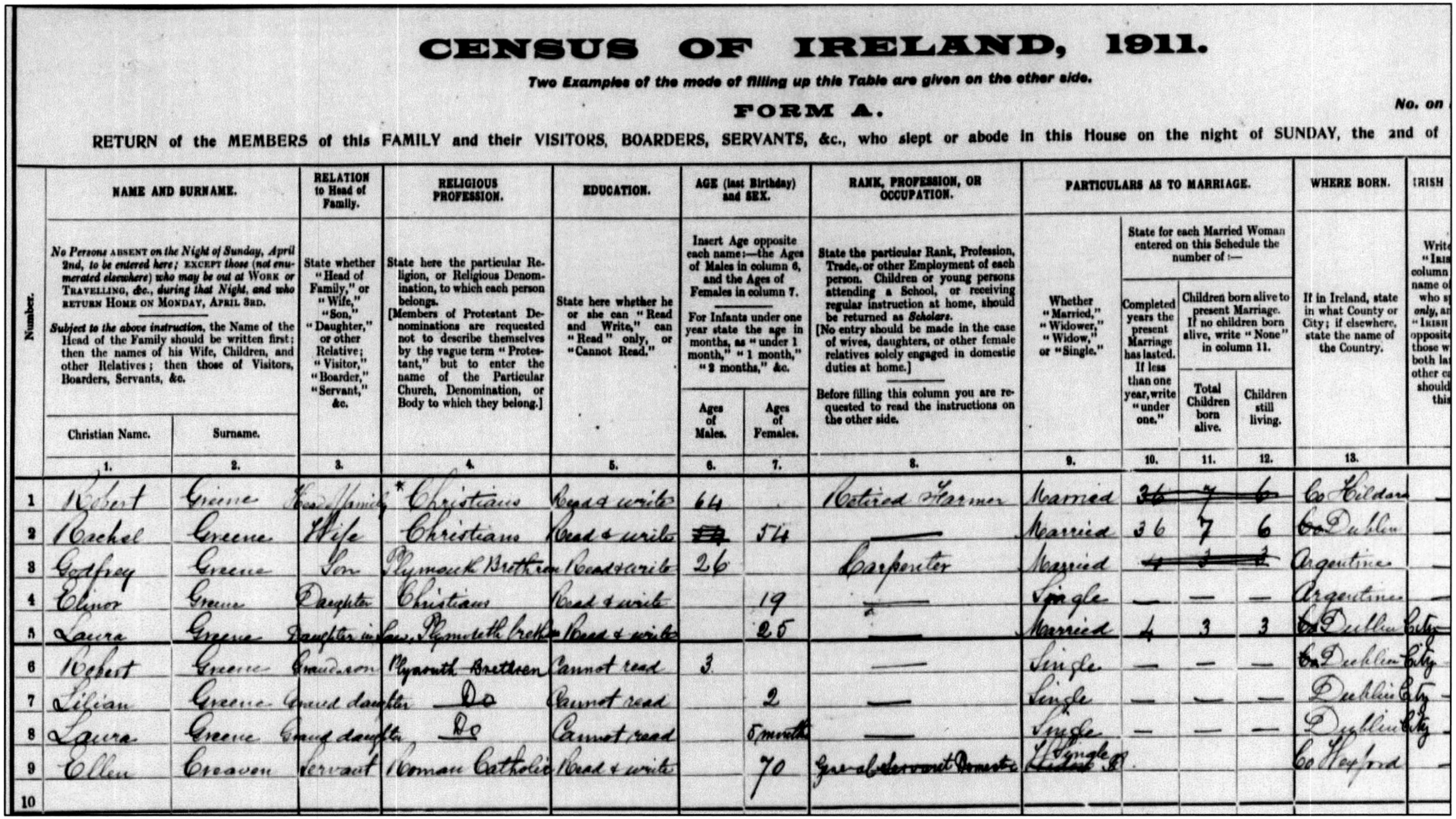

CENSUS OF IRELAND, 1911.

Two Examples of the mode of filling up this Table are given on the other side.

FORM A.

No. on

RETURN of the MEMBERS of this FAMILY and their VISITORS, BOARDERS, SERVANTS, &c., who slept or abode in this House on the night of SUNDAY, the 2nd of

Number.	NAME AND SURNAME. Christian Name.	Surname.	RELATION to Head of Family.	RELIGIOUS PROFESSION.	EDUCATION.	AGE (last Birthday) and SEX. Ages of Males.	Ages of Females.	RANK, PROFESSION, OR OCCUPATION.	PARTICULARS AS TO MARRIAGE. Whether "Married," "Widower," "Widow," or "Single."	Completed years the present Marriage has lasted.	Children born alive to present Marriage. Total Children born alive.	Children still living.	WHERE BORN.	IRISH
	1.	2.	3.	4.	5.	6.	7.	8.	9.	10.	11.	12.	13.	
1	Robert	Greene	Head of family	* Christians	Read & write	64		Retired Farmer	Married	~~36~~	~~7~~	~~6~~	Co Kildare	—
2	Rachel	Greene	Wife	Christians	Read & write	~~64~~	54	—	Married	36	7	6	Co Dublin	—
3	Godfrey	Greene	Son	Plymouth Brethren	Read & write	26		Carpenter	Married	~~4~~	~~3~~	~~3~~	Argentine	—
4	Elinor	Greene	Daughter	Christians	Read & write		19	—	Single	—	—	—	Argentine	—
5	Laura	Greene	Daughter in Law	Plymouth Brethren	Read & write		25	—	Married	4	3	3	Co Dublin City	—
6	Robert	Greene	Grandson	Plymouth Brethren	Cannot read	3		—	Single	—	—	—	Co Dublin City	—
7	Lilian	Greene	Grand daughter	Do	Cannot read		2	—	Single	—	—	—	Dublin City	—
8	Laura	Greene	Grand daughter	Do	Cannot read		5 months	—	Single	—	—	—	Dublin City	—
9	Ellen	Creavon	Servant	Roman Catholic	Read & write		70	General Servant Domestic	Single				Co Wexford	—
10														

Figure 12: 1911 Census sample. On the original, a notation at the bottom of the page clarified that the term "Christians," as applied to these parents, referred to a "small sect who meet in 'ancient concert rooms' on Sunday mornings." Also listed in the family, some of whom were born in Argentina and moved back to Ireland, were those affiliated with the Plymouth Brethren and Roman Catholic denominations. For clarification about the term Plymouth Brethren, see information on the following page. (Image courtesy of the National Archives of Ireland. Permission received.)

Ireland in 1901 and 1911, the chance is good that the emigrant's descendants retained some legend about him or her. Names of an uncle, aunt, or cousin might have lingered in lore, and, therefore, to find those who stayed may be to find the ancestral home.

Some important elements need to be kept in mind when using these censuses. One is that people relocated within Ireland during this period. They left farms for jobs in urban areas such as Belfast, Cork, Dublin, Galway, and Waterford, and so the counties of birth in the censuses can be helpful in sorting through common names. The findings from the censuses can be compared with civil registrations, directories, and gravestone compilations as well as wills and administrations. If people were in Ireland from 1901 to 1911, they were most likely in at least one or both of those important censuses.

Another misrepresentation that might confuse a search, if not careful, is religion. If the family in Ireland was known or suspected to have been "Plymouth Brethren," it might or might not have been noted with that description in the Irish censuses. The faith tradition or lore about it was familiar among immigrants to Australia, Canada, New Zealand, and the United Kingdom. Even though there is no such denomination as a "Plymouth Brethren," it is a colloquial term that has stuck with this form of conservative Protestants. The faith group has an aversion to denominationalism, and its church name was a description. It could have been recorded as Brethren (Open or Closed), Christian Brethren, Christians,

Gospel Hall, non-denominational, or simply Plymouth Brethren. All the labels, within reason, refer to the same expression of the congregations and are found in the Irish censuses.

In another example, alternative designations for the Church of Ireland are English Church or Church of England, an illustration that is easier to understand than the "Plymouth Brethren." Just be aware that the information is not always straightforward.

Do not assume that the ages are exact. Even though the expectation is that most are within reason, do not overlook the correct family, as it can be ten years off or more! Many people did not know how old they were, or they were not the ones giving the information.

In another immigration strategy, birthplaces should be noted. Often, people associated with the British Army, Royal Navy, or Merchant Marines were in Ireland with children born globally. Also, it is not completely uncommon for someone in the family to return to Ireland for a variety of reasons. While such homecomings traditionally are not believed to have occurred, consider that once an immigrant branch of the family became established in Canada, South Africa, or the United States, funds could have been available to go back to Ireland. Some did so to take care of family matters.

After the Potato Famine, those who remained and survived in Ireland progressed over time toward a class of people who had estates upon their deaths. By the turn of the twentieth century with the Lands Purchase Act, people could buy their farms and keep adding to them, again contributing to estates. Thus, those abroad needed to travel to Ireland to settle estates. Many stayed. Money earned in the immigrant countries allowed people to do things that were impossible decades before, further adding far-flung birthplaces to the 1901 and 1911 census reports.

Both the 1901 and 1911 enumerations are worth exploring from an immigration perspective. Lost relatives still might have been on the old home place in those years, or someone might have returned to settle the estate and stayed. If so, in effect, immigration questions would be solved.

Using Census Alternatives for Immigration Research

Most researchers consult census substitutes with the goal of locating where in Ireland their families lived. If the immigrants cannot be found in the church registers or if they left before church registers began, an alternative record may solve the problem. When trying to decide what will or will not work to locate immigrants, it is best to:

- Identify potential sources
- Determine coverage of the sources
- Consider the arrangement of the sources
- Establish the relative importance of the sources

If Ireland alone is known, a source that covers the entire island with a good selection of the population represented needs to be consulted. Certainly, Griffith's Primary Valuation (1847-1864) qualifies as perhaps the best. Strategies can address where families were located during the Griffith's period. If nothing but a county is known, a combination of smaller sources possibly can identify where families were living.

When thinking about census alternatives, often records are needed that indicate where surnames are located in Ireland. This approach is more of a surname distribution survey rather than one to find ancestors in an odd source. For more common surnames, such as Kelly and Sullivan, the plan does not work well, if at all. However, even with ordinary surnames, island-wide reports can still be utilized if a given name is unique. With a distinctive given name as a guide, an assessment similar to a surname search can be performed. The assumption is that, although the surnames found may or may not be the ancestor, a rare given name in various branches of the family may be determined to have originated from a specific county or even a few parishes within a county. A cousin of a cousin whose branch of the family continued to use the unusual first name that belonged to the immigrant family may be the key needed for where everyone was from.

Many novice researchers do not consult Griffith's Primary Valuation because they do not recognize its value if their ancestors emigrated before it was published. They need to consider that it does not

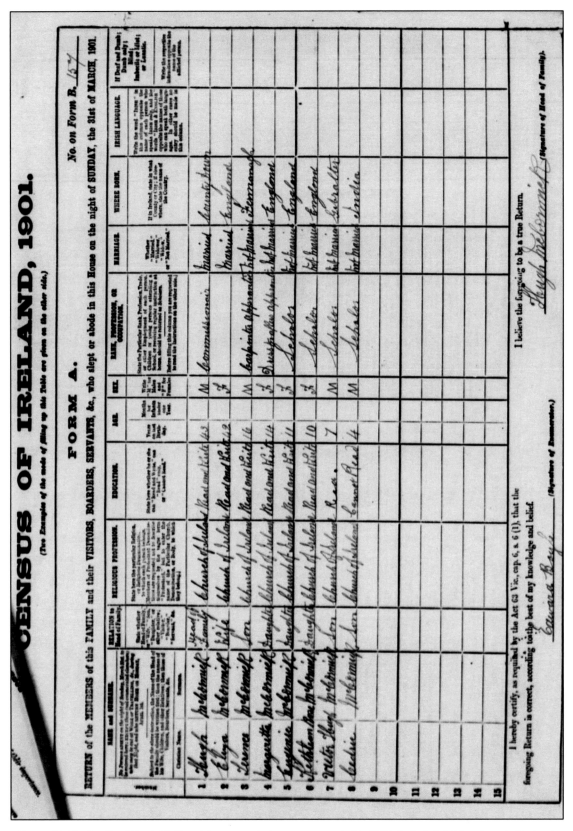

Figure 13: The family of Hugh McCormick, a commissioner, enumerated in 1901, included children born in England, Gibraltar, and India. Image courtesy of the National Archives of Ireland. Permission received.

matter, even if ancestors were gone for 100 years. Not all relatives emigrated, and someone might have been left on the family's property. Becoming preoccupied with only those who left instead of those who stayed is unwise. Sometimes, family members did remain behind. They could include parents, siblings, cousins, or those further removed. Accessing the geographical area is essential because it opens more records to search even in a census substitute strategy.

Thinking that all parish registers have all christenings and marriages is natural. Irish research is so unlike English, German, or Swedish research that comparisons are hard to find. *Not* finding ancestors in the church records databases for Ireland is not infrequent despite the parish registers being extant for the period the ancestors were there. Thus, census alternatives are necessary. Here, they are not substituting for missing census enumerations but for missing and incomplete church registers!

Aside from a general surname search of island-wide databases, rare first names or less common surnames can be used in conjunction with spouses' surnames to limit potential origins. In this tactic, a viable substitute can document the locations of the husband's surname and the wife's surname, which is why the birth names of women are indispensable. Maiden names of wives are ordinarily discovered not in the Irish records but in those in the immigrant countries. With

both names, how common they are becomes less important. The two surnames can be triangulated to a reasonable geographical distance from each other. Remember, not all marriage registers from which to document the events have survived in Ireland's parishes. Only the civil registrations of Protestant marriages from 1845 and all marriages from 1864 are generally available.

In the triangulation approach, the theory is that the future groom and the future bride had to have lived near each other to have met. Because an average tenant farmer might not have owned a horse, walking distance has to be judged. How far could the young man and young woman have walked to engage in a courtship? As logical and as simple as it seems, maybe five miles is more than a generous estimation. The real distance is probably within a couple of miles.

Another possibility for a couple to have become acquainted, other than catching a ride on someone's wagon to travel a few miles, was not in church and not in the neighborhood but often on the designated market day at the local market town. If they did meet at the market town, they could have been from opposite sides of the county or from different counties depending on from where the market town drew people on that day. Consequently, to continue a search in such a record as Griffith's, a wife's surname may be discovered five miles on one side of the market town and the husband's surname, five miles on the other side, or ten-plus miles between the two families. Therefore, be careful when thinking about a logical distance for couples to meet during the period. Distance can be an unquestionable factor when considering a surname distribution survey.

When a family is found in the church records' indexes, the problem is solved with maybe no need to consult a census alternative at all. However, when a family was not recorded in the registers, thinking creatively has to be the next step.

In most genealogy instruction books, the chapters on census substitutes typically present an array of sources by year. Most start with what is available from the 1600s and work forward to the 1911 census. Yet, most of the records, maybe with the exceptions of the Tithe Applotment, Griffith's Valuation, and the 1901 and 1911 censuses, were in communities instead of covering entire counties—assuming research already has produced a county name. In examples from County Monaghan, an inventory of sources from which a census substitute strategy can be developed could look something like the following:

1630: Muster Roll of Ulster.

1654: The Down Survey for Kilmore and Drumsnat Parishes in Eamonn Mulligan and Fr. Brian McCluskey, *The Replay: A Parish History* (Monaghan: Sean McDermotts G.F.C., 1984), pp. 343-346.

1659: Seamus Pender, *Census of Ireland* (Dublin: The Stationary Office, 1939), pp. 149-160.

1661-1859: "Members of the Irish Parliament for the Co. Monaghan," in Denis Carolan Rushe, *History of Monaghan for Two Hundred Years, 1660-1860* (1921 Revised. Monaghan, Ireland: The Clogher Historical Society, 1996), pp. 349-350.

1661-1800: "List of M.P.'s of Borough of Monaghan," in Denis Carolan Rushe, *History of Monaghan for Two Hundred Years, 1660-1860* (1921 Revised. Monaghan, Ireland: The Clogher Historical Society, 1996), pp. 350-351.

1663-1665: Hearth Money Roll in Denis Carolan Rushe, *History of Monaghan for Two Hundred Years, 1660-1860* (1921 Revised. Monaghan, Ireland: The Clogher Historical Society, 1996), pp. 291-338, 360-414.

1666-1668: Colony of Protestants to whom Catholic lands were made over by Letters Patent or Certificate in Killeevan Parish in Rev. J. E. M'Kenna PP. *Diocese of Clogher. Parochial Records. Monaghan* (Enniskillen: Fermanagh Herald, 1920), p. 576.

1751: List of members (subscribers) in the Ballyalbany Presbyterian Church in Rev. S. Lyle Orr and Alex. Haslett. *Historical Sketch of Ballyalbany Presbyterian Church* (Belfast: Steam-Printing Co., 1939), pp. 11-13.

1758-1759: Thomas Greer's (of Dungannon) Market Book for Crown Linen. Monaghan Town, Monaghan Parish (#771-799, 886-912, 980-1009).

[2]

Prſh. of AUGHALOW.

John Crozier—ONE LOOM.

	Wheels.
David Carroll	4
Alexander Pringle	4
Revd. David Holmes	4
Alexander Daviſon	4
William Thompſon	4
John Potter	4
William Lundy	4
Henry Hughes	4
Edward Hazleton	4
George Bell	4
Archibald M'Maſter	4
Joſeph Means	4
James Brown	4
Henry Kelly	4
James Hughes	4
George M'Cleery	4
James Douglas	4
James Robinſon, ſen.	4
James Robinſon, jun	4
Hariſon Marſhall	4
James Daviſon	4
Moſes M'Guffin	4
William Cullen	4
James M'Croden	4
John Henderſon	4
Phelix M'Kenna	4
James Pelligrew	4
Samuel Campbell	4
Samuel Johnſton	4
William Johnſton	4
James Hughes	4
Samuel M'Cheſney	4
John Auld	4
James Fleming	4
Widow M'Anallon	4
William Fleming	4
Matthew M'Guiffen	4
John M'Michael	4
Mary Beatty	4
William Coulter	4
John Daviſon	4
Robert Divin	4
John Caldwell	4
Alexander Beatty	4
John Loughran	4
John Bruſh	4
William Martin	4
Andrew Kyle	4
John Bruſh	4
John Hamill	4
James Murphy	4
Andrew M'Clelland	4
William Irwin	4
Thomas Montgomery	4
Revd. James Daviſon	4
Phelix Caſſidy	4
Francis M'Maghan	4
Barnaby Murphy	4

	Wheels.
Robert Leeſon	4
William Fleming	4
Adams Maxwell	4
Hugh Donaldſon	4
William Aken	4
James M'Mullen	4
Philip M'Guire	4
Robert Happer	3
Charles Higgins	3
John Oliver	3
David Wright	3
Robert Brown	3
Thomas Daviſon	3
Mary Moore	3
John Hamill, jun.	3
Robert Happar	3
Samuel Irwin	3
John Hetherinton	3
James M'Mullan	3
Richard M'Williams	3
William White	3
Margaret Bell	3
Robert Miller	3
James Begs	3
James Buchannan	3
John Brown	2
Robert Dixon	2
Joſeph Irwin	2
Hugh Warden	2
William Veaney	2
Widow Willſon	2
Thomas Ritherford	2
John Stewart	2
Patrick M'Kenna, ſen.	2
Daniel M'Cann	2
Robert Potter	2
Joſhua Wright, ſen.	2
Hugh Campbell	2
James Bell	2
Richard Barton	2
James Wright	2
Daniel Dougherty	2
John Campbell	2
James Hamill	2
John Walker	2
Joſeph Willſon	2
Thomas Willſon	2
John Hadden	2
John Tagert	2
Richard Bevins	2
Robert M'Ginn	2
Hugh Scott	2
Arthur Scott	2
Robert Riddle	2
Peter M'Kenna	2
James Campbell	2
William Irwin	2
Robert Johnſton	2
Thomas Kelly	2
Murtagh M'Ginn	2
Patrick Kerran	2

	Wheels.
John Hamill, ſen.	2
Robert Williamſon	2
Michael Dixon	2
Williams Williamſon	2
John Lowry	2
David M'Michael	2
Robert M'Michael	2
Denis Dawley	2
Hugh Loughran	2
Matthew Beatty	2
Robert Briſban	2
Patrick Grimley	2
Robert Sloan	2
William Sloan	2
Robert Beaty	2
William Mains	2
James M'Maghan	2
Alexander Jackſon	2
William Burnet	2
David Barnet	2
John Dixon	2
George Agnew	2
John M'Veigh	2
William M'Williams	2
Benjamin Smith	1
William Sherkey	2
Bryan M'Kenna	2
William Bell	2
George Little	2
George Caford	2
Moſes Little	2
James Adams	2
Barnaby M'Kenna	2
John Anguiſh	2
William M'Kenna	2
Mary Lunday	2
Widow Linn	2
James Clerk	2
William Delaney	2
Robert Todd	2
James Todd	2
Robert M'Cleery	2
Hugh Branigan	1
Edward M'Veigh	1
John Wright	1
William Cooper	1
Robert Willſon	1
Patrick M'Cluſkey	1
Samuel Ritherford	1
Samuel M'Kenna	1
Mary Black	1
Samuel Cooper	1
Patrick M'Kenna, jun.	1
James Burns	1
Robert Stevenſon	1
William Irwin	1
Robert Bryers	1
Francis M'Guncheſon	1
Neil Gilgranew	1
Widow O'Donald	1
Elizabeth Brown	1

Figure 14: 1796 spinning wheel entitlement list for "Aughalow" Parish (Agahloo), County Tyrone, Ireland. Such lists serve as excellent census substitutes. Produced by the Linen Trade Board. (Image courtesy of the National Library of Ireland. Irish copyrights apply for the life of the author plus 70 years. No permissions required.)

1761: Militia Officers in County Monaghan, pp. 61-62.

1772: "Castleblayney Rent Book" in *Clogher Record* 10, #3 (1981), pp. 414-418.

1777: "Petition for a Protestant Church in Carrickmacross 1777," in *Clogher Record* 6, #1 (1966), pp. 121-123.

1782: The gentlemen of the Home Rule Grand Jury of County Monaghan in Denis Carolan Rushe. *Monaghan in the Eighteenth Century* (Dublin: M.H. Gill & Sons, 1916), pp. 63-64.

1784-1789: Rental of the Anketeel Estate in Donagh and Errigal Truagh parishes in *Clogher Record* 11, #3 (1984), pp. 403-420.

1785: Male Protestants of 17 Years and Upward in Magheracloone, Killanny, Errigal Trough parishes.

1786: List of landholders on the Ballybay Estate taken from rental records in *Clogher Record* 11, #1 (1982), pp. 73-76.

1787: List of members (subscribers) of the Ballyalbany Presbyterian Church in Rev. S. Lyle Orr and Alex. Haslett. *Historical Sketch of Ballyalbany Presbyterian Church* (Belfast: Steam-Printing Co., 1939), pp. 48-50.

1790-1830: Tenants on the Ker Estate (Newbliss), Aghabog, and Killeevan parishes in *Clogher Record* 12, #1 (1985), pp. 110-126.

1794: "County Monaghan Subscribers to the Sixth Edition of the Troy Bible Issued 1794" in Denis Carolan Rushe, *History of Monaghan for Two Hundred Years, 1660-1860* (1921 Revised. Monaghan, Ireland: The Clogher Historical Society, 1996), pp. 355-356.

1796: Spinning Wheel Premium List.

1797-1825: "A List of the Officers of the Several District Corps of Ireland," – Monaghan: 1797 (p. 75); 1804 (pp. 93-95); 1820 (pp. 43-44); 1825 (pp. 36-37).

1804: Names of Officers in Monaghan Militia in Denis Carolan Rushe, *History of Monaghan for Two Hundred Years 1660-1860* (Monaghan, Ireland: The Clogher Historical Society, 1996), p. 166.

1804: List of seat holders in the Ballyalbany Presbyterian Church in Rev. S. Lyle Orr and Alex. Haslett. *Historical Sketch of Ballyalbany Presbyterian Church* (Belfast: Steam-Printing Co., 1939), pp. 64-69.

1805: "List of Officers of the Militia and the Gentlemen and Yeomanry Cavalry and Volunteer Infantry" from County Monaghan in the Groves Collection Box 17, pp. 91-93.

1807: County Monaghan Yeomanry and Volunteers (one manuscript page) in the Groves Collection Box 17.

1815: County Monaghan Yeomanry Crops on their return to Athlone in Denis Carolan Rushe, *History of Monaghan for Two Hundred Years 1660-1860*

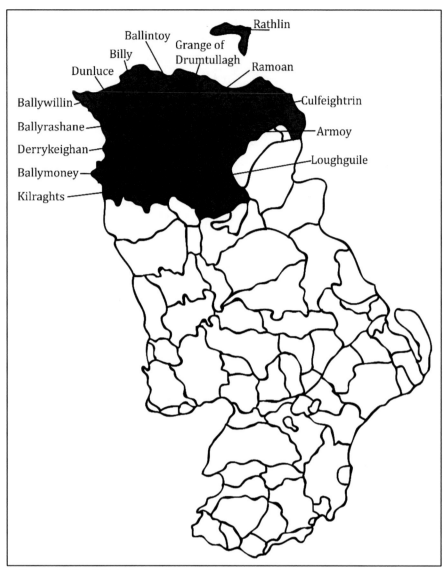

Figure 15: The 1803 Agricultural Census for County Antrim is one source to use when the county of origin is known. Surviving for only 14 civil parishes (shaded), it nonetheless can limit origins if the ancestors can be found in this collection.

1821: Census extracts See Theo McMahon's article "Some County Monaghan Extracts from the 1821 Census" in *Clogher Record* 14, #1 (1991), pp. 92-110.

1823: "Church of Ireland Members in the Aghadrumsee Area in 1823," in *Clogher Record* 15, #1 (1994), pp. 107-121.

1823-1834: Tithe Applotment Books.

1825: "Yeoman Cavalry and Volunteer Infantry" County Monaghan in the Groves Collection Box 17, pp. 36-37.

(Monaghan, Ireland: The Clogher Historical Society, 1996), p. 165.

1818: List of tenants in Kilnaclay, Drumsnat Parish in Eamonn Mulligan and Fr. Brian McCluskey. *The Replay: A Parish History* (Monaghan: Sean McDermotts G.F.C., 1984), p. 357.

1820: "Yeoman Cavalry and Volunteer Infantry" County Monaghan in the Groves Collection Box 17, pp. 43-44.

1826: Parochial Returns of school master and mistresses in Ulster – Monaghan in *Second Report of the Commissioners of Irish Education Inquiry* (Dublin: The House of Commons, 1826), pp. 448-471.

1832: Census of Donagh Parish with the Church of Ireland records.

1834: List of teachers and students of the Ballyalbany Presbyterian Church in

Rev. S. Lyle Orr and Alex. Haslett. *Historical Sketch of Ballyalbany Presbyterian Church* (Belfast: Steam-Printing Co., 1939), pp. 127-129.

1837-1838: Pawnbrokers in Ireland, Volume 17 *British Parliamentary Papers*.

1841: Selected families from the Gertrude Thrift Genealogical Abstracts (Bundle 18) including three families from Donagh Parish.

1841, 1851: Old Age Pension Applications. Indexed in Joseph Masterson, *Ireland: 1841/1851 Census Abstracts (Northern Ireland)* (Baltimore, Maryland: Genealogical Publishing Co., 1999).

1846-1863: Parish Register Printout of Loughmourne Presbyterian Church christenings, 1846-63. Loughmourne is in Aghnamullen Parish.

1847: Poor Law Rate Book, Castleblayney in *Clogher Record* 5, #1 (1963), pp. 131-148.

1850: List of Millers taken from the Ordnance Survey Memoirs in William E. Hogg's *The Millers & the Mills of Ireland of About*

1850 (Sandycove, Co. Dublin, Ireland: Millbrook Printing, 1998), pp. 301-305.

1858-1861: Griffith's Primary Valuation.

1901: Census of Ireland

1911: Census of Ireland

Certainly, the preceding records are varied, but they are not the only ones. They do demonstrate that except for the obvious sources, such as Griffith's, the Tithe Applotment, and the national censuses, each of the others standing on its own is not much help in either identifying surnames or solving immigration problems. Nevertheless, if they and additional documents from County Monaghan were

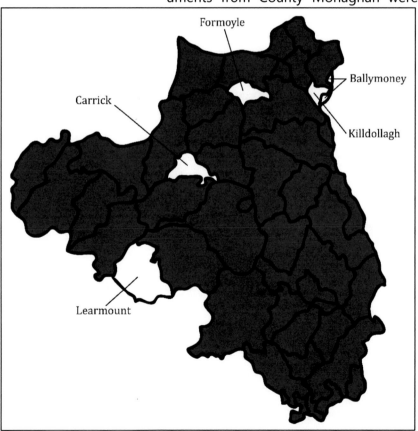

Figure 16: As can be seen, Londonderry (Derry) is unique, missing only five civil parishes from the 1831 census. The rest of the county remains intact, while the remainder of the country does not.

combined into one database, some serious study can be undertaken from several angles in a surname distribution survey. County-wide indexes are starting to be offered online. Some are appearing on RootsIreland.ie, where the entire range of odd and scattered records can be searched together. One major compilation is on the Ulster Historical Foundation's website Ancestryireland.com, but it is limited to the six counties of Ulster. Regardless, wherever such combined compilations of anomalous sources can be found, they can be exceptionally valuable.

If a County is Already Known

If the county of origin is already known, unfamiliar sources that have some coverage of the county can assist research. Two of interest are the 1803 Agricultural Census of Antrim and the 1831 Census of Londonderry. They can solve immigration problems for those two counties, but they require understanding their purposes, the kinds of people listed, and the range of reporting within the counties.

The 1803 Agricultural Census was a survey of fourteen civil parishes in northern County Antrim: Armoy, Ballintoy, Ballymoney, Ballyrashane, Ballywillin, Billy, Culfeightrin, Derrykeighan, Dunluce, Grange of Drumtullagh, Kilraghts, Lough-guile, Ramoan, and Rathlin. The information includes individuals' names, townlands, civil parishes, inventories of livestock, agricultural equipment and crops/ stores, and occupations for a minority of individuals. It did not encompass the entire county, but for 1803 and for that section of County Antrim, it is

amazing. This 1803 census is on Ancestryireland.com as well as indexed on other websites, which a simple internet search can easily identify.

The 1831 Census for County Londonderry (Derry) listed heads of households only for the following civil parishes: Aghadowy, Aghanloo, Agivey, Arboe, Artrea, Ballinderry, Ballyaghran, Ballynascreen, Ballyrashane, Ballyscullion, Ballywillin, Balteagh, Banagher, Bovevagh, Clondermot, Coleraine, Derryloran, Desertlyn, Desertmartin, Desertoghill, Drumachose, Dunboe, Dungiven, Errigal, Faughanvale, Kilcronaghan, Killelagh, Killowen, Kilrea, Lissan, Lower Cumber, Macosquin, Maghera, Magherafelt, Tamlaght, Tamlaghtard, Tamlaght Finlagan, Tamlaght O'Crilly, Templemore, Termoneeny, and Upper Cumber. This provides the names of the heads of households, parishes and townlands of residences, numbers of males and females, numbers of servants, and religions. It is on the websites of the National Archives of Ireland, FamilySearch.org, and Findmypast.com. Many researchers have solved immigration problems through this source, but they needed to know in advance the ancestors were from County Londonderry (Derry).

Again, odd and random documents, especially ones similar to the 1803 Agricultural Census, are not prevalent throughout all of Ireland, but any of the instruction books in their census substitute chapters have clues about what is available and the geographical areas encompassed. The census substitute chapters in these books are thus noteworthy.

1834 General Demographics for Primary Protestant Expansion in Ireland

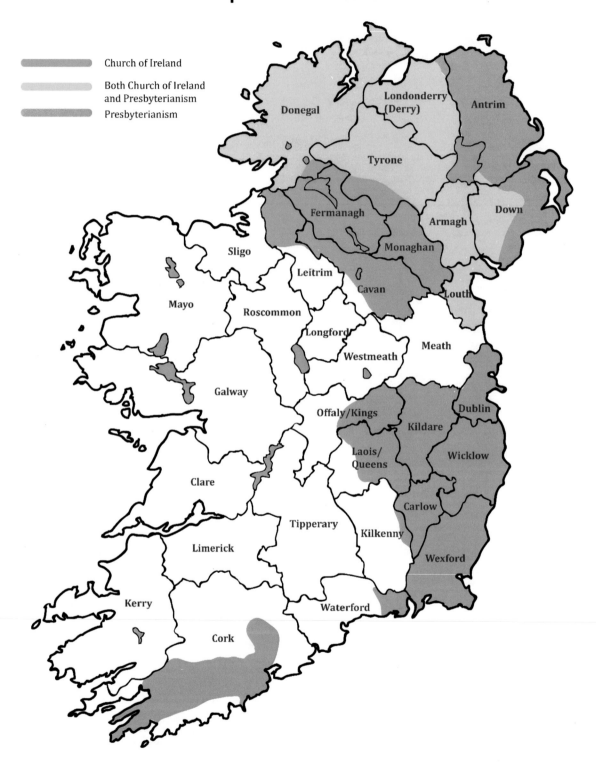

Figure 19: Although the predominant religion of Ireland remained Catholic, expansions of Protestant faiths, most notably the Church of Ireland (Anglican) and Presbyterianism, were significant by 1834.

Chapter Four

Church Records

To begin the search for Irish origins in church registers, determining whether the immigrant was Catholic or Protestant is essential because of the different research approaches to each denomination. If the answer is unknown, the accepted rule is that he or she likely was Protestant. The rationale is that Catholicism is a culture as well as a religion, and so an awareness of its relationship with the family usually was passed down in some form through the generations. This was not the same case for Protestants because Protestantism is different in its very foundation, that is, more individual in character, than Catholicism. Salvation is not based on the church as an institution or ritual but on personal faith, and although this conviction certainly has variations, it is a basic understanding. Denominational loyalty within Protestantism does not affect one's status as a Christian, and a Protestant denomination can be changed simply by transferring membership. Both church and rituals are essential for Catholics, and, consequently, the memories of their connections to the Church endure for generations, whether those images are positive, negative, or neutral.

From the Irish perspective, many books treat various denominations separately. One that encompasses the major and a few minor groups is James G. Ryan's *Irish Church Records: Their History, Availability and Use in Family and Local History Research*, 2nd ed. (Glenageary, Ireland: Flyleaf Press, 2001). As with any book published in today's market, it is dated the moment it is published. However, to place the situation in perspective, age only applies to the availability of digitized records and current databases. Church records remain, and the information about them is always relevant. Ryan's is a standard work in the field of Irish genealogy.

Even today, when discussing the religious lives of people in the Republic of Ireland and Northern Ireland, the major churches are:

- Roman Catholic
- Church of Ireland
- Presbyterian
- Methodist

The numbers of members in each denomination are in the above order. All four have had a tremendous historical influence on Ireland.

The roles of minority faiths are often ignored by researchers. Their impact was hidden from history for plentiful reasons, the most notable being emigration, which kept their already small populations at such a low level that they appear to have had no noticeable growth or significance. Therefore, a more holistic assessment of their true contributions is repeatedly missed. Minority faiths that have been chosen for an immigration discussion, in alphabetical order, are:

- Christian Brethren (Plymouth Brethren) and Gospel Hall
- Church of Jesus Christ of Latter-day Saints (Mormons)
- Congregational Church
- Moravians (United Brethren)
- Religious Society of Friends (Quakers)

Other than the Quakers, most of the minority faiths tend to be neglected in Irish reference books. Certainly, other denominations are also worthy of discussion, but for present immigration purposes, the ones listed are of immediate interest.

Mixed Marriages and Religious Conversions

Researchers who have spent time in church registers are aware of conversions to and from Catholic and Protestant churches. The conversions were sometimes for economic reasons because Catholics had their civil rights restricted until full Catholic Emancipation in 1829. Yet, logically, if a person was poor, regardless of religion, he or she had nothing to gain or lose in a Catholic-Protestant marriage.

Nonetheless, many conversions were motivated by marriage. It is usual to find in the Catholic registers that someone had "denounced the errors of Protestantism." It is also common in Protestant registers, especially those of the Church of Ireland, to see that someone "denounced the papacy" or the "errors of the papacy." Regardless of the way it was listed, it is an amazing clue about how it affected generations of immigrants and a point from where research should proceed.

In some cases, no mention of a conversion is in the church registers. Instead, the marriage was in one church or the other. The children's christenings might have been in either denomination or in several churches! The assortment of churches can certainly raise an entirely new set of questions as researchers try to decide if they have the same family or two different families with parents of the same names. Especially problematic is not knowing a wife's maiden name ahead of time to help sort through the entries in an index.

During the infamous Penal Laws, which were intended to force Irish Catholics and Protestant dissenters to accept the Church of Ireland, a Protestant of any denomination had no advantage from converting to Catholicism. Conversely, Catholics and non-Anglican Protestants converting to the Church of Ireland did have many benefits. For families of wealth, such as the landed Catholic families, financial security was more important than religious loyalty.

That the Protestant Reformation came to Ireland through conquest rather than through missionary work can be easily forgotten. At that victory, the old and majestic Catholic buildings, which still dot the land, became Church of Ireland parishes. It is so even to this day. For example, Dublin has two cathedrals, St. Patrick's Cathedral and Christ Church Cathedral. Both were originally Catholic structures and now are Church of Ireland. The same happened in England and Wales.

The Penal Laws were gradually dismantled between 1778 and 1793 and fully repealed with Catholic Emancipation in 1829. Throughout Ireland, new faiths came from missionaries and ministries from outside. They included the Mormons from the United States, the Religious Society of Friends (Quakers), and the United Brethren (Moravians) from England. Most conversions to any of them were from the already established Protestant denominations. Methodism is unique in its example of how incongruous and fascinating conversion can be.

Methodism spread swiftly throughout Ireland but remained embedded within the Church of Ireland as study groups. The denomination arose late in Ireland when compared to other religions, beginning about 1817-1818, and so conversion must be thought of a little differently when speaking of Methodists. It affects immigrant research because the first Irish Methodist congregations were in the 1760s in what became the United States and Canada. Thus, early Methodist research in Ireland, before 1817, may involve Anglican research. From an immigration perspective, do not assume that the denomination to which an ancestor belonged in the immigrant country was his or hers in Ireland as well.

Using Indexes and Databases

The availability of church record indexes and scanned images online has revolutionized Irish research. What once took months to obtain by mail systems can now be studied firsthand in minutes. While this technology has provided solutions to any number of immigrant problems, it has also brought new challenges to light, namely, the propensity of novice researchers to quickly connect to families that may share the same names but if caution were exercised, are clearly not ancestors.

The main indexes of Irish church records can be found on Ancestry.com, Findmypast.com, Irishgenealogy.ie, and RootsIreland.ie. Whether a database has both Catholics and Protestants or simply Catholics varies. FamilySearch.org has some church records also indexed. Because there is typically only one copy of each church register, all the websites are indexing from the same register or a modern transcript of that record. Therefore, each must be studied on its own merits and search capabilities.

For example, Ancestry.com and Findmypast.com both have the same index to the same Catholic registers, furnished to them by the National Library of Ireland from its microfilm collections. Technically, a search in one of the databases should be the same as that in the other, but because each has its unique way of searching the massive database, the results found may be dissimilar. Consulting both is wise. In addition, to obtain a clear picture, a third database of Catholic registers on RootsIreland.ie needs to be consulted. It has its own indexing method, done locally, from, theoretically, the original registers. The results can be unlike those found on Ancestry.com and Findmypast.com.

Surprisingly, when approaching church databases, many researchers forget to ask the basic question, What is on them? Only Catholic register indexes are on the aforementioned databases at Ancestry.com and Findmypast.com. RootsIreland.ie, on the other hand, hosts indexes from regional heritage centers, which can include a variety of denominations.

The next logical question is: When did the records begin? For example, if a Presbyterian christening in 1750 is required for research, after determining that no Presbyterian records are in a particular county or in the entire database before 1820, means a new strategy needs to be developed. In short, there is no christening document – period.

With any church records' database, some preliminary research needs to determine what has been indexed and when those records started. If a website does not have some version of an inventory page with this information, conduct a general search elsewhere. RootsIreland.ie has an excellent inventory page for each county for what is on its databases for all denominations. One quick way, at least for Catholic records, is to consult the maps on the JohnGrenham.com website, which lists the parishes, when their records began, where they are located, and the websites on which they are indexed.

What is reported on the databases is also an issue. Although the databases on Ancestry.com, Findmypast.com, and RootsIreland.ie are massive, they are not complete. RootsIreland.ie has county maps of Ireland showing which areas are covered and which are not. Typically, what is not included in the scope of its website can be found on Irishgenealogy.ie.

Keep in mind that theology creates records, and the subject of baptism provides a perfect example. Quakers, as an illustration, do not baptize, and so only birth records are what can be viewed on a database. Baptists theologically hold to believers' baptisms, performed by full submersions of believers upon confessions of faith. A "believer's baptism" is often referred to as "adult baptism" in some indexes. Consequently, infants are not christened. Methodists baptize by sprinkling, pouring, or full body submersion. Infants, young adults, or adults can be baptized. Catholics baptize by sprinkling or pouring water on infants or adult converts. Mormons not only baptize by full submersion but also on behalf of ancestors by living proxies in "baptisms for the dead." All these practices are centered on the facet of theology of each denomination, which in turn affects the records generated.

Perhaps being critical of findings is most important. In an era of easy and fast answers, the tendency among novice researchers is to attach to the wrong family, which is one of the most common problems in genealogy. The findings are added to someone's online tree, and they are spread, perpetuating incorrect information at record speed.

Do not accept a family from a database as your ancestor unless enough information confirms that those are the correct people. The difficult part from an immigration perspective is that the ages in the immigrant records seldom match the Irish records. The first names do not always match either because nicknames and variant names were often used, such as Delia for Bridget and Owen for Eugene. Also, even in the indexes, the original indexers might not have been familiar with Latin and could have confused the Latin for John for Joan or vice versa. The issues need to be heeded.

Therefore, it is imperative to have all the basic research completed in the immigrant country first. Get all the facts in line, the names of all the siblings of an ancestor, and, by all means, try to find a mother's maiden name. All will greatly assist in assuring the correct family has been identified in the Irish church databases. If there is still some uncertainty from the index results, trace the family discovered forward for those who stayed. If its members remained in Ireland when they were supposed to be in, for instance, Chicago, the wrong family has been targeted.

A final word about indexes is necessary. Not finding ancestors in church records' indexes is frequent, even if records are extant for the period in question. Many reasons for their absences exist, including gaps in records or unreadable and sloppy record-keeping practices by ministers and priests. The fact christenings and marriages are missing from the registers is, unfortunately, more common than researchers think. In such cases, immigrant origins may have to be located without the use of church registers.

Roman Catholic

Researchers who have spent time in Roman Catholic registers in many European countries are aware of how informative they can be. In fact, the details can be stunning. The situation is not the same for Irish Catholic registers.

Fortunately, most Catholic registers for all of Ireland are indexed on Ancestry.com, Findmypast.com, Irishgenealogy.ie, and RootsIreland.ie. They are also available on the website of the National Library of Ireland. Through all of them, except for a few stray parishes that have not been microfilmed or digitized yet, the coverage is excellent. More than one database having the same records is to the advantage of the research because errors and omissions can be identified.

Entries for christenings and marriages in Catholic registers are usually one or two lines, sometimes abbreviated, and can be written sloppily in either Latin or English. The typical record does not begin until the late 1820s or early 1830s, and these are incomplete as well. A practical rule is to never expect to find all the marriages and baptisms being sought. Discovering only part of the family in registers is a good day in Irish research and solves the immigration problem at hand. While certainly, in many cases, an entire family can be documented, there are also just as many cases where the family can only be partially documented. A partial documentation of a family is still fine because in theory, the family had all their children in the same parish. Of course, that fact is not universal but is a place to start, and so knowing who other siblings are from the immigrant country records is extremely helpful.

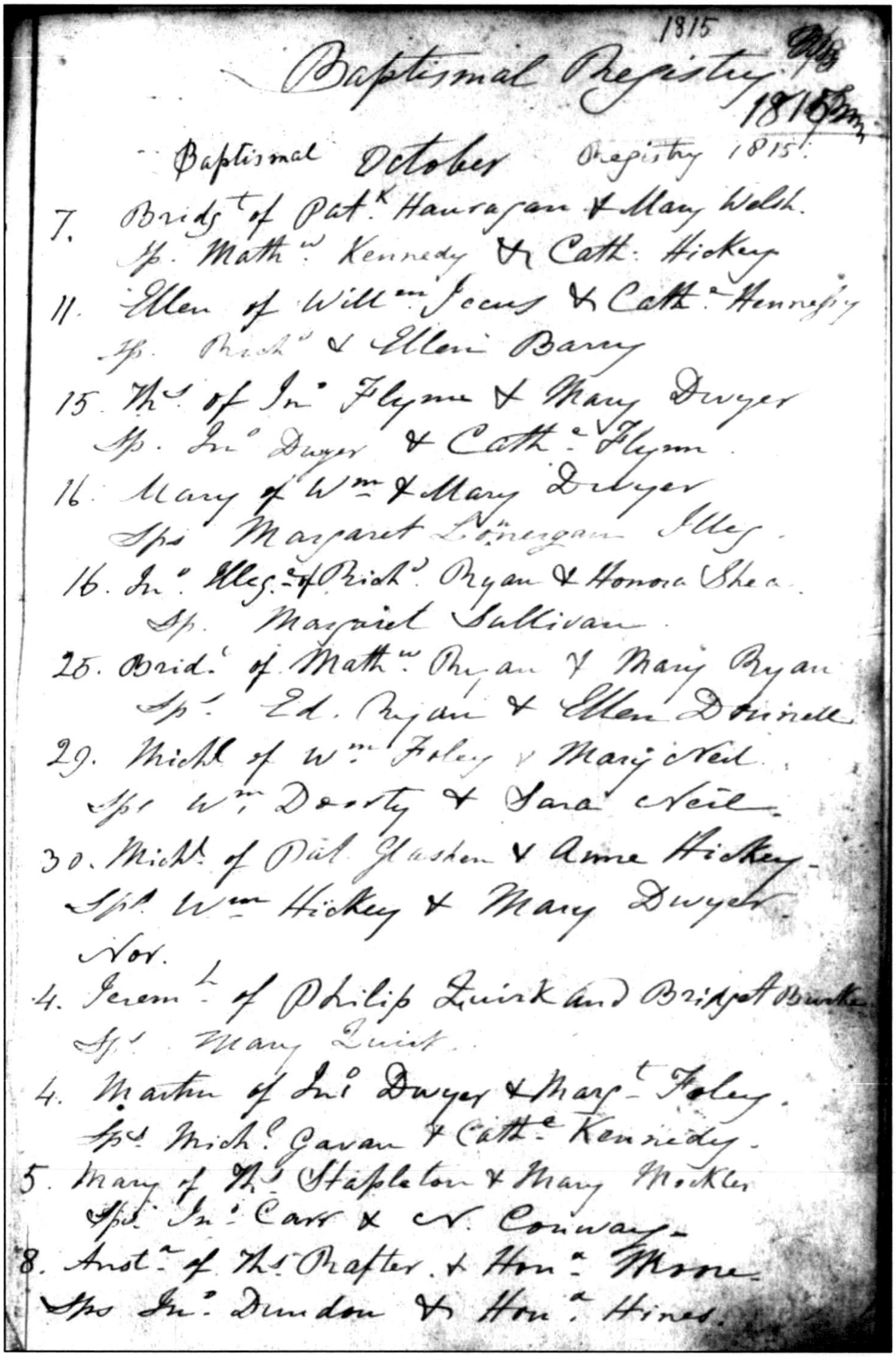
1815
Baptismal Registry 1815
Baptismal October Registry 1815.
7. Bridt of Patk Hanragan & Mary Walsh.
Sp. Mathw Kennedy & Cath. Hickey
11. Ellen of Willm Jeens & Cathe Hennessy
Sp. Richd & Ellen Barry
15. Ths of Jno Flynn & Mary Dwyer
Sp. Jno Dwyer & Cathe Flynn.
16. Mary of Wm & Mary Dwyer
Sps Margaret Lonergan Illeg.
16. Jno Illeg. of Richd Ryan & Honora Shea.
Sp. Margaret Sullivan.
25. Brid. of Mathw Ryan & Mary Ryan
Sp. Ed. Ryan & Ellen Donnell
29. Michl of Wm Foley & Mary Neil.
Sps Wm Dorty & Sara Neil.
30. Michl of Pat Gleshen & Anne Hickey.
Spt Wm Hickey & Mary Dwyer.
Nov.
4. Jeremh of Philip Quirk and Bridget Burke
Sps Mary Quirk.
4. Martin of Jno Dwyer & Mary Foley.
Sps Michl Gavan & Cathe Kennedy.
5. Mary of Ths Stapleton & Mary Mockler
Sps Jno Carr & N. Conway.
8. Anste of Ths Rafter & Hona Moore
Sps Jno Dundon & Hona Hines.

Figure 20: Catholic baptisms for Cappawhite, County Tipperary, Ireland. Note that these registers provide the names of the children, names of the parents (including maiden names of the mothers), and names of sponsors (godparents). Other parish registers may contain more or fewer details. (Image courtesy of the National Library of Ireland. Refer to https://registers.nli.ie/about#about_usage_rights_header)

A typical marriage entry has the names of the couple, the date, sometimes residence, and the witnesses. A typical christening has the baptismal date (sometimes a birth date), names of the child and parent or parents, the mother's maiden name, sometimes residence, and sponsors' (godparents') names. Burials are seldom noted in registers because baptisms and marriages are sacraments of the Catholic Church and burials are not. Again, the reasons records were generally created about vital events were theological.

Causes vary for the poor record-keeping practices. The most incomplete registers can be found on the western coast. There, priests trained in dioceses often served the parishes. The priests went to the countryside to perform their religious duties. In rural Ireland, especially in poor areas, people did not own horses, and so travel to church buildings to have children christened was a hardship. Scraps of paper with notations or the memories of the days' events then were brought back by the priests, who added them to the main church registers. The jottings frequently were forgotten.

Immigration Strategies
Even though the Irish Catholic registers may not meet the standards of other countries, they remain invaluable and may be the source that solves the question of immigrant origins. However, care needs to be taken when using them and maneuvering through the properties that each database offers. Researchers must be more creative in how they approach information and the indexes that accompany it.

For example, when trying to find an ancestral entry, it is also necessary to determine whether the search capability of a database can effectively sift and discern the information being sought. As a model, a theoretical couple named Patrick Sullivan and Mary O'Donnell in the original parish register page could appear as parents as:

- Patrick Sullivan & Mary O'Donnell
- Patrick & Mary Sullivan
- Patrick O'Sullivan & Mary his wife
- Patrick Sullivan & wife
- Patrick Sullivan & Mary Donnell (or Donald or Donel)
- Ptk Sullivan & My O'Donnell
- P. Sullivan & M. Don.

Regardless, to find all children, carefully test each of them in a "parent search," leaving the first name of the child blank. Normally, a good search feature should automatically correlate O'Sullivan and Sullivan. Where it might have trouble is with *Ptk* and *My*. Often, the indexers cannot tell *My* from *Mg* for Margaret; therefore, it becomes indexed under Margaret instead of Mary. Be aware that the database searches are not as straightforward as often advertised.

To ascertain how sophisticated a search feature is, pick a surname that can be spelled numerous ways and see if one search finds them all. A good one is Byrne, Burns, Beirne, and Bierne, and then with *O'B** in the name. Once the researcher identifies the limitations of a given database search, efforts can proceed accordingly.

But even in the same register, the same priest might have recorded two different names for a surname. For example, Cassidy and Casserly are interchangeable, and the search engines may or may not pick up both together. If a *Cass** or *Cas*y* can be used, the problem would be solved but would also create another because the common name Casey would be mixed into the findings.

If a parish is known, discovered, for instance, from a tombstone in a Catholic cemetery abroad or a death certificate, but the index is of no assistance, look page by page at the digitized version of the register. The pages are online at the National Library of Ireland website, Ancestry.com, and FamilySearch.org. Afterward, research efforts can state with confidence whether the family was listed in the registers or not.

Female Names in the Records

One area that is never very certain and can throw off any search for immigrant ancestors is how women's names were recorded, by their married names or their birth surnames. In marriage records, the goal is not the ones for the brides but for any female witnesses. The same is true for christenings. Whether a female sponsor (godmother) was listed by her married or birth surname can make a tremendous difference in research, and both names appearing for her is possible.

In the quest to identify the correct family and not just one that seems correct, the sponsors' names are vital pieces of information. Godparents are chosen from among the friends and relatives of the parents. They often also immigrated to the same place the parents did. Hence, if it is uncertain that the exact family has

---

Abbreviations for Selected Religious Orders of Women Active in Ireland Before 1920

CHF	Holy Faith Sisters
CSB	Congregation of St. Brigid (Brigidine Sisters)
DC	Daughters (Sisters) of Charity of St. Vincent de Paul
IBVM	Institute of the Blessed Virgin Mary (Loreto Sisters)
OCD	Order of Discalced Carmelite Nuns
OP	Nuns of the Order of Preachers (Dominican Sisters)
OSB	Sisters of the Order of St. Benedict (Benedictine Nuns)
OSU	Order of St. Ursuline (Ursuline Nuns)
PBVM	Sisters of the Presentation of the Blessed Virgin Mary (Presentation Sisters)
PCC/OSC	Poor Clares
RSC	Religious Sisters of Charity (Irish Sisters of Charity)
RSM	Religious Sisters of Mercy
RGS/CGS	Good Shepherd Sisters

been found in the indexes, the witnesses' and godparents' names can be used as a guide. Ask who they were, whether the ancestors acted as godparents for their children, and whether all were together in one location, for example, San Francisco.

No rule governs the use of female surnames in the records. Technically, the beginning assumption is that females were listed by their birth surnames because in christenings, the mothers' maiden names were habitually recorded. Exceptions must be carefully considered. It is easier to use the male godparents' names because their surnames do not change.

Researching Catholic Religious
The background of a priest, nun, or other religious in the family should be examined. It is a recurrently overlooked immigration strategy. Religious are prime candidates for exploration because they were educated, creating records. The records are held by the order to which

Abbreviations for Selected Religious Orders of Men Active in Ireland Before 1920

CFC	Congregation of Christian Brothers (of Ireland)
CM	Congregation of the Mission (Vincentians)
CP	Congregation of the Passion (Passionists)
C.S.Sp	Holy Spirit (Holy Ghost) Congregation
C.SS.R	Congregation of the Most Holy Redeemer (Redemptorists)
FPM	Presentation Brothers
FSC	Brothers of the Christian Schools (De La Salle Brothers)
FSP	Congregation of the Brothers of St. Patrick (Patrician Brothers)
IC	(prev. OC) Institute of Charity (Rosminians) (prev. Order of Charity)
O.Carm	(prev. OCC) Order of Carmelites of the Ancient Observance (prev. Caleed Carmelites)
OCD	Order of Discalced Carmelites
OCSO	(prev. Cist.) Cistercian Order of the Strict Observance (Trappists)
OFM	(OSF until 1897) Order of Friars Minor (Franciscans)
OFM.Cap	(prev. OSFC) Capuchin Friars
OFM.CONV	Conventual Franciscans
OH	Hospitaller Brothers of the Order of St. John of God (St. John of God Brothers)
OMI	Oblates of Mary Immaculate
OP	Order of Preachers (Dominican)
OSA	Order of St. Augustine (Augustinians)
OSB	Order of St. Benedict (Benedictine Monks)
OSF	Brothers of the Third Order Regular of St. Francis (Franciscan Brothers)
SJ	Society of Jesus (Jesuits)
SM	Society of Mary (Marists)
SMA	(prev. AM) Society of African Missions

the religious belonged and are not part of the parish registers. It is customary for the ordination documents to have birthplaces, regardless of where the priest, nun, or brother served in the world.

If researching male religious, remember that they might have been well-educated, well-traveled, authors of books, and, most significantly, might have left behind that all-important paper trail. At the very least, these men may have been mentioned in newspapers either before emigration or in the place where they settled, and perhaps both. These men in the family history should be among the first to be researched in any Catholic family tree. The key to accessing religious records about a man is to identify the order he joined. It can be found in a history book or, in all probability, in an obituary. The letters after his name identify his order and training, but they can be baffling, especially for people unfamiliar with Roman Catholic orders.

If a religious man was trained in Ireland, the orders and corresponding letters refer to an order operating in Ireland or that was at one time. For example, the OP is the Order of Preachers (Dominicans), SJ for the Society of Jesus (Jesuits), and the SM for the Society of Mary (Marists). Once the Religious Order has been identified, conduct an Internet search for a website or contact the Central Catholic Library in Dublin, or even the archive of that order.

For women religious trained in Ireland, the same principle applies. They had educations, could have traveled extensively, and could have left writings behind.

Many were teachers in parochial schools globally. Their religious records should be with their orders' motherhouses. As with the men, each order has initials, which are in obituaries for the women. For example, CSB for the Congregation of St. Brigid (Brigidine Sisters), OP for Nuns of the Order of Preachers (Dominican Sisters), OSU for Order of St. Ursuline (Ursuline Nuns), and PBVM for Sisters of the Presentation of the Blessed Virgin Mary (Presentation Sisters) or IBVM, the Institution of the Blessed Virgin Mary of the Loreto Order. Once identified, search the Internet for a website if the order is still operating in Ireland. Otherwise, contact the Central Catholic Library in Dublin or each order's archives. Within the records of the order, the nun's birthplace in Ireland may be preserved, thus solving the immigration question for everyone in the family. For further reference to Irish orders and the abbreviations for them, Kyle J. Betit's article "Priests, Nuns and Brothers in Ireland" in *The Irish At Home and Abroad* 5, No. 2 (2nd Quarter 1998), pp. 70-76, is difficult to surpass in scope.

Church of Ireland

The Church of Ireland is a member of the Worldwide Anglican Communion. In different countries and regions, the church has different names. An Anglican Province could encompass several countries. Examples within the Anglican Communion are: Church of England, Episcopal Church of the United States, Anglican Church of Australia, Anglican Church of Canada, Anglican Church of Southern Africa, Church in Wales, The Scottish Episcopal Church, and the subject of this discussion, the Church of Ireland. They are all the same denomination even though they are diverse culturally, theologically, and socially. National churches and the parishes range from extreme conservative to extreme liberal, with everything in between.

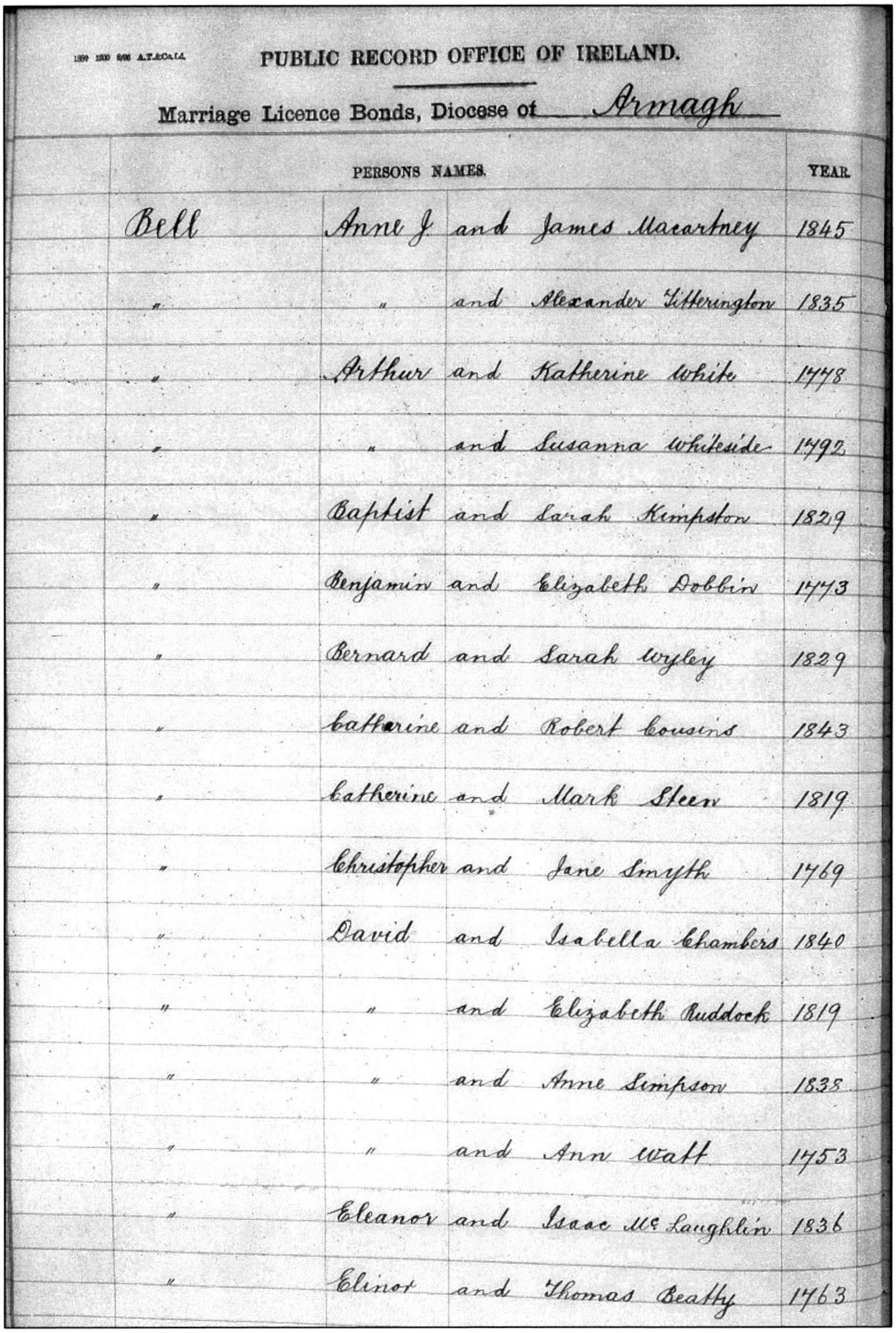

1890 1820 500 A.T.&Co.Ld.	PUBLIC RECORD OFFICE OF IRELAND.		
	Marriage Licence Bonds, Diocese of *Armagh*		
	PERSONS NAMES.		YEAR.
Bell	*Anne J* and *James Macartney*		*1845*
"	" and *Alexander Titterington*		*1835*
"	*Arthur* and *Katherine White*		*1778*
"	" and *Susanna Whiteside*		*1792*
"	*Baptist* and *Sarah Kimpston*		*1829*
"	*Benjamin* and *Elizabeth Dobbin*		*1773*
"	*Bernard* and *Sarah Wyley*		*1829*
"	*Catherine* and *Robert Cousins*		*1843*
"	*Catherine* and *Mark Steen*		*1819*
"	*Christopher* and *Jane Smyth*		*1769*
"	*David* and *Isabella Chambers*		*1840*
"	" and *Elizabeth Ruddock*		*1819*
"	" and *Anne Simpson*		*1838*
"	" and *Ann Watt*		*1753*
"	*Eleanor* and *Isaac McLaughlin*		*1836*
"	*Elinor* and *Thomas Beatty*		*1763*

Figure 21: A Church of Ireland marriage bond index from Armagh Diocese. (Image courtesy of the National Archives of Ireland. Permission received.)

In Ireland, Anglican was the state religion, also termed the "established church," meaning it was *the* Protestant Church on the island from 1536 through 1870. After it was disestablished, on 1 January 1871, it became one of many churches operating in Ireland, and after 1922, in Northern Ireland, it accounted for more than 12 percent of the population. Its history is different from Anglicanism in other parts of the world. As a minority faith, it was surrounded by and responsible for often hostile and uncooperative Catholics and Presbyterians or both, depending on the part of Ireland. Their congregations were on the edge of Europe, resulting in them repeatedly being ignored and underfunded from the home base in Canterbury, England.

Before its disestablishment as the state religion, the term Protestant was used in its narrowest sense, referring strictly to members of the Church of Ireland. All others were dissenters, also termed nonconformists. As the state religion, it had certain privileges as well as responsibilities. Not only were people of all faiths in a parish expected to pay tithes (such as the Tithe Applotment) but also the church, with those funds, was expected to undertake certain civic duties for all in the local community, such as caring for the poor of all faiths; the upkeep of the streets, security, and lighting throughout the parish watch; and burials of the dead.

The place of the Church of Ireland in Irish society is complex, and understanding how it affected everyone in Ireland can explain records. Anglicans see themselves as a "reformed catholic church," using the word catholic not in a denominational sense but in a historical and traditional sense. The church shares many of the same saints with the Roman Catholic Church in Ireland. Its place as the state religion came through English conquest, not through missionary work. It splits the difference between Catholics and evangelicals, being neither and both at the same time. As the established church, everyone was affected by it to some degree. In immigrant research, some of the more obvious ways it did so that affect genealogical efforts and explain some oddities are:

- As the state religion, everyone had the right to be buried in the parish graveyards, and so expect to find people of all faiths interred in the oldest Church of Ireland cemeteries for parishes. Many have their own traditional Catholic sections. Always look in the Church of Ireland cemeteries for burials before dedicated Catholic graveyards were established.

- Catholic families who had arrived from England in the Middle Ages intermarried with the local Irish. Being Catholic, and so to protect assets, many in this class of Catholics converted to the Church of Ireland. Preserving wealth took precedence over religious loyalty. Affluent Catholic, now Protestant, families left many records, genealogies, and histories behind.

- To maintain what they had, Catholics of means regularly

married in the Church of Ireland and had some or all children christened by Anglican ministers. It was also common for them to have some or all children christened by Roman Catholic priests. In other words, look in the registers of both churches for this class of people. A clue to the family's social status is its being listed in the indexes of church records.

- Methodism, which in Ireland began as study classes within local parish churches, remained within the Church of Ireland later than it did in other parts of the British Isles. It was not until 1818 that the Wesleyan Methodist Church separated from it. The Primitive Wesleyan Methodists continued as part of the parish system until 1878, when the two versions of Methodism joined, and so early Irish Methodist research is intertwined with Anglican research.

- Presbyterians, although they were Protestant dissidents, have a long history with the Church of Ireland. In Scotland, most were Presbyterians, and most arrived in the 1600s to Ulster as Presbyterians. However, intermarriages were usual, and so many of the Scots-Irish (Ulster-Scots) emigrants left as Anglicans, not as Presbyterians.

- If tracing an Anglican family abroad, assume that in Ireland, it had some status and accumulated some wealth. This was not always the case. Many were tenant farmers, like their neighbors, but it is a starting point because the denomination was conducive to upward mobility.

- Before 1782, marriages performed by dissident ministers were not legal, and before 1845, those ministers could not perform mixed marriages. Also, Methodist chapels or preaching houses were not licensed by the government until 1863. Accordingly, a Methodist marriage most likely occurred in the Church of Ireland parish.

Determining What Has Survived

After 1 January 1871, when the church was disestablished, its registers as public property began to be deposited at the Public Record Office in Dublin, now the National Archives of Ireland in Dublin. When the Four Courts, where the archives were housed, was burned in the 1922 Irish Civil War, about half of the Church of Ireland registers, approximately 1,006, from throughout Ireland were destroyed.

For the family historian seeking Anglican registers, the first task is to determine what has and has not survived and whether any second copies were made before 1922. The quickest way to verify record survival is to consult the online edition of "Table of Church of Ireland Parish Registers" on the Representative Church Body Library (RCBL) website, which is updated periodically. This online work codes in color the status of parish registers. Once it has been established whether a record still exists, a research strategy can be developed and indexes searched.

Major repositories for Church of Ireland registers are the RCBL in Dublin and the PRONI in Belfast. Some parish registers remain with local parish churches, but an excellent effort to gather and preserve them has been made.

Registers and Indexes

Not all Church of Ireland registers currently have been indexed. Places to begin the search are RootsIreland.ie, which has indexes for large collections of parish registers. The inventory on the website for each county shows exactly what parishes and what years are on the database. The Representative Church Body Library in Dublin is also indexing some parish registers in its custody, and they are on its RCBL website. The website Irishgenealogy.ie has major Church of Ireland indexes for County Carlow, Dublin City, and County Kerry.

Parish registers consist of births/christenings, marriages, and burials and are the record types that are found in the various indexes. The vestry minutes, which are the business books of the parishes, may or may not contain vital information. They typically are not indexed unless any vital information has been extracted from them.

Vestry Minutes

The vestries were committees responsible for the upkeep of churches and welfare of all the people within the parish boundaries irrespective of religion. Their records can provide a great deal of personal detail about who lived where. As manuscript books, they are usually arranged chronologically. As business minutes of the parish, they can include a wide range of data. The parish committees or vestries before the disestablishment of the church on 1 January 1871 acted as local councils. They levied taxes for general services, such as the upkeep of roads, relief for the poor, and security.

The record-keeping process varies from parish to parish. Some are neat and chronological. Others are haphazard, with a poor dating system to mark off new days, months, or even years.

At times, the minutes have vital information. Sometimes, rare items such as emigration lists, property owners, and ratepayers were included as well as parish censuses. Some vestry minutes were deposited at the Public Record Office before 1922 because they did contain vital information. Most were not turned in, though, and so they may be the only remaining collections for parishes whose other records were destroyed in 1922.

Church of Ireland Marriage Bonds Indexes (pre-1845)

Before 1845, people wishing to obtain a marriage license without having banns in the parish churches were required to place bonds with the bishops of the dioceses. The original licenses and bonds did not survive, but the bond indexes have for most of the Diocesan Courts. Transcripts of the Prerogative Court were made before the 1922 fire.

Church of Ireland Diocesan Courts by County

County	Diocesan Courts
Antrim	Connor, Derry, Down, Dromore
Armagh	Armagh, Dromore
Carlow	Leighlin
Cavan	Ardagh, Kilmore, Meath
Clare	Killaloe & Kilfenora, Limerick
Cork	Ardfert & Aghadoe, Cork & Ross, Cloyne
Donegal	Clogher, Derry, Raphoe
Down	Connor, Down, Dromore, Newry & Mourne
Dublin	Dublin
Fermanagh	Clogher, Kilmore
Galway	Clonfert, Elphin, Killaloe & Kilfenora, Kilmacduagh, Tuam
Kerry	Ardfert & Aghadoe
Kildare	Dublin, Kildare, Leighlin
Kilkenny	Leighlin, Ossory
Leitrim	Ardagh, Kilmore
Leix (Queen's)	Dublin, Kildare, Leighlin, Ossory
Limerick	Cashel & Emly, Killaloe & Kilfenora, Limerick
Londonderry (Derry)	Armagh, Connor, Derry
Longford	Ardagh, Meath
Louth	Armagh, Clogher, Drogheda
Mayo	Killala & Achonry, Tuam
Meath	Armagh, Kildare, Kilmore, Meath
Monaghan	Clogher
Offaly (King's)	Clonfert, Kildare, Killaloe & Kilfenora, Meath, Ossory
Roscommon	Ardagh, Clonfert, Elphin, Tuam
Sligo	Ardagh, Elphin, Killala & Achonry
Tipperary	Cashel & Emly, Killaloe & Kilfenora, Waterford & Lismore
Tyrone	Armagh, Clogher, Derry
Waterford	Waterford & Lismore
Westmeath	Ardagh, Meath
Wexford	Dublin, Ferns
Wicklow	Dublin, Ferns, Leighlin

From an immigration purpose, the marriage bond indexes are important for locating people. While the names of the grooms and brides along with the dioceses are listed, more exact locations within the dioceses are not given. When using the source, remember that, generally, the people were moneyed Protestants because obtaining a marriage license bond required a payment. Therefore, the lists are not complete for all Protestant marriages.

The indexes are on the National Archives of Ireland website as well as on FamilySearch.org and Findmypast.com, but it is necessary to know which dioceses are in which counties. Without this knowledge, the indexes are not helpful. The chart on page 51 will assist.

Not all the manuscript diocesan indexes have survived. Again, knowing which books did or did not will aid in sorting through what is being viewed on the online indexes. Those that have survived are indicated with the included years in the chart below.

Prerogative Court Indexes

The Prerogative Court issued marriage license bonds and covered all of Ireland. Like the diocesan marriage bonds, the marriage license bonds were also destroyed in the 1922 Four Courts Fire, but the indexes survive as do abstracts made before 1922. They are indexed on the National Archives of Ireland website, FamilySearch.org, and Findmypast.com.

Surviving Marriage Bond Indexes for Each Diocese

Diocesan Court	Years
Ardfert & Aghadoe	---
Armagh	1727-1845
Cashel & Emly	1664-1857
Clogher	1709-1866
Clonfert	1739, 1815-1844
Cloyne	1630-1866
Cork & Ross	1623-1845
Derry	---
Down, Connor, Dromore	1721-1845
Dublin	1672-1741
	1638-1800
	1630-1825
Elphin	1709-1845
Kildare	1790-1865
Killala & Achonry	1787-1842
Killaloe	1718-1845
Kilmore & Ardagh	1697-1844
Limerick	1827, 1833, 1844
Lismore Peculiar Jurisdiction	1779-1802
Meath	1655, 1702-1845
Newry & Mourne	---
Ossory, Ferns & Leighlin	1691-1845
Raphoe	1710-55, 1817-30
Tuam	1769-1845
Waterford & Lismore	1649-1845

The Prerogative Court documented moneyed Protestants.

Presbyterian Church

Presbyterians arrived en masse to Ulster throughout the 1600s. About 200,000 emigrated from Scotland to Ulster. Most of the incoming settlers were Lowland Scots farmers, and most came from Ayrshire, Galloway, Lanarkshire, Renfrewshire, and along the border with England. They were tenant farmers in Scotland who went to Ulster for better lives, only to continue as tenant farmers under the English landlord system. They were planted by the Crown as loyal Protestants on lands cleared during the wars that desolated Ulster and left it in ruin. This process is referred to as "Ulster Plantations."

As a result of their immigration history and their concentration in Ulster Province, some fascinating strategies have been developed that can assist in locating Ulster origins. While not all Presbyterians were confined to Ulster, the region is the focus of this chapter's section. It includes the six counties that now comprise Northern Ireland (Antrim, Armagh, Down, Fermanagh, Londonderry, and Tyrone) and three in the Republic of Ireland (Cavan, Donegal, and Monaghan). Today, the various branches of Irish Presbyterianism remain the third largest religious group in all of Ireland.

Often called Ulster-Scots, or in the United States, Scots-Irish, the people developed into an ethnic group, separate and isolated from their counterparts in Scotland. Yet, what exactly constitutes an Ulster-Scot is complicated. While it is true that most arrived as Presbyterians in the 1600s, a classification becomes far more complex if religions and Scottish surnames are used as a guide. For this reason, a broader definition of Scots-Irish needs to be taken because of conversions and intermarriages with other faith groups. At the time of immigration, a Scot-Irish rooted family might have been Anglican, Christian Brethren (Plymouth Brethren), Methodist, Moravian, Mormon, Quaker, or even Roman Catholic and might have been named Smith, Jones, or Williams. For researchers seeking immigrant origins, it is sensible to treat any Ulster lineage as potentially having Ulster-Scots lines intermixed. They may not be, but an expanded description of who the Ulster-Scots were needs to be considered. Using surnames and religions only as a guide may convey part of the picture but perhaps not all of it.

Presbyterian Registers and Indexes

If an ancestor's county or origin is not known, church records' indexes are the first places to begin research. Presbyterian registers are still in the process of being indexed. For Ulster, most of the locally produced indexes are online at RootsIreland.ie. Always check its online inventory of church records to see how complete it is and when the registers began. Presbyterian registers in Ireland cannot be judged by the standards of Scotland. In Ireland, they typically started in the 1820s and 1830s, and so if registers are of no assistance, a new research strategy has to be developed.

One important work for determining when Presbyterian registers and session

Guide to Church Records

	Ref No.
[see under NEWRY]	
S	
SAINTFIELD, CO. DOWN	
C.I. Saintfield (Down diocese)	
Baptisms, 1724-57 and 1793-1961; marriages, 1724-57, 1798 and 1813-45; burials, 1824-1831 and 1834-78; confirmations, 1832; vestry minutes, 1730-1920, which include accounts; minutes of Saintfield Auxiliary Bible Society, 1837-57.	**MIC1/69; CR1/4; D1759/1D/1 - available on MIC637/2**
Churchwardens' accounts, 1871-; cess applotment, 1833-; register of vestrymen, 1870-; preachers' books, 1849-69 and 1877-1924.	**In local custody**
P. 2nd Boardmills	
Baptisms, 1846-1950; marriages, 1847-1902; session minutes, 1857-1908 and 1931-66, [session minutes, 1931-66, relate to the congregations of 2nd Boardmills and Killaney].	**MIC1P/102; D1759/1D/2 - available on MIC637/2**
Marriage notice books, 1871-1901.	MIC1P/230/5/1-2
P. 1st Saintfield	
Baptisms, 1854-1986; marriages, 1845-1905; marriage notice book, 1871-77.	**MIC1P/298; T2320; MIC1P/230/5/1**
Session minutes, 1845-69; treasurers' book containing a list of seatholders, 1855-60.	T1184
Volume of manuscript notes giving dates and places of death of members, c. 1950-c.1961.	D1693/3
P. 2nd Saintfield	
Baptisms, 1831-1902; marriages, 1831-1930; burials, 1831-84; details of elders, 1831-9.	**MIC1P/289**
R.C. Carrickmannon and Saintfield (Down and Connor diocese)	
Baptisms, 1837-81; marriages, 1845-83.	**MIC1D/63**
SALLAGHY CHURCH OF IRELAND PARISH, CO. FERMANAGH	

338
Public Record Office of Northern Ireland
© Crown Copyright 2019

Figure 22: Inventories from PRONI's Guide to Church Records. Note the Presbyterian congregations prefaced with the letter P. This source addresses areas mainly in Ulster. (This work is produced and copyrighted by the Crown Copyright©. Meeting Open Government License qualifications for this content, no additional permissions required.)

minutes began is online at the PRONI as *Guide to Church Records*. The listing of church registers is by civil parish and details the Presbyterian denomination, when its records began, and where they are located. Presbyterian registers or copies of registers are usually at the PRONI, Presbyterian Historical Society of Ireland, or in local custodies. It is a principal resource and is updated periodically, but to use it, researchers need to know the ancestors' home places. If they are not known, and indexes, such as on RootsIreland.ie or AncestryIreland.com, do not help, other strategies have to be utilized.

Probably the most effective plan is a surname distribution survey, with records, such as Griffith's Primary Valuation (1847-1864), to determine in which civil parishes surnames were located. Even if an ancestor was gone long before Griffith's, a surname distribution survey can still be essential because not all relatives emigrated. Once potential civil parishes are identified, the church records that are not indexed can be searched if they date back far enough. This strategy is effective when two or more surnames are known to have come from the same area. A husband's surname with his wife's birth name can work. Odd or uncommon surnames also produce good results. Common surnames are not as successful without the second surname.

Even if registers are present for the appropriate period, they may not be indexed yet. If they are not, consult the Ulster Historical Foundation in Belfast through its website AncestryIreland.com to seek assistance. Most deposited

Presbyterian registers are either at the PRONI or at the Presbyterian Historical Society of Ireland, which can be contacted through the Presbyterianhistoryireland.com website.

Many researchers have solved immigrant origins' problems by using online indexes, such as on RootsIreland.ie, but all options must be evaluated. One approach is a search in the Church of Ireland indexes since it was the state religion, but because half of the registers were destroyed in the 1922 Four Courts Fire, it may not be an option. Realize that finding Presbyterians in the Church of Ireland registers is expected, even though Presbyterian marriages performed by Presbyterian ministers were legalized in 1782. It was not until 1844 that these same Presbyterian ministers could legally perform marriages between Presbyterians and Anglicans, thus bringing research back to Church of Ireland registers for mixed-denomination marriages during the interim.

Presbyterian registers consist of a variety of record types. Indexed predominantly are the christenings, marriages, and burials. Of the three, christenings and marriages are found most frequently.

The baptisms tend to be basic. The names of the children and the fathers were given. Usually, but not always, the names of the mothers and the addresses of the families were also provided. The occupations of the fathers and the birth dates of the children were sometimes added. Each congregation kept its own registers, which explains the inconsistency of information among congregations.

Before 1845, marriage records are simple as well, with the names of the grooms, brides, and the dates of the marriages. Sometimes, other information is contained in them, for instance, names of the couple's fathers and witnesses, occupations of fathers, and residences. The information became standard for Protestant marriages after 1845 and for all marriages after 1864 because of the introduction of civil registrations for everyone. From 1845, one copy of the marriage register was retained by the church, and the other was sent to the Registrar General's Office to become a government record.

Burial records are rare. When they exist, they usually have only the names of the deceased, dates of burials, and sometimes, ages and residences. The tombstones in Presbyterian graveyards may, therefore, have to be the records of deaths for the church communities before 1864, when civil registration of deaths began.

Session Minutes

Session minutes of Presbyterian churches are the daily affairs of the congregations and often predate the registers of births and marriages by as much as a century. Within the body of the minutes, lurid details about congregants may be found as church leaders dealt with disciplinary matters. Session minutes sometimes contain references to vital events such as baptisms and marriages. The PRONI and the Presbyterian Historical Society of Ireland, both in

Belfast, have large collections of session minutes from all branches of the Presbyterian faith in Ireland. Each organization has an online catalog. If not deposited, then session minutes still may be with local congregations. The *Guide to Church Records* on the PRONI website also has the inventory of session minutes.

Typical session minutes' books are in manuscript form and arranged chronologically. They have communion lists, some vital information, disciplinary actions, accounting records, membership records, transfers in and out of the congregations, and emigration lists, all interwoven with business minutes for the congregations.

Tracing Presbyterian Ministers

One proven immigration strategy in Presbyterian research is to focus efforts on the immigrant ministers of congregations because many ministers would enlist their congregants to emigrate as groups. Not everyone in an Ulster congregation left at the same time, but at least a portion of the communicants along with their minister contracted a ship and left together. To learn where the minister served in Ireland would, therefore, point closely to where his congregants lived.

This immigration strategy of following a minister back across the ocean to his origins to determine origins of his congregation is particularly useful for Colonial American research because birth or origins' information will almost never be in a Presbyterian record from Ulster in the 1700s. Not all immigrant Presbyterian ministers brought their congregations

Select Presbyterian Evolution in Ireland

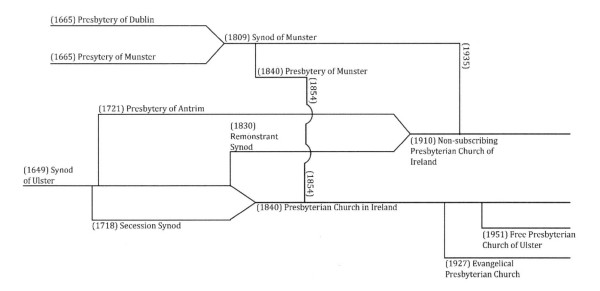

Figure 23: Select Presbyterian Evolution in Ireland.

with them, but the strategy should be explored if research predates the advent of most church registers in Ulster.

The first indication that such an approach needs to be considered is in the immigrant country itself. If the minister was trained and was a pastor in Ireland, were any of his Irish-born members in the immigrant congregation from his home congregation in Ireland? If so, that, by itself, helps solve the immigration origins' question.

Biographical lists of ministers are known as fasti books. They are excellent sources for tracing Irish Presbyterian pastors and conventionally mention whether the ministers emigrated and where they pastored abroad. Sometimes, the fasti books state they took part of their congregations with them, but since that is not the purpose of the books, those details are generally omitted. The various branches

of Irish Presbyterianism have produced their own fasti books. The ones most used are:

Bailie, W.D. and L.S. Kirkpatrick, eds. *Fasti of Seceder Ministers Ordained or Installed in Ireland 1746-1948*. Belfast: Presbyterian Historical Society of Ireland, 2005.

Barkley, John M. *Fasti of the General Assembly of the Presbyterian Church in Ireland, 1840-1910*. Belfast: Presbyterian Historical Society, 1986-1987.

Loughridge, Adam. *Fasti of the Irish Reformed Presbyterian Church*. [S.l.]: Reformed Presbyterian Synod of Ireland and Presbyterian Historical Society, 1970.

McConnell, James and Samuel G. McConnell. *Fasti of the Irish Presbyterian Church*. Belfast: Presbyterian Historical Society, 1951.

Presbyterian Historical Society of Ireland. *A History of Congregations in the Presbyterian Church in Ireland, 1610-1982.* Belfast: Presbyterian Historical Society, 1982.

Stewart, David. *The Seceders in Ireland with Annals of Their Congregations.* Belfast: Presbyterian Historical Society, 1950.

A History of Congregations in the Presbyterian Church in Ireland, 1610-1982 is technically not a fasti book. It is a brief history of all the congregations with their successions of ministers, the dates when the congregations were formed, and whether the churches merged or closed. The Presbyterian Historical Society of Ireland published a supplement and index to the book in 1996, and such works, fasti books, and information on immigrant ministers can be found on its website. The published works also are at major repositories for Presbyterian records and history outside of Ireland.

Methodist Church

The Methodist Church in Ireland is a movement that should not be ignored in research. It has an unusual history in Ireland, but its impact was enormous. Methodist missionaries arrived from England to Ireland, and the Church began as study classes within the local Church of Ireland parish system. To a lesser degree, it took root in Presbyterian congregations. Methodists were the radicals of the 1700s and early 1800s, and they spread throughout Ireland. Their zeal and enthusiastic worship style, along with their revivals, were not always appreciated by the Anglican clergy, but they revitalized local parishes.

By 1817-1818, the gap between Methodism and Anglicanism was so great in Ireland that Methodists separated from the local parishes, forming the Wesleyan Methodist Church. The Primitive Wesleyan Methodists remained part of the Anglican parish system until 1878, when the two versions of Methodism combined into one denomination. Today, the Methodist Church is the fourth largest denomination throughout Ireland. Sometimes, the power of Methodism in Ireland is overlooked because it is hidden within the Church of Ireland. However, Methodism assisted in transforming the religious landscape in the British Isles as well as in the United States and Canada. Its co-founders, John Wesley and Charles Wesley, did not have a political or academic power base. They simply spoke the language of the common people and brought their message directly to the masses.

Although Methodist Societies were planted throughout Ireland, Ulster became their most fertile ground. The relationship of Methodism and the Church of Ireland was complex, with the potential to affect genealogy research the most. The Methodist Societies were allowed to operate as auxiliaries of local parish churches. Therefore, they could have been recorded among the records of various congregations, particularly the Church of Ireland, which leads research back into Anglican records. Methodists were tolerated if they kept within certain bounds. They were warned not to say anything against the established church, to keep their enthusiasm under control, and not to draw people away from Anglicanism. The Anglican clergy complained that Methodist class meetings resembled Catholic confessions with their emphasis on prayers and testimonies. They also protested about Methodist meetings frequently interfering with Anglican services. Many in the clergy disdained Methodism. However, the Anglican clergy did welcome the earnestness of the Methodists and their ability to reinvigorate the parishes. Even so, Methodists' study classes were not allowed to be in Church of Ireland buildings.

The Methodist Societies were permitted the use of Presbyterian meeting houses as long as they did not say anything that would undermine evangelical growth within Irish Presbyterianism. The Methodist example taught the Presbyterian clergy how to conduct evangelistic meetings. From this perception, Methodism aided in spreading the messages of orthodox Presbyterian ministers during the turn of the nineteenth century. Methodism also set the example for the Presbyterian clergy to strongly emphasize a personal conversion and to tone down Calvinist end-time millenarianism, helping to prepare the way for the great Ulster Revival of 1859.

As a result, before 1817-18, eighteenth-century Methodism was different than it was after it became a denomination. The earliest Methodists were based in homes, not in chapels. In early Methodism, older, unmarried, or widowed women were the first to convert. They brought other family members to the classes. Methodism did not shift from women to men until the nineteenth century, when chapels began to be built, institutions were founded, and formal theological training became a standard.

Irish Methodist membership declined because of emigration. Even though it was a separate denomination by 1817-1818, the steady stream of congregants departing, especially for North America, caused Methodism to wane by the 1830s. By that time, as many as 1,000 Methodists per year had left, stripping the movement of its younger and most energetic people.

Methodist Records

Methodist Church government in Ireland is dissimilar from that in some other countries. The form of government is not an episcopal (bishopric) in Ireland but is tiered in the following manner, as adapted from Steven C. ffeary-Smyrl's *Irish Methodists – Where Do I Start?* (Killester, Dublin, Ireland: Council of Irish Genealogical Organizations, 2000) and the "Methodist Church in Ireland" website:

Class: A small group of Methodists with lay leadership, which always has been the very life of the Methodist movement. In today's church, classes tend to go by names such as Home Group, Prayer Triplet, and Bible Study. Their goal is to encourage one another in faith.

Society: Many small classes from a given area governed by the leaders from each class. They act as a board. Usually, one chapel for each society (congregation) is

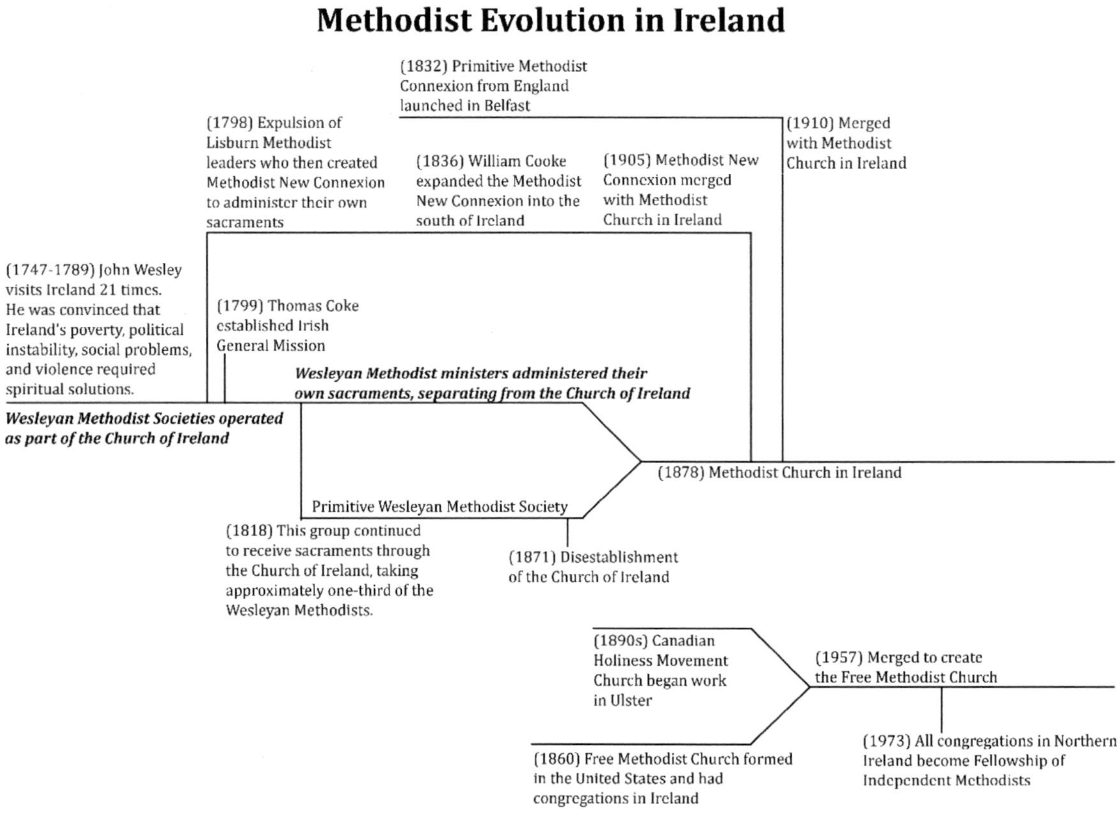

Methodist Evolution in Ireland

(1832) Primitive Methodist Connexion from England launched in Belfast

(1798) Expulsion of Lisburn Methodist leaders who then created Methodist New Connexion to administer their own sacraments

(1836) William Cooke expanded the Methodist New Connexion into the south of Ireland

(1905) Methodist New Connexion merged with Methodist Church in Ireland

(1910) Merged with Methodist Church in Ireland

(1747-1789) John Wesley visits Ireland 21 times. He was convinced that Ireland's poverty, political instability, social problems, and violence required spiritual solutions.

(1799) Thomas Coke established Irish General Mission

Wesleyan Methodist ministers administered their own sacraments, separating from the Church of Ireland

Wesleyan Methodist Societies operated as part of the Church of Ireland

(1878) Methodist Church in Ireland

Primitive Wesleyan Methodist Society

(1818) This group continued to receive sacraments through the Church of Ireland, taking approximately one-third of the Wesleyan Methodists.

(1871) Disestablishment of the Church of Ireland

(1890s) Canadian Holiness Movement Church began work in Ulster

(1957) Merged to create the Free Methodist Church

(1860) Free Methodist Church formed in the United States and had congregations in Ireland

(1973) All congregations in Northern Ireland become Fellowship of Independent Methodists

Figure 24: The introduction and progression of Methodism in Ireland.

on each circuit. A chapel has several trustees.

Circuit: A number of societies (congregations) form a circuit that is governed by a quarterly meeting over which the Superintendent Minister of the circuit presides. In urban areas, circuits are smaller in geographical size.

District: A group of Circuits form a district that is overseen by a District Superintendent and administered by a District Synod. The District Synod is composed of the ministers stationed in the district.

Conference: The governing body of the Irish Methodist Church is the Conference. It meets once a year.

Methodism has had its own Conferences in Ireland since 1752, giving it an identity and missionary zeal while remaining close to the Methodists in Great Britain. This does mean that records, such as periodicals, were produced by Irish Methodism before its separation from the Church of Ireland in 1817-1818.

Be attentive to some essential facts in Methodist records when developing a viable research strategy. Among them is that marriages in Methodist chapels or preaching houses were not licensed until 1864. From 1845 to 1863, marriages could have been conducted within Methodist chapels, but they had to be in the presences of District Registrars, who retained the records. Consequently, few

Methodist marriage records began before 1845, with most after 1864.

Few Methodist churches had graveyards attached to them. Thus, on the local level, records of concern are society and circuit registers. Circuit records consist of baptisms, memberships, and minutes. Society records include board minutes.

Many Methodist records are being indexed on the RootsIreland.ie website. If a county of origin is already known, look over the website's inventory of what is on the database for how far the indexing projects have progressed. Remember, early Methodists were documented in the Church of Ireland parish registers; therefore, check the RootsIreland.ie inventories for the status of those registers as well.

Records for all Methodist denominations can be found at the PRONI, but most of its collection is concentrated on the counties contained in the old Ulster province. For areas outside of Ulster, registers still may be in local custody. Various Methodist collections also are at the Wesley Historical Society (now the Methodist Historical Society of Ireland) located at Edgehill Theological College in Belfast. Contact information can be found at Methodisthistoryireland.org.

If an area has been targeted through a surname distribution search and it is found that no early Methodist or Church of Ireland registers have survived, a new research strategy is required, one that often does not involve church registers.

Methodist record-keeping practices always have been established and formal, which is the opposite approach to Irish Presbyterianism. To a degree, Methodist record keeping followed that of the Church of Ireland of the nineteenth century. In Irish Methodism, patterns of lists and statistics were compiled, and the results were returned to a central repository, originally in Dublin but now in Belfast.

Methodist records of assistance include class lists (lists of members of each class in the society), baptismal registers, and after 1863, more complete marriage registers. The class lists (membership rolls) establish when people joined, and they could have been organized by family units. In the margins of the register books, notations about, for instance, marriages, transfers, and deaths often were made. Nearly all baptismal registers were arranged on a circuit basis, but marriage registers were on a congregational basis. The congregations that constituted a circuit changed frequently, possibly complicating the search for the relevant circuit register.

Within the circuit records are the baptisms. It was not until the 1820s that most Methodists had their children baptized by Methodist circuit clergy instead of Church of Ireland clergy, which is when most of the Methodist baptisms began. Baptismal registers are simple. The names of the children, their parents, and the dates of baptisms were recorded. Additional details could have been added by the minister. Rarely were maiden names of mothers recorded. A consolidated baptismal register, dating from about 1816 to 1845, known as the "Irish Wesleyan Methodist Connexional Baptismal Register," is on microfilm at the PRONI and includes most Methodist circuits and missions (MIC 429/1).

Not all Methodist records are in the form of circuit/mission or congregation registers. For example, a history that can shed light on individual Methodist ancestors is Charles H. Crookshank's three-volume *History of Methodism in Ireland* (London: 1885-1888). It includes information about preachers and prominent members of the Methodist societies from 1747 to 1859. Crookshank's history indexes persons and places, and the book is on several websites that digitize public domain works.

Methodists and an Immigration Strategy

The largest concentration of Methodists was in Ulster and along its border. By 1830, 43 percent of all Irish Methodists lived within two concentrated areas. The following descriptions of these two geographical districts have been adapted from David Hampton's essay "Methodism in Irish Society, 1770-1830" in *Transactions of the Royal Historical Society* 5th Series 36 (1986): 117-142:

Linen Triangle: The region formed a triangle on the north from Dungannon, County Tyrone in the west, to Lisburn on the Antrim-Down border in the east, and both met at Newry on the Armagh-Down border in the south. Growth occurred in the 1780s and in 1800-1802, 1809-1810, and 1819-1821. The Linen Triangle shared in the great evangelical revivals of Southern Ulster from 1809 to 1810 and

1819 to 1820, but the Methodist memberships fell until the great Ulster revival of 1859.

Lough Erne Rectangle: The geographical area stretched from Ballyshannon, County Donegal, in the west to the County Cavan towns of Cavan and Ballyhaise on the eastern side, and then from Irvinestown, County Fermanagh, in the north, to the southern line, running from Manorhamilton, County Leitrim, to Cavan Town. Periods of explosive growth occurred in 1772-1773, in 1783, and in 1785-1787, 1799-1802, and 1819-1820. During this last period, Methodism became its own denomination. The revival of 1799-1802 saw large numbers of Methodist converts in Cavan and Fermanagh.

Tracing Methodist Ministers

Ministers who preached to all classes in societies, making no distinctions between them, were pivotal in spreading the Methodist message. Thus, the common people found the message appealing because it provided hope in desperate circumstances. A Methodist minister should, therefore, be a prominent person in a family history, and something was likely written about him, hopefully preserving birthplaces.

If a Methodist minister was in the family, the database "Index to Methodist Ministers" hosted by the University of Manchester Library should be one of the first places to consult. The database covers 1819-1968. The source is "Ministers and Probationers who Have Died in the Work," which appeared in the back of the

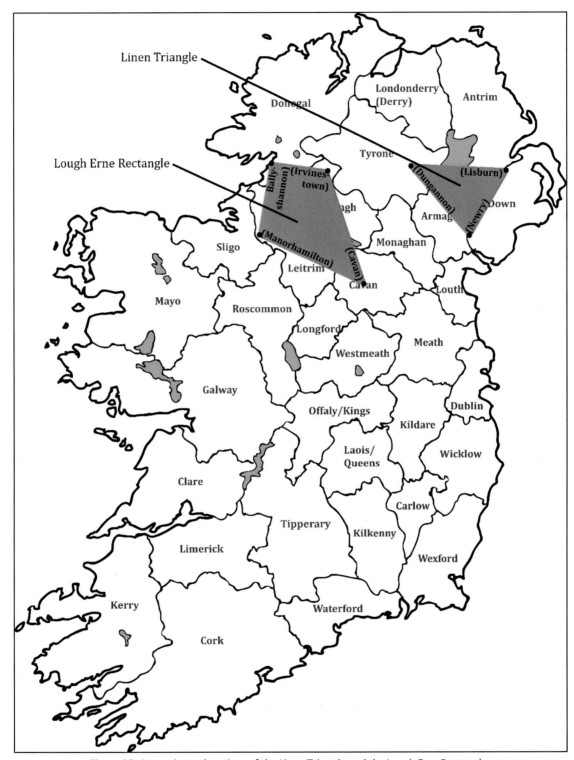

Figure 25: Approximate locations of the Linen Triangle and the Lough Erne Rectangle.

1968 edition of *Ministers and Probationers of the Methodist Church,* printed by the Methodist Publishing House in London. A search feature on Ancestry.com under the database "UK, Methodist Ministers Death Index, 1800-1963" provides the basic information and a link to the university's website.

The Methodist Historical Society of Ireland at Edgehill College in Belfast has an index to all ministers from all the branches of Irish Methodism. They have indexes to biographical information in the following Irish Methodist magazines: *Armenian Magazine* (1778-1797), *The Methodist Magazine* (1798-1821), and *Wesleyan Methodist Magazine* (1822-1839). These, as expected, include details about ministers and some lay members. Biographies of early ministers also were published by the Wesley Historical Society (now the Methodist Historical Society of Ireland) in the *Irish Christian Advocate,* and of those who died before 1840 in Robert H. Gallagher's *Pioneer Preachers of Irish Methodism Who Were Called to Their Eternal Reward During the First Century of Methodism* (Belfast: Wesley Historical Society [Irish Branch], 1965). If an immigrant was an Irish minister, searching these resources is necessary.

Christian Brethren (Plymouth Brethren) and Gospel Hall

What is popularly called the "Plymouth Brethren" is a movement that began in Ireland in the 1820s. Plymouth Brethren is the term that often is found and that stayed in the minds of many immigrants although no such denomination existed. Even so, it has to be used in any Internet and library catalog search.

The movement began in Dublin around 1827 and was carried to Plymouth, England, in 1831. The earliest Brethren came from many denominations, meeting together to move beyond sectarianism. Because the Dublin group referred to one another as "brother" to avoid titles, they

were nicknamed Brethren. The movement became so well known in Plymouth that these Christians were nicknamed Plymouth Brethren.

In some areas, the movement appealed to and grew among the lower middle-class segment of British and Irish society. In other areas, it attracted the working class with more skills. Nevertheless, the leaders of the initial movement were drawn almost exclusively from the upper ranks of society that included Anglican clergy, Oxford teachers, lawyers, doctors, sons of country families, and wealthy merchants. This first generation of leaders were alike because they were all young men in their twenties or early thirties, nearly all of them well educated and several of them classical or biblical scholars of their day. They sought to heal the divisions within Protestantism under the banner of a restored apostolic Christianity, *not* through an ecumenical approach.

In its various expressions, the Brethren have influenced evangelical Protestantism to no small degree. The Brethren are a conservative evangelical Christian body and provided the beginning of what is today a defined and recognizable fundamentalist wing of evangelical Christianity. The present section focuses on the Brethren Movement; the interrelated Churches of God (Needed Truth Brethren), who emerged in 1892; and the Gospel Hall Brethren. The Gospel Hall Brethren came from the 1859 Revival that swept through Ulster and Scotland.

Some important factors pertain to Brethren research and records, the first of which is that the topic is uncharted with little written about it for genealogists. Also, few of the Brethren records have been gathered in archives. Some are beginning to appear on RootsIreland.ie, but without a centralized index from which to draw, researchers abroad have to know a place where an ancestor lived before searching for records. While finding immigrant origins is the goal of the pursuit in most cases, locating at least a county in Ireland certainly is an exceptional lead. This is where a surname distribution exploration using tax lists may be practical in targeting areas in which to continue the investigation.

Details to consider when beginning this type of research and looking for records are:

- Many terms for this collection of congregations include Christian Brethren, Gospel Hall, and Brethren Assembly.

- From 1848, two strains of the Brethren appeared and exist to this day. The two branches have popularly been referred to as Open and Exclusive. From this point, all Brethren history can be understood as Open and Exclusive. Both Open and non-open Brethren were involved in missions at the same time.

- The majority of Brethren today are Open. Their churches have no headquarters. Active Brethren meetings are in both the Republic of Ireland and Northern Ireland. The largest concentration is in Northern Ireland.

- In Brethren assemblies, a distinction between clergy and laity is not recognized, nor is a clergy even acknowledged. The church is overseen by designated elders (also called overseers). In some cases, all male members may supervise. The elders come from within the local assembly. Among Open assemblies, elders are appointed, and they rule. In most non-open assemblies, they are recognized and lead the Brethren but often are not referred to as elders at all.

- Baptism and the Lord's Supper are the two basic ordinances. Baptism is typically by total immersion. A believer's baptism is commonly held within an Open Brethren assembly, where an individual upon a confession of faith is baptized. In about half of the assemblies of the Exclusive Brethren, household baptisms are practiced, wherein if the head of each household is converted and baptized, all in the household can be baptized.

Apart from a few separatist groups, theological differences between the Open and non-open Brethren are small except when it comes to the "independency" (open) or "interdependency" of local assemblies. Practices are less uniform among non-open Brethren since each assembly is autonomous, whereas they are more uniform among Open Brethren because of their belief in interdependency. However, neither has a central authority or headquarters.

While practices do differ between assemblies, probably the clearest dissimilarities between Open and Exclusive branches are the ways various assemblies relate to one another. The Open Brethren meetings are local assemblies that are autonomous but often informally linked to the others. Exclusive Brethren generally are "connexional" in approach, that is, the assemblies recognize and adhere to the disciplinary actions of the associated assemblies. Disciplinary actions, after other avenues failed, denied the breaking of bread on Sunday and sometimes ostracism in some Brethren groups.

Brethren and Gospel Hall Records

At this writing, studies of Brethren and Gospel Hall records, which, as a whole, are not centralized, microfilmed, or digitized, are still in their infancy. Nobody, not even the Brethren, knows what is available. The Christian Brethren Archive housed at the John Rylands University Library in Manchester, England, has a large collection of Brethren history, newspapers, and documents. Its book and manuscript collection concentrates on the Brethren in the British Isles, including Ireland, and its website lists many valuable references and aids for continuing research.

Since the status of Brethren records in their entirety remains unknown, the purpose of this section is to help document where assemblies meet and how to contact them for information about ancestors. Most of the primary records are still with the local assemblies and as private records, are subject to the policies of the local assemblies.

The Internet currently has a wealth of information on the history of the related movements, and Brethren studies are flowering. A central website with additional links and reference books is "The Brethren Archivist and Historians Network," abbreviated as BAHN. Individual assemblies sometimes have websites with contact information. The website "Gospelhalls UK and ROI" also has a list of assemblies with contact information. The best way to find material held by a local assembly may be as simple as sending an e-mail or conducting an Internet search.

Because the Brethren see themselves as being simply Christians, not as a Christian denomination, their identity in the records is often obscured. The religious statistics that accompanied the 1901 and 1911 censuses of Ireland demonstrate this point. The Brethren were labeled as Christian, Christian Brethren, Brethren, Plymouth Brethren, undenominational Christian Protestant, Exclusive Brethren, Open Brethren, or some other term. Also, remember that if a family is listed as "no religious denomination" in the census, this cannot be interpreted as not attending church. Always remember that Brethren were hostile toward denominationalism.

Even though their exact numbers have not been determined, genealogists in Ireland have estimated that by 1901, approximately 5,000 Brethren were dispersed throughout Ireland. It is important to understand that the identification of who is Brethren and who is not may not be as straightforward as it is with other evangelicals. The 1901 and

1911 censuses online need to be searched with care.

Before looking at Brethren records, attention to some of the distinctive features that will affect research is beneficial. Among these are:

- The buildings of Open Brethren are customarily referred to as Gospel Chapels, Bible Chapels, Christian Assemblies, and commonly in Ulster, Gospel Halls. The buildings of the Exclusive Brethren usually are labeled as Meeting Rooms, Gospel Halls, or assemblies, which is important because a Christian Brethren assembly may be designated by one of these, and even others, which is one way to identify a Brethren assembly. However, also be aware there are numerous non-Brethren gospel halls, some independent and some run by the Faith Mission. Some of these non-related gospel halls are also outreaches of denominational churches.

- In the nineteenth century, Brethren commonly did not vote. Many nineteenth-century Brethren held nonresistance positions. Brethren missionaries would preach at the Army barracks in Ireland. As a result of their beliefs, upon converting, many officers in the British Army and Royal Navy resigned their commissions. By the end of the nineteenth century, many new officer-converts ceased to follow this stance. The Brethren rejected involving themselves with governments and sought to remain a separate people. While they obeyed earthly governments, they did not participate in them.

- The Brethren do not link baptism to salvation; baptism plays no role in salvation from sins. It is usually performed by immersion as an outward expression of an inward cleaning, its symbolism being a death, burial, and resurrection. In some cases, a person is considered part of an assembly upon baptism and is often regarded as a witness to others. A record of a baptism depended upon the assembly.

- Brethren were less likely to belong to the Loyal Orange Lodge than were other Protestants in Ulster. They had a strong belief in the separation of church and state. The tendency was not to become involved in politics. This is a generalization only and could be applied to the Freemasons also. While a few might have become Orangemen or Freemasons, historically, the majority did not join these fraternal organizations.

Participation among both Open and Exclusive Brethren can be thought of as a fellowship instead of a membership. Traditionally, the assemblies do not have the concept of persons joining a local gathering of believers, affecting what is called membership records in other churches because some assemblies kept them and some did not. For practical matters, though, lists of who attends services are maintained on an informal basis within the Open Brethren. Such lists were compiled for internal use or to produce directories. The term *member* generally is rejected among Open Brethren, although it is used by outside writers.

Among Exclusive Brethren, the concept of official membership is somewhat unclear. Because anyone who wishes to break bread must be affiliated with an assembly, local assemblies are

---

Brethren Directories Housed at the Brethren Archives, John Rylands University, Manchester, England

Branch	Years
Open Brethren	
General	1897, 1904, 1922, 1927, 1933, 1951, 1959, 1968, 1971, 1975, 1983, 1990, 1991, 1995, 1997, 2002, 2006
Vernalite Brethren	1922 (List of Assemblies of God)
Exclusive Brethren	
Darby Meetings	1873, 1877
Stoney Meetings	1882, 1884, 1885
Kelly Meetings	1892, 1925 [Glanston], 1930 *(Glanstons were a separate group from the Kellys, like the Lowes; Kellys and Lowes reunited in 1926, adding the Glanstons in 1974, and then split again about 1999.)*
London/Taylor Meetings	1903, 1906, 1911, 1917, 1927, 1929, 1938, 1941-1945, 1949, 1951, 1956-1957, 1959-1963
Croydoen/Frost Meetings	1974/1980 (cover page missing on directory)
Lowe Meetings	1901
Kelly-Lowe-Continental-Tunbridge Wells-Mory Meetings	1959
Kelly-Lowe-Continental-Tunbridge Wells-Grant-Stuart-Glanton Meetings	1975, 1982, c.1987, 1992

responsible for determining whether a member is in good standing. A Brethren visiting other assemblies must have a letter of commendation from the home assembly assuring his or her good standing and that he or she is not under discipline. The practice also can be found among conservative Open Brethren. Any lists of members are with local assemblies.

One method of approaching a Brethren family when its self-identity is undenominational is by locality. To know where various Brethren assemblies were meeting is always advantageous. A Christian Brethren family is possibly distinguished by the geographical area. Early directories for both the Open and Exclusive Brethren were published to inform travelers where the assemblies were located, a first step in identifying Brethren Assemblies because they were listed by county or city. The Open Brethren directory provides more geographical descriptions, but the Exclusive directory has the names of contacts. Contact names, in turn, are a method to access the 1901 and 1911 Irish censuses online. Sometimes, they have several references and their addresses and occupations. The Exclusive directory thus is, in effect, more than a list of assemblies. The directories are at the Christian Brethren Archive housed at the John Rylands University Library, Manchester, England, and include those locations noted in the chart on the previous page.

Church of Jesus Christ of Latter-day Saints (Mormons, LDS)

The Church of Jesus Christ of Latter-day Saints (colloquially known as the LDS Church or Mormons) was founded in Upstate New York in 1830 by Joseph Smith (1805-1844), who claimed to be a

Figure 26: Logan Temple, Logan, Cache County, Utah, United States. This LDS temple was completed in 1884. (Photograph courtesy of Alexandria Radford, 2020. Permission received.)

prophet, seer, and revelator. Mormons began seeking converts in Ireland in 1840 and had mission stations in Belfast and Dublin. The message they presented to potential Irish converts was that of a restored Christian religion, neither Catholic nor Protestant, and one in which God spoke through modern prophets, revealing scriptures to accompany the Bible. The Mormons, as a group, provide an important example of one or more siblings converting while the rest of the family did not. Consequently, Irish origins may be preserved for an entire lineage with the Latter-day Saint branch of a family.

"Mormon" originally was a prejudicial term created outside the church, but it became part of the English language as a reference point. The church tolerated the term until 2018, when the current prophet-president in Salt Lake City instructed members not to use it to describe themselves or the church.

The majority of early Mormon converts had Protestant backgrounds, and they were expected to immigrate to the Mormon colonies in the United States. However, although LDS missionaries had some success in Ireland, their greatest numbers of Irish-born converts were among those who had already immigrated elsewhere. Scotland and areas around Lancashire, England, were especially fertile grounds for conversions of Irish-born Protestants. In addition, Wales, other parts of the United Kingdom, and places as far away as Australia yielded Irish-born converts. In these other locales, the new members would prepare to immigrate to the Mormon colonies in the Rocky Mountains. Many

converts in Ireland went to Liverpool, where they united with other Latter-day Saints, and then left for the United States on the same ships.

After 1847, official church policy encouraged converts to settle in the Salt Lake Valley in Utah. Once there, they either stayed in the area or moved to another Mormon colony in the West. Many converts were assigned to a specific colony for an economic purpose, which benefited the church as a whole in a type of Christian Socialism. Without the idea of kingdom building, a complete understanding of early Mormons and the drive that sent converts packing for a second time is not possible. The early Mormons believed that they were building the spiritual and physical Kingdom of God on earth.

From an immigration evaluation, finding a Latter-day Saint branch of the family in one's genealogy may be the key to identifying from where the entire family came in Ireland. Genealogy is such an integral part of the religion that Latter-day Saints practice baptism on behalf of dead ancestors, giving the deceased the opportunity to accept or reject that ordinance after death. Proxy marriages for the dead also are performed in the church's temples, which are different than chapels. The proxy baptisms and marriages for ancestors are reflected in the online genealogy databases of the church.

Pertinent to research is that all the converts' journeys have paper trails. When converts were preparing to submit names for "temple work" on behalf of their ancestors, questions were asked

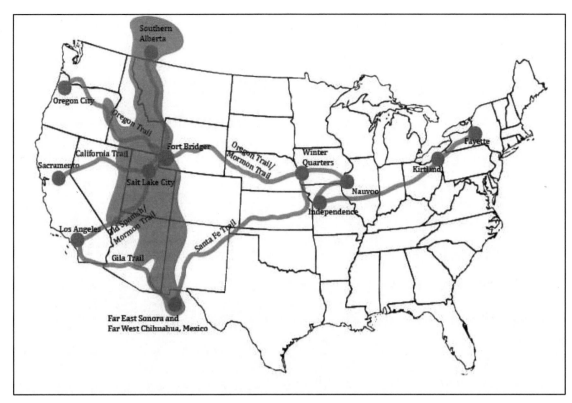

Figure 27: Mormon Corridor, showing origins, migrations, and long-term settlement areas.

about the deceased, such as when and where they were born. Thus, knowledge of lineages could be preserved far beyond when the average church register began in Ireland. Even if an ancestor never became a Latter-day Saint but their sibling or cousin did, the related convert is a prime person to research so that Irish origins for the ancestor can be identified.

Researchers worldwide typically discover their "Mormon branch of the family" through the Internet, a published family history, or an online tree on one of the major websites. The massive "Family Tree"-linked pedigree program through FamilySearch.org is maintained by the church. Many pioneer Mormon pedigrees have also been added to the Member Trees on the commercial websites of

Ancestry.com and Myheritage.com. If attempting to determine whether a pedigree found online is for Mormons, some good geographical clues to consider are:

- Western United States, especially in Arizona, Idaho, Nevada, Utah, and Wyoming, where the Church of Jesus Christ of Latter-day Saints remains either the largest or second-largest church. Mormon colonies also are in California, Colorado, and New Mexico, but they are not as numerous as they are in the former states named.

- Southern Alberta, centered around Cardston, Lethbridge, and Raymond, because Mormons colonized that region of

Canada after arriving from the Latter-day Saint communities in the Intermountain West of the United States. They are a strong presence there today.

- Northern Mexico, in the states of Chihuahua and Sonora, where some of the Mormon colonies that survived the Mexican Revolution (1910-1920) are still found. The areas are more mixed today, but the Anglo-American presence is still there.

Latter-day Saint records, including those generated through the Belfast and Dublin missions, are in two main repositories, the Family History Library and the Church History Library, both in downtown Salt Lake City. A third can be added, the secular Daughters of the Utah Pioneers, a lineage society open to anyone who can trace an ancestor to before the completion of the Transcontinental Railroad in 1869. The society is in downtown Salt Lake City.

Genealogy Meets Religion

With LDS theology, take into account that genealogy is part of the faith. The church operates the Family History Library, the largest of its kind in the world and which is open to the public at no cost. It collects records from all over the world and from all religions so that members and others can research their ancestries. Because the faith has been gathering genealogies for theological reasons since the 1840s, Irish origins can be found among the submitted family histories of the members. An early pioneer to the American West might have left a diary or simply recounted his or her genealogy as part of the "temple work" theology. Regardless of the reason, it is preserved. As with any family history, it needs to be authenticated and documented. Contemporary members who are at various levels in their research skills are seeking to accomplish the same tasks. Any record about Irish-born converts to Mormonism in Ireland or those who converted in a second country is a potential treasure in the search for Irish origins.

Congregational Church

The beginnings of the Congregational Church were within the Separatist movement from the Church of England during the reign of Queen Elizabeth after 1558. Its members believed in liberty of conscience and the independence of each congregation. They first appeared in Ireland in 1646-1647 and returned in force with Oliver Cromwell.

The church was a minority one in Ireland with six Independent congregations in 1695, and it remained a small denomination until the nineteenth century, during which time it experienced a revival. The Revival began in Scotland and expanded to Ireland. Within this period, many of the congregations still in existence were founded. In 1829, the numerous congregations formed the Irish Congregational Union, and in 1899, the denomination absorbed the Irish Evangelical Society.

By the time of the Potato Famine, many Congregational churches had dwindled through the congregations' deaths and emigrations. However, because of a great evangelical revival that swept through Ulster in 1859, the Congregational Church in that province saw its attendance explode. Open-air services had to be held in summers to host the attending crowds. The 1859 revival impelled the large growth of the Irish Congregational Church after it was reanimated.

Congregational Church Records

According to the 1901 Irish census, the declared membership was 10,000.

Congregational Churches in Ireland

From an immigration assessment, although records began late and are incomplete, knowing where churches were located can be a first step toward identifying origins in Ireland. The list below has the locations of the Congregational churches in Ireland before 1864, the year country-wide civil registrations of births, marriages, and deaths for the population began. The list has been adapted from Malcolm Coles's *I Will Build My Church: The Story of the Congregational Union of Ireland*. Civil parishes have been added for easier reference:

County	Civil Parish	Town	Formation
Antrim	Ballynure	Straid	1816
	Carnmoney	Ballycraigy	1805
	Carrickfergus	Carrickfergus	1816
	Shankill	Albertbridge, Belfast	1862
	Shankill	Donegall St., Belfast	1801
	Shankill	Rugby Ave., Belfast	1854
Armagh	Armagh	Armagh	1793
	Kilmore	Richhill	1800
	Newry	Newry	1820
Cork	Cork City	Cork City	1760
Donegal	Donegal	Donegal	1833
Down	Bangor	Bangor	---
	Kilkeel	Kilkeel	---
Dublin	Dublin City	Kilmainham, Dublin	1815
	Dublin City	King's Inn Street, Dublin	1820
	Dublin City	Merrion Hall, Dublin	1863
	Dublin City	Plunkett Street, Dublin	1772
	Dublin City	York Street	1802
Londonderry	Coleraine	Coleraine	1836
	Templemore	Londonderry	1821
Sligo	Easkey	Easkey	---
Tyrone	Donaghenry	Donaghey	1860
	Donaghmore	Donaghmore	1834
Wexford	Enniscorthy City	Enniscorthy City	---

Congregationalists kept membership lists with details about members emigrating or transferring to other congregations. The records also include baptismal and marriage registers. Congregational records are appearing on the RootsIreland.ie website.

The records can be sketchy because many registers survived from only the 1880s. Others start early but still have gaps because of many factors. Some records were lost for the Ulster congregations during World War II in the bombing raids. Others are gone because the individual congregations did not appreciate the need to preserve them. Records for the Congregational Church are housed at the PRONI.

In addition to the records of individual congregations are the registers of the Congregational Union of Ireland, which date from 1829 to 1843. There is a large gap in the minutes from 1843 to 1860 because the Union was dissolved. It was reorganized in 1860, but the minute books did not begin again until 1889. They are located at the PRONI (CR/7/1), which has published the online guide to the collection as *Introduction: Congregational Union of Ireland* (2007).

Other records include the denominational magazine, *The Irish Congregational Magazine* (1861-1876), with copies at the Linen Hall Library in Belfast. The Ministers' Provident Fund established in 1867 (CR/7/2/D) is at the PRONI.

The Congregational Union of Ireland (CR/7/1) records overlap the Irish Evangelical Society records, also at the PRONI

(CR/7/2), and began in 1814. The PRONI has an online guide, *Introduction: Irish Evangelical Society* (2007), describing the collection of the society and its successor, the Irish Evangelical Society and Congregational Home Mission.

Moravian Church (United Brethren)

The Moravian Church is a pre-Reformation body. Organized in 1457 in Bohemia, it, along with the Waldenses, was founded in 1170 in what is now Italy, and the two were the precursors of the Protestant Reformation. At the birth of the Reformation, the Moravians stood alongside Martin Luther and other Reformation leaders who were merging into the rising tide of Protestantism. The Moravian Church arrived in Ireland in 1746 through missionaries from England.

Several Moravian congregations were in Ireland, most in Ulster. Their Christian piety attracted Presbyterians, Anglicans, and Roman Catholics. The number of Moravians in Ireland during the eighteenth and nineteenth centuries is uncertain, but historians have estimated it at about 5,000 in 1834. In the past, congregations have been several areas.

Of the several congregations in Ireland, only one, Gracehill, County Antrim, was a part of a full-scale Moravian congregational settlement. It is not the oldest Moravian Church, but it has been the "Mother Church" for all of Ireland. Gracehill is located about two miles from Ballymena. Knowing where congregations were located is helpful from an immigration perspective because any church member will be attending one of these congregations, automatically restricting the regions for Irish origins.

While the Moravian Church as an organization dates from 1759, Gracehill was founded in 1765 upon land initially leased from Lord O'Neill. The town was built in the grid-like pattern traditional to villages in Europe at the time. At the center of the town was the Moravian Church. God's Acre was established as the burial place, and surrounding the central area were homes for the residents of the congregation. The buildings included brethren houses, communal houses for single sisters and single brethren and widows, and schools for boys and girls, all radiating outward from the central point, the church. A farm, shop, and inn for parents accompanying their children to and from boarding schools completed Gracehill. The community was highly structured and utopian, and all residents were Moravians. The goal of Gracehill was to become entirely self-sufficient so that time could be devoted to evangelical work. Among its other affairs, Gracehill is remembered for its educational standard. The Moravian school became famous throughout Ireland and attracted pupils from the highest segments of Irish society.

Moravians are a record-keeping faith community. Most surviving church registers are at the PRONI and often extend back into the mid-eighteenth century. These collections are valuable in emigration research because connections between Moravians who emigrated and the Irish congregations can be made.

For example, Irish Moravians arriving in America tended to settle first among other Moravians, even if that meant they spread out later. In this example, two very prominent clusters of Moravian communities were in the United States. One was the Winston-Salem, North Carolina, area on the Moravian Tract. The other was the migration to three towns in southeastern Pennsylvania: Bethlehem and Nazareth in Northampton County and Lititz in Lancaster County. The emigration from the Irish congregations thus

Known Moravian Church Congregations in Ireland

County	Civil Parish/City	Town/Location
Antrim	Ahoghill	Gracehill
	Ballinderry	Ballinderry
	Belfast City	Belfast (2 congregations)
Cavan	Drumgoon	Coothill
Clare	Kilneboy	Corofin
Down	Kilkeel	Kilkeel
	Hillsborough	Kilwarlin (Corcreevy Townland)
Dublin	Dublin City	Bishop Street
		Stafford Street (closed 1777)
Londonderry	Artrea	Gracefield (Ballymaguigan Townland)

ties into specific American migrations. Other Moravians went first to the Caribbean, where missionaries had been operating for years.

If an immigrant Moravian record does not provide the birthplace in the registers or in a memoir read at the death of a member, the Irish records can answer the origins' question. Some congregation registers are being indexed on RootsIreland.ie.

Religious Society of Friends (Quakers)

The Religious Society of Friends, or Quakers, originated in England as a radical religious movement. The first Quaker meeting was organized in 1652 under the leadership of George Fox (1624-1691). Fox's family belonged to the Church of England. As a young man, he became dissatisfied with the ceremonies of Anglicanism. From simple beginnings, the tenets of the Quakers began to unfold: no clergy, no liturgy, no tithes, no religious leaders, civil liberty for all, and the equality of men and women. Quakers swore no oaths, did not take up arms, and had a simple lifestyle. Every day was to be a communion and experience with God. These were radical views for the time. From their pacifists' stances to their equal treatment of women, the Quakers were not only considered a danger to the society as a whole but also a threat to the authority of the state religion. The Quakers suffered a great deal of persecution and imprisonment for their convictions.

The roots of their radical stand against the grain of society had to do with the doctrine of the "Inward Light" (Inner Light), the key to understanding Quaker culture and belief. The Inward Light, a metaphor to express that all people have access to the inspiration of the Holy Spirit, guides individuals and groups with no need for a clergy. For "Silent Quakers," whose meetings are based upon silence, no one speaks unless directed by the Inward Light. At that point, any man or woman can share promptings with the Monthly Meeting (MM) in an unedited format. The practice is the opposite of traditional Protestantism, wherein the clergy delivers messages to be heard in edited formats. When a message from the Inward Light was accepted by the MM, it was spread far and wide, in affect influencing the attitudes of the larger culture. The social areas in which it was most prominent were war, abolition, and women's suffrage.

The first meeting in Ireland was held at Lurgan, County Armagh, in 1654. Many of the earliest Quakers were from England and had settled in Ireland, some as former Cromwellian soldiers who were horrified by what they saw under Cromwell. Others were farmers and merchants who immigrated to Ireland after the English Civil War (1641-1651). Between 1660 and 1690, between five and six thousand Quakers were in Ireland, throughout the country. Although the Quaker faith progressed among Protestants in Ireland, native, Gaelic-speaking Quakers were few.

Quakers provide an extraordinary insight into tracing a family in Ireland into the 1600s and even back into England. Their record-keeping practices included births, marriages, and deaths/burials. The MM registers hold transfers in and out of the MM and can be correlated with the transfer in records of the MM when a member immigrated. Because Quakers do not baptize, birth registers are for entire families.

Another factor making a Quaker branch of the family important in research is that they began emigrating early to the American colonies. Emigration can be divided into three periods: 1682-1710, 1710-1729, and 1729-1750. The first period was caused mainly by religious persecution; the second, by economic depression; and the third began with the failure of crops in 1729. Because Pennsylvania was founded as a Quaker refuge, it was the first choice for immigration, although certainly not the only one. Large colonies of Quakers also went into English settlements.

An estimated two thousand Quakers emigrated during the 1682-1750 period, creating a significant drain of people, talent, and resources. During these last years of emigration (1729-1750), many Quaker MMs either closed or merged into other MMs. In Ireland by 1845 were about 3,000 Quakers and in 1690, approximately 5,000 to 9,000.

Much has been written about Irish Quakers from a historical and genealogical perspective. The standard genealogical works certainly include:

Goodbody, Olive C. *Guide to Irish Quaker Records, 1654-1860.* 2 vols. Dublin, Ireland: Irish Manuscript Commission, 1967.

Falley, Margaret Dickson. "Quaker Records" in *Irish and Scotch-Irish Ancestral Research.* Vol. 1. 1962 Reprint. Baltimore, Maryland: Genealogical Publishing Co., 1988, pp. 412-428.

Harrison, Richard S. Harrison, edited by James G. Ryan. "Irish Quaker Records" in *Irish Church Records,* 2nd ed. Dublin, Ireland: Flyleaf Press, 2001, pp. 15-40.

Quaker Records and Indexes

Irish Quaker records are in several repositories. The main ones are the Dublin Friends Historical Library (DFHL) and the PRONI. The DFHL collections do not necessarily contain what is held at the PRONI. The Family History Library is a secondary library that has some Quaker vital record extractions digitized.

The largest boon for Irish Quaker research is the indexed and digitized collections on Findmypast.com, and so it may be among the first sources that should be consulted in research. Included are the original MM records as well as periodicals. The collections came from the DFHL, which has additional indexes to records and families not on Findmypast.com.

For the Quakers in Ulster, though, the collections are not part of the DFHL or Findmypast.com, but they have been indexed in a most unusual place. Family History Library has a 1990 microfilm of the "PRONI Card Index to Names." It has the Quaker abstracts as *part* of the index and, consequently, acts as an index to the Ulster Quaker collections.

On the FamilySearch.org website is a massive, digitized collection of cards. Over the decades, it was the index to many collections housed at the PRONI. The index provided short extractions of the records as they were deposited and the reference numbers to the manuscripts at the archive. Because it is of such value and was always an expanding collection of index cards over the decades, FamilySearch.org microfilmed it three times (in 1959, 1978, and the last, in 1990). In the FamilySearch.org catalog, it is named "Card Index to Names, 1990 Edition" and comprises the Quaker abstracts with the manuscript references in the PRONI.

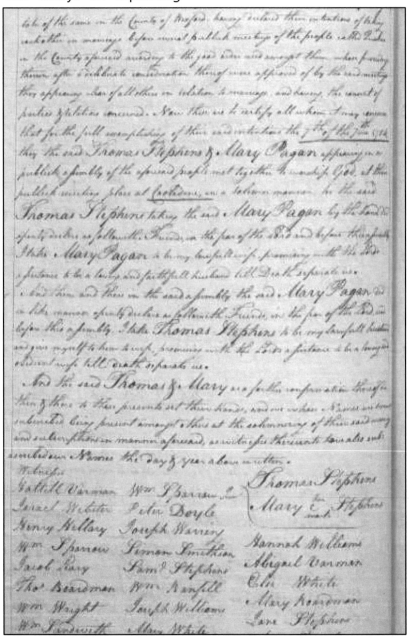

Figure 28: A Quaker marriage record. (Image courtesy of Friends Historical Library Dublin. Permission received.) Also available through FindMyPast.com.

Chapter Five

Civil Registration

The Irish government began recording Protestant marriages in 1845 and all births, marriages, and deaths for the entire population in 1864. These amazing documents have helped countless researchers discover the Irish origins of their families. As with all Irish records in general, though, they do not come without their inconsistencies and challenges.

Many people do not realize that civil registrations can address the origins' question even if ancestors were gone before the general 1864 recording. For example, not everyone left Ireland, and thinking that all family members did is a mistake. Lore in a family could be about Uncle Patrick who did not emigrate, and so tracking him and his descendants can determine from where the ancestors came. Typically, those who stayed took over the family farms, and if they were of the tenant class, they owned their homes and farms by around 1900. They might

have married and had children in Ireland, and so the civil registrations are pertinent. Before working with this vast archive of records, some basic information is essential, which is:

- Registrations of births and deaths can be incomplete, even up to 1900. If all expected records are not found, the nature of the source is the fault.

- Do not suppose a birth will correlate with immigrant records of the birth. Most people during this time never thought about how old they were, nor was it a concern for them. Also, civil birth dates possibly were recorded after children were christened. The church records should be believed instead of the civil records.

- Registrations of marriages were all-inclusive for Protestants from 1845 onward and for all marriages from 1864. Always expect to find a marriage, but in the rare case when one was not registered, adjust the research strategy.

- Birth records have the mothers' maiden names and the addresses of the families, and townlands were used as the addresses. All are keys to accessing other records, such as tax lists.

- Informants were at births and deaths, and witnesses were at marriages. They might have been important people in the family and could be new clues.

First Page.   Superintendent Registrar's District of _____ 05293857

113

19 27. Marriage solemnised at the Roman Catholic _Cathedral_ of _Monaghan_ in the Registrar's District of _Monaghan_ in the Union of _Monaghan_ in the County of _Monaghan_

Marriage No. 7

Registered by me, this 16th day of July 19 27.

J. C. Ward, Registrar.

No. (1)	When Married. (2)	Name and Surname. (3)	Age. (4)	Condition. (5)	Rank or Profession. (6)	Residence at the Time of Marriage. (7)	Father's Name and Surname. (8)	Rank or Profession of Father. (9)
7	6th July 1927	Charles Jas. McCabe Brigid Winters	28 25	Bachelor Spinster	— —	Greaghglass Greaghglass	James McCabe James Winters	Policeman Farmer

Married in the Roman Catholic _Cathedral_ of _Monaghan_ according to the Rites and Ceremonies of the Roman Catholic Church by me, _P V Mallon C. C._

This Marriage was solemnized between us, { _Charles James McCabe_ / _Brigid Winters,_ } in the Presence of us, { _Peter Paul McPhillips_ / _Florrie Winters_ } 113

19 27. Marriage solemnised at the Roman Catholic _Chapel_ of _Monaghan_ in the Registrar's District of _Monaghan_ in the Union of _Monaghan_ in the County of _Monaghan_

Marriage No. 8

Registered by me, this 16th day of Oct. 19 27.

J. C. Ward, Registrar.

No. (1)	When Married. (2)	Name and Surname. (3)	Age. (4)	Condition. (5)	Rank or Profession. (6)	Residence at the Time of Marriage. (7)	Father's Name and Surname. (8)	Rank or Profession of Father. (9)
8	July 4th 1927	James Fowler Kathleen Slevin	full full	Bachelor Spinster	Farmer —	Ardaghey Dunalsdron	Patrick Fowler (deceased) James Slevin (deceased)	Farmer Shop manager

Married in the Roman Catholic _Chapel_ of _Monaghan_ according to the Rites and Ceremonies of the Roman Catholic Church by me, _A H Boylan Adm_

This Marriage was solemnized between us, { _James Fowler_ / _Kathleen Slevin_ } in the Presence of us, { _William Fowler_ / _Ellie Slevin_ }

19 27. Marriage solemnised at the Roman Catholic _Cathedral_ of _St Macartin_ in the Registrar's District of _Monaghan_ in the Union of _Monaghan_ in the County of _Monaghan_

Marriage No. 9

Registered by me, this 12th day of August 19 27.

J. C. Ward, Registrar.

No. (1)	When Married. (2)	Name and Surname. (3)	Age. (4)	Condition. (5)	Rank or Profession. (6)	Residence at the Time of Marriage. (7)	Father's Name and Surname. (8)	Rank or Profession of Father. (9)
9	11 August 1927.	Patrick Murray Mary Anne Murray	38 29	Bachelor Spinster	Teacher Nurse	Monaghan Monaghan	Thomas Murray John Murray	Farmer Farmer

Married in the Roman Catholic _Cathedral_ of _St Macartin_ according to the Rites and Ceremonies of the Roman Catholic Church by me, _P V Mallon c c_

This Marriage was solemnized between us, { _Patrick Murray_ / _Mary A Murray_ } in the Presence of us, { _Hugh McEnaneyEileen Murray_ }

19 27. Marriage solemnised at the Roman Catholic _Church_ of _Tyholland_ in the Registrar's District of _Monaghan_ in the Union of _Monaghan_ in the County of _Monaghan_

Marriage No. 10

Registered by me, this 6th day of August 19 27.

J. C. Ward, Registrar.

No. (1)	When Married. (2)	Name and Surname. (3)	Age. (4)	Condition. (5)	Rank or Profession. (6)	Residence at the Time of Marriage. (7)	Father's Name and Surname. (8)	Rank or Profession of Father. (9)
10	August 16th 1927	Peter Cassidy Mary McGarry	full full	Bachelor Spinster	Farmer —	Drumuck Drumskirmon	Charles Cassidy (deceased) Thomas McGarry	Farmer Farmer

Married in the Roman Catholic _Church_ of _Tyholland_ according to the Rites and Ceremonies of the Roman Catholic Church by me, _Patrick McQuaid P.P._

This Marriage was solemnized between us, { _Peter Cassidy_ / _Minnie McGarry_ } in the Presence of us, { _James Cassidy_ / _Rose McGarry_ }

I, _Francis C Ward_ * Registrar of Marriages, in the District of _Monaghan_ in the Union of _Monaghan_ in the County of _Monaghan_, do hereby Certify, That this is a true copy of the Registrar's Book of Marriages within the said District from the Entry of the Marriage of _Charles Jas McCabe_ and _Brigid Winters_ Number _7_, to the Entry of the Marriage of _Peter Cassidy_ and _Minnie McGarry_ Number _10_. Witness my hand, this _22nd_ day of _October_ 19 27. _J C Ward_ * Registrar.

I have examined the above, and have compared it with the said original Registrar's Book, and hereby certify that it is a true copy. Witness my hand this _26th_ day of _October_ 19 27. _Peter Maguire_ * Superintendent Registrar.

Figure 29: Page from a 1924 civil register of marriages. (Image courtesy of the General Record Office. Permissions received.)

- Only the names of the fathers of brides and grooms appear on marriage records. If a father was deceased, a record may or may not state this.

When studying civil records, immediately apparent is that they were filed by Civil Registration Districts, which are the same as the Poor Law Unions. The districts do cross county boundaries, and so appreciate that once an entry is found, the townland of residence still needs to be correlated with a civil parish or Catholic parish to begin accessing its records.

When creating an online tree or writing a book, researchers not familiar with Irish place names have difficulty knowing how to list information from the civil records. Where were the places of births, marriages, or deaths? The townlands in which the events occurred are the solutions. To standardize information, the civil parishes are named most often as the units. If a christening also is found in a church record, the denomination and congregation or parish is appropriate to use. How to list information has no rule. The practical guide is whether any researcher anywhere in the world could follow the information and duplicate it from the record. The civil registration districts are likely meaningless to people outside Ireland because they have little reason to know the geography of the localities.

Districts and Databases

From an immigration perspective, the civil registration indexes and digitized images online are a boon for identifying immigrant origins, but the searches still are unpredictable. The major collections of indexes and images are on Irishgenealogy.ie, whose records are from the main sets held by the government. However, they are not the only collections available. Partial ones are on FamilySearch.org and RootsIreland.ie. The RootsIreland.ie collection comprises copies of the records from registers' districts, not the government copies, and what is on the index depends on the counties. The FamilySearch.org group is from the government certificates. Each of the three has its own search potential, which affects what is found. The differing database search capabilities can be manipulated, such as where wildcards can be placed in a name. Thus, if a family birth, marriage, or death is not found in one, explore the others for additional clues.

To compare findings between the three databases, it is helpful to know what years are covered. From 1845 to 1863, only Protestant marriages were registered, but from 1864, all marriages were.

FamilySearch.org: "Ireland, Civil Registration Indexes, 1845-1958" database excludes Northern Ireland from 1922 onward; "Ireland, Births and Baptisms, 1620-1881" database has civil registrations of births for 1864-1881; "Ireland, Marriages, 1619-1898" database has civil registrations of marriages for 1864-1870; "Ireland, Deaths, 1864-1870" database has civil registrations of deaths for those years. The indexes and databases also are shared with Ancestry.com.

Irishgenealogy.ie: Digitized images and indexes in the database include births for 1864-1919; marriages for 1845-1944; and deaths for 1864-1969. As they become available, images are added by the General Registers Office [GRO], Dublin. Northern Ireland records from 1922 are not included.

RootsIreland.ie: If the civil records for a county have been indexed, the years are listed in the inventory under the County/Online Sources. The extracted records are under the Birth/Baptism, Marriage, Burial/Death searches and can include the ones up to 1900 or later for some counties.

With civil registration indexes and databases, guidelines need to be considered to distinguish the correct family and not an unrelated family with matching names. The issue is predominant, especially among novices. Some suggestions are:

- Civil registration districts do cross county boundaries, which are reflected in the chart on the following pages. (Also, see pp.10-11, images 5a-5b for a district map.) Therefore, if an entry of interest is found, the townland of residence is the means of identifying the civil parish located within it. It then can be correlated with the Catholic parish serving that area.

- Birth dates in the immigrant country, for instance, those on tombstones, likely will not match the ones found in the civil births. Be open-minded about ages.

Immigrants commonly did not know how old they were or when they were born, and the relatives burying them may not have known either.

- Civil birth dates are consistently incorrect because fines were levied for late registrations. In other words, the informants, usually one of the parents, lied. Church registers' accounts of births or christening dates are more accurate.

- The registering of births and deaths was not complete from their starting date of 1864 to, often, around 1900. Sometimes, no birth records were registered with the government for families or only some of the births were registered. Consequently, the immigration question can be solved if any of the children are identified in the civil registration databases. Make sure all the siblings of an immigrant ancestor who also might have immigrated are verified for this purpose.

- Although sometimes a marriage simply was not registered with the government, such a circumstance is rare. Most marriages were registered: Protestants, from 1845, and Catholics, from 1864. If all the births of a couple's children were not registered, always look for the marriage of the parents. It will solve the immigration question.

- Do not hesitate to manipulate information during a search of the databases. One that works well is a "parent search." If the names of the parents are known, including the mother's maiden name, leave the name of the child blank and put in the parents' names only. The approach should bring up all children registered with those parents. If a mother's maiden name is not known, no option is left but to leave it blank. However, narrow the search to a ten-year period either side of a targeted year, which, at least, makes the pursuit manageable.

- If a county in Ireland and a mother's maiden name are not known, certainly conduct the parent search with the years defined for anything that might make sense. If nothing does, try adding the known children of the couple one at a time to the parent search. Usually, this hunt brings results that are otherwise lost in large numbers of entries.

Because the registration districts cross county boundaries, some databases are reluctant to add counties to the names in the collections, designating just the districts. Where boundaries cross county lines in the certificates, often two counties are listed in the headers. For someone not familiar with Irish towns, attempts to locate the registrars' offices can be confusing. Registration districts have the same names and boundaries as the Poor Law Unions, and thus boundaries are defined for where births, marriages, and deaths were registered in geographical areas. If a county of origin is known from the immigrant records, some databases allow a search to be restricted to the county name. Counties and their corresponding districts are in the chart below. Note that some districts appear in multiple counties, and a few have variant spellings (Corrofin or Corofin). In addition, name changes may have occurred before the present day (Parsonstown is now known as Birr). Also refer to the civil registration map on pp. 10-11, figures 5a-5b.

Superintendent Registers' Districts to 1921

County	District
Antrim	Antrim, Ballycastle, Ballymena, Ballymoney, Belfast, Coleraine, Larne, Lisburn, Lurgan
Armagh	Armagh, Banbridge, Castleblaney, Dundalk, Lurgan, Newry
Carlow	Baltinglass, Carlow, Enniscorthy, New Ross, Shillelagh
Cavan	Ballieborough, Bawnboy, Cavan, Cootehill, Enniskillen, Granard, Kells, Oldcastle

Superintendent Registers' Districts to 1921

County	District
Clare	Ballyvaughan, Corofin, Ennis, Ennistimon, Killadysert, Kilrush, Limerick, Scarriff, Tulla
Cork	Bandon, Bantry, Castletown, Clonakilty, Cork, Dunmanway, Fermoy, Kanturk, Kilmallock, Kinsale, Lismore, Macroom, Mallow, Middleton, Millstreet, Mitchelstown, Skibbereen, Skull, Youghal
Donegal	Ballyshannon, Derry (Londonderry), Donegal, Dunfanaghy, Glenties, Inishowen, Letterkenny, Millford, Strabane, Stranorlar
Down	Banbridge, Belfast, Downpatrick, Kilkeel, Lisburn, Lurgan, Newry, Newtownards
Dublin	Balrothery, Celbridge, Dublin North, Dublin South, Dunshaughlin, Naas, Rathdown
Fermanagh	Ballyshannon, Clones, Enniskillen, Irvinestown, Lisnaskea
Galway	Ballinasloe, Ballinrobe, Clifden, Galway, Glenamaddy, Gort, Loughrea, Mount Bellew, Oughterard, Portumna, Roscommon, Scarriff, Tuam
Kerry	Cahersiveen, Dingle, Glin, Kenmare, Killarney, Listowel, Tralee
Kildare	Athy, Baltinglass, Celbridge, Edenderry, Naas
Kilkenny	Callan, Carrick-on-Suir, Castlecomer, Kilkenny, New Ross, Thomastown, Urlingford, Waterford
Laois (Queens)	Abbeyleix, Athy, Carlow, Donaghmore, Mountmellick, Roscrea
Leitrim	Ballyshannon, Bawnboy, Carrick-on-Shannon, Manor Hamilton, Mohill
Limerick	Croom, Glin, Kilmallock, Limerick, Mitchelstown, Newcastle, Rathkeale, Tipperary,
Londonderry/Derry	Ballymoney, Coleraine, Londonderry, Magherafelt, Newtownlimavady
Longford	Ballymahon, Granard, Longford
Louth	Ardee, Drogheda, Dundalk

Superintendent Registers' Districts to 1921

County	District
Mayo	Ballina, Ballinrobe, Belmullet, Castlebar, Castlereagh, Claremorris, Clifden, Killala, Newport, Oughterard, Swineford, Westport
Meath	Ardee, Celbridge, Delvin, Drogheda, Dunshaughlin, Edenderry, Kells, Navan, Oldcastle, Trim
Monaghan	Carrickmacross, Castleblayney, Clogher, Clones, Cootehill, Dundalk, Monaghan
Offaly (Kings)	Edenderry, Mountmellick, Parsonstown, Roscrea, Tullamore
Roscommon	Athlone, Ballinasloe, Boyle, Carrick-On-Shannon, Castlereagh, Glennemaddy, Roscommon, Strokestown, Swineford
Sligo	Ballina, Boyle, Dromore West, Sligo, Tobercurry
Tipperary	Borrisokane, Callan, Carrick-On-Suir, Cashel, Clogheen, Clonmel, Nenagh, Parsonstown, Roscrea, Thurles, Tipperary, Urlingford
Tyrone	Armagh, Castlederg, Clogher, Cookstown, Dungannon, Enniskillen, Gortin, Irvinestown, Omagh, Strabane
Waterford	Carrick-On-Suir, Clogheen, Clonmel, Dungarvan, Kilmac-thomas, Lismore, Waterford, Youghal
Westmeath	Athlone, Ballymahon, Delvin, Granard, Mullingar, Tullamore
Wexford	Gorey, Enniscorthy, New Ross, Shillelagh, Wexford
Wicklow	Baltinglass, Naas, Rathdown, Rathdrum, Shillelagh

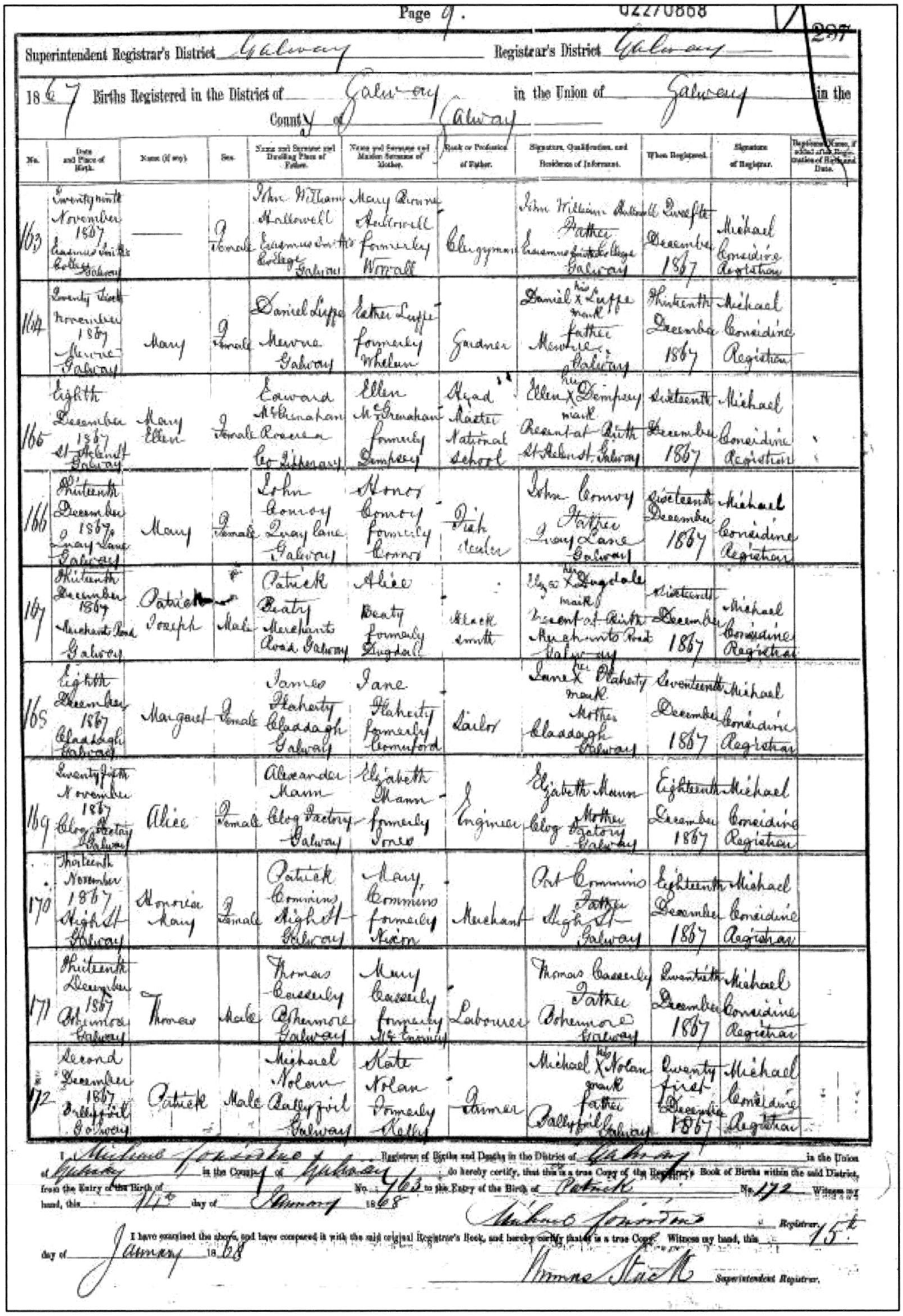

Page 9. 02270868 287

Superintendent Registrar's District Galway Registrar's District Galway

1867 Births Registered in the District of Galway in the Union of Galway in the County of Galway

No.	Date and Place of Birth.	Name (if any).	Sex.	Name and Surname and Dwelling Place of Father.	Name and Surname and Maiden Surname of Mother.	Rank or Profession of Father.	Signature, Qualification, and Residence of Informant.	When Registered.	Signature of Registrar.	Baptismal Name, if added after Registration of Birth, and Date.
163	Twenty ninth November 1867 Erasmus Smith's College Galway	—	Female	John William Hallowell Erasmus Smith's College Galway	Mary Brown Hallowell formerly Worrall	Clergyman	John William Hallowell Father Erasmus Smith's College Galway	Twelfth December 1867	Michael Considine Registrar	
164	Seventy third November 1867 Newne Galway	Mary	Female	Daniel Luffe Newne Galway	Esther Luffe formerly Whelan	Gardener	Daniel x Luffe his mark Father Newne Galway	Thirteenth December 1867	Michael Considine Registrar	
165	Eighth December 1867 St. Helens St Galway	Mary Ellen	Female	Edward McGrenahan Roscrea Co Tipperary	Ellen McGrenahan formerly Dempsey	Head Master National School	Ellen x Dempsey her mark Present at Birth St Helens St Galway	Sixteenth December 1867	Michael Considine Registrar	
166	Thirteenth December 1867 Quay Lane Galway	Mary	Female	John Conroy Quay Lane Galway	Honor Conroy formerly Connor	Fish dealer	John Conroy Father Quay Lane Galway	Sixteenth December 1867	Michael Considine Registrar	
167	Thirteenth December 1867 Merchants Road Galway	Patrick Joseph	Male	Patrick Beaty Merchants Road Galway	Alice Beaty formerly Dugdall	Black smith	Eliza x Dugdale her mark Present at Birth Merchants Road Galway	Sixteenth December 1867	Michael Considine Registrar	
168	Eighth December 1867 Claddagh Galway	Margaret	Female	James Flaherty Claddagh Galway	Jane Flaherty formerly Comerford	Sailor	Jane x Flaherty her mark Mother Claddagh Galway	Seventeenth December 1867	Michael Considine Registrar	
169	Twenty fifth November 1867 Clog Factory Galway	Alice	Female	Alexander Mann Clog Factory Galway	Elizabeth Mann formerly Jones	Engineer	Elizabeth Mann Mother Clog Factory Galway	Eighteenth December 1867	Michael Considine Registrar	
170	Thirteenth November 1867 High St Galway	Honoria Mary	Female	Patrick Commins High St Galway	Mary Commins formerly Nixon	Merchant	Patt Commins Father High St Galway	Eighteenth December 1867	Michael Considine Registrar	
171	Thirteenth December 1867 Bohermore Galway	Thomas	Male	Thomas Casserly Bohermore Galway	Mary Casserly formerly McEnany	Labourer	Thomas Casserly Father Bohermore Galway	Twentieth December 1867	Michael Considine Registrar	
172	Second December 1867 Ballyfoil Galway	Patrick	Male	Michael Nolan Ballyfoil Galway	Kate Nolan formerly Kelly	Farmer	Michael x Nolan his mark Father Ballyfoil Galway	Twenty first December 1867	Michael Considine Registrar	

I, Michael Considine, Registrar of Births and Deaths in the District of Galway in the Union of Galway in the County of Galway do hereby certify, that this is a true Copy of the Registrar's Book of Births within the said District, from the Entry of the Birth of Mary No. 163 to the Entry of the Birth of Patrick No. 172. Witness my hand, this 11th day of January 1868

Michael Considine Registrar.

I have examined the above, and have compared it with the said original Registrar's Book, and hereby certify that it is a true Copy. Witness my hand, this 15th day of January 1868

Thomas Stack Superintendent Registrar.

Figure 30: Page from an 1867 civil register of marriages. (Image courtesy of the General Record Office. Permissions received.)

Chapter Six

Emigration Lists

Consulting passengers' lists is not a priority in developing a pre-1890 immigration strategy because they are scarce in Ireland before that year. Some unusual collections substituting for them can solve the question of Irish origins, but before accessing those records, a few ideas about leaving Ireland should be considered.

Hearing researchers abroad cite family lore about ancestors being from County Cork is quite common. It could be true, but numerous people other than those born and brought up in County Cork left Ireland at the port of Queenstown. This port historically was also known as the Cove of Cork and is today known as Cobh. It is located at the southern tip of the county. The names that remained in the minds of the immigrants, passed down through the generations, were County Cork or just Cork. From an immigration perspective, even though Cork

might not have been accurate as the place of origin, at the least, the ancestors informed their descendants that they had lived in that area of Ireland. If they had not been from the region, they would have left through Londonderry (Derry), Belfast, or Dublin, none of which are close to Cork.

The port of Queenstown (Cobh) can be compared to those of Liverpool, New York City, Cape Town, and Sydney. Cobh was a huge harbor, servicing vessels worldwide. Docked in Queenstown were ships waiting to transport people and goods as well as ships arriving to pick up additional crews, passengers, and cargoes. To place Cobh emigrations in perspective, between 1848 and 1950, an estimated 6 million people left Ireland. Of those, 2.5 million sailed from Queenstown (Cobh) alone. Although Cork is the example, similar statistics for the other major Irish harbors, those being Belfast, Dublin, and Londonderry (Derry), are plentiful as well. If family relayed through generations that the ancestor came from one of these areas, be a bit skeptical.

Passengers' Departure and Arrival Records

Before 1890, the lists for Irish ports are almost totally lacking, and so the main source for that period is often the ancestors' arrivals in their new countries. To research departures from Ireland, the focus must be on records not associated with the ports that document persons leaving or arriving. Two major collections of them have been indexed and digitized. They are on Ancestry.com, Findmypast.com, and are part of the Board of Trade (BT) series at The National

Archives, Kew, outside London. The outward lists are in the papers of BT27, and the incoming are BT26:

- UK, Outward Passenger Lists, 1890-1960
- UK, Incoming Passenger Lists, 1878-1960

These are United Kingdom collections through 1921, when the Irish Free State (Republic of Ireland) was established. Irish Free State ports were recorded as a segment of the BT records for only a few short years after 1921. The ports in Northern Ireland are administered by the Board of Trade.

Ships leaving Ireland in BT27 record series are:

- Belfast, County Antrim
- Dublin, County Dublin
- Galway, County Galway
- Londonderry (Derry), County Londonderry
- Moville, County Donegal
- Queenstown (Cobh), County Cork

The records for incoming ships that often contain names of tourists are in the BT26 series and are for the following ports:

- Bangor, County Down
- Bantry, County Cork
- Belfast, County Antrim
- Cork, County Cork
- Dublin, County Dublin
- Londonderry (Derry), County Londonderry (Derry)
- Moville, County Donegal
- Queenstown (Cobh), County Cork
- Sligo, County Sligo
- Tralee, County Kerry

Many of the inbound records were destroyed by the BT around 1900, and so the series is by no means complete. Also, the collection documents only the ships arriving from foreign countries, excluding those from Europe and the Mediterranean. Exceptions included ships from European and Mediterranean ports that picked up passengers who were en route to destinations other than the United Kingdom. Separate lists were kept for British, Commonwealth, and alien passengers.

Although both outbound and incoming records began late, they cannot be deemed inconsequential in immigrant research. Typically, if someone was traveling after 1890, the place of origin in Ireland may, but not assuredly, already be known by his or her descendants. Because the people who left long before 1890 might have acquired some wealth, having escaped poverty through emigrating, they could travel. People who departed when they were young thus in adulthood could visit families in Ireland (incoming list) and return to their home countries (outward lists).

The inward and outward lists provide only basic information. However, because they are indexed and ages are given, they assist in sorting through people with common names. Sometimes, it is possible to discover persons traveling back and forth over the years. Appreciate that even though the records may be for dates too late for emigrations, they can be used for tracing homes of ancestors. Clues of great worth are: the ports through which they entered; whom they might have gone to see; and what was noted in the port records in the immigrants' home countries to complement these two BT series of records.

Miscellaneous Emigration Records

While departure lists can be useful, they represent a mere fraction of the people who left Ireland. In fact, before 1890, the

Figure 31: Port locations for emigration and immigration for which records have survived in Board of Trade collections BT26 and BT27.

only government records are from 1803 to 1806. Additional documents are from businesses, churches, institutions, or other sources. Noteworthy collections, or all the ones that can be classified as "major collections" from the many odd and localized ones, are:

1803-1806: Between March 1803 and March 1806, masters

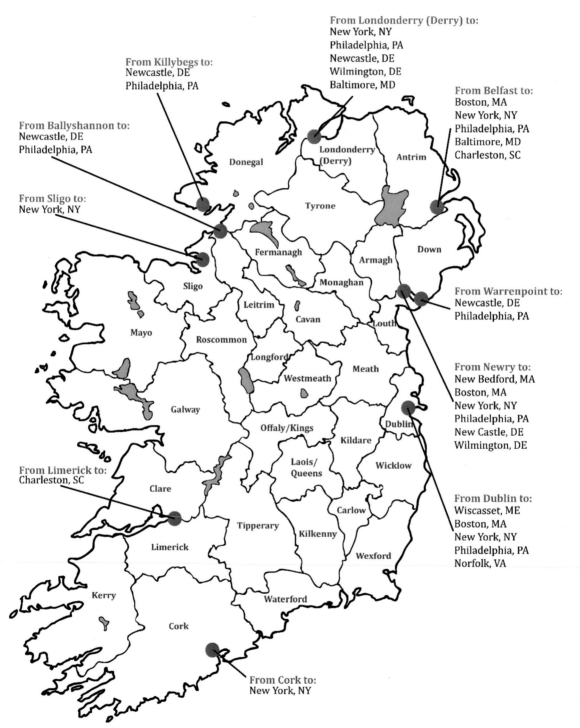

Figure 32: Ports of departure with surviving records between 1803 and 1806, together with lists of destinations.

of ships were required by law to provide registers of the passengers on their ships sailing from Irish ports. The majority of ships were leaving from Dublin (28 ships), Londonderry (26 ships), Belfast (22 ships), Newry (19 ships), and Sligo (6 ships). The lists are called the Hardwicke Papers, and they have each passenger's name, age, occupation, and residence. The law was intended to keep skilled laborers from leaving the country, and so the occupations reported may be questionable since people tried to avoid the law. Brian Mitchell extracted and indexed these records in *Irish Passenger Lists, 1803-1806: Lists of Passengers Sailing from Ireland to America Extracted from the Hardwicke Papers* (Baltimore, Maryland: Genealogical Publishing Co., 1995). They are available on Ancestry.com.

1833-1839: The Ordnance Survey project started to note emigrants in each parish, but the effort was abandoned in 1840 after completing lists for County Londonderry and County Antrim. Brian Mitchell published the lists for the two counties in *Irish Emigration Lists, 1833-1839: Lists of Emigrants Extracted from the Ordnance Survey Memoirs for Counties Londonderry and Antrim* (Baltimore, Maryland: Genealogical Publishing Co., 1989).

Also recorded were seasonal harvest workers bound for England and Scotland who worked in and around the ports of Liverpool and Glasgow. The lists are arranged by parish with a general index of all names. In addition to names are ages, years of emigrations, townlands of residences, destinations, and religions. As with all pre-1890 emigration records, this collection is limited. Extractions can be found on several online databases, including Ancestry.com, as "Irish Emigration Lists, 1833-1839."

1847-1871: Surviving records of two shipping companies that took passengers from the port of Londonderry to Canada and the United States are available at the PRONI. The lists are indexed in Brian Mitchell's *Irish Passenger Lists 1847-1871: Lists of Passengers Sailing from Londonderry to America on Ships of the J & J Cooke Line and the McCorkell Line* (Baltimore, Maryland: Genealogical Publishing Co., 1988), available on Ancestry.com as the database "Irish Passenger Lists, 1847-1871." During the first seventy years of the nineteenth century, about 200,000 passengers left through the port of Londonderry, yet the surviving shipping records include 27,495 emigrant names, or 13.74% of the projected 200,000 figure. From 1847 to 1867, the shipping line sent 21,199 passengers to North America. As an example, in 1847, a famine year, 5,071 passengers left, and of those, 1,197 (23%) went to Philadelphia; 2,210 (44%), to St. John, New Brunswick; and 1,664 (33%), to Quebec. It is safe to conclude that most of the passengers leaving Londonderry through this shipping line were from the heavy concentrations of people in the counties of Donegal, Londonderry (Derry), and Tyrone.

Of course, the foregoing records do not comprise other types, such as the ones for people sent to the Australian colonies as convicts. Those categories of records initiate a new discussion because the transported persons were not willing emigrants.

Mellon Centre for Migration Studies

Housed at the Ulster American Folk Park in Omagh, County Tyrone, Northern Ireland, is the Mellon Centre for Migration Studies. Over the last forty years, the center has assembled sources to document migration to North America, specifically to the United States and Canada. The findings are being compiled into the "Irish Emigration Database," which covers 1700 to 1950, even though about three-quarters of them are from 1820 to 1920. Thirteen categories of sources are included, for instance, emigrant letters, newspaper articles, advertisements, and passenger lists. The geographical areas encompassed in the database are all the counties in Ireland, the United States, and Canada. The database is free to the public at the Centre, the public libraries in Northern Ireland, and the PRONI.

A link to the "Irish Emigration Database" and explanations about the database can be found on the Mellon Centre website. Part of the database is on the website, and collections such as emigrant letters have been extracted for it. The sources for each paper and where it is deposited are also provided. The database holds over 33,000 records, and the online version can be consulted first and then, if needed, at the Centre. Realize that as massive as it is, only a fraction of the emigrants are documented.

Newspapers

During the 1700s, the passengers on ships from Ulster customarily signed "letters of thanks" to the ships' captains for good voyages. The letters with the names of the passengers were published in Ulster newspapers to encourage others to enroll for passages with the captains. In other words, they were free advertising. Not every ship did this, however.

Between 1737 and 1772, the major newspaper in Ulster was the *Belfast Newsletter,* which published notices regarding ships (including the "letters of thanks") from ports throughout the north of Ireland. A detailed index to this paper, *Belfast Newsletter Index, 1737-1800* (Ann Arbor, Michigan: UMI, 1993), compiled by John C. Greene, is a five-part index on microfiche to surnames, places, ships, general topics, and advertisements. The index is also on the University of Louisiana Lafayette website and on Irishnewsarchive.com. In the online edition, every significant word and date in the 20,000 surviving pages is indexed, but the website does highlight some limitations. For example, only one-quarter of the newspaper editions survived from 1737 to 1750, yet it is nearly complete from 1750 to 1800. The database contains 300,000 items of news and advertisements.

The same kind of emigration material may be found in the *Londonderry Journal*, which began publication in 1772. Notes about passengers, along with other items, dating from 1772 to 1784, were abstracted in Donald M. Schlegel's *Irish Genealogical Abstracts From the Londonderry Journal, 1772-1784* (Baltimore, Maryland: Clearfield Co., 1990).

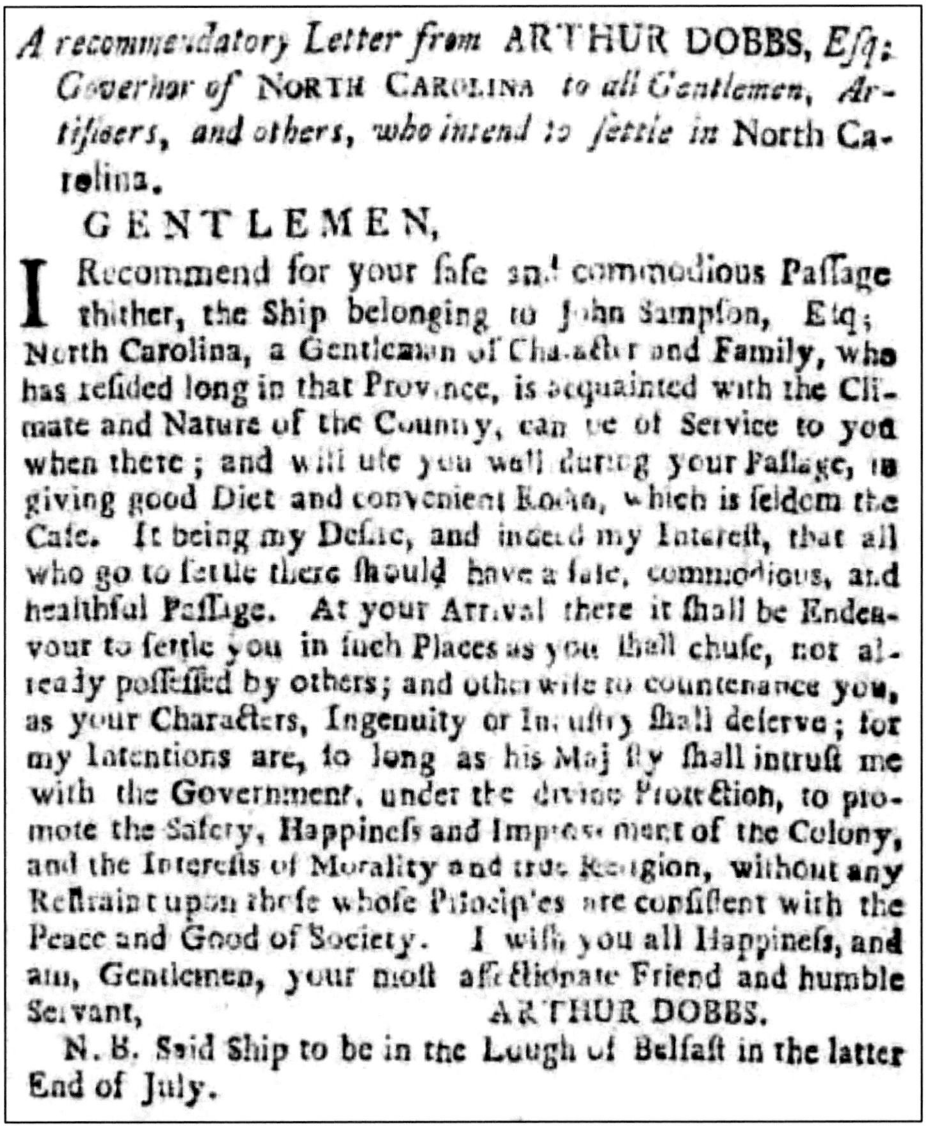

A recommendatory Letter from ARTHUR DOBBS, *Esq; Governor of* NORTH CAROLINA *to all Gentlemen, Artificers, and others, who intend to settle in* North Carolina.

GENTLEMEN,

I Recommend for your safe and commodious Passage thither, the Ship belonging to John Sampson, Esq; North Carolina, a Gentleman of Character and Family, who has resided long in that Province, is acquainted with the Climate and Nature of the Country, can be of Service to you when there; and will use you well during your Passage, in giving good Diet and convenient Room, which is seldom the Case. It being my Desire, and indeed my Interest, that all who go to settle there should have a safe, commodious, and healthful Passage. At your Arrival there it shall be Endeavour to settle you in such Places as you shall chuse, not already possessed by others; and otherwise to countenance you, as your Characters, Ingenuity or Industry shall deserve; for my Intentions are, so long as his Majesty shall intrust me with the Government, under the divine Protection, to promote the Safety, Happiness and Improvement of the Colony, and the Interests of Morality and true Religion, without any Restraint upon those whose Principles are consistent with the Peace and Good of Society. I wish you all Happiness, and am, Gentlemen, your most affectionate Friend and humble Servant, ARTHUR DOBBS.

N. B. Said Ship to be in the Lough of Belfast in the latter End of July.

Figure 33: Belfast Newsletter, 7 June 1754, p.2. An advertisement in the form of a recommendation letter from North Carolina's Governor Arthur Dobbs to promote Irish emigration from Belfast. "At your arrival there [North Carolina] it shall be endeavor[ed] to settle you in such places as you shall chuse [sic], not already possessed by others...as your characters, ingenuity or industry shall deserve." (Image courtesy of Linen Hall Library, Belfast. Under UK Copyright law, a publisher's work is protected for 25 years from the end of the year in which the publication occurred. No permissions required.)

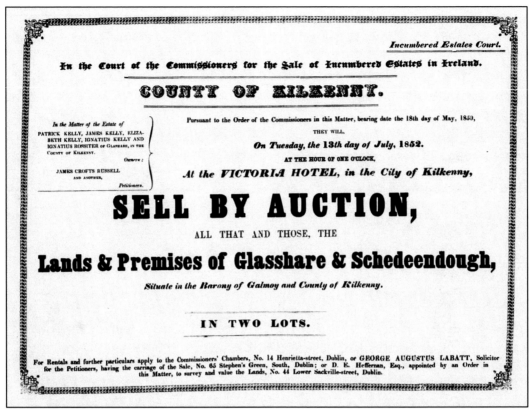

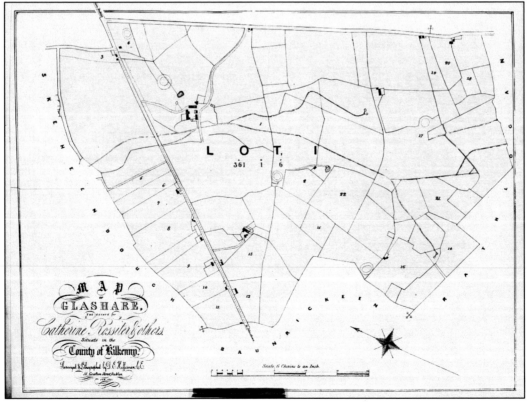

Figures 34-35: Encumbered (Incumbered) Irish Estate records found within the database titled "Landed Estate Court Rentals 1850-1885" on www.Findmypast.com. Lot numbers on the map relate to the list found on p. 97, also taken from the same source. (Images courtesy of Findmypast.com. Permissions received.)

Chapter Seven

Estate Records

Before the twentieth century, most of the people in Ireland leased or rented the lands and houses they occupied instead of owning them. Their rental arrangements might have been directly with the property holders or from intermediaries who held leases and then sublet or rented the lands to successions of tenants. Estate landowners were usually Protestant, often members of the nobility, landed gentry, or Church of Ireland clergy. Lands also were held by the Crown, the Church of Ireland, London guilds, and various companies.

Estate records were essentially the private papers of the landlords of Ireland, and they can be massive sets, especially for the larger, well-established estates. Each estate, as a private business, had its own name and kept its registers in its own manner. Some were quite detailed, and some were simply the accounts of the estates. Unless they have been indexed or an inventory has been created, conjectures cannot be made about what is in the records, particularly concerning the tenants. Fortunately, many archival inventories have been produced for the larger estates. They can be found on the websites of the National Library of Ireland and the PRONI, whose catalogs can facilitate locating records on deposit at other archives.

Although many of the smaller estate records have not survived, the ones for the larger estates usually have been archived. Records generated by estate owners are often the last source researchers consult to trace common persons in the era before the advent of parish registers. Most people read estate records for the rental agreements. These detail the rights of the tenants on the properties. However, accessing them requires either an index or knowing the places in Ireland so that the names of the landlords can be discovered.

For solving questions about immigrant origins, the indexes for the records of various estates can be of assistance. Without an index, estate records are limited for purposes of immigration. Even so, state-sponsored plans were initiated, whereby the passages out of Ireland were paid by the landlords to evict tenants from their lands. Interest in estate records is frequently stirred by research in the immigrant country that uncovers a reference to one of the assisted emigrations. Much about the schemes has been published or is online because historians and genealogists are intrigued by them. For an immigration strategy, it is the rest of the estate papers, such as the rentals and leases, that need to be searched once a landlord and a family from the estate have been identified.

Assisted Emigration Schemes

The records for the estates where the tenants lived can document the departures of families or individuals. Each estate record is distinctive. Some have lists of those leaving, and others have records of tenants who petitioned the landlords for funds to emigrate. Some landlords paid the total costs of their tenants' emigrations while others paid only portions of the expenses. Often, if funds were not available and the estate could not afford to keep the tenants, they were simply evicted. A record of eviction may be at the end of a lease or rental agreement between the estate holder and the tenant.

Importantly, within these types of estate records are addresses for families being assisted. The exact addresses, such as townlands, often were not given in academic studies. Rather, the emphasis was on the general histories of the emigrations, not the individuals on the estates. Therefore, if articles or books have been found documenting assisted emigrations, realize that not all records from estates might have been extracted. If the authors were genealogists, the lists of those assisted probably were included because the immigrants were the focus of the studies. If written by historians, the addresses might or might not have been noted. Perhaps only the statistical data was pertinent to the research projects.

Marie E. Daly discusses the relationship of the tenants to the estates and emigrations in her article "Evictions & Forced Emigration: Landlord-Assisted Passage from Ireland" in *New England Ancestors* 8, #4 (Fall 2007), pp.19-24. She calculated that between 1846 and 1855, landlords paid for the passages of approximately 100,000 Irish.

As examples, estate-sponsored emigrations sent tenants to Saint John, New Brunswick, and to New York City, but the cheapest route into North America was through Quebec. From there, tenants could move elsewhere. In 1848, because of the desperate conditions of the famine, so many tenants arrived in British Canada that the government curtailed the practice by imposing a levy for each immigrant on every ship. Because groups of tenants were coming from the same estate, it is customary to find historical information about who these people were and to which estate-sponsored plan they belonged.

One of the most famous assisted migrations was out of the Shirley Estate in County Monaghan. The 26,000-acre estate was owned by Evelyn John Shirley, Esq., in Farney, County Monaghan. Between 1842 and 1852, about 1,300 tenants were sent to Liverpool, Quebec, and Australia. Many eventually settled in Upstate New York and in the upper Midwest of the United States. This assisted emigration is so well known because the lists of persons leaving are thorough and amazing in detail, similar to the lists of passengers that any researcher has seen from any large port. The manuscript records of the Shirley Estate are at the PRONI. Patrick J. Duffy's article, "Assisted Emigration from the Shirley Estate 1843-

54" in *Clogher Record*, XIV, #2 (1992): 7-62, contains extracts from the estate's archive. Consequently, because assisted emigration schemes were somewhat renowned, finding extracted information about them in databases and published in books or journal articles is common.

Encumbered Estate Court Records

About 25 percent of the estates went through the Incumbered (Encumbered)

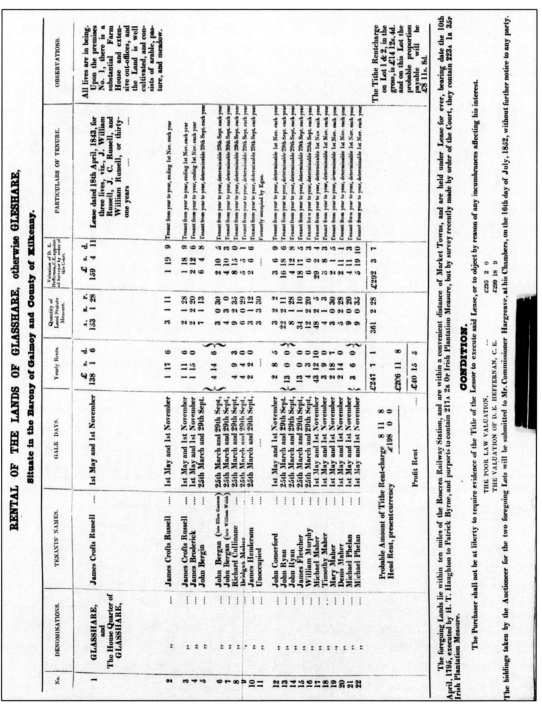

Figure 36: List of tenants matching the lot numbers found on maps for the same lands. From Encumbered Irish Estates. See p. 94 for correlating images. (Images courtesy of Findmypast.com. Permissions received.)

Estates Court. The sales brochures for bankrupt estates are indexed and online at FamilySearch.org in its database "Ireland, Landed Estates Court Files, 1850-1885" and at Findmypast.com in its database "Landed Estates Court Rentals, 1850-1885." The huge collection of records includes over 500,000 tenants in over 8,000 estates throughout Ireland. It is fully indexed, and so researchers do not have to know the estate or even the county where an ancestor lived. However, the search is limited because only 25 percent of the Irish estates are in the collection. Unless more information is known ahead of time, such as an ancestor coming from a specific landlord's estate, care does have to be taken to assure the person found in the index is indeed the ancestor. Knowing a county of origin certainly helps.

The Encumbered Estates Act of 1849 created a court to sell debt-ridden estates. In 1852, it was replaced by the Landed Estates Court, which was replaced in 1877 by the Land Judges Court that was part of the Chancery Division of the High Court. All these courts had the same purpose, to sell insolvent estates, and over 3,000 estates were processed between 1849 and 1857 alone.

Each of the estate sales through a court had a brochure that accompanied the sale, which informed prospective buyers about what they were purchasing. Printed sales brochures for estates being sold by the courts ordinarily had the names of the bankrupt landowners, maps of the estates, and listings of the tenants on the properties. Included were the tenants' yearly rents and the types of tenures by which they occupied their lands. The information about the tenants corresponded to the accompanying townland maps showing exactly where each person's property was located.

The indexes to the estate sales are the perfect immigration source. The days of the sales at the courthouses are listed and so provide dates from which to judge when ancestors were on the estates. After the sales, if tenants were marked off the tax lists, such as Griffith's Primary Valuation (1847-1864) or the subsequent revision books, deaths or emigrations from the estates can be confirmed. However, because names are common, if a tenant is found on the estate after the ancestor is known to have emigrated, he or she may simply be a person with the same name.

The Encumbered Estate brochures are useful even if an ancestor emigrated before the process began in 1849. If an ancestor left before the estate went bankrupt, relatives who were still on the land might be listed in the records. When the lands were auctioned, the tenants remained as part of the estate if they held a lease agreement. The tenants' rights can be spelled out for as far back as the 1700s, but, generally, they date to the early 1800s. Therefore, even when an ancestor emigrated, a sibling might have stayed and assumed the tenant's entitlement to the farm. It is the sibling who would have been reported in the brochure as having the right to the farm, thus solving the question of Irish origins.

This source could be used as part of a surname distribution search. If the target surname, or even a first name, is unusual, the Encumbered Estate sales brochures along with other records, such as the taxes, can be studied to locate where the names appear in Ireland. The results are frequently successful when indexes of church records do not reveal the ancestral family.

Estate Records Database
The National University of Ireland Galway (NUI Galway) has developed the "Connacht and Munster Landed Estates Database" for estates in Counties Clare, Cork, Galway, Kerry, Leitrim, Limerick, Mayo, Roscommon, Sligo, Tipperary, and Waterford. It documents historical estate houses, families, and records from about 1700 through 1914, opening new research avenues for family historians. The database is maintained by the Moore Institute for Research in the Humanities and Social Studies at the NUI Galway.

Most researchers consult this database for Connacht and Munster Provinces if they already know landlords' names or specific places in Ireland. Otherwise, it would not be a usable database. This is an inventory of estate records, not an index to what is in the records themselves. The inventory is helpful in determining what happened to estates. If they went through bankruptcies, series of owners can also be listed.

However, if an estate is not known but the civil parish is, probably through Griffith's Valuation or the Tithe Applotment, the database can be searched with the name of the parish.

Estates associated with that civil parish should be revealed, bringing the investigation one stage closer to accessing the estate books themselves.

Remember, before the advent of church registers, estate records may be the only remaining Irish source for either confirming immigrants' origins or extending their pedigrees. The landlords' estate records are especially valuable for the tenant class. They may have notations about the tenants' emigrations or provide insight into how the lands were cleared of the tenants through assisted emigration schemes.

Figure 37: The Estates Records Database developed by the University of Ireland Galway, which includes the provinces of Connaught and Munster.

BLA

30 April, 1675, when he was s. by his two surviving sisters, Eleanor and Martha; the latter m. Arthur Squibb, Esq., and ELEANOR, the elder, m. EDWARD ASPINWALL, Esq. of Aspinwall and Ormskirk, whose grandson, Edward, left a son and heir, and a dau., Mary. Ireland Aspinwall, the son, d. unm. in 1733, and Mary s. as heir to her brother: she m. Isaac Green, Esq., who died Lord of Childwall and Hale, 9 July, 1749, leaving three daus., of whom the eldest d. unm.; Ireland Green, the second, m. Thomas Blackburne, Esq. of Orford, who thus acquired Hale and Halewood; and Mary, m. Bamber Gascoyne, Esq.

⁎ From a younger son of the Irelands of the Hutt, descend the Irelands of Robertstown, co. Kildare. (*See that family.*)

BLACKER OF CARRICK BLACKER.

BLACKER, WILLIAM, Esq. of Carrick Blacker, co. Armagh, M.A., Lieutenant-Colonel of the Armagh militia, and a deputy-lieutenant of that shire, b. in 1780, m. in 1810, Anne, eldest dau. of Sir Andrew Ferguson, Bart., M.P. for Londonderry. Col. Blacker was appointed Vice-Treasurer of Ireland in January, 1817, and held office until 1829, when he resigned. He s. his father in 1826.

Lineage.

CAPTAIN VALENTINE BLACKER, of Carrick, in the parish of Seagoe and co. of Armagh, b. in 1597, m. Judith, dau. of George Harrisson, Esq. of Ballydorgan, and had one son, GEORGE, and a dau., Violetta. Captain Blacker purchased the manor of Carrowbrack, with courts leet &c., from Anthony Cope, Esq. of Loughall, 22 Aug. 1660. This manor is commonly known by the name of Carrick-Blacker. He d. 17 Aug. 1677, and was interred in Seagoe Church. His only son and successor,

MAJOR GEORGE BLACKER, of Carrick, a firm adherent of King WILLIAM III., m. Rosa, dau. of Rowland Young, Esq., of Drakestoun, co. Louth, and by her, who d. in 1689, left two sons; the younger, Robert, was ancestor of the BLACKERS of Drogheda, and of the co. Meath; the elder, WILLIAM BLACKER, Esq. of Carrick and Ballytroan, m. 1st, before the year 1666, Elizabeth, daughter of the Hon. Robert Stewart, of Irry and Stewart Hall, in the co. of Tyrone, third son of the first Baron Castlestewart, and by her, who d. in Jan. 1678, he had an only son, STEWART, his heir. Mr. Blacker espoused, 2ndly, late in life, Miss Mathers, and had another son,

Samuel, of Tandragee, who m. in 1734, Mary, dau. of Corry, of Rock Corry, co. Monaghan, and by her (who d. 30 Oct. 1771,) he left issue.
ST. JOHN BLACKER, in holy orders, rector of Moira, co. Down, and afterwards prebendary of Inver, in Donegal, b. in 1743, m. 1st, in 1767, Grace, dau. of Maxwell Close, Esq. of Elm Park, in Armaghshire, and 2ndly, Susan, dau. of Dr. Messiter, of London. By his first wife he had five sons and four daus., viz.,
  I. SAMUEL, in holy orders, LL.D., prebendary of Mullabrack, co. Armagh, b. 1771, m. 1st, Mary-Anne, dau. of David Ross, Esq. of Rosstrevor, by whom he had, with a son, Henry, who d. s. p., one dau., Elizabeth, m. to the Rev. N. Calvert, of Hunsdon House, Herts. Dr. Samuel Blacker wedded, 2ndly, Elizabeth, dau. of Thomas Douglas, Esq. of Grace Hall, co. Down, and has issue, St. John, Thomas, Theodosia, and Elizabeth.
  II. Maxwell, of Dublin, Q.C., late chairman of Kilmainham, b. 14 March, 1773, d. s. p. in 1843.
  III. William, of Armagh, b. 1776.
  IV. Valentine, C.B., lieut.-col. of the 1st regiment of light infantry in the E. I. Co.'s service, quartermaster-general of the Madras army, surveyor-general of India, &c., b. in 1778, m. 22 Dec. 1813, Emma, dau. of Robert Johnson, Esq. of Liverpool, and had three sons, Valentine-Samuel-Barry, Maxwell, and Murray, and one daughter, Emma-Louisa-Rosa. He d. in 1823.
  V. St. John, lieut.-col. in the 1st regiment of Madras Native infantry, b. 14 March, 1786, m. in 1828, Anne-Hammond, only child of Sir Charles Morgan, and has two sons, Maxwell and William, and two daus., Charlotte and Isabella.
  VI. Mary.
  VII. Catherine, m. 1st, 10 January, 1804, to the Rev. Charles Barker, canon of Wells, and 2ndly, to the Rev. Robert Ball.
  VIII. Grace, m. 6 May, 1809, to Robert Alexander,
101

BLA

Esq., representative of the elder branch of the Caledon family, and has issue.
  IX. Charlotte, m. 8 Dec. 1808, to Lieut.-Col. John Munro, and has issue.

William Blacker, of Carrick, was s. at his decease, in 1732, by his elder son,
STEWART BLACKER, Esq. of Carrick, b. in 1671, who m. in 1704, Elizabeth, dau. of the Rev. Henry Young, A.M., and niece and heiress of William Lathum, Esq. of Brookend, in the co. of Tyrone, and had issue,
  I. WILLIAM, his heir.
  II. Lathum, b. 1711, m. Martha, dau. of Peter Beaver, Esq. of Drogheda, by whom (who d. in Sept. 1802) he left issue,
    1. William-Lathum, m. Miss Hamlyn, and d. in 1810, leaving issue.
    2. Henry, captain 65th regiment, d. s. p.
    3. Beaver, who m. his cousin, Miss Susan Blacker, and d. in 1808, leaving, with other issue, a son,
      Lathum Blacker, Esq., solicitor to his Majesty's Customs, Ireland, who m. 13 April, 1820, Catherine, dau. of the Rev. George Miller, D.D., late Fellow of Trinity College, Dublin, rector of Dennyvollen, co. Fermanagh, and has Beaver-Henry, A.B., and other issue.
    4. Lathum, major 65th regiment, Newent, co. Gloucester, m. Catherine, dau. of Col. Maddisson, of Lincolnshire, and has had issue,
      George, d. unm. ensign 65th regiment.
      Martha, m. to the Rev. John Fendall, Meserdine, Gloucestershire.
      Catherine, m. to Richard Onslow, Esq., son of Archdeacon Onslow.
      Mary.
      Theodosia, m. in 1832, to Lord Monson, who died in 1841.
    5. Elizabeth, m. to Henry Coddington, Esq., M.P., of Oldbridge, and had issue.
  III. Henry, in holy orders, b. 10 July, 1713, m. Miss Martin, and had a dau. Frances, who d. unm. in 1829.
  IV. George, of Hallsmill, in Downshire, b. 26 Sept. 1718, m. 1st, in 1744, Mary, only surviving dau. of Joseph Nicolson, LL.D., and 2ndly, in 1746, Alicia, only child of Edward Dowdall, Esq. of Mowntoun, in Meath, (by Alicia Haughton, relict of — Parsons, Esq., brother of Sir William Parsons, Bart., father to the Earl of Rosse,) and had, with other issue, James Blacker, magistrate of Dublin, b. 14 Aug. 1759, who m. Miss Mansergh, and had, *inter alios*, the Rev. George Blacker, chaplain to the city of Dublin, and rector of Taghadoe, co. Kildare.
  V. Barbara, b. 23 Oct. 1706, m. to James Twigg, Esq. of Rohan Castle, co. Tyrone.

Mr. Blacker d. in 1751, aged eighty, and was buried at Sego. He was s. by his eldest son,
WILLIAM BLACKER, Esq. of Carrick and Brookend, b. 12 Sept. 1709. He espoused, 8 Aug. 1738, Letitia, dau. of Henry Cary, Esq. of Dungiven Castle, M.P. for the co. of Londonderry, and d. in 1783, leaving issue,
  I. STEWART, his heir.
  II. William, captain 105th regiment, served in the American war. He m. the dau. and heiress of Arthur Jacob, Esq. of Killane, co. Wexford, and had, with another son, and four daus., his heir,
    WILLIAM BLACKER, Esq. of Woodbrook, co. Wexford, who m. Anne Carew, dau. of the late M.P. for the county of Wexford, and sister to Robert, Lord Carew, lord-lieutenant of that shire, by whom he left, at his decease in the year 1831, two sons and two daus., viz.,
      1. WILLIAM-JACOB, of Woodbrook, b. in 1823.
      2. Robert-Shapland-Carew.
      1. Anne.
      2. Susan, m. in 1840, to the Rev. A.-L. Kirwan, Dean of Kilmacduagh.
      3. Ellen-Letitia.   4. Hannah-Dorothea.
      5. Jane-Mary.
  III. Henry, a captain in the 62d regiment, who served in the American war, and was wounded and taken prisoner with General Burgoyne, at Saratoga. He inherited from his maternal uncle, the Right Hon. Edward Cary, the house and property of Milburn, co. Derry. He d. 1 Sept. 1827, and was buried at Coleraine, leaving his estates to his nephew, the Rev. Richard Olpherts.
  IV. George, in holy orders, who d. vicar of Sego, 1 May, 1810, aged forty-six.
  V. Eliza, in 1739, m. Sir William Dunkin, judge of the Supreme Court of Judicature in Bengal.
  VI. Barbara, m. to Richard Olpherts, Esq. of Armagh, and had issue.
  VII. Martha.
  VIII. Alicia, m. in 1772, to General Sir James Stewart Denham, Bart., G.C.H.
  IX. Jane, m. to James Fleming, Esq. of Belleville, co. Cavan, and has issue.
  X. Letitia, m. General the Hon. Edward Stopford, brother to the Earl of Courtown, and has issue.
  XI. Lucinda.

Figure 38: A page from "A Genealogical and Heraldic Dictionary of the Landed Gentry of Great Britain and Ireland, Vol.1. (UK copyrights apply for the life of the author plus 70 years. No permissions required.)

Chapter Eight

Genealogies and Pedigrees

A popular impression is that everyone in Ireland was impoverished. Ireland is the opposite of other countries, for instance, England, where royalty and wealth have been idealized in the public imagination. Poverty has been romanticized in Ireland, and wealth, disdained. The relationship between the gentry and the common people was probably the same in England and in Ireland, but in Ireland, horrifying famines, deaths, and massive emigrations were added to the history. The current chapter is about the category of people who were scorned, those who were regarded as prosperous and thriving because of the dispossessions of the common people.

Families did not always emigrate because they were desperate and hungry. People with money or who came from families with money also emigrated.

They were businesspeople, clergy, educators, missionaries, and sometimes adventurers. They are a part of a less sentimentalized version of Irish history.

People who descend from moneyed and landed families may have files that trace lineages several hundred years or more! The task is identifying ancestral families from this class of people and then tying them into published or manuscript pedigrees. A lot of their pedigrees were often compiled from sources that were destroyed in the 1922 Four Courts Fire. When the archive in Dublin burned during the Civil War, large collections of records for the wealthy families became ash. The pedigrees are all that are left as proofs of relationships.

Some considerations about whether to pursue pedigree research should be:

- The class of families who left pedigrees such as those housed at the Genealogical Office were almost always Protestant. However, do not assume that a Catholic family in the immigrant country did not at some point have well-to-do Protestant ancestors.

- The family in the immigrant country likely was Protestant. This class of families was almost always Protestant, but conversions to Catholicism somewhere in Ireland or abroad should not be discounted. Even so, the Protestant aspect is an indication for where to begin research.

- Upon immigrating, the family had funds to purchase land or set up a viable business. Unless someone is descended from a branch that lost all the family wealth along the way, the people in question should have had income. They were not immigrating because they were poor. Using land as a sign of money or social status can extend all the way into the 1600s because the wealthy set up businesses and plantations in the Caribbean and American colonies.

- If a family was educated upon immigrating, assume that it was from a wealthier class. A solid education beyond that which most people received in Ireland, especially at the university level, is an excellent sign of social status in Ireland.

- If the families were prominent persons in their communities or in their churches through their educations and wealth, they certainly were in a higher social class in Ireland. These people, even in the immigrant countries, were probably, although not exclusively, Anglican.

- Evidence of a higher class of families was their prominence in organizations such as the Freemasons, an organization that required funding and was utilized by higher classes around the world to build and maintain business and social connections.

All imply that the published and manuscript genealogies in Ireland can be a sensible research pursuit.

The Anglo-Irish

Many people are descendants of what is termed the Anglo-Irish. Although the label is mainly from the nineteenth and twentieth centuries, it refers to the families who arrived in Ireland from England as early as the 1200s. They might or might not have merged with the Anglo-Irish (New English) who immigrated in the sixteenth and seventeenth centuries. Primarily through intermarriage with the incoming wealthy families, the Anglo-Normans, in effect, became Anglo-Irish and thus the Protestant Ascendancy in Ireland.

The Anglo-Irish were landed and wealthy families who had intermarried with each other and with Irish noble families. During the Reformation in Ireland and the subsequent Penal Laws that restricted the rights of non-Anglicans, the Anglo-Irish converted to the Church of Ireland. Their memberships allowed them to retain their holdings and social statuses. Records of conversions can be found in the Catholic Qualification Rolls & Convert Rolls, which include documents filed with the various courts along with the conversions to the Church of Ireland. The original records were destroyed in the 1922 Four Courts Fire, but the calendars for them survive. They are indexed on FamilySearch.org in the database "Ireland, Catholic Qualification & Convert Rolls, 1705-1845" and on Findmypast.com in a database with the same name. The National Archives of Ireland also has a database "Catholic

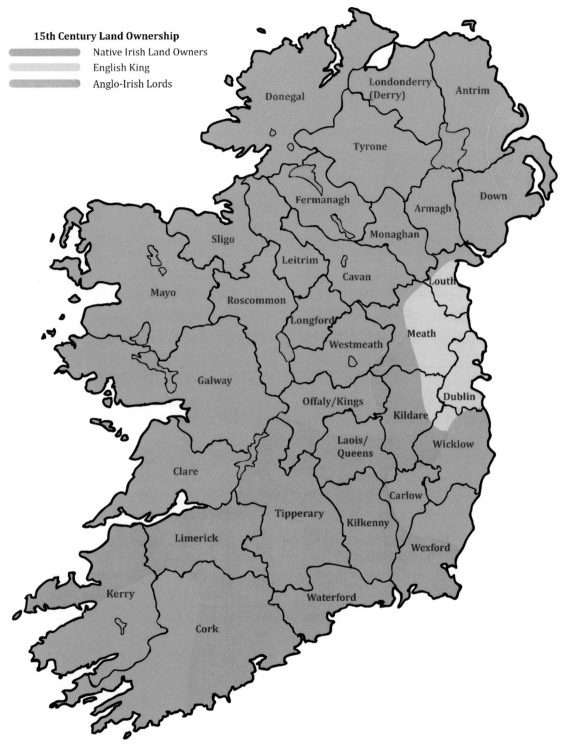

15th Century Land Ownership
Native Irish Land Owners
English King
Anglo-Irish Lords

Figure 39: Dated about 1450, this map represents the people of the landed class who, if they conformed to the Church of Ireland, which became the state religion in 1536, might have had their pedigrees recorded or Arms registered. The areas are superimposed on a later county map of Ireland for easier reference.

Qualification Rolls 1700-1845." Interestingly, many of the conversions took place after Catholic Emancipation, when restrictions against Catholics were lifted. The records, those being the calendars, are basic, but they afford enough information to sort through people and places. They contain names, addresses, occupations, dates of conversions or qualifications, dates of enrollments or court hearings, and the courts' names.

The Anglo-Irish people, as the professional class of citizens from the 1600s, commonly were documented in the history books and in published genealogies. Records of them may be found in the manuscripts of the Genealogical Office in Dublin, sometimes dating into the distant past. Websites documenting gentry, such as "Burke's Peerage" on Burkespeerage.com, are excellent resources as well, although they may be somewhat dated and, in some instances, even made up.

Even today, busts, statues, and tombs, most of which are marble, of the Anglo-Irish can be found in Church of Ireland cathedrals. Portraits and statues of them still speckle government buildings and universities. Many of their castle-like estate houses are tourist attractions. Both the honorable and unscrupulous of their population were a part of the tapestry that built modern Ireland. Their descendants influenced politics, economies, and religions throughout the British Empire.

Genealogical Office Dublin

One of the more unique repositories in Dublin is the Genealogical Office (GO). It is a section of the National Library of Ireland, and within its vast collections are miscellaneous extracts, histories, genealogical collections, and pedigrees. At the library, many people find resources despite the 1922 Four Courts Fire, which destroyed so many primary records.

The Genealogical Office has collections of pedigrees and other documents of wealthy and landed families. Many of these genealogies include ancient English and Gaelic families. In other words, they are pre-Reformation genealogies. However, it remains mainly a Protestant source, and so genealogies for common tenant farmers cannot be found. The exceptions are marriages between non-gentry and gentry families, for instance, a marriage of a Presbyterian minister's daughter to a son from a more prominent Church of Ireland family. Nevertheless, it could be properly argued that the Presbyterian family was not of the common class. Continuing with this illustration, the Presbyterian line may be traced into Scotland before the large-scale Ulster-Scots (Scots-Irish) plantings of the 1600s.

Even though pedigrees for ordinary tenant farmers are not at the Genealogical Office, various papers housed there relate to common people. For example, copies of destroyed records for the tenant class are at that location. They may be in the form of manuscripts of the 1740 and 1766 censuses for given parishes. Therefore, while the Genealogical Office is not the first place to look for tenant families, these and other sources found during research may lead back to Genealogical Office manuscripts.

Because of the manner in which they were gathered and classified, the records of the Genealogical Office on their own are difficult to access even though they are all digitized on the FamilySearch.org website. They were never meant to be primary sources, but since 1922, that is exactly what they have become. The original manuscripts are often the hand-written notebooks of historians or genealogists who were researching in the extant records before 1922. Sometimes, the notes are scraps of paper or outline pedigrees in the notebooks. All kinds of records were extracted before 1922 to accompany whatever research was being conducted. An excellent index to the collections as originally microfilmed and made available is at the Family History Library, Virginia Wade McAnlis's *The Consolidated Index to the Records of the* *Genealogical Office, Dublin, Ireland, 4 vols.* (Issaquah and Port Angeles, Washington: by author, 1994-1997). She indexed the Family History Library microfilms alphabetically by surname. The entries include the Genealogical Office collection reference numbers and the corresponding microfilm numbers. Now that the microfilms are digitized on the FamilySearch.org website with new digital folder numbers, they can also be easily translated from the old microfilm numbers to the new digital folder numbers.

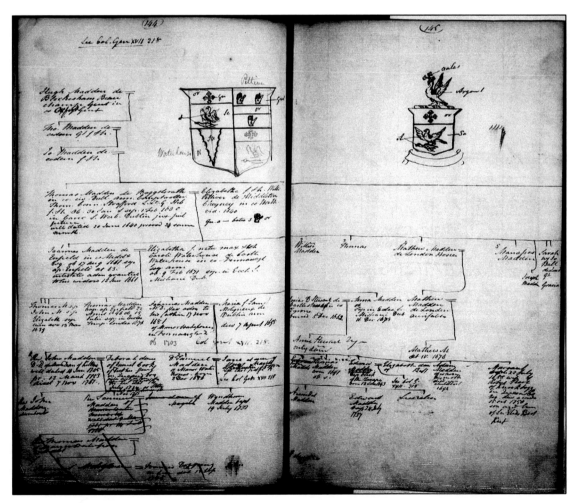

Figure 40: Hand-drawn pedigree and coat of arms. (Image courtesy of the Genealogical Office of Ireland, now part of the National Library of Ireland. Irish copyrights apply for the life of the author plus 70 years. No permissions required.)

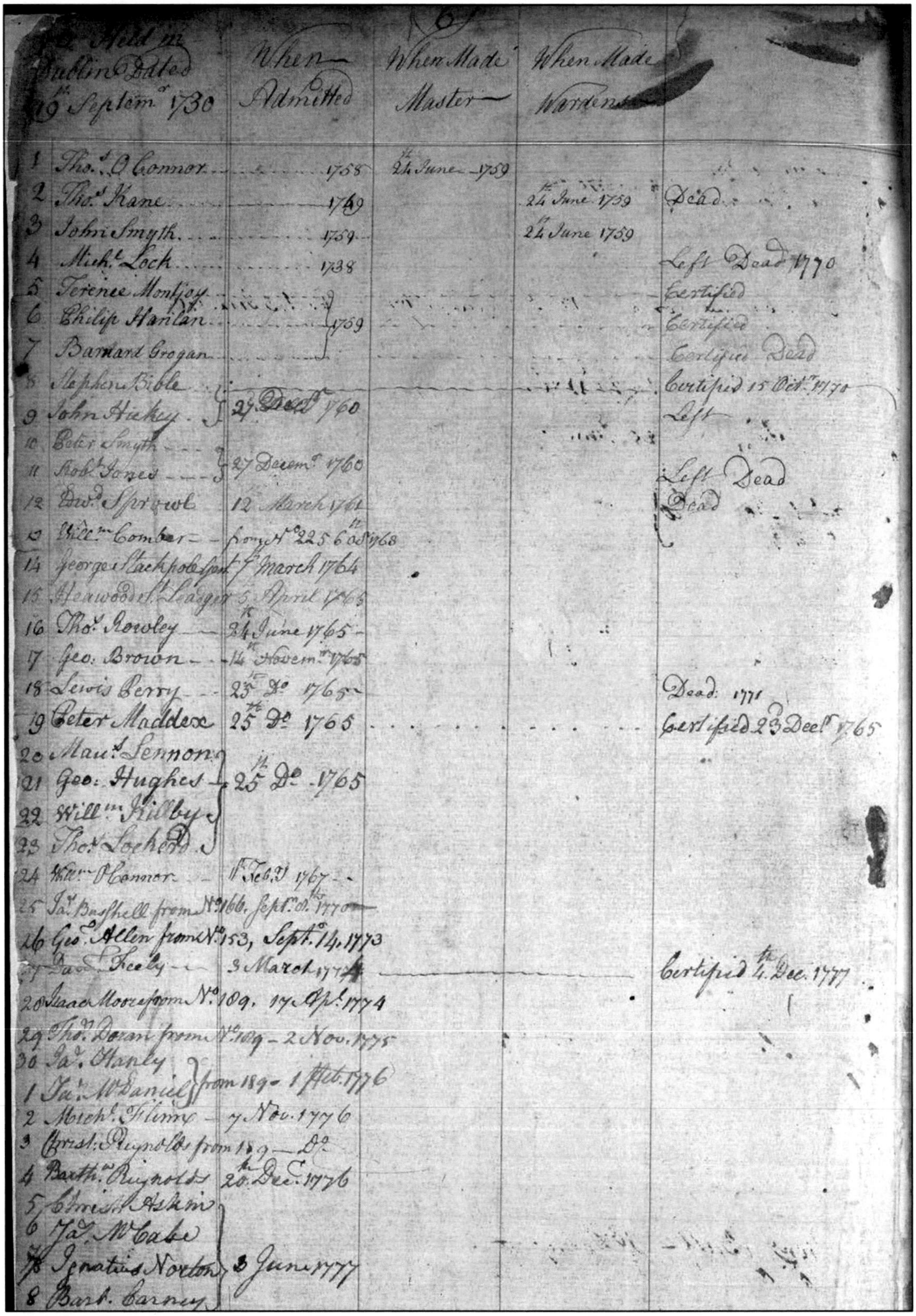

Held in Dublin Dated 19th Septem. 1730	When Admitted	When Made Master	When Made Wardens	
1 Thos. O Connor	1758	24th June 1759		
2 Thos. Kane	1749		24th June 1759	Dead
3 John Smyth	1759		24th June 1759	
4 Michl. Lock	1738			Left Dead 1770
5 Terence Montjoy				Certified
6 Philip Hanlan	1759			Certified
7 Barnard Grogan				Certified Dead
8 Stephen Bible				Certified 15 Oct. 1770
9 John Hickey	23 Decr. 1760			Left
10 Peter Smyth				
11 Robt. Jones	27 Decemr. 1760			Left Dead
12 Edwd. Sprowl	12 March 1761			Dead
13 Willm. Comber	from No. 225 6 Octr. 1768			
14 George Stackpole	5 March 1764			
15 Heawood ... Leadger	5 April 1765			
16 Thos. Rowley	24th June 1765			
17 Geo. Brown	14th Novemr. 1765			
18 Lewis Perry	23th Do. 1765			Dead 1771
19 Peter Maddex	25th Do. 1765			Certified 23 Decr. 1765
20 Maut. Lennon				
21 Geo. Hughes	25th Do. 1765			
22 Willm. Killby				
23 Thos. Lockett				
24 Wm. O Connor	1 Feb. 1767			
25 Jas. Boshell from No. 166,	Septr. 1770			
26 Geo. Allen from No. 153,	Sept. 14, 1773			
27 Danl. Feely	3 March 1774			Certified 4th Dec. 1777
28 Isaac Moore from No. 189,	17 Apl. 1774			
29 Thos. Doran from No. 189	2 Nov. 1775			
30 Jas. Hanly				
1 Jas. McDaniel from 189	1 Feb. 1776			
2 Michl. Flinn	7 Nov. 1776			
3 Christ. Reynolds from 189	Do.			
4 Barthw. Reynolds	20th Dec. 1776			
5 Christ. Askin				
6 Jas. McCabe				
7 Ignatius Norton	3 June 1777			
8 Bart. Carney				

Figure 41: A page from Lodge 6, Dublin, from the Grand Lodge of Freemasons of Ireland Membership Registers, 1733-1923, a collection now found on Ancestry.com. (Image courtesy of The Grand Lodge of Ireland. Permissions received.)

Chapter Nine

The Grand Lodge of Ireland

During the eighteenth and especially the nineteenth centuries, belonging to various societies was popular. Brotherhoods of men operating in fraternal organizations, such as the Freemasons and Orange Lodges in Ireland, traditionally served many purposes, as they do currently. Some, whether organized or through the associations of members, were for charitable, social, and political affiliations or for forming and retaining business contacts. The Freemasons were open to persons of any background, but the Orange Lodges' members were strictly Protestant.

Historically, other types of societies were vehicles of rebellion, for example, the United Irishmen of both Catholic and Protestant members. The Orange Lodges left their mark on Canadian society, whereas the Freemasons bequeathed a large imprint on American history. Many of the defeated United Irishmen were transported to Australia, contributing to its history. This chapter addresses only the Grand Lodge of Ireland serving Freemasons because its records are now easily accessible online.

Before exploring the records for the Grand Lodge of Ireland, take note that it should not be confused with other societies in Ireland. For example, many researchers have some knowledge of the Freemasons, even if only of an ancestor or a living relative being a member. However, the Orange Lodge can remain elusive for many, and so from an immigration perspective, to which organization, if either, an ancestor belonged could be a source of confusion. To begin the search demands recalling what is known about an immigrant ancestor's fraternal associations. Among some of the initial questions to pursue are:

- Did an ancestor leave personal papers, pictures, emblems, or written works that indicate he had lodge or society membership?

- Did an ancestor's obituary state anything about lodge membership?

- Did the ancestors have any attitudes about Roman Catholics? This can be an important clue.

- Did ancestors have any distinctive political opinions about the British or, later, Northern Ireland, in general? An ancestor in

Australia, Canada, or New Zealand would have had a different estimation than an ancestor in the United States did.

- Were an ancestor's personal stances or personal papers tied into politics or mysticism? They may define whether an ancestor was an Orangeman or a Freemason.

The preliminary questions, listed above, are but a few that can be guides to resolving uncertainties. For example, Irish immigrants upon arriving in the United States had lodge memberships mainly in the Freemasons because even though the Loyal Orange Lodges functioned in the United States, they had to drop their pro-British position. After all, renouncing allegiance to a former government is part of the entire United States naturalization process, whereas immigration to a British Commonwealth country required no such procedure.

Attitudes toward Roman Catholics are a little more complex. Into the twentieth century, anti-Catholicism was common throughout Protestantism, although it had nothing to do with a fraternal society. The Orange Lodge was more intolerant because of its political goals. Freemasons did not discuss religion in the Lodge. Therefore, on paper, Freemasonry welcomed everybody who subscribed to its principles, and it had no religious qualifications. In reality, the viewpoints within any given local lodge might have varied from those of others. Especially in Australia, Canada, New Zealand, South Africa, and the United Kingdom,

strong political judgments among immigrants about the United Kingdom and, later, Northern Ireland may point to Orange Lodge membership. Freemasons had little reason to have a political position about British politics. Once some of these general subjects are settled, a research strategy can be formulated.

Other considerations are important concerning lodge memberships, perhaps foremost of which is that not everybody belonged to societies. Private fraternities charged dues, and so if an ancestor was a poor tenant farmer, living from hand to mouth in Ireland, a lodge membership was implausible. Without this tradition in the family, it might not have been one worth seeking in the immigrant country. Also, many men saw the world in practical terms with no need to further their knowledge through the mysticism, or at least inner reflection, offered through a Masonic organization. In short, lodge membership was not for every man in Ireland or abroad, but one such as the Freemasons had a financial and social appeal to the men of the middle and upper classes of Irish society.

Grand Lodge of Ireland

The Grand Lodge of Ireland, the second oldest organization of Freemasons in existence, was established in 1725 and is entirely male. England had the first and Scotland, the third. Ireland had lodges throughout the island and even administered ones overseas, especially in countries of the British Empire. The majority of them, though, have always been in Ulster and around Dublin City.

The Masons traditionally are open to persons of all religious affiliations. Many researchers are surprised to learn that the Grand Lodge of Ireland before 1826 had both Catholic and Protestant members. Moreover, some of the earliest Grand Masters in Ireland were Roman Catholics. Catholic membership drastically declined in the 1820s after Papal Bulls (official pronouncements of the Pope) condemned Freemasonry. Although the Papal Bulls had been published in Ireland in 1826, they were ignored in some areas, and Catholic members continued their lodge activities. It is possible that Catholic ancestors who were Freemasons upon immigration retained their memberships. In some parts of the world, especially where the Church was weak or priests were scarce, Catholics as Freemasons were not uncommon. Where the Catholic Church is strong in the world, Catholics joining their local lodges is rare.

Although Catholics were not supposed to be Freemasons after the 1820s, that they continued to be speaks of an often-forgotten principle, that is, what is preached from the pulpit and what is practiced in the pews are not necessarily the same. This truth is universal in all churches, organizations, societies, and cultures, all being composed of people who make their own choices.

History and Purpose of Freemasonry
Freemasonry consists of various fraternal organizations with currently millions of members worldwide. Its present form dates from the late sixteenth to early seventeenth century, with modern beginnings in the founding of the Grand Lodge of England in 1717. Because the topic is new for many researchers, some background is advantageous. The Grand Lodge of Ireland is just one aspect of the wider Freemasonry. Grand Lodges from various organizations may or may not recognize one another based upon certain landmarks of practices because no overall body governs all Freemasons or Grand Lodges.

Non-Masons should understand several facts about Freemasonry. It is not a religion, but it is religious. It is not a political movement, although some of its members have been among the greatest political and societal reformers in history. It is not a charity, but it operates excellent and unsurpassed charity programs. It can be thought of as a secret society, or as many Masons term it "a society with secrets." However, no Masonic practices are secret, and more are public knowledge than are private.

The secrets mainly comprise methods of identification (passwords and handshakes) and some details from the various degree ceremonies themselves. At its core, Freemasonry is a men's society whose philosophy is concerned with moral and spiritual values. The values are taught through allegories, symbols, oaths, mythologies, and secrecy, all of which are accomplished by progressing through three degrees. The members interpret the symbols and lessons on an individual basis.

The Grand Lodge governs regional, individual lodges within its jurisdiction. The Grand Lodge of Ireland in Dublin, for example, oversees lodges in both Northern

Ireland and the Republic of Ireland. To operate, each local or subordinate lodge must receive a warrant or charter from the Grand Lodge, and each elects, initiates, and promotes its members and officers. Every one keeps its own records. It is appropriate to say that Freemasons meet *as* a Lodge, not *in* a Lodge. There are also "Lodges of Research," with membership drawn from Master Masons only. These Lodges of Research are warranted but do not initiate new candidates. They are for research purposes only, exploring topics such as history and philosophy.

Each local Masonic lodge is led by a Worshipful Master (basically, the President) who is always an elected officer. Most jurisdictions elect the Senior and Junior Wardens (in essence, Vice-Presidents), the Secretaries, and the Treasurers. Every lodge has a Tyler or Tiler who guards the door to the lodge room while the lodge is in session, along with other appointed officers, such as Deacons, Stewards, and a Chaplain. The officers can be the same on the Grand Lodge level, but the word Grand is added to the titles occasionally.

Before 1717, the origins of Freemasonry are somewhat enveloped in myth, mystery, theory, speculation, and, sometimes, misinformation. Freemasonry certainly did exist before 1717, and it had a different character than it did after it began to be regulated through various Grand Lodges. The first period is known as "Operative Freemasonry," when masons, as a society or guild, literally worked with stones, chisels, and hammers. At the end of this era, operative masons began to be replaced by

"admitted" or "gentlemen" masons, and the society became fraternal with the focus on philosophy and charity work, known as "Speculative Freemasonry."

Documentation on Operative Freemasonry before 1717 is sparse, which is why its origins have many perspectives. Systematic record keeping of the Speculative Freemasonry began with the founding of the Grand Lodge of England. While many look to the stonemasons of the Middle Ages for origins, others seek more ancient beginnings, including King Solomon and the construction of the temple in Jerusalem, Moses, the Essenes, Druids, Gypsies, Rosicrucian, ancient mystery schools, or the Gnostics. All have their supporters and detractors.

Generally accepted Masonic history traces modern Freemasonry to the stonemason guilds of the Middle Ages in Scotland, England, and France. In France, the stonemasons were organized by the eighth century, and records prove they were organized in York, England, in the year 926. The oldest surviving document recording the rules of the Freemasons is called the *Regius Manuscript* (housed at the British Museum), and it dates from 1390. Historians think it was copied from an older text. Although some of the rules have changed over the years, the governance outlined in this manuscript is essentially the same structure as that of today's Masonic lodges.

The word Freemason is thought to have been derived from European craft guilds, which were *free,* not bound to the land or indentured. Masons' skills in building complex stone structures, especially churches and cathedrals, allowed them to travel and find work at will. They *lodged* in temporary structures near the main stone buildings being constructed. (In the modern usage, a lodge is both a building and the group of Masons who meet there. Technically, a lodge meets in a lodge.) Historically, they resided at the lodges and received their work assignments from the *masters* of the work. To maintain their freedom, their skill requirements had to remain exclusive. They *apprenticed* and trained certain men in moral values and in the tools of the trade, binding them to the craft. The transition from these skilled craft guild stonemasons to a speculative fraternity is believed to have started in the Scottish lodges during the seventeenth century. By 1717, the Grand Lodge of England was founded, bringing the fraternity out of the shadows and into the modern mainstream of society.

The moral lessons of Freemasonry are told through the performance of an allegorical ceremony, known as a ritual, in which the candidate progresses through degrees. Each degree brings knowledge and understanding of the member and his relationship with others and the Supreme Being. The various symbols encountered in these rituals, about which Masons are expected to speculate, do not have only one meaning. Some lodges use a Tracing Board, a painted or printed illustration of various Masonic emblems, which are teaching aids that follow each of the three degrees. At the advancement time, an experienced member explains Masonic concepts to new members. Tracing Boards, placed on the floors or upright, also can be self-

reminders for experienced members. The metaphors of the stonemasons' tools and implements are coupled with the allegory of building King Solomon's Temple.

A Masonic lodge building itself, usually facing east, is patterned after King Solomon's Temple. The ceremonies of the lodge take place in the center of a rectangular room with seating around the perimeter and with the Officers' chairs in specific positions. In the room are an altar with the Volume of Sacred Law lying open with candles illuminating it and two tall pillars with globes on their tops patterned after the two bronze columns that were prominent features of Solomon's Temple. The letter *G* is often suspended over the Master's chair in the east or over the altar and represents both God and geometry (the original secret knowledge of the stonemasons). This custom can be found in the English-language lodges. The lodge buildings are often built where more than one lodge can meet and hold ceremonies at the same time.

Masonic symbols can be recognized in any number of places once people realize what they are. The square with the compass is the most popular, but the sun, moon, stars, handshakes, pillars, ark, swords, aprons, beehives, altars, the letter *G*, coffins, ladders, anchors, and the All-Seeing Eye, to name a few, are all Masonic symbols. They are meant to teach the philosophies of Freemasonry, not Freemasonry, to the public.

Although politics and religion are forbidden as discussions within Masonic lodges, candidates are required to declare a belief in a Supreme Being, one who is not defined further. Masons are not placed in a position of having to defend a personal interpretation of faith. Most Christians who are also lodge members equate the Supreme Being to their own ideas of God or the Trinity, but other Masons hold a more complex or philosophical interpretation of what a Supreme Being is. In the Masonic ritual itself, the Supreme Being is referred to as the Great Architect of the Universe.

A Volume of the Sacred Law is always displayed. It does not have to be the Bible. A candidate, according to his beliefs, is given his choice of a religious text. In lodges where members are of mixed religions, it is common to find more than one sacred text on exhibit.

The Three Degrees of Craft or Blue Lodge Freemasonry are: 1) Entered Apprentice, the degree of an Initiate that makes one a Freemason; 2) Fellow Craft, an intermediate degree involving learning; and 3) Master Mason, the Third Degree and necessary for participating in most aspects of Freemasonry. The Three Degrees represent stages of personal development—youth, manhood, and age—and are meant to convey the most fundamental principle of Freemasonry, how a man lives and how he dies.

Each degree has signs (gestures), grips or tokens (handshakes), and words to gain admissions to meetings and identify legitimate visitors, and each Grand Lodge is free to create its own rituals, signs, grips, and passwords. Part of the rituals is Obligations, in which candidates swear to follow the rules and to keep the secrets of Freemasonry. Obligations also include how to act toward others in accordance with the principles of Freemasonry. Obligations are sworn on the Volume of the Sacred Law and in the witness of the Supreme Being with the assurance that it is of the candidates' free wills. Obligations vary, and not one represents all Freemasonry. Penalties, interpreted symbolically, are associated with the Obligations.

Catholic Membership

No discussion of Irish Freemasonry is complete without an examination of its relationship with the Roman Catholic Church and how the organization became almost exclusively Protestant. The Grand Lodge of Ireland before 1826 had both Catholic and Protestant members. No distinction was made between the two groups, nor was religious affiliation discussed in the records. The Most Rev. Doctor Troy, Catholic Archbishop of Dublin, published the Papal Bulls (official pronouncements) against Freemasonry in 1799. As other Irish Catholic dioceses distributed the Papal Bulls, Catholic membership began to decrease but did not wholly disappear.

It was not until two additional Papal Bulls condemning Freemasonry were printed in the 1820s that Catholic membership in Ireland drastically fell. In 1821, Pope Pius VII issued the *Ecclesiam a Jesu Christo,* and in 1825, Pope Leo XII published *Quo graviora.*

Although the Papal Bulls denouncing Masonry had been circulated in Ireland in 1826, they were ignored in some areas, and Catholic members continued their lodge activities for many years. Nonetheless, stating that the lodge had mostly Protestant members beginning in the 1830s is a fair assessment. It is also important to remember that Catholic membership was retained in the British Army.

For background on the Catholic Church's position on Freemasonry from the Masonic point of view, see the series of articles by W. J. Chetwode Crawley, Grand Treasurer, Ireland, titled "The Old Charges and The Papal Bulls," published in the *Transactions of the Quatuor Coronati Lodge #2076, England* beginning in 1911. He included the full text of the various Papal Bulls.

Masonic Records

The Grand Lodge of Ireland generated many records. Before its establishment in 1725, records for individual Masonic lodges are incomplete. A tombstone in the immigrant country may signify the man was a Freemason, but the question at that point was whether he became a member in the immigrant country or whether he was one in Ireland as well.

Several Internet sites detail the history and many manuscript collections of Irish Freemasonry. The website "Irish Masonic History and the Jewels of Irish Freemasonry": Irishmasonichistory.com is requisite as new material continues to be added to it. It also documents the worldwide aspect of Irish Freemasonry.

Records began to be produced from the establishment of the Grand Lodge of Ireland as it started to reorganize the existing local lodges. However, Masonic records cannot be thought of in terms of what one finds in church registers because their purpose was to document other concerns. Manuscript material by the Grand Lodge, such as membership reports, are all centralized at the Grand Lodge of Ireland Library in Dublin, located just a couple of blocks from the National Library of Ireland. Printed material is there as well, but it is also in other sizable Masonic libraries. Two of the largest Grand Lodges with enormous libraries are the United Grand Lodge of England in London and the Grand Lodge of Iowa A.F. & A.M. in Cedar Rapids. The Iowa library is one of the biggest Masonic libraries in the world.

When considering the Grand Lodge of Ireland records or those of the subordinate lodges, keep in mind some rudimentary facts:

- Individual lodges warranted under the Grand Lodge in Dublin usually consisted of members from one community or group of geographically close townlands. Estimates are that the lodge drew its membership from a three- to five-mile radius of the lodge building. Bear in mind that in the eighteenth century, most lodges met at their local inns, taverns, and coffee houses.

- Irish Masonic lodges were attached to various British Army regiments, partly because so many Irish were in the British Army. As a consequence, the Grand Lodge of Ireland had more military lodges than did the United Grand Lodge of

England and the Grand Lodge of Scotland in Edinburgh combined.

- When studying Masonic records, be aware that sometimes the Masonic date is given, arrived at by adding 4,000 years to the year in question. (e.g., 1847 = 5847).

- Freemasonry in Ireland was open to all males over the age of twenty-one.

- Although most of the membership was Protestant, do not assume that an Irish ancestor was. Roman Catholics were commonly members in Ireland because the Grand Lodge does not count religion as a test of membership. It was the Catholic Church that discouraged men to join with threat of excommunication in 1826.

- During the 1798 Rebellion and the founding of the Society of United Irishmen, many lodges in Ulster had to openly disavow violence for solving problems. Others were rebellious in their attitudes, and others completely disassociated themselves from the Rebellion. Many of the United Irishmen were Freemasons. The Grand Lodge had to send notices to members forbidding them to bring religion or politics through the doors of the lodges.

Assumptions about whether an ancestor might have been a Freemason can be based on several points. The artisan and shopkeeper classes often joined, and Protestants with more moderate or affluent incomes might have had Masonic connections. If an ancestor was poor, he likely was not a Mason since lodge membership required dues. With these guidelines, a decision can be made about whether an ancestral family fit the profile of a Freemason.

The Grand Lodge of Ireland in Dublin has a library open to the public, although its book collection is limited in genealogical value. Its archive houses the membership records and other manuscripts, which are significant for the family historian. The records included are for both the Republic of Ireland and Northern Ireland lodges and members.

A variety of documents were made either by the Grand Lodge of Ireland or others connected to it at some level. Besides locating residences of ancestors by the sites of the Lodges, this archive of records should be explored for other reasons.

The membership lists can substitute to fill in gaps for destroyed census schedules and nonexistent church records or to document emigrations or perhaps deaths in the absences of tombstones or wills. Because the Lodge was often a multi-generational fraternal society, records can provide new clues about possible relationships among the men, once more becoming substitutes for nonexistent censuses and church records. The most helpful records from a genealogical perspective are:

Membership Records: Each subordinate (local) lodge submitted to the Grand Lodge copies of its membership records, and so, in theory, two copies of membership records are in existence. Membership records deposited at the Grand Lodge have been digitized and are on Ancestry.com in their database "Ireland, Grand Lodge of Freemasons of Ireland Membership Records, 1733-1923." However, membership records generally began in the 1760s. More complete membership records date from the 1780s to the present. The membership registers are basic, but they do place men in specific localities at specific times. They do not provide birth information, ages, or parents' names. The manuscripts are by lodge numbers, but the Ancestry.com edition has an index to them.

Irish Masonic Records: To learn more about local lodges, an invaluable work is Keith Cochrane's *Irish Masonic Records* on CD. This is the 3rd version of the book, updating Philip Crossle's former edition of the book from 1973, which is now out of print. It is an eminent reference because it provides the numbers of lodges with their locations. This work extracts notable Masonic references from newspapers and all 27 volumes of the "Grand Lodge Registers," an index of warrants and newspaper and historical articles. Still published in CD format, more information about this resource can be found on the Irishmasonichistory.com website.

Deputy Grand Secretary Correspondence Files (1820-1880): These records, filed by the lodge number, are the correspondence of the individual lodges with the Grand Lodge. Typical correspondence has minutes, officers' business, and charity petitions. The emigrations of individual members may be noted because funds were gathered to assist emigrations. Since the lodge number has to be known, the Ancestry.com index to the membership records is invaluable.

Over the years, a large quantity of material has been published about Irish Masonry. Three requisite sources are: 1) the two-volume set by R. E. Parkinson, *History of the Grand Lodge of Free and Accepted Masons of Ireland*, Vol. 2. (Dublin: Lodge of Research, 1957), the standard work for Irish Masonry. Volume 1 was written by Lepper and Crossle, and volume 2, by R.E. Parkinson; 2) *Transactions of the Lodge of Research #200 of the Grand Lodge of Ireland*, containing specific aspects of Irish Masonry. This publication of various articles has been produced by Lodge #200 continuously since 1914; 3) *Transactions of the Quatuor Coronati Lodge #2076, England*, a periodical of articles and papers written by Lodge #2076 of the Grand Lodge of England that has been published continuously since 1890. It deals with the international facets of Masonry, especially English Freemasonry, with many articles about Irish Freemasonry.

Since many of the records must be searched by Lodge number, the task can be approached in two ways. The first is through the Ancestry.com index, which gives the page number on which the member is recorded by the lodge number, thus linking the member with a specific lodge. However, this does not necessarily help locate that lodge in Ireland. To solve that dilemma, the most important one for Irish origins, the lodge number has to be attached to a location and county.

The chart below has been created as a locator for lodges warranted through the Grand Lodge of Ireland as of 1804. For the location of each lodge in 1804, the corresponding civil parish has been added as a reference point. Remember that lodges often moved to other sites or even to neighboring counties. Many lodges were closed by 1804, and others, after 1804. If searching beyond the 1804 period, consult Keith Cochran's *Irish Masonic Records*.

After the number and locality are identified, many other record types are opened. For example, in solving immigrant origins, the civil parish or a neighboring one was where the member was residing. The civil parish is the foundation from which Irish research proceeds from record type to record type because it was a stable government administrative unit. Also, the civil parish is a guide to connecting men in a geographical area who might or might not have been relatives. In addition, tax and land records and church registers can be found to further situate the parish area where the ancestor lived. For this reason, instead of placing the lodges in numerical order, geographical order was deemed of more assistance to the family historian. It will simply take a little more time to find the lodge number in the chart once it is found through the Ancestry.com membership database.

Irish Masonic Lodges in Ireland in 1804

The following list of Masonic Lodges is from the *List of Lodges of the Most Ancient & Honorable Fraternity of Free and Accepted Masons Held Under the Sanction of the Right Worshipful Grand Lodge of Ireland . . .* (Dublin: Brother C. Downes, 1804). The directory carries the lodges' locations but not those of the civil parishes, which have been added in alphabetical order. Urban areas with multiple lodges have been listed separately.

Irish Masonic Lodges in Ireland in 1804

#	Location	Civil Parish
Antrim		

Masonic lodges for Belfast City include: 182, 257, 272, 484, 491, 550, 587, 621, 684, 687, 761, 762, 763, 783, 793, 845, 926, 949

#	Location	Civil Parish
918	Massereene	Addergoole
490	Aghagallon	Aghagallon
487	Ahoghill	Ahoghill
537	Cullybracky	Ahoghill
704	Drumramer	Ahoghill
784	Garvaghy	Ahoghill
736	Portglenone	Ahoghill
313	Antrim	Antrim

Irish Masonic Lodges in Ireland in 1804

#	Location	Civil Parish
Antrim (cont.)		
529	Antrim	Antrim
805	Dunsilly	Antrim
627	Killead (near Antrim)	Antrim
776	Parkgate (near Antrim)	Antrim
365	Armoy	Armoy
404	Upper Ballinderry	Ballinderry
772	Ballinderry	Ballinderry
408	Ballintoy	Ballintoy
905	Kilmahamogue	Ballintoy
135	Ballymoney	Ballymoney
240	Ballymoney	Ballymoney
655	Ballymoney	Ballymoney
703	Ballymoney	Ballymoney
818	Stranocum	Ballymoney
746	Ballynure	Ballynure
915	Ballynure	Ballynure
430	Ballyclare	Ballynure, Doagh Grange
543	Grange	Ballyscullion
583	Aghavary	Ballyscullion Grange
636	Falls of Belfast	Belfast City
229	Bushmills	Billy, Dunluce
414	Bushmills	Billy, Dunluce
811	Hillhall (near Lisburn)	Blaris
112	Lisburn	Blaris
178	Lisburn	Blaris
193	Lisburn	Blaris
716	Lisburn	Blaris
749	Lisburn	Blaris
800	Crumlin	Camlin
645	Carnmoney	Carnmoney
651	White House	Carnmoney, Shankill
253	Carrickfergus	Carrickfergus
270	Carrickfergus	Carrickfergus
923	Straid (near Carrickfergus)	Carrickfergus
802	Connor	Connor
829	Carey Mill	Culfeightrin
602	Milltown	Derryaghy
403	Stoneyford	Derryaghy
294	Doagh	Doagh Grange
590	Doagh	Doagh Grange
539	Randlestown	Drummaul
574	Carn-beg	Dunaghy

Irish Masonic Lodges in Ireland in 1804

#	Location	Civil Parish
Antrim (cont.)		
597	Artlone	Duneane
890	Moneyrod	Duneane
658	Staffordstown	Duneane
942	Shanaghy	Finvoy
571	Vow	Finvoy
725	Glenwhirry	Glenwhirry
901	Muckamore	Grange of Muckamore
615	Larne	Inver, Larne
825	Larne	Inver, Larne
317	Ballymena	Kirkinriola
676	Ballymena	Kirkinriola
775	Ballymena	Kirkinriola
752	Clough (near Ballymena)	Kirkinriola
652	Lambeg	Lambeg
700	Cushendal	Layd
429	Magheragall	Magheragall
629	Magheragall	Magheragall
424	Broughshane	Racavan
431	Ballycastle	Ramoan
432	Ballycastle	Ramoan
380	Carrowreagh (near Ballycastle)	Ramoan
841	Ballymaconnelly	Rasharkin
593	Carnfinton	Rasharkin
258	Rasharkin	Rasharkin
418	Malone	Shankill
598	Ballyutoag	Templepatrick
551	Templepatrick	Templepatrick
917	Glenarm	Tickmacrevan
426	Glenavy	Tickmacrevan
428	Glenavy	Tickmacrevan
499	Dundrod	Tullyrusk
Armagh		
16	Armagh	Armagh
104	Armagh	Armagh
409	Armagh	Armagh
623	Armagh	Armagh
695	Armagh	Armagh
459	Clare	Ballymore
394	Poyntzpass	Ballymore
315	Tanderagee	Ballymore
361	Tanderagee	Ballymore

Irish Masonic Lodges in Ireland in 1804

#	Location	Civil Parish
Armagh (cont.)		
612	Baltylum	Drumcree
516	Portadown	Drumcree, Seagoe
592	Portadown	Drumcree, Seagoe
789	Portadown	Drumcree, Seagoe
680	Richmount	Drumcree
938	Aughantarragh	Eglish
924	Diamond	Keady
463	Keady	Keady
540	Keady	Keady
766	Keady	Keady
678	Markethill	Kilclooney, Mullaghbrack
696	Mullaghglass	Killevy
527	Ballintagart	Kilmore
328	Richhill	Kilmore
757	Richhill	Kilmore
395	Charlemont	Loughgall
743	Clonmain	Loughgall
603	Grange O'Neil	Loughgall
944	Kennaghan	Loughgall
582	Levalleglish	Loughgall
618	Tullyherron	Loughgilly
393	Hamiltonsbawn	Mullaghbrack
933	Ballybott (near Newry)	Newry
134	Lurgan	Shankill
747	Lurgan	Shankill
266	Maghery	Tartaraghan
665	Margaraty	Tartaraghan
349	Killylea	Tynan
671	Killylea	Tynan
681	Killylea	Tynan
264	Middletown	Tynan
437	Middletown	Tynan
601	Tynan	Tynan

Carlow

Masonic lodges for Carlow City in Carlow Parish include: 111, 116, 493, 524, 555, 741, 838

#	Location	Civil Parish
565	Leighlinbridge	Agha, Wells

Cavan

#	Location	Civil Parish
515	Belturbet	Annagh
560	Belturbet	Annagh

Irish Masonic Lodges in Ireland in 1804

#	Location	Civil Parish
Cavan (cont.)		
452	Bailieborough	Bailieborough
667	Bailieborough	Bailieborough
796	Bailieborough	Bailieborough
842	Ashfield	Drumgoon
795	Ashfield	Drumgoon
184	Cootehill	Drumgoon
181	Cootehill	Drumgoon
628	Cootehill	Drumgoon
561	Corrinary	Drumgoon
753	Roosky	Drumgoon
451	Kingscourt	Enniskeen
310	Killashandra	Killashandra
904	Killashandra	Killashandra
912	Killashandra	Killashandra
920	Ballynanagh	Kilmore
405	Ballyconnell	Tomregan
417	Shercock	Shercock
90	Cavan	Urney
545	Cavan	Urney
Clare		
60	Ennis	Drumcliff
238	Tulla	Tulla
Cork		

Lodges in Cork City include: 1, 27, 28, 41, 67, 71, 95, 130, 167, 221, 267, 277, 347, 383, 385, 520

#	Location	Civil Parish
504	Skibbereen	Abbeystrowry, Creagh
84	Bandon	Ballymodan, Kilbrogan
413	Bandon	Ballymodan, Kilbrogan
259	Kanturk	Castlemagner, Clonfert, Kilroe
742	Doneraile	Kilroe
31	Kinsale	Kinsale, Ringcurran
156	Kinsale	Kinsale, Ringcurran
325	Mallow	Mallow
49	Charleville	Rathgoggan
19	Youghal	Youghal
Donegal		
670	Newtown Cunningham	Allsaints
448	Rathmelton	Aughnish
614	Castlefin	Donaghmore

Irish Masonic Lodges in Ireland in 1804

#	Location	Civil Parish
Donegal (cont.)		
434	Killygordon	Donaghmore
588	Donegal	Donegal, Killymard
644	Tawnawully Mts	Donegal
939	Buncrana	Fahan Lower
882	Fahan	Fahan Upper
589	Island of Inch	Inch
287	Ballyshannon	Inishmacsaint, Kilbarron
558	Bruckless	Kilaghtee
346	Raphoe	Raphoe
442	Ballybofey	Stranorlar
641	Ballybofey	Stranorlar
215	Pettigo	Templecarn
814	Pettigo	Templecarn
Down		
808	Glascar Hill	Aghaderg
391	Loughbrickland	Aghaderg
715	Loughbrickland	Aghaderg
737	Scarva	Aghaderg
815	Strangford	Ballyculter
682	Ballintine	Blaris
335	Broomhedge	Blaris
316	Maze	Blaris
427	Maze Bridge	Blaris
608	The Maize	Blaris
477	Waringstown	Donaghcloney
735	Waringstown	Donaghcloney
75	Donaghadee	Donaghadee
343	Downpatrick	Down
367	Downpatrick	Down
371	Waringsford	Dromara
507	Dromore	Dromore
508	Dromore	Dromore
662	Dromore	Dromore
732	Dromore	Dromore
372	Gill Hall	Dromore
807	Thornyford Bridge	Dromore
410	Rathfryland	Drumballyroney, Drumgath
654	Rathfryland	Drumballyroney, Drumgath
314	Drumbo	Drumbo
659	Lisnode	Drumbo
941	Drumadonnell	Drumgooland

Irish Masonic Lodges in Ireland in 1804

#	Location	Civil Parish
Down (cont.)		
683	Ballykeel	Hillsborough
606	Cabragh	Hillsborough
927	Kircubbin	Inisnargy
755	Kilkeel	Kilkeel
840	Kilkeel	Kilkeel
624	Killinchy	Killinchy
180	Killyleagh	Killyleagh
843	Crossgar	Kilmore
861	Ballymacarret	Knockbreda
931	Ballymacarret	Knockbreda
947	Ballymacarret	Knockbreda
609	Newtownbreda	Knockbreda
446	Ballynahinch	Magheradrool
822	Cumber	Magheradrool
549	Moira	Moira
702	Moira	Moira
447	Newtown Ards	Newtownards
521	Ballybot	Newry
269	Donaghmore (near Newry)	Newry
77	Newry	Newry
706	Newry	Newry
914	Newry	Newry
925	Newry	Newry
425	Saintfield	Saintfield
336	Banbridge	Seapatrick
734	Banbridge	Seapatrick
943	Banbridge	Seapatrick
126	Gilford	Tullylish
526	Hall's Mill	Tullylish
764	Knocknagore	Tullylish
771	Tullylish	Tullylish
544	Ballykeel	Warrenspoint
697	Warrenspoint	Warrenspoint

Dublin

The lodges for Dublin City include: 2, 6, 7, 54, 64, 100, 118, 137, 141, 153, 155, 171, 189, 190, 198, 202, 206, 207, 209, 324, 348, 353, 402, 489, 584, 620, 916, 930.

#	Location	Civil Parish
535	Balbriggan	Balrothery
721	Black Rock	Monkstown
945	Islandbridge	St. James

Irish Masonic Lodges in Ireland in 1804

#	Location	Civil Parish
Fermanagh		
889	Lisnaskea	Aghalurcher
894	Maguires Bridge	Aghalurcher
416	Brookeborough	Aghavea
804	Cleffany	Aghavea
928	Belleek	Belleek
891	Belleek	Belleek
436	Lisbellaw	Cleenish
913	Lisbellaw	Cleenish
831	Ardlougher	Derryvullan
457	Ballinamallard (near Irvinestown)	Derryvullan
386	Irvinestown	Derryvullan
513	Irvinestown	Derryvullan
674	Irvinestown	Derryvullan
810	Irvinestown	Derryvullan
830	Irvinestown	Derryvullan
870	Irvinestown	Derryvullan
892	Irvinestown	Derryvullan
303	Lisnarrick	Derryvullan
707	Lisnarick	Derryvullan
871	Tullynagarn	Derryvullan
893	Whitehill	Devenish
782	Cahore	Drumkeeran
473	Ballinalack (near Enniskillen)	Enniskillen, Rossory
17	Enniskillen	Enniskillen, Rossorry
468	Enniskillen	Enniskillen, Rossorry
595	Enniskillen	Enniskillen, Rossorry
481	Tempo	Enniskillen
834	Tempo	Enniskillen
853	Tempo	Enniskillen
896	Tempo	Enniskillen
439	Newtown Butler	Galloon
919	Belmore	Killesher
453	Callowhill	Kinawley
648	Craghan	Magheracross
827	Magheracross	Magheracross
797	Tullyrain	Magheracross
819	Ederney	Magheraculmoney
366	Kesh	Magheraculmoney
758	Kesh	Magheraculmoney
937	Mantlin	Magheraculmoney
778	Tullanaguiggy	Magheraculmoney
859	Laragh	Rossorry

Irish Masonic Lodges in Ireland in 1804

#	Location	Civil Parish
Fermanagh (cont.)		
899	Drumgarrow	Trory
464	Gublusk	Trory
Galway		
358	Ahascragh	Ahascragh
331	Headford	Cargin, Kilkilvery, Killursa
326	Ballinasloe	Creagh, Kilcloony
455	Eyrecourt	Donanaghta
275	Gort	Kiltartan
87	Loughrea	Loughrea
248	Loughrea	Loughrea
281	Loughrea	Loughrea
357	Loughrea	Loughrea
329	Summerville	Moylough
14	Galway	Rahoon, St. Nicholas
70	Galway	Rahoon, St. Nicholas
274	Galway	Rahoon, St. Nicholas
368	Galway	Rahoon, St. Nicholas
29	Tuam	Tuam
501	Tuam	Tuam
Kerry		
373	Killarney	Killarney
886	Tralee	Ratass, Tralee
Kildare		
444	Kilcullen Bridge	Carnalway, Kilcullen
142	Castledermott	Castledermot
116	Athy	Churchtown, St. Johns, St. Michaels
498	Athy	Churchtown, St. Johns, St. Michaels
341	Maynooth	Laraghbryan
801	Leixlip	Leixlip
220	Kill	Monasterevin
276	Monasterevan	Monasterevin
283	Monasterevan	Monasterevin
Kilkenny		
496	Callan	Callan
278	Pilltown	Fiddown
261	Kilkenny	Kilkenny City
55	Kilkenny	Kilkenny City
642	Kilkenny	Kilkenny City

Irish Masonic Lodges in Ireland in 1804

#	Location	Civil Parish
Kilkenny (cont.)		
250	Ashgrove	Pollrone
Offaly (King's County)		
519	Frankford	Ballyboy
163	Birr	Birr
321	Tullamore	Kilbride
858	Tullamore	Kilbride
820	Edenderry	Monasteroris
511	Ballycumber	Lemanaghan
306	Banagher	Reynagh
Leitrim		
744	Carrigallen	Carrigallen
866	Newtowngore	Carrigallen
600	Manor Hamilton	Cloonclare, Killasnet
767	Cloone	Cloone
262	Carrick on Shannon	Kiltoghert
472	Ballinamore	Oughteragh
Leix (Queen's County)		
660	Mountmellick	Ardea, Rosenallis
398	Maryborough	Borris
357	Maryborough	Borris
291	Castledurrow	Durrow
334	Portarlington	Lea
712	Stradbally	Stradbally
Limerick		
94	Newcastle	Kilmurry
13	Limerick	Limerick City
9	Limerick	Limerick City
271	Limerick	Limerick City
563	Rathkeale	Rathkeale
Londonderry (Derry)		
839	Craigmore	Aghadowey
572	Tamlaght	Aghadowey
525	Ballynenagh	Artrea
567	Ballyronan	Artrea
423	Chapel of Artrea	Artrea, Desertlynn
826	Littlebridge	Artrea, Desertlynn
880	Maghadone	Artrea

Irish Masonic Lodges in Ireland in 1804

#	Location	Civil Parish
Londonderry (Derry) (cont.)		
531	Moneymore	Artrea, Desertlynn
701	Moneymore	Artrea, Desertlynn
769	Moneymore	Artrea, Desertlynn
647	Salterstown	Artrea
460	Ballynascreen	Ballynascreen
728	Cahore	Ballynascreen
586	Bellaghy	Ballyscullion
650	Bellaghy	Ballyscullion
932	Tamniaran	Ballyscullion
123	Coleraine	Coleraine, Killowen
138	Coleraine	Coleraine, Killowen
235	Coleraine	Coleraine, Killowen
754	Coleraine	Coleraine, Killowen
940	Coleraine	Coleraine, Killowen
745	Desertmartin	Desertmartin
785	Knocknagin	Desertmartin
719	Newtown Limavady	Drumachose
638	Dungiven	Dungiven
669	Dungiven	Dungiven
730	Garvagh	Errigal
779	Garvagh	Errigal
844	Garvagh	Errigal
594	Tobermore	Kilcronaghan
397	Kilrea	Kilrea
634	Claragh	Kilrea
821	Tamlaght	Kilrea
781	Annaghmore	Magherafelt
422	Ballinderry (near Magherafelt)	Magherafelt
387	Castle Dawson	Magherafelt
581	Castle Dawson	Magherafelt
691	Castle Dawson	Magherafelt
573	Magherafelt	Magherafelt
613	Magherafelt	Magherafelt
777	Magherafelt	Magherafelt
824	Crew	Maghera
532	Curran	Maghera
534	Maghera	Maghera
729	Maghera	Maghera
851	Swatragh	Maghrea
132	Londonderry (Derry)	Templemore
362	Londonderry (Derry)	Templemore
640	Londonderry (Derry)	Templemore

Irish Masonic Lodges in Ireland in 1804

#	Location	Civil Parish
Longford		
505	St. Johnstown	Clonbroney
284	Granard	Granard
813	Granard	Granard
579	Edgeworthstown	Mostrim
312	Ballymahon	Noughaval, Shrule
406	Ballymahon	Noughaval, Shrule
131	Longford	Templemichael
20	Longford	Templemichael
Louth		
482	Ardee	Ardee
786	Ardee	Ardee
237	Drogheda	Drogheda
411	Drogheda	Drogheda
469	Drogheda	Drogheda
222	Dundalk	Dundalk
384	Dundalk	Dundalk
934	Dundalk	Dundalk
934	Dunleer	Dunleer
Mayo		
176	Castlebar	Aglish
625	Castlebar	Aglish
233	Ballinrobe	Ballinrobe
330	Ballinrobe	Ballinrobe
21	Newport	Burrishoole
526	Killala	Killala
619	Killala	Killala
548	Ballina	Kilmoremoy
585	Ballina	Kilmoremoy
677	Westport	Oughaval
803	Foxford	Toomore
Meath		
107	Navan	Athlumney, Donaghmore, Navan
607	Kells	Kells
509	Crossakeel	Kilskeer
556	Summerhill	Laracor
494	Trim	Trim
862	Trim	Trim

Irish Masonic Lodges in Ireland in 1804

#	Location	Civil Parish
Monaghan		
419	Ballybay	Ballybay
693	Ballybay	Ballybay
790	Clones	Clones
881	Clones	Clones
688	Emyvale	Donagh
751	Emyvale	Donagh
488	Glaslough	Donagh
611	Glaslough	Donagh
694	Glaslough	Donagh
794	Glaslough	Donagh
201	Rockcorry	Ematris
673	Rockcorry	Ematris
731	Rockcorry	Ematris
301	Carrickmacross	Magheross
454	Castleshane	Monaghan
951	Lattigar	Monaghan
401	Monaghan	Monaghan
564	Monaghan	Monaghan
352	Castleblayney	Muckno
868	Castleblayney	Muckno
Roscommon		
338	Boyle	Boyle
363	Boyle	Boyle
340	Strokestown	Bumlin, Kiltrustan
242	Roscommon	Roscommon
Sligo		
568	Tobercurry	Achonry
355	Sligo	Calry, St. Johns
530	Sligo	Calry, St. Johns
566	Sligo	Calry, St. Johns
626	Sligo	Clary, St. Johns
Tipperary		
268	Carrick-on-Suir	Carrick
308	Carrick-on-Suir	Carrick
296	Tipperary	Cordangan, Corroge, Tipperary
288	Nenagh	Nenagh
307	Roscrea	Roscrea
541	Cashel	St. John Baptist, St. Patrickrock
770	Cashel	St. John Baptist, St. Patrickrock

Irish Masonic Lodges in Ireland in 1804

#	Location	Civil Parish
Tipperary (cont.)		
96	Clonmel	St. Mary's, Clonmel
279	Clonmel	St. Mary's, Clonmel
5	Thurles	Thurles
Tyrone		
333	Caledon	Aghaloo
711	Dyan	Aghaloo
850	Lismulladown	Aghaloo
639	Ardstraw	Ardstraw
835	Drumnahoe	Ardstraw
717	Kilmore	Ardstraw
666	Knockroe	Ardstraw
833	Moyle	Ardstraw
547	Newtown Stuart	Ardstraw
900	Newtown Stewart	Ardstraw
718	Gorticashel	Bodoney Lower
798	Sion Bridge	Camas, Leckpatrick, Urney
438	Strabane	Camas, Leckpatrick, Urney
569	Strabane	Camas, Leckpatrick, Urney
630	Strabane	Camas, Leckpatrick, Urney
832	Gortinagin	Cappagh
483	Aughnacloy	Carnteel
502	Aughnacloy	Carnteel
599	Aughnacloy	Carnteel
657	Carnteel	Carnteel
946	Drummond	Carnteel
883	Moorefield	Carnteel
812	Augher	Clogher
720	Fivemiletown	Clogher
906	Fivemiletown	Clogher
909	Killyfaddy	Clogher
911	Murley	Clogher
557	Benburb	Clonfeacle
760	Benburb	Clonfeacle
780	Benburb	Clonfeacle
461	Blackwatertown	Clonfeacle
722	Curran	Clonfeacle
205	Moy	Clonfeacle
232	Moy	Clonfeacle
465	Moy	Clonfeacle
576	Moy	Clonfeacle
605	Moy	Clonfeacle

Irish Masonic Lodges in Ireland in 1804

#	Location	Civil Parish
Tyrone (cont.)		
553	Cookstown	Derryloran
610	Cookstown	Derryloran
668	Cookstown	Derryloran
739	Cookstown	Derryloran
768	Cookstown	Derryloran
869	Lissan	Derryloran
710	Sandholes	Derryloran
369	Fintona	Donacavey
633	Carrickatane	Donaghedy
480	Coal Island	Donaghenry, Tullyniskan
756	Coal Island	Donaghenry, Tullyniskan
318	Stewartstown	Donaghenry
396	Stewartstown	Donaghenry
479	Stewartstown	Donaghenry
554	Stewartstown	Donaghenry
698	Stewartstown	Donaghenry
765	Stewartstown	Donaghenry
708	Castlecaulfield	Donaghmore
740	Donoghmore	Donaghmore
849	Kilnaslee	Donaghmore
922	Meenagowan	Dromore
884	Tullywee	Dromore
726	Bush House	Drumglass
421	Dungannon	Drumglass
663	Dungannon	Drumglass
689	Dungannon	Drumglass
750	New Mills	Drumglass
774	New Mills	Drumglass
806	The Rock	Drumglass
724	Aghaleag	Drumragh
787	Cloghog	Drumragh
476	Dromore (near Omagh)	Drumragh
809	Dromore (near Omagh)	Drumragh
902	Drumragh	Drumragh
897	Garvagh	Drumragh
910	Garvagh	Drumragh
672	Glenally	Drumragh
332	Omagh	Drumragh
679	Ballygawley	Errigal Keerogue
723	Ballygawley	Errigal Keerogue
727	Ballygawley	Errigal Keerogue
475	Trillick	Kilskeery

Irish Masonic Lodges in Ireland in 1804

#	Location	Civil Parish
Tyrone (cont.)		
828	Drumquin	Longfield East & West
350	Cappagh	Pomeroy
836	Pomeroy	Pomeroy
470	Coagh	Tamlaght
471	Coagh	Tamlaght
415	Killeter	Termonamongan
664	Killeter	Termonamongan
799	Lislaird	Termonamongan
523	Six Mile Cross	Termonmaguirk
908	Tiroony	Termonmaguirk
705	Castlederg	Urney
823	Crane's Hill	*unidentified*

Waterford

All Masonic lodges were in Waterford City and included: 43, 194, 230, 265, 286.

Westmeath

#	Location	Civil Parish
904	Finnea	Foyran
304	Moat Granogue	Kilcleagh
773	Kinnegad	Killucan
337	Kilbeggan	Kilnbeggan
145	Mullingar	Mullingar
360	Mullingar	Mullingar
433	Mullingar	Mullingar
885	Mullingar	Mullingar
467	Castlepollard	Rathgarve
101	Athlone	St. Mary's
342	Athlone	St. Mary's
874	Athlone	St. Mary's

Wexford

#	Location	Civil Parish
817	Duncannonfort	St. James & Dunbrody
93	Enniscorthy	St. Mary's, Enniscorthy
344	New Ross	St. Mary's
517	New Ross	St. Mary's
591	New Ross	St. Mary's
872	New Ross	St. Mary's
596	Wexford	Wexford City
632	Wexford	Wexford City

Irish Masonic Lodges in Ireland in 1804

#	Location	Civil Parish
Wicklow		
879	Arklow	Arklow
497	Newbridge	Arklow
713	Baltinglass	Baltinglass
748	Wicklow	Drumkah, Kilpoole, Rathnew

County Militia Lodges

#	Location
289	Antrim Militia
888	Armagh Militia
212	Downshire Militia
903	Carlow Militia
495	Cork (South) Militia
865	Donegal Militia
374	(Dublin) Irish Artillery
864	Fermanagh Militia
847	Kildare Militia
855	Kilkenny Militia
948	King's Co. Militia
854	Leitrim Militia
898	Meath Militia
552	Monaghan Militia
200	Monaghan Militia
242	Roscommon Militia
837	Sligo Militia
856	Tipperary Militia
562	Tyrone Militia
846	Tyrone Militia
791	Westmeath Militia
935	Wexford Militia
877	Wicklow Militia
848	Wicklow Militia
877	Wicklow Militia

Chapter Ten

Internet Database Searches

Today's technology has revolutionized genealogy research, allowing the possibility of finding information that was hidden just a few years ago. Nevertheless, with the upsurge of indexing and databases, some new problems have been created. One challenge is that technology uniting with Irish ancestral research has resulted in innumerable choices because of the prevalence of so many common Irish names.

As people type a surname or given name into a database, they too often instinctively think that the record for the person they are seeking will or will not automatically appear. They hunt no further when they should. Instead of searching a database and recording negative results in logs, some relevant subjects need to be addressed. The main one should be about the database itself. Is the answer there but hiding? Some practical and logical methods can test databases for the authenticity of positive or negative results.

Testing a Database

Before the technological revolution, searching name alterations from printed indexes in the backs of books was fairly straightforward. In printed indexes, all one had to do was scrutinize, for example, *G* surnames to determine what would pass for Garriety or all *B* entries for Bryan or *O* for O'Bryan variations. Reading them takes time, but the old-fashioned route worked, although it did not come without its frustrations.

In the new and fearless technology, with which researchers are cruising through databases at a rapid pace, people tend to forget how the outdated way worked. Is the database picking up the differences between Bryan, Brian, O'Bryan, Bryant, and so forth? Never assume that a database search can recognize all variations. Therefore, examining the drive capability of any database is wise. Sometimes, researchers forget that most of the population of Ireland was illiterate or semi-literate. Irish ancestors did not know how to spell their names, nor did the clerks or clergy ever expect or ask them to do so. To no small degree, accents also played a part in the mutilations of surnames.

Two names that soundly assess a search capability are Byrne and McDonald. Any surnames can be chosen, but the idea of the beginning test is that they must have multiple spellings. Does the search engine on Ancestry.com, FamilySearch.org, Findmypast.com, RootsIreland.ie, or

Irishgenealogy.ie pick up the modifications of Byrne, for instance, Burn, Bierne, and Beirne and then add an *O* in front of the name and an *s* on the end? How is it reading the space between the *O* and the *B*? Does Patrick O'Byrne become Patrick O. Byrne or, better yet, Patrick Obryne?

McDonald provides an example that is equally as muddled. In church registers, especially Roman Catholic, McDonald for the same family can be O'Donald, Donald, and the ever-present O'Donnell, McDonnell, and Donnell. It can be extraordinarily frustrating. A researcher needs to be creative and consider whether the priest or minister in church records was mistaking Donnelly for Donnell. In its case, what does the search or the indexing process do with the *Mc*? As with an *O*, the *Mc* must have some attention. Did the indexers or the search engine read Thomas Mc [space] Donald? Was it reading Thomas M. Donald? The parish registers often use an abbreviation such as this to denote *Mc* names. What about MacDonald? Will *Mc* and *Mac* be construed as the same prefix? If not, it is necessary to search them separately as if they are two different names.

Typically, a more sophisticated website has the capability to restructure some of these problems. Yet, some websites are basic, without any means of distinguishing names other than those typed into the search engine.

How to Determine Variations in Surnames

Another question is whether the database allows a search to include a wild card. Usually, this is an asterisk or maybe a percent sign to circumvent several problems. If the engine does not accept *L** as a search, think of options for Leddy. In a case such as this, narrowing the hunt to a parish and then looking at all *L* surnames is a reliable plan. Probably researchers will recognize the targeted name even if it is defectively indexed. Depending on how the *L* was interpreted by the indexers, it could look like an *S* or maybe an *F*, certainly alternatives any standard search feature will not detect for Leddy. However, will a search engine decipher Libby as Leddy? The question is appropriate because indexers can only write what they interpret from the original registers.

Surname inconsistencies sometimes can be identified by conducting a basic search of the tax list Griffith's Primary Valuation (1847-1864) for what it reveals. Another good database is RootsIreland.ie, which has an explanation of surnames and their disparities encountered in its database. Even so, not all variations of surnames are presented because indexing errors are not taken into account. As an illustration, the indexes were worthless for the Sutherland family from a particular Church of Ireland in Offaly (Kings County) until it was discovered that Suderland, Southern, Southran, or some other implausible spellings were written for Sutherland, resulting in difficulty in searching the indexes. Without being able to look at all *S** names, the alterations to Sutherland might not have been revealed if it had not been known ahead of time. In this case, Suderland and Sutherland are more obvious than Southern and Southran.

Comparing Various Indexing and Search Engines

The question occasionally is posed about why the different commercial companies and private organizations are indexing the same records. Sometimes, they are not, but, rather, they share a single index of the same source. Indexing has several issues.

Realizing that two or three different indexes are from the same source is to the researchers' advantage. One indexing might have picked up something another one did not. For example, if Rootsireland.ie indexed the same parish register now online at Ancestry.com and Findmypast.com, search them all. The fact that they are duplicates is exactly what is essential to a thorough investigation.

Some may argue that a subscription to Rootsireland.ie is no longer required since the majority of Catholic records are now on Ancestry.com and Findmypast.com. On the contrary, RootsIreland.ie is needed now more than ever as a balance to the other two websites. It has Protestant records, whereas the other two have only Roman Catholic ones. Moreover, Rootsireland.ie is an entirely different indexing program, offsetting the Catholic registers' databases on Ancestry.com and Findmypast.com, both of which are the same. Therefore, accuracy can be checked between the two programs.

Utilizing Internet Databases Effectively

During the scurry through the sphere of Internet information, researching before today's computer wonders seems too distant to remember. As profoundly as global interconnection has changed the way genealogy is conducted, it also has led to novel issues. Part of the journey through the myriads of databases and websites has instigated a new set of questions about manipulating the technology and often about determining what is not disclosed.

A foremost principle that should not be forgotten is that books and microfilm are by no means products of the past and worthless. Because of copyright restrictions, many major resources currently in book formats or on microfilm cannot be digitized until the copyrights are released or they become properties of the public domain. The legal aspects of genealogy are becoming more prevalent and are significant discussions in the industry. Before placing a book, article, or microfilm image online, ensure that it has no copyright restrictions. The large nonprofit and commercial websites have to do the same when they develop their databases.

This section concentrates on deriving the most information from databases. Even though they all may seem uncomplicated, and are often advertised that way, they can be anything but so.

What the Records Are Not Telling You

A main issue with databases as they appear on any website is people thinking all documents are contained in them. In the research process, it is fundamental to keep asking questions. People tend to give up too quickly when something is not found in a database. What they are inclined to forget is that each record source must be approached with a measure of education and even skepticism.

Researchers often go to the "general search" feature on websites such as FamilySearch.org, Ancestry.com, or Findmypast.com with the trust that findings are all-inclusive. When the method is effective, it is amazing, but just as many times, it is not because of distinct reasons. One problem in searching in this manner is the overwhelming results, hundreds and even thousands that have nothing to do with the research. With common Irish names, a general search can be the most frustrating of all. Which Mary Kelly is the one in question? Maybe none of them!

Sometimes, instead of choosing a general search, finding the catalog or inventory on the website about what it hosts can lead to educated choices. With this approach, one site may look better than another. Once some databases of interest are found, they can be studied individually. A typical Web page has a card catalog that presents not only its subject matter, for instance, marriages, but also the dates for when those records began. It is an important feature, especially for church records.

A model is RootsIreland.ie, a noteworthy website hosting both Catholic and Protestant indexes that is continually expanding with new records. For example, if it is already known that a Scot-Irish (Ulster-Scot) immigrant to Colonial America was born in the 1720s, study when Protestant records began for the Ulster region. If the online inventories reveal

the Protestant records did not begin until the 1820s, no birth or baptism record from which to document that event is in Ireland or Northern Ireland. Therefore, searching for it is not an issue. Church records will be of no assistance, and so a lineage has to be explored without the use of church registers. The website did not state the situation, but it can be inferred through analysis after studying the inventory on the website.

Also, enormously perplexing in the research process is appraising a specific source. The database explanation may or may not impart what types of people are covered, but it is a valid question in evaluating the worth of a database. How comprehensive are the original records? Do they include all the population, only heads of households, or are they incomplete in general? Are they for specific occupations or social classes? Two good examples of these are Griffith's Primary Valuation (1847-1864) and the Tithe Applotment Books (1823-1837).

Griffith's Valuation is looked upon as a census alternative or census substitute, but it is not as comprehensive as people using the databases often think it is. Griffith's has data only for those who were heads of households or responsible for properties. If more than one family lived in a house, only one was accountable for the tax and subsequently valued for that tax payment. In many cases, documenting the townlands where families lived is possible. This is easy when the church registers provide the townland of residence for the family. However, never finding them in Griffith's Valuation or the succeeding revision books is frustrating.

One reason is that no one in that family was paying the tax because no one was the head of the household. How many people are missed because of this, and how many wrong assumptions are made when what is expected is not found in the records? Consequently, a study of what Griffith's is and why it was made should be undertaken before searching the databases.

The Tithe Applotment Books are not like Griffith's, and confusion is further created when the two are treated as if they are of equal service. While Griffith's indeed does have its inconsistencies, its assistance in tracing ancestors remains solid and reliable, which is not necessarily true with the Tithe Applotment. The latter source was generated to document the people who personally were paying cash for holdings in rural Ireland. The funds supported the Church of Ireland, the state religion through 1870. People of all faiths paid the tithes, but not all who paid are listed in the records. For example, "and co. [company]" and "and oths [others]" are common after names because those persons collected the tithes on behalf of their neighbors in townlands. Only the persons paying are listed in the books. Therefore, assumptions should be made with caution about who were in townlands and who were not.

In the case of Griffith's and the Tithe, understand that the entire population was not included. Both still can be of inestimable service with a proper understanding of why an ancestor was not listed but might have been living there. The same applies to many records because they and the databases do not state that people are missing for various reasons. Comprehending what the databases and sources themselves are not imparting is as essential as knowing what they are.

What is in a Database?
In the pursuit of inexpensive and speedy answers in databases, failing to notice a necessary layer of questioning is easy. What is certain about the sites being searched? In the rush for immediate solutions to difficult problems, the habit is to type a name into the search engine, and whether it is there or not, the case is closed. The haste, not unusual, misses the reality that many databases are evolving works. The ones on FamilySearch.org note the last times they were revised. RootsIreland.ie has "new" attached to its inventory of records. If a database is not complete, review it periodically. Findmypast.com is a classic example because it has some leading databases being updated around the world. Sometimes, the website will supply digital images for browsing online while the indexing progresses.

If indexes to Church of Ireland records, for instance, for those on RootsIreland.ie, do not reveal the ancestral families, recall that half the Church of Ireland records were burned in the Four Courts Fire in Dublin. A deeper layer of research thus should be performed for what has and has not survived, a guide to which is on the website of the Representative Church Body Library. Afterward, the contents of the databases make sense.

Duplicate Databases

Since one organization cannot digitize and index everything a genealogist wants, the principal websites frequently join forces to accomplish specific tasks. For example, either FamilySearch.org or Findmypast.com indexes images and then shares them with the other. FamilySearch.org is nonprofit and free to users whereas Findmypast.com is commercial and has a subscription membership. Which of the two hosts the digitized images is a copyright issue. Another case in point is the Catholic parish registers from the National Library of Ireland collection that have been digitized and indexed on both Ancestry.com and Findmypast.com. Both have the same index and records and are commercial services.

In the example of the Catholic register databases, they are National Library of Ireland compositions and not from Ancestry.com or Findmypast.com. Technically, a search in one should produce the identical results the other does. Yet, each has its own search engine with separate methods of maneuvering data, and, therefore, if something is not found on one, it may be on the other. Furthermore, a totally separate indexing of most the Catholic records is on RootsIreland.ie, and so a third way can verify the conscientiousness of indexers in reading the records. It must be stated that RootsIreland.ie is a vital aid in checking accuracy because it was compiled from the original registers, not the National Library of Ireland microfilm. In innumerable cases, the microfilm images may not be as clear as the original pages.

When possible, inspecting multiple indexes of the same material is sensible. If the indexing is different, the variations can be shocking. The search can be unchanged but with only partially matching results. While this advice may not be applicable to records such as Griffith's Primary Valuation because the original was printed, it is vital in manuscripts such as church registers. Indexers can have dissimilar interpretations of one record, especially when the old Latin scribbles from the Catholic registers are being indexed. Often, it is challenging for anyone, especially an indexer, to distinguish between John and Joan in Latin or an abbreviated *My* (Mary) versus *Mg* (Margaret). And what does an inexperienced indexer do with *Ptk* (Patrick)? Did the transcriber read it as *Ptk,* let alone Patrick? All are valid questions when trying to manipulate the search feature on any database.

The General Internet Search

Some websites function as an index to indexes and websites and are continually being revised. Accordingly, they have to be referenced at regular intervals. One good one is GenUKI.org.uk (Genealogy UK and Ireland), which can be viewed by county or for all of Ireland. Sometimes, the oddest items can be found as links, and they can be amazing. Another well-known, standard source is "Cindi's List" on Cindislist.com. Both should be consulted periodically for updates.

A general Internet search should not be excluded. Astonishing snippets that are unfamiliar, unexpected, intriguing, and mysterious can disclose themselves. Remember that smaller databases or websites are not included or linked to the large, commercial, or nonprofit websites but that a family historian with a passion for a given surname or geographical area might have created the exact Web page needed. Try a general exploration with "Ireland Cemetery Records" or "Leitrim Graveyards." Certainly, interchange graveyards, cemeteries, tombstones, and monumental inscriptions in the searches.

Because a wealth of information is housed locally, such as in county libraries, enter the words "Tipperary County Library" and note what comes up. If looking for a specific record, try "Irish workhouse records" or "Kildare poorhouse records." Note what comes up.

Surnames or specific families can be sought as well. Depending on word choices in combination with a place name or county name, someone's family computer pages somewhere in the world may be discovered. For many family historians, personal genealogy websites have replaced books. These Internet family sites normally have additions as research continues, and so they need to be consulted from time to time.

Linked Genealogies Online

A great cause of amusement for genealogists, whether they are professionals or amateurs, is the online pedigrees on all the major websites. People often do not deliberate about the material they insert, and most never document anything. People at five years old can be married, and deceased women can give birth. Almost all family historians are dismayed over what they have observed for years through these linked pedigree pages.

As entertaining as the pedigrees are, they are not totally worthless; perhaps they are thoughtless but not enough so to be entirely discounted. Foremost is identifying the correct family on these databases so that the information, and, hopefully, the citations, can be evaluated. Directing the hunt can be by trial and error and may require starting with the person *after* he or she immigrated to the new country so that the various lineages leading back to Ireland can be studied. If a researcher is not familiar with Irish place names or how to list them, what is in the files can be hidden. For example, did the submission have "Ulster" instead of "County Fermanagh?" Was Fermanagh even spelled correctly? Maybe the search feature can pick this up, and maybe it cannot.

Even with all the totally incorrect information and weak links on the linked pedigree sites, they should be consulted for clues. The tenet is that possibly someone knows something about a listing that is not referenced, such as precise day of birth. The date came from somewhere, conceivably a family Bible, a tombstone, a death certificate, or an old family letter. An exact date should not be ignored and may signal the need to contact the submitter.

APOTHECARIES LICENSED IN DUBLIN.   115

— 4. —

A RETURN of the Number of Prosecutions, the Name of the Person prosecuted, the Date of each Prosecution, together with the Offence committed against the Act of 31st Geo. 3, from the 24th June 1791 until the 25th of March 1829; also, the number of Penalties, with the Name of the Person from whom recovered, and Date of recovery of said Penalty.

NAME.	RESIDENCE.	OFFENCE.	Date of Prosecution.	OBSERVATIONS.	Penalty Recovered.		
					£.	s.	d.
John Riddle	Monaghan	Commencing without license	Nov. 1791	Capias served	20	—	—
Samuel Kennedy	Cavan	ditto ditto	—	ditto.			
Samuel Taggart	Donegal	ditto ditto	Feb. 1792	Proceedings discontinued.			
Michael Drew	Dublin	Taking an unqualified apprentice	—	Capias served	20	—	—
John Boyd	Kilkenny	ditto ditto	—				
Arthur Valely	Middleton, Armagh.	Commencing without license	Mar. —	Capias served	20	—	—
Thomas H. Justice	Cork	ditto ditto	—	Exculpated himself by affidavit.			
William Johnston	Middleton, Armagh.	Illegally selling arsenic and keeping oils, &c.	—	Ditto - in part, fine mitigated.	10	—	—
Samuel Howes	Slane	Commencing without license	none	Admitted his offence	20	—	—
George Shegog	Castleblayney	ditto ditto	Nov. —		20	—	—
Bartholomew Connor	Lanesborough	ditto ditto	Nov. —	Capias served	20	—	—
Samuel Morton	Swadlinbar	ditto ditto	—		20	—	—
Frederick Price	Cavan	ditto ditto	Apr. 1793		20	—	—
Alexander Cairns	Carrickfergus	ditto ditto	May —		20	—	—
Thomas Kelly	Monaghan	ditto ditto	—		20	—	—
Roger Best	Tyrone	Illegally selling oils and colours.	—		5	—	—
Adam Gillespie	Derry	Taking an unqualified apprentice	—	Fine mitigated on exculpation to	1	2	9
James Reynolds	Antrim	Illegally selling oils and colours.	—		20	—	—
James M'Adam	Caledon	Keeping oils and colours illegally.	—		5	—	—
William Philips	Down	Commencing without license	June —	Exculpated himself in part, fine mitigated.	1	2	9
Joseph Berney	Tyrone	Selling arsenic illegally	—	ditto ditto	1	2	9
Hutton	Down	Unqualified assistant	—	ditto ditto	1	2	9
John Nesbitt	ditto	Commencing without license	—	ditto ditto	1	2	9
James D. Campbell	Tyrone	ditto ditto	July —	ditto ditto	1	2	9
Robert Bell	Down	Selling arsenic illegally	—	ditto ditto	1	2	9
Alexander Patton	Tanderagee	Unqualified apprentice	—	ditto ditto	1	2	9
Campbell Miller	Antrim	Commencing without license	Sept. —	ditto ditto	1	2	9
Arthur Clarke	Monaghan	Selling arsenic illegally	Oct. —		5	—	—
P. Blackburn	Antrim	ditto ditto	Nov. —		5	—	—
Robert Gomell	Cork	Commencing without license	Feb. 1794		20	—	—
Patrick M'Dermott	ditto	ditto ditto	—		20	—	—
William Spear	Meath	ditto ditto	Apr. —		20	—	—
William Harkur	Roscommon	ditto ditto	May —		20	—	—
Richard M'Clelland	Antrim	Selling oils and colours illegally.	June —	Fine mitigated on exculpation to	1	2	9
James Blair	Raphoe	Taking an unqualified ap-	Aug. 1795				

Figure 42: A page with penalties for individuals' offenses extracted from the section of the report Listings from the Apothecarie's [sic] Hall, Dublin, 1791-1829. (Under UK Copyright law, a publisher's work is protected for 25 years from the end of the year in which the publication occurred. No permissions required.)

Chapter Eleven

Occupations

If ancestors emigrated before the publication of Griffith's Primary Valuation (1847-1864) and their records are not in church indexes, occupations can indicate where they may have lived in Ireland. The subject of occupation also arises when a young person immigrated alone, the parents' names are unknown, and he or she cannot be connected to anyone in a community. The area of interest depends on how specialized the work was and the age of the ancestor at the time of emigration. The younger someone was, the less likely a skill was acquired in Ireland instead of in the immigrant country.

The principle for researching an occupation is always to ask whether the training for stone mason, pewter maker, goldsmith, distiller, or another occurred in Ireland. If it was not, it could have been obtained in a country such as the United Kingdom before the family moved again and settled in North America, Australia,

or South Africa. Where the instruction was acquired can assist in developing an immigrant strategy to find origins.

Most researchers have the same question about eighteenth- and nineteenth-century occupations: What does that term mean? Other topics such as medical terminology are no different. The English language has evolved over the centuries, leaving many official and accepted designations in the dust heaps of history. To compensate for this, family historians have gone through the historical directories and dictionaries to compile practical reference tools and websites for genealogists. A notable work is Colin Waters's *A Dictionary of Old Trades, Titles and Occupations* (Newbury, Berkshire, UK: Countryside Books, 1999), which contains entries from the English language, sources dating back to the Norman Conquest, and terms outside the British Isles, such as those from Australia and the United States.

One research tactic often overlooked is the use of published studies on particular occupations. Some of them are focused on Ireland and have lists of people with their addresses who were engaged in the skills. These books, though, also are published more generally about occupations in Great Britain or the United Kingdom with Ireland included or with a special Irish section in the book. Before 1921, separating the affairs in Ireland from the rest of the United Kingdom was difficult at times, and so do not neglect the books concentrating on the British Isles. They may not be cross-referenced to Ireland in a library catalog, but, rather, listed as United Kingdom or Great Britain books.

Outside the United Kingdom and Ireland, this category of books should be at any major public or academic library that has a large British or Irish collection.

Immigration Strategy

Identifying immigrant origins from occupations has to be viewed from several perspectives. Some may not apply to the targeted ancestor and some have to be tailored. The goal is to develop a method that is successful and through which questions can be properly addressed.

One approach is to consider the market towns. They were all over Ireland and held fairs or market days at selected times, during which people gathered to buy, sell, and mingle with one another. Young people from opposite sides of the town might have become acquainted at one of those events. A family might have had a small shop in the town where the children met customers whom they eventually married. A blacksmith or grocer's town occupation and store could easily explain how the son of a small businessperson married a farmer's daughter.

Moreover, the market towns can be significant before all civil registrations began in 1864 or when church records are nonexistent, incomplete, or start late. When comparing the vicinities of market towns to tax lists, such as Griffith's Primary Valuation (1847-1864), some meaningful patterns can emerge, especially in a surname distribution study. Lists of counties' fairs and market towns are in Irish directories, which are on the database "Ireland, City and Regional Directories, 1847-1946" on Ancestry.com.

For example, for County Leitrim, the *Thom's Irish Almanac and Official Directory for the Year 1850* (p. 502) printed the following fairs with their dates, shown in the chart on next page. With a minimal effort of studying modern county maps on the internet, such as the one below for County Leitrim, market towns and surrounding potential residences of ancestors can be platted.

In this circumstance, County Leitrim already would need to be known from the records of the immigrant country. That is not necessarily unusual. However, if the family cannot be documented in either the Catholic or Protestant registers, an occupation may aid in solving the problem. If the ancestor had a barrel making business or was a wheelwright, the most likely towns where the shops were located can be determined. From there,

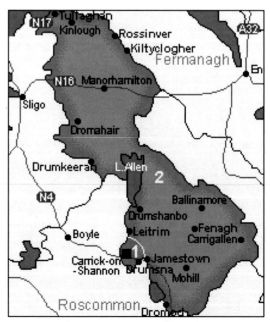

Figure 43: County Leitrim. (Image courtesy of Ireland GenWeb—County Leitrim. Permission received.)

Markets/Fairs for County Leitrim as Published for 1850

Town	Dates
Ballinamore	12 May, 12 Nov.
Carrick-on-Shannon	18 Jan., 20 Mar., 6 Jun., 11 Aug., 14 Sep., 22 Oct., 21 Nov., 16 Dec.
Carrigallen	Easter Mon., 7 May, 9 Aug., 8 Oct., last Friday in Dec.
Cashcarrigan	1 Feb., 17 Mar., 1 and 28 May, 29 Jun., 1 Aug., 21 Sep., 8 Oct., 1 Nov., 21 Dec.
Cloone	12 Feb., 5 Apr., 26 May, 13 Jun., 10 Jul., 26 Aug., 29 Sep., 2 Nov., 20 Dec.
Dromahair	13th of every month
Dromod	1 Jan., 28 Mar., Sat. after 12 May, 29 Jun., 10 Oct., Sat. before 12 Dec.
Drumkeeran	27 Jan., 28 Mar., Easter Mon., 27 May, 24 Jun., 18 Jul., 18 Aug., 16 Sep., 19 Oct., 11 Nov., 9 Dec.
Drumshanbo	15 Feb., 1 Apr., 16 May, 2nd Fri. in Jun., 16 Jul., 6 Oct, 16 Nov.
Drumsna	20 May, 22 Jun., 25 Aug, 7 Oct, 13 Dec.
Jamestown	28 May, 8 Jul. 1 Sep., 20 Dec.
Kinlough	6th of every month
Leitrim Town	22 Jan., 20 Feb., 25 Mar., 5 May, 16 Jun., 23 Jul., 1 Sep., 13 Oct., 1 Dec.
Longfield	17 May, 10 Oct., last Mon. in Dec.
Lurganboy	15 May, 21 Jun., 21 Aug., Thurs. before Michaelmas Day, 21 Oct.
Manorhamilton	12 Jan., 12 Feb., 12 Mar., 12 Apr., 12 Jun., 1st Thurs in Aug., 12 Sep., 12 Dec.
Mohill	14 Feb., 28 Apr., 21 Jul., 9 and 10 Oct., 4 Dec.
Newtown	25 Feb., 25 May, 25 Aug., 25 Nov.
Newtowngore	26 Jun., 15 Oct.

Griffith's Primary Valuation or a directory could be examined for where the surnames are found in those towns. Knowing more than one surname, such as a wife's maiden name, can narrow the search further.

In cases where the county is not known, if an occupation in the immigrant country is unusual, directories may be helpful. The early directories were for the professions in the towns and cities. They were not every-name directories for all residents, nor were they rural or farming directories. By using the odd occupation as a keyword, it is possible to manipulate a database such as that on Ancestry.com for where the targeted name or surname appears in these types of directories. Remember, some occupations were more suited to towns than to countrysides. By narrowing all the entries from the various directories by occupation, how common the surname is in the country will not matter. Possibly, the method can link the immigrant printer to the Irish printer or the immigrant hat maker to the Irish hat maker.

The present chapter will focus on a few, chosen occupations requiring levels of skills that could have been obtained through training in Ireland. The list is by no means comprehensive but only demonstrates the immigrant strategies

Historic Dublin Guilds

Free Citizens of Dublin (a person had to belong to a guild to join)

Apothecaries

Bakers

Barber-Surgeons

Brewers and Maltsters

Bricklayers and Plasterers

Butchers

Carpenters, Millers, Masons and Heliers

Cooks and Vintners

Coopers

Curriers

Cutlers, Painters, Paper-Stainers and Stationers

Feltmakers

Glovers and Skinners

Goldsmiths

Hosiers and Knitters

Joiners, Ceylers and Wainscotters

Merchants

Saddlers, Upholders, Coach and Coach-Harnessmakers, Bridle-Cutters and Wheelwrights

Sheermen and Dyers

Shoemakers (Corvisers or Cordwainers)

Smiths

Tailors

Tallow Chandlers, Soap Boilers and Wax-Light Makers

Tanners

Weavers

that could be developed. Occupations such as attorneys and doctors are not addressed because the chance of the people engaged in them leaving behind biographical information or obituaries listing birthplaces is good. Also discussed in this chapter are the important Dublin Guilds, which licensed and apprenticed craftsmen from throughout Ireland.

The rule when embarking upon occupations as a viable immigration method concerns proficiency level: Was the immigrant's occupation in the immigrant country accomplished to the degree that training might have been acquired in Ireland? In some cases, the answer could certainly be yes, as examples, for an apothecary or a bookbinder. For others, such as miners, the answer might not be as clear. Yet even with miners, the question remains valid.

The Guilds

Guilds were mutual benefit associations and have been in Europe since the eleventh century. The four kinds of guilds were:

- Guild merchants, also known as merchant guilds, were responsible for regulating commerce.

- Craft guilds, also known as trade guilds, set the standards within professions.

- Religious guilds were created for the spiritual welfare of members.

- Military guilds assisted the army in times of war.

Dublin was a major center for the guilds in Ireland, and the city's twenty-five chartered trade and craft guilds dominated commercial aspects of the city until 1841. There were eleven religious guilds and two military guilds. Mary Clark and Raymond Refaussé's *Directory of Historic Dublin Guilds* (Dublin: Dublin Public Libraries, 1993) specifies what was not destroyed in the 1922 Four Courts Fire, providing the needed inventory before approaching this topic. It designates which records survived, where they are deposited, and where transcripts were made of records before 1922.

Surviving records or transcripts may include the people who took oaths, minute books, admissions of freemen, and apprentices' lists. Although the foregoing guilds listed were limited to Dublin City, ancestors might not have been living in Dublin since people throughout Ireland were licensed through the Dublin guilds. However, Dublin was a major center of commerce in the Irish economy, and so it would not be surprising if an ancestor with an occupation necessitating training was from Dublin or had spent time in Dublin because of the economic powers the guilds held. All the guilds were specialized and produced skilled, licensed emigrants.

Apothecaries

An apothecary made and dispensed medicines to physicians, surgeons, and patients. In modern English, a pharmacist or chemist is what was historically called an apothecary. Through investigations of herbs and chemicals, the craft of the apothecary became chemistry and pharmacology. The products were sold from local stores and were typically family businesses. In 1791, with the Irish Apothecary's Act, apothecaries in the British Isles were first regulated nationally, and the Company of Apothecaries' Hall was established in Dublin.

Apothecaries in Ireland were apprenticed as well as licensed through the Apothecaries' Hall in Dublin. A printed list of approved and licensed businesses and practitioners in Ireland is in chronological order from 1791 to 1829, and an ancestor in the immigrant country who was an apothecary may be found on it. Typical information contained is basic and is arranged in this fashion:

- Licensed Apothecaries (pp. 2-80), listing dates, names, residences, and counties (pp. 2-80).

- Those certified to become assistants or journeymen, listing dates, names, residences, and counties (pp. 82-91).

- Persons certified to open shops and practice as apothecaries in Ireland, listing dates, names, residences, and counties (pp. 92-114).

- Those prosecuted for offenses, listing names, residences of offenses, dates of prosecutions, observations, and penalties recovered (pp. 115-119).

Because each of the four categories has details of the residences and counties of the men, the information is invaluable in developing an immigrant origins' strategy.

Among the apothecaries prosecuted for offenses were some operating without licenses while others were taking on unqualified apprentices or keeping or selling oils illegally. From 24 June 1791 to 25 March 1829 there were 239 prosecutions, of which 194 were "commencing without a license," 12 for "selling arsenic," 7 for "selling oils and colors," 22 for "taking unqualified apprentices," 2 for "taking unqualified assistants," 1 for taking an apprentice for less than seven years," and 1 for "taking an unqualified partner."

These records were ordered to be printed by the House of Commons in 1829 and are at the Genealogical Office in Dublin (Ms no. 648). They also are digitized through FamilySearch.org under the title "Apothecaries' Hall, Dublin: 1791-1829."

Bookbinders
The bookbinder presents a fascinating study of how an occupation can lead to another. For example, if an immigrant ancestor was a bookbinder, which is a skilled profession, it deserves consideration about it being learned in Ireland. However, the trade itself in the British Isles requires some explanation because historically, it could have been either a full-time or part-time job. That alone opens some interesting possibilities.

Charles Ramsden's *Bookbinders of the United Kingdom (Outside London) 1780-1840* ([England]: C. Ramsden, 1954), pp. 228-250, has a section on Irish bookbinders. He presented the names of the bookbinders; their addresses, including city and street addresses; the years they practiced; and the references from where the entries were derived. While some of the entries are detailed, most are limited but with information sufficient for situating individuals at exact places and times, making this an important source for tracing an occupation as an immigrant strategy. A typical entry has Alexander Drennan at Bridge Street, Sligo. The reference is listed as PIG/SIN/20, which interprets as the Pigot's *Commercial Directory of Scotland, Ireland, and the Four Northern Counties of England for 1820*.

Ramsden pointed out that compiling a list of bookbinders in smaller country towns was an issue. The incorrect assumption is that small towns did not have binders. Often, orders to local binders were passed on to larger, more established ones who normally operated in major cities. Frequently, they are found listed as "Binders to" someone else. Smaller bookbinders did have connections with leather dealers, cutters, and the local saddlers, and so those binders were able to do some of their own work in small towns.

In the countrysides, even though binders may have been committed to their trade, they probably did not have enough business. Thus, they often had other occupations, such as a victuallers (licensed to sell liquor), grocers, umbrella makers, parish clerks, tailors, or librarians. Stationers, printers, and booksellers were the most common occupations for those who did bookbinding because the three businesses naturally accompanied the craft. Consequently, people who were skilled bookbinders may be hidden in various directories that list businesses, which can affect a research program.

Knowing that bookbinders might not have been dedicated to only their craft in small towns opens doors to other occupations as main focuses of searches. Records from the main occupations may be keys to immigrant origins, and they were discovered through bookbinding in the immigrant country! Perhaps they were in a related field of work, for instance, leather maker, stationer, saddler, printer, or even umbrella maker in Ireland. The island-wide business directories for the smaller towns are a viable option in the strategy for identifying the correct immigrant ancestor.

Merchant Marine (Merchant Navy)
At almost every point in immigrant research, families have lore about ancestors who arrived as stowaways. Most of the stories cannot be proved, but they have to be investigated if only because the prevalence of them is amusing.

It must be wondered if perhaps part of the rumor of the stowaway may be true, but it is not the stowaway element. Conceivably, the young man worked on a ship or was an apprentice, from where the tale became convoluted over the years. Maybe deserting his ship would be relayed in the narrative as stowaway, a much more acceptable term than deserter.

The topic is so important that many databases help sort through the different types of records generated about men or, interestingly, also about women involved in the maritime trades. The occupation being discussed herein is that of a Merchant Mariner or Merchant Navy. King George V bestowed the title of Merchant Navy on the merchant ships after their services in WWI.

Merchant mariners worked on commercial or merchant vessels and transported cargoes and people during times of peace and war. The Merchant Marine was also referred to as the Merchant Navy, and during the height of the British Empire, it was the largest merchant fleet in the world. Men can be found as boatswains, captains, mariners, mates, seamen, or super cargoes. The industry took men and women from all over the world. If an immigrant worked as a Merchant Mariner in the immigrant country, he might have been a mariner in Ireland. During the period in question, Irish men were part of the British Merchant Marine. The records generated about these men and their qualifications are part of the Board of Trade (BT) series at The National Archives, Kew, London. While not all the papers are indexed, some major collections have been, and they could provide

the link between an immigrant mariner and an Irish mariner. The databases, which at least are a beginning to the search into this profession, include the following series of records:

> Crew Lists (BT 98)
> Apprentices (BT 150/1-53)
> Merchant Seamen (BT 112-116, 120)

Maritime codes are used in the records, such as 3 M for 3rd mate, EDH for Efficient Deck Hand, or P Boy for Pantry Boy. A list of these is on the Findmypast.com website in the article "Merchant Seamen Abbreviations." In some of the registers, ports were assigned specific numbers. The Irish ports were:

#	Port
10	Belfast
28	Coleraine
34	Drogheda
35	Dublin
37	Dundalk
43	Galway
50	Westport
65	Londonderry (Derry)
67	Limerick
73	Newry
89	Sligo
98	Waterford
102	Wexford
111	New Ross
119	Tralee
122	Ballina
160	Youghal

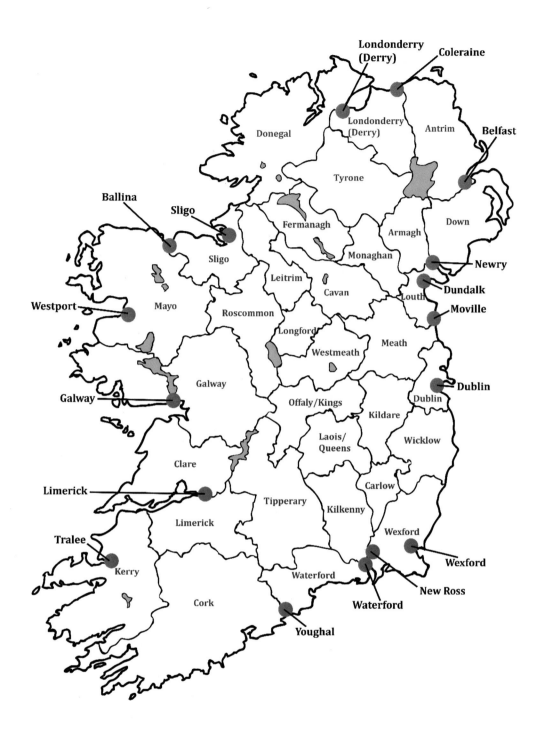

Figure 44: Merchant Marine Ports in Ireland for which records are currently known.

Each port authority in Ireland had agreements with the ships from the Merchant Navy, resulting in the crew lists (BT 98). Every year, each ship registered at these ports had to submit a report to the Registrar General of Shipping and Seamen, who kept the records for the Merchant Navy. The registers are detailed and

Registered Foreign Ports for Merchant Marines of Ireland

Australia

Port #	Port Name
207	Sydney, New South Wales, Australia
208	Hobart Town, Tasmania, Australia
211	Launceston, Van Diemen's Land (Tasmania), Australia
263	Melbourne, Victoria, Australia
294	Geelong, Victoria, Australia

Caribbean

Port #	Port Name
217	Kingston, Jamaica
218, 223	St. Lucia
219	Montego Bay, Jamaica
232	Kingstown, St. Vincent, Windward Islands
245	St. Johns, Antigua
250	Bermuda
287	Antigua

Mediterranean and Africa

Port #	Port Name
224	Malta (plus Gibraltar?)
225	Louis, Mauritius
237	Sierra Leone
259	Cape Town, South Africa
288	Cape of Good Hope, South Africa

Asia

Port #	Port Name
257	Bombay, India
258	Calcutta, India
260	Cochin, India
262	Madras, India
275	Hong Kong
277	Moulmein, Burma

South America

Port #	Port Name
254	Demerara, Guiana
296	Stanley, Falkland Islands

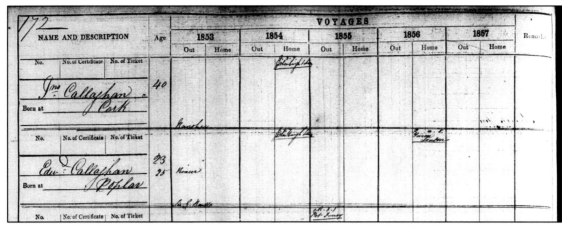

Figure 45: Merchant seamen records from collection BT116 at The National Archives in London. Note the presence of birthplaces and ages. (This work is produced and copyrighted by the Crown Copyright©. Meeting Open Government License qualifications for this content, no additional permissions required.)

Registered Foreign Ports for Merchant Marines of Ireland

Canada

Port #	Port Name
200	Halifax, Nova Scotia, Canada
201	Liverpool, Nova Scotia, Canada
202	Pictou, Nova Scotia, Canada
203	Yarmouth, Nova Scotia, Canada
228	Miramichi Bay, New Brunswick, Canada
229	Prince Edward Island, Canada
230, 243	St. John, New Brunswick, Canada
231, 244	St John's, Newfoundland, Canada
236	Bathurst, New Brunswick, Canada
242	St. Andrews, Newfoundland, Canada
251	Arichat, Cape Breton Island, Nova Scotia, Canada
252	Montreal, Quebec, Canada
253	Quebec, Quebec, Canada
271	Gaspé, New Brunswick, Canada
272	Windsor, Nova Scotia, Canada
273	St. Stephen, New Brunswick, Canada
274	Digby, Nova Scotia, Canada
276	New Glasgow, Pictou, Nova Scotia, Canada
278	Lunenburg, Nova Scotia, Canada
279	Parrsboro, Nova Scotia, Canada
281	Grand Island, Cape Breton Island, Nova Scotia, Canada
282	Weymouth, Nova Scotia, Canada
289	Medway, Nova Scotia, Canada
290	Port Wallace, Nova Scotia, Canada
291	Guysborough, Nova Scotia, Canada
293	Richibucto, New Brunswick, Canada
295	St. Mary's, Newfoundland, Canada

document crews, agreements with seamen regarding wages, conditions of services, and information about the ships. The ships were registered with the individual ports. The merchant marines were instrumental in the valuable trade of commodities, such as opium, spices, sugar, and tea.

One index is the National Archives of Ireland database "Records of the Registrar General of Shipping and Seamen, 1860-1921" and concerns only ports in what is today the Republic of Ireland. A second database edition, "Ireland Merchant Navy Crew Lists 1863-1921," is on Findmypast.com and holds information about the crews from throughout Ireland, incorporating ports in what became Northern Ireland in 1921. Both websites have digitized images.

The guide to the Findmypast.com database points out that it includes crew members born in Ireland and in other parts of the world as well as females from when the ships began to employ them as stewardesses, in the latter part of the nineteenth century. As the women's duties expanded, their services on board were as laundresses, matrons, hairdressers, catering personnel, and shop assistants. Because they had no maritime training, their career opportunities were limited.

Within the records are birthplaces of crews; the last ships on which they served; and services that were discontinued with the reasons, dates, and places.

The apprentices' personal information includes names, ages, dates of indentures, ports of indentures, dates of assignments, and ports of assignments. The birth and death information on the crews can supply parents' names, mothers' maiden names, and last residences of parents. If members of the crews or passengers died, the information was recorded.

Under the Merchant Seamen Act 1823, the masters of ships of 80 tons or over were required to carry a given number of indentured apprentices. They were enrolled with the local Customs Officers. The records contain most of the same information as that for crew members, but they do vary in content depending on the period. The records have dates and for the apprentices, names and ages, birthplaces, terms for which they were bound, names and residences of Masters or those to whom they were bound, names of vessels and ports where they enrolled, deaths or cancellations, and remarks. Apprentices' desertions were noted also, which could explain the "stowaway" lore that is so common!

The Ancestry.com database "UK, Apprentices Indentured in Merchant Navy, 1824-1910" (BT 150/1-53) has both the indexes and digitized images. Since not all the apprentices' birthplaces were recorded, especially in the early years, do not assume that an ancestor is not listed in the database because a search with "Ireland" did not yield desired results.

In the Findmypast.com database "Britain, Merchant Seamen, 1835-1857" (BT 112-116, 120), which contains digital images, are the registers from the time the British Government was monitoring the potential reserves of sailors for the Royal Navy. The records can include dates, names, birth years, birthplaces, birth counties, discharges, and reference numbers. Sometimes, the records have only "Ireland," but they can have counties or places within counties. There is no way of knowing until they are searched. Although basic, these registers can be narrowed to the birth dates of the sailors. Another version of this set, with the addition of BT 119, is the FamilySearch.org database "United Kingdom, Merchant Navy Seamen Records, 1835-1941."

As part of a worldwide immigration strategy, knowing the ports of call where the Merchant Marines were registered may be beneficial. If an apprentice deserted or a former mariner emigrated, it might have been to one of these port towns. Pages 150 and 151 present a list of ports adapted from the Findmypast.com website in the article "Merchant Seamen Abbreviations." Each port was assigned a number, which can be reflected in the registers.

Millers

Millers operated mills and were a skilled and important part of regional economies. If an ancestor was successfully operating a mill in an immigrant country, there is good reason to believe the person had this occupation in Ireland.

Different types of mills were in Ireland, and they sometimes operated close together because of the water sources. Corn mills and flax mills are examples. Nevertheless, insufficient water supplies hindered the ability of multiple mills to operate at the same time. Therefore, in certain areas, these mills had to take turns using the water power. This practice fell out of use.

An island-wide guide to mills and millers is William E. Hogg's *The Millers & the Mills of Ireland of About 1850* (Sandycove, Ireland: William E. Hogg, 1998). Hogg designed his work with the family historian in mind, using Valuation Office Mill Books (housed at the National Archives of Ireland), Griffith's Primary Valuation, and Ordnance Survey Memoirs of Ireland as the three main sources for compiling his inventory. He covered about 3,600 mills, with the names of the millers or mill proprietors.

The Valuation Office Mill Books encompass Ireland with the exception of counties Antrim, Carlow, Donegal, Dublin, Fermanagh, Kildare, Londonderry, Meath, Monaghan, Roscommon, and Tyrone, and no books were found for any of these at the time of Hogg's research. Hogg gives the locations of the mills and the names of the proprietors along with some figures and statistics. He clarifies a few types of historic mills for the modern reader:

> ***Beating Mill***: subjects raw linen fabric to a continuous

hammering process to flatten the weave and provide finish.

Grist Mill*:* a term most often used in reference to County Cork mills. Grist is a word that applies to corn or other mills to which people brought their grain to have it ground. However, grist mills were found throughout Ireland.

Tuck Mill*:* improved woolen fabric (which was often home-woven) by subjecting it to repeated scouring or thickening processes through wheels and machinery operating a variety of combs.

If an ancestor was a miller in the immigrant country, a study of Hogg's work may identify either the miller in Ireland or perhaps a relative who took over the mill when the owner or proprietor emigrated. Because addresses of the mills are in the book, the logical assumption is the millers did not live far from their businesses, thus solving the question of the immigrant's place of birth.

Mining

Ireland typically is not associated with the mining industry, but ignoring its mining history in the search for immigrant origins is shortsighted. A list adapted from the 1855 edition of *Thom's Irish Almanac and Official Directory* (Dublin: Alexander Thom and Sons Printers and Publishers, 1855), pp. 425-428, displays how widespread mining was in Ireland.

The chart shows the types in operation, the ones formerly worked, or where deposits were identified with their yields yet to be determined in 1855. The *Thom's Directory* presents additional information, such as the townlands and the Ordnance Survey Maps where the deposits or mines were located. It also provides the names of the mines that were in operation, omitting coal mines and collieries. As of 1855, no metallic lodes had been discovered in counties Carlow, Londonderry (Derry), and Westmeath.

Exploring the Beara Peninsula of County Cork is an example of solving immigrant origins with mining as an occupation. Although emigrants from this area went worldwide, an exact migration pattern is linked to the copper industry on the peninsula. As an illustration, if ancestors mined in the United States in several locations in and around Butte, Montana, and Park City, Utah (or in all mining regions in Montana and Utah in general), some basic strategies can be developed. First, both Butte and Park City are historically recognized for mining and are well known in their states' annals for the influxes and departures of miners. Copper was in Butte, and gold and silver, in Park City. The work attracted people from all over, but groups of Irish can be verified travelling between the two towns. The chief question is whether they were all from the same section of Ireland and were miners before emigrating. In this set of circumstances, they were.

Locations of Metallic Deposits or Mines

County	Post Town	Mines or Indications
Antrim		
	Ballycastle	Coal, Clay-Ironstone, Hematite
	Carrickfergus	Rocksalt, Gypsum
	Larne	Iron
Armagh		
	Belleeks	Lead
	Crossmaglen	Copper, Lead
	Keady	Lead, Manganese
	Middletown	Lead
	Newry	Copper, Lead
	Newton Hamilton	Lead
	Pointzpass	Lead
Cavan		
	Cavan	Copper
	Cootehill	Lead
	Shercock	Lead
	Swanlinbar	Clay-Ironstone
Clare		
	Ballyvaughan	Argentiferous Lead, Copper, Manganese
	Feakle	Copper, Lead
	New Market on Fergus	Antimony, Argentiferous Lead, Lead
	Quin	Argentiferous Lead, Copper with Zinc
	Roadford	Argentiferous Lead
	Sixmilebridge	Lead and Sulphur ore
	Tuamgraney	Lead
	Tulla	Argentiferous Lead, Copper, Lead, Silver, Sulphur Ore
Cork		
	Ballydehob	Copper, Lead
	Bantry	Argentiferous Lead, Copper, Lead, Sulphate of Barytes
	Carrigtohill	Lead with Zinc
	Castletown-Bearhaven	Copper, Lead
	Castle Townsend (Townshend)	Antimony, Copper, Lead
	Clonakilty	Copper, Lead, Sulphate of Barytes,
	Cloyne	Iron
	Cork	Copper
	Crookhaven	Argentiferous Lead, Auriferous Gossan, Copper, Lead, Silver
	Dunmanway	Copper, Mundic

Locations of Metallic Deposits or Mines

County	Post Town	Mines or Indications
Cork		
	Glengarriff	Copper
	Millstreet	Copper
	Nohaval	Argentiferous Lead, Lead
	Ross Carbery	Copper, Iron, Manganese, Sulphate of Barytes
	Skibbereen	Copper
	Skull	Copper
Donegal		
	Ballybofey	Lead, Iron
	Ballyshannon	Argentiferous Lead with Zinc, Copper, Lead
	Bundoran	Copper, Lead
	Carndonagh	Argentiferous Lead with Zinc, Copper, Sulphur Ore
	Dunfanaghy	Copper, Iron, Lead, Sulphur Ore,
	Glenties	Lead, Lead with Zinc, Sulphur Ore
	Killybegs	Argentiferous Lead, Manganese
	Letterkenny	Lead
	Naran	Copper, Lead
Down		
	Annalong	Copper and Lead
	Ardglass	Copper and Sulphate of Barytes, Lead
	Bryansford	Lead
	Crawfordsburn	Lead
	Dromara	Iron
	Dromore	Lead and Manganese
	Dundrum	Lead
	Hillsborough	Iron
	Kilkeel	Copper and Lead
	Killough	Copper and Sulphur Ore, Lead
	Killyleagh	Lead
	Newtownards	Lead
	Strangford	Argentiferous Lead and Copper
Dublin		
	Dublin	Lead, Lead with Zinc
	Golden Ball	Argentiferous Lead with Zinc, Lead, Native Silver
	Howth	Lead, Manganese
	Kingstown	Copper, Lead, Lead with Zinc, Tin
	Rush	Copper

Locations of Metallic Deposits or Mines

County	Post Town	Mines or Indications
Fermanagh		
	Belleek	Copper and Iron
Galway		
	Ardrahan	Argentiferous Lead, Bismuth, Copper, Lead
	Clifden	Copper, Lead, Iron
	Galway	Lead, Mundic
	Kinvarra	Argentiferous Lead
	Moycullen	Lead
	Oranmore	Lead with Zinc, Sulphur Ore
	Oughterard	Argentiferous Lead, Copper, Lead, Lead with Zinc, Iron, Manganese, Mundic, Silver, Sulphur Ore
	Roundstone	Lead
Kerry		
	Ardfert	Lead
	Castleisland	Copper, Lead, Silver
	Castlemaine	Argentiferous Lead with Zinc, Copper, Lead
	Causeway	Copper, Lead
	Dunquin	Copper
	Kenmare	Argentiferous Lead, Copper, Lead
	Killarney	Argentiferous Lead, Cobalt, Copper, Lead With Zinc, Sulphur Ore
	Sneem	Copper
	Tralee	Copper, Lead, Silver
Kildare		
	Celbridge	Lead, Lead with Zinc
	Edenderry	Lead
	Newbridge	Copper
Kilkenny		
	Castlecomber	Clay-Ironstone
	Inistioge	Argentiferous Lead
	Kilmacow	Lead
	Knocktopher	Copper, Lead, Silver
	Thomastown	Iron, Micaceous
King's Co.		
	Edenderry	Lead
	Kinnitty	Copper, Lead

Locations of Metallic Deposits or Mines

County	Post Town	Mines or Indications
Leitrim		
	Drumkeeran	Clay-Ironstone
	Lurganboy	Argentiferous Lead, Copper
	Mohill	Iron
Limerick		
	Askeaton	Argentiferous Lead, Silver
	Doon	Lead
	Oola	Argentiferous Lead, Copper, Sulphur Ore
	Newcastle	Lead
	Pallaskenry	Argentiferous Lead
	Rathkeale	Argentiferous Lead
Longford		
	Longford	Argentiferous Lead
	Scrabby	Iron
Louth		
	Clogherhead	Copper
	Drogheda	Copper, Lead
	Dundalk	Lead
	Jonesborough	Antimony
	Togher	Copper, Lead
Mayo		
	Ballycastle	Copper, Geevraun
	Ballyhaunis	Lead
	Louisburgh	Copper, Sulphur Ore
	Newport	Argentiferous Lead, Copper, Mundic, Sulphur Ore
	Westport	Argentiferous Lead
Meath		
	Ardcath	Lead
	Athboy	Lead
	Slane	Copper, Lead
	Walterstown	Copper
Monaghan		
	Ballybay	Lead
	Bellanode	Lead with Zinc
	Bellatrain	Manganese
	Carrickmacross	Gypsum
	Castleblayney	Argentiferous Lead, Lead, Sulphate of Barytes
	Monaghan	Antimony, Argentiferous Lead with Zinc, Lead, Lead with Zinc, Sulphate of Barytes

Locations of Metallic Deposits or Mines

County	Post Town	Mines or Indications
Queen's Co.		
	Maryborough	Iron
Roscommon		
	Keadew	Clay-Ironstone
Sligo		
	Ballysadare	Lead, Silver
	Sligo	Copper, Lead, Sulphate of Barytes
Tipperary		
	Borrisoleigh	Lead
	Cappaghwhite	Copper
	Dunkerrin	Copper
	Newport	Copper
	Portroe	Copper, Lead
	Silvermines	Argentiferous Lead, Copper, Lead, Lead with Zinc, Silver, Sulphur Ore
	Tipperary	Argentiferous Lead, Copper, Manganese
Tyrone		
	Coal Island	Clay-Ironstone
	Cookstown	Iron
	Gortin	Antimony, Lead
	Pomeroy	Copper
Waterford		
	Annestown	Copper
	Bunmahon	Argentiferous Lead, Argentiferous Lead with Zinc, Colbalt, Copper, Native Copper
	Ballynamult	Copper
	Carrick-on-Suir	Iron, Lead, Micaceous
	Dungarvan	Iron
	Stradbally	Copper
	Tramore	Copper
	Waterford	Copper
	Youghal	Lead
Wexford		
	Enniscorthy	Argentiferous Lead with Zinc, Copper, Iron, Lead, Mundic, Sulphur Ore
	Riverchapel	Iron
	Wexford	Copper
Wicklow		
	Annamoe	Argentiferous Lead, Copper, Copper with Zinc, Lead
	Arklow	Copper, Iron, Lead, Particles of Gold, Tin

Locations of Metallic Deposits or Mines

County	Post Town	Mines or Indications
Wicklow (cont.)		
	Ballinalea	Copper
	Baltinglass	Lead,
	Bray	Copper
	Enniskerry	Copper, Lead
	Hollywood	Lead
	Kiltegan	Copper, Lead
	Rathdrum	Antimony, Arsenic, Auriferous Silver, Copper, Copper with Zinc, Iron, Lead, Lead with Zinc, Particles of Gold, Sulphur Ore, Tin
	Redcross	Copper, Iron, Sulphur Ore
	Roundwood	Copper, Lead, Lead with Zinc
	Shillelagh	Lead
	Tinahely	Lead

This approach is different from, for instance, a similar group who might have gone to southern Wales for employment in the heavy industry around Glamorganshire. They learned the work in the foundries in Wales and not in Ireland and then took those skills to mining districts like those in Pennsylvania. The industrialized area of Ireland was Belfast, and the rest of the island was somewhat bypassed by the Industrial Revolution that transformed the countryside in the United Kingdom. In the case of the Beara Peninsula, the men already had the skills.

Riobard O'Dwyer published four volumes on the people of the Beara Peninsula in the remarkable series *Who Were My Ancestors?*:

Who Were my Ancestors?: Genealogy (Family Trees) of the Allihies (Copper Mines) Parish, County Cork, Ireland. [S.l.: s.n.], 1988.

Who Were my Ancestors?: Genealogy (Family Trees) of the Bere Island Parish, County Cork, Ireland. [S.l.: s.n.], 1989.

Who Were my Ancestors?: Genealogy (Family Trees) of the Castletownbere (Killaconenagh) Parish County Cork, Ireland. [S.l.: s.n.], 1989.

Who Were my Ancestors?: Genealogy (Family Trees) of the Eyeries Parish, Castletownbere, County Cork, Ireland. [S.l.]: R. O'Dwyer, 1976.

O'Dwyer accessed the civil records, Catholic and Church of Ireland parish registers, and other documents to gather primary evidence, but the bulk of his information was obtained from interviews with the local people. Thus, the *Who Were my Ancestors?* series is a virtual "who went where" resource for this region of County Cork. The work has several paragraphs on each individual or

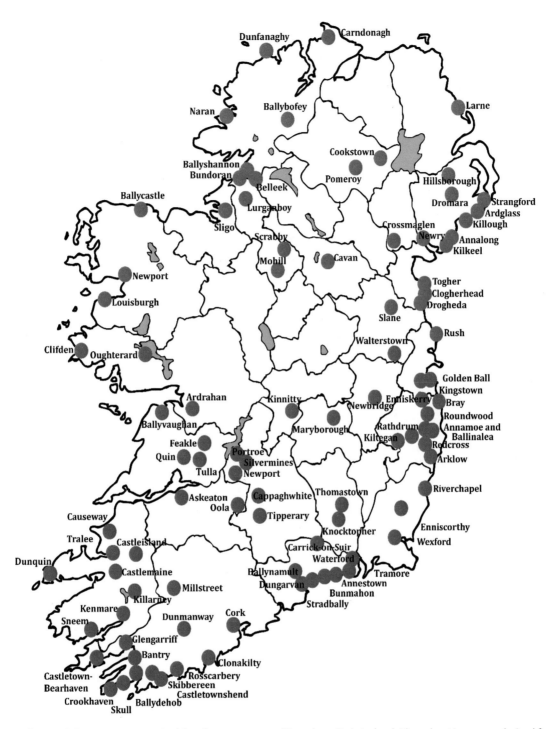

Figure 46: Post towns recognized for silver, copper, and iron deposits in Ireland. These locations were derived from the charts on pages 155-160.

family with names, dates, and events related to them.

Continuing with the Butte and Park City examples, the further the descendants

were removed from those locales, the greater the chance was that all knowledge of the Beara Peninsula origins might have been lost. Yet, in developing an immigration research strategy,

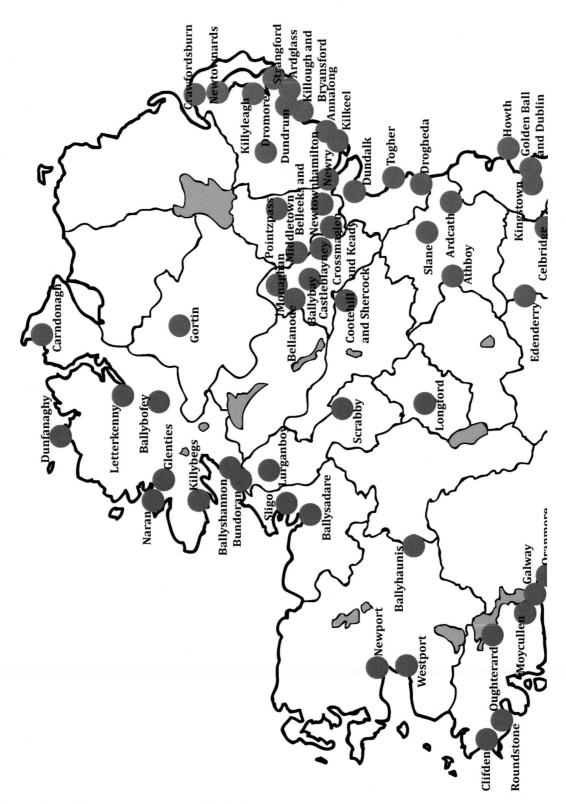

Figures 47a and 47b: Post towns recognized for lead deposits in Ireland. These locations were derived from the charts on pages 155-160.

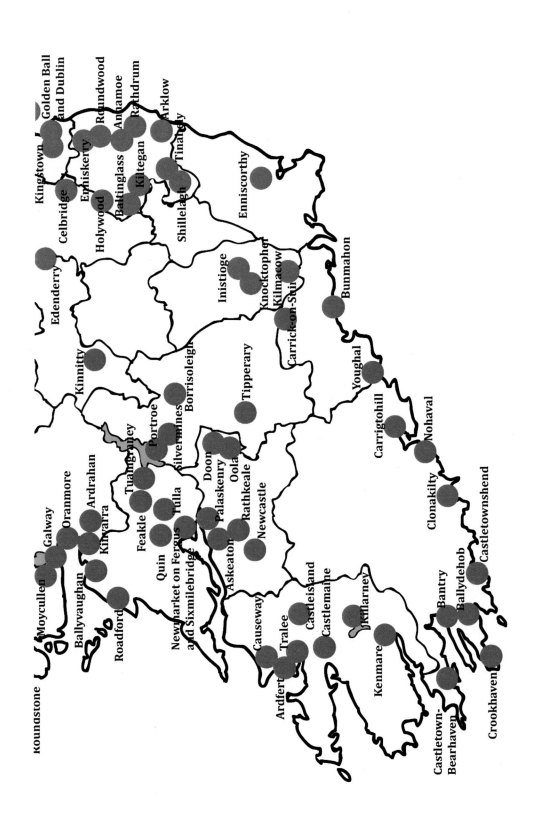

the quest for immigrant origins is in the occupation itself. If ancestors in Montana and Utah were Irish Catholic miners, the sites of mining in Ireland should be considered, especially with copper, as in Butte. Copies of O'Dwyer's books are available in several libraries that can be located through WorldCat.org.

While O'Dwyer provides an excellent model of how an occupation can transfer to the immigrant country, the Butte and Park City example is only one of "who went where." Another occupational migration mentioned in O'Dwyer's work is the Upper Peninsula of Michigan in Marquette County, where the iron ore mines drew immigrants.

The idea is to identify the occupation of the ancestor and then determine if a group of Irish might have gone to that area because they had the same or similar occupation in Ireland. If such was suspected in the Butte and Park City cases, the search is narrowed to mining regions of Ireland. Also, an overabundance of miners from the County Cork seemed to have been in the districts, potentially confining the investigation considerably by separating Cork from the heavy mining operations in Tipperary or Wicklow. From there, the search could be limited even further until eventually the Beara Peninsula migration is discovered by way of Montana and Utah.

No discussion of the Irish mining industry is complete without including coal because so many immigrants worked in the coal mines. Because Ireland is not thought of as a coal producing country and does not extract much of it, coal is almost always ignored in ways that copper and silver are not in developing an immigration plan. Even though Ireland did not have many coal mines, the possibility of the occupation for identifying immigrant origins should be considered carefully. A coal miner in Ireland might or might not have been a coal miner in Pennsylvania or West Virginia, United States, or in northern England.

The counties and the post towns in Ireland where coal was mined or had been mined are listed below and are adapted from *Mineral Statistics of the United Kingdom of Great Britain and Ireland for the Year 1865* (London: Longmans, Green, Reader & Dyer, 1866), pp. 208-209. The places are reliable for research. Some of the mines were not working as of 1865. Collieries, that is, the coal mines with their equipment and buildings, were part of the industry. The directory presents the companies or owners of the collieries as shown on the next few pages.

The number of post towns, only 23 of them, is limited because in each district, several collieries had the same town addresses. An immigrant coal miner may not have worked as such in Ireland, but the counties and post towns can be geographical references to a surname distribution survey through Griffith's Primary Valuation to determine whether the targeted surname(s) is in the vicinity.

Directory of Collieries for 1865

County	District	Post Town	Colliery
Antrim	Ulster	Ballycastle	Ballycastle
		Ballycastle	Murlough Bay
Cavan	Ulster	Kilnaleck	Kill
Carlow and Queens	Castlecomer	Carlow	Agharue
		Carlow	Bilboa
		Carlow	Ridge
Cork	Dunhallow	Banteer, Mallow	Dromagh
		Dromagh, Mallow	Dromingh
		Dromagh, Mallow	Drumskehy
		Dromagh, Mallow	Lisnacon
Kilkenny	Castlecomer	Castlecomer	Broom Park
		Castlecomer	Coolbawn
		Castlecomer	Coolcullen
		Castlecomer	Crutt
		Castlecomer	Curragh
		Castlecomer	Firdoa
		Castlecomer	Jarrow
		Castlecomer	Massford
		Castlecomer	Monala
		Castlecomer	Monteen
		Castlecomer	Rock
		Castlecomer	Skehana
		Castlecomer	Upper Riesk
		Kilkenny	Baurnafea
		Kilkenny	Coolcullen
Leitrim, Sligo and Roscommon	Lough Allen	Boyle	Gobarudda
		Drumkeeran	Geevagh
		Drumkeeran	Greaghnageeragh
		Drumkeeran	Meenashammer
		Drumkeeran	Seltanaskeagh
		Drumkeeran	Tullymurry
		Drumkeeran	Tullynaha
Limerick	Limerick	Abbyfeale	Crataloe
		Abbyfeale	Tulligoline
		Glin	Glin
		Loghill	Coalhill
		Loghill	Knockaboula
		Loghill	Rockview
		Newcastle	Sugarhill

Directory of Collieries for 1865

County	District	Post Town	Colliery
Queen's (Laois, Leix)	Castlecomer	Ballylinan, Athy	Aughamafa
		Ballylinan, Athy	Mullaghmore
		Ballylinan, Athy	Wolfhill
		Ballickmoyler, Carlow	Towlerton
		Ballickmoyler, Carlow	Modubea
		Carlow	Ardataggle
		Carlow	Coorlaghan
		Crettyard, Carlow	Geneva
		Crettyard, Carlow	Glen
		Crettyard, Carlow	Holly Park
		Crettyard, Carlow	Kilgory
		Crettyard, Carlow	Meeragh
Tipperary	Slieve Ardagh	Ballingary	Ballingary
		New Birmingham	Ballycurry
		New Birmingham	Ballynastick
		New Birmingham	Boulea
		New Birmingham	Coalbrook
		New Birmingham	Coolquill
		New Birmingham	Earl's Hill
		New Birmingham	Foilacamin
		New Birmingham	Glengoole
		New Birmingham	Kilcooly
		New Birmingham	Killenaisle
		New Birmingham	Knockanglass
		New Birmingham	Lickfinn
		New Birmingham	The Commons
		New Birmingham	Williamstown
		Stradbally	Kingcote
Tyrone	Ulster	Stewartstown	Annahone
		Dungannon	Coal Island
		Dungannon	Drumglass

It employs the identical strategy as for copper, iron, lead, or zinc mines listed above. Identifying where the mines were operating can help in the absence of church registers in some areas and definitely assists in sorting through some of the common names even if church registers do survive!

Pawnbrokers

A pawnbroker as a profession may not occur to many researchers as an Irish career, but historically, it was. Therefore, if an ancestor was a pawnbroker in the immigrant country, the occupation might have been his or hers before emigration.

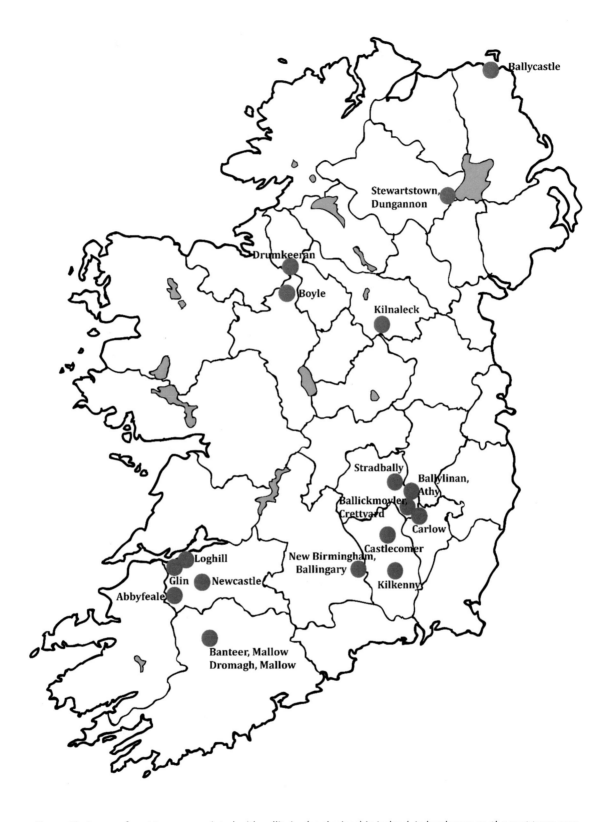

Figure 48: A map of post towns associated with collieries (coal mines) in Ireland. In border areas, the post town may be in one county while the colliery may be in another county.

Pawnbrokers lend money, charging interest, to others based upon goods deposited with them, and many had reputations for being ruthless and operating businesses hidden from public scrutiny. In Ireland, they did not escape the press or the authorities.

In 1837 to 1838, a "Select Committee on Pawnbroking," after investigating the industry, submitted to the House of Commons its findings, which can be found in the *Parliamentary Papers*. The inquiry started because the newspapers in Ireland were reporting that pawnbrokers were charging extortionate and illegal rates of interest on the money lent to their clients. The industry and its damaged reputation were placed under inspection. The probe revealed that the pawnbrokers themselves, especially in Dublin, had been extorted by the organization set up to regulate and protect their interests, the Marshal of Dublin. What resulted for the family historian was not only a public accounting of an industry that often operated in the shadows but also a valuable list of pawnbrokers in Ireland as of December 1837.

The investigation of Irish pawnbrokers can be found online for purchase as a download, and it has been photocopied from the *Parliamentary Papers* and sold as a bound book, which is available in many libraries. However, it is not the only list of pawnbrokers in Ireland. On the Ulster Historical Foundation website on AncestryIreland.ie is the database "Pawnbrokers Registered in Ireland

1832-1833." It also was extracted from the *Parliamentary Papers* and includes names, towns, dates of registrations, tickets issued, sums lent, and comments. Some of the papers mention people's deaths or those who were refused licenses.

Pawnbrokers are a perfect example of how to manipulate information and create a virtual directory of possible relatives of an ancestor. Consult the Ancestry.com database "Ireland City and Regional Directories, 1847-1946" with "pawnbroker" as a keyword with a specific name or surname in the search. Using "pawnbroker" will have results because it was such an unusual occupation. It will collect all the entries from the various directories by occupation and perhaps link an immigrant pawnbroker who might have been one in Ireland. If the pawnbroker ancestor was known to have been from County Cork, a list of all pawnbrokers can be narrowed further, focusing only on those from Cork.

Royal Irish Constabulary

The Royal Irish Constabulary (RIC) was Ireland's police, an armed paramilitary force controlled by the British Government in Ireland. Some 85,028 men passed through its ranks, stationed in 1,400 barracks throughout Ireland. It operated alongside the Dublin Metropolitan Police (1836-1925), which had its own forces. Londonderry and Belfast had their own forces as well, but they were disbanded by 1870, the RIC assuming their duties. The RIC included both

Catholic and Protestant men, with the numbers being almost equal in 1841. Afterward, the number of Catholic RIC members began to rise. In 1851, the RIC was 64% Catholic, and by 1910, 77% Catholic.

Former RIC members who immigrated to other parts of the British Empire were instrumental in establishing police forces. The RIC was the model for the Canadian North West Mounted Police, the Victoria Police force in Australia, and the Royal Newfoundland Constabulary in what is today Newfoundland, Canada (Newfoundland and Labrador joined Canada as the tenth province in 1949), New Zealand, and South Africa. The RIC was disbanded in 1922 and replaced with the Garda Síochána in the Irish Free State (now Republic of Ireland) and with the Royal Ulster Constabulary in Northern Ireland.

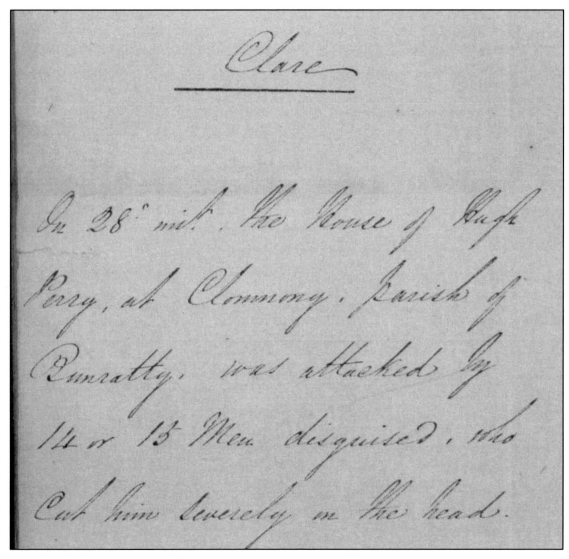

Figure 49: A page from the Outrage Reports, 1836-1840. The claim was dated 28 August 1838 and was formally summarized and logged on 4 September 1838. (This work is produced and copyrighted by the Crown Copyright©. Meeting Open Government License qualifications for this content, no additional permissions required.)

Appendix, Nº 11.—List of Roman Catholic Day Schools

PROVINCE OF MUNSTER:		NAME of Townland or Place at which the School is held.	NAME of Master or Mistress.	RELIGION of Master or Mistress.	Free or Pay School.	TOTAL ANNUAL INCOME of Master or Mistress, arising in all ways from the School.
COUNTY.	PARISH.					
CORK - - (continued.)	Mallow, Female School.	Deal-yard-lane.	Jane Carey - -	Roman Catholic	Free & in part pay.	£. 19. - - - -
	Ballymartyr	Ballintonlas	John Carrol - -	Roman Catholic	Free & in part pay.	£. 10. - - -
	Castlemartyr	Castlemartyr	Redmund Joyce -	Roman Catholic	Pay	£. 38. Scholars pay from 2 s. to 6 s. per quarter, some 1 penny a week.
	Killeagh -	Killeagh -	Patrick Henesy -	Roman Catholic	Pay	£. 5. to 60 l. Scholars pay from 2 s. 6 d. to 4 s. 4 d. per quarter.
	Youghall -	Strand-street	David Burke, John Fitzgerald and Mary Keefe.	Roman Catholics	Free & in part pay.	Burke about 30 l.; Fitzgerald, 20 l. to 30 l., arising from payments of 6 boys, at the rate of 2 l. 13 s. per annum. Mistress from 12 l. to 13 l. received at chapel, and 400 l. bequeathed for that purpose.
	Ballymoodane	Gallowshill, East Gully.	Jeremiah Brien -	Roman Catholic	Free	£. 33. 16 d. - - -

Figures 50a-50b (see following page): School Masters and Mistresses, 1826, from Education in Ireland: Reports from Commissioners, 1801-1826, Vol. 121. (Under UK Copyright law, a publisher's work is protected for 25 years from the end of the year in which the publication occurred. No permissions required.)

The RIC was created in 1816 and consisted of Irish-born men. After 1900, it recruited men from England, Scotland, the United States, and Wales. The original records can be quite detailed, comprising not only recruitment information but also birth information and emigration data.

Historians and genealogists for years have had an interest in the RIC. Its emigration aspect and how it affected law enforcement in various countries is even more intriguing.

The RIC records are indexed and digitized in two databases on Ancestry.com, which are "Ireland, Royal Irish Constabulary Pensions, 1873-1925" and "Ireland, the Royal Irish Constabulary 1816-1921." The pension collection has the digitized images and can be searched by place in Ireland or the place the pension was given. The RIC general database is only the index and provides the FamilySearch.org microfilm numbers. The microfilm is now digitized, and a film/fiche search on the FamilySearch.org catalog using the microfilm number from the Ancestry.com database will link to the collection "Irish Constabulary, General Registers of Services, Returns of Personnel and Intelligence Notices, 1816-1922."

COMMISSIONERS OF IRISH EDUCATION INQUIRY. 121

Founded or Maintained wholly or in part by Subscription—*continued.*

Description of SCHOOL HOUSE, and probable Cost thereof.	Number of Pupils in Attendance:		SCRIPTURES, whether read or not.	OBSERVATIONS.
	By the Protestant Returns.	By the Roman Catholic Returns.		
a room in the before mentioned house.	143	143	not read.	£. 9. 10s. is paid from a subscription fund.
part of a cabin, roofed with straw.	35	70	not read.	£. 2. 5s. 6d. is paid by the parishioners through the Rev. Ja' Walsh, P. P. for the instruction of some poor children.
held in the master's house; cost 50l.	85	110	not read.	£.18. 10s. of the master's income is paid by subscriptions made at the chapel; some R. Catholic inhabitants contribute 5 s. annually. (One pupil of the Established Church in this school.)
house built of clay and clay mortar; similar one would cost 16 to 20 pounds.	108	107	not stated.	The Rev. Rob' Riordan, P. P. pays the master 22 l. 15 s. per annum.
school house is an old dwelling house, built with stone and mortar.	486	486	not read.	Superintended by a committee of subscribers.
house adjoining the chapel -	140	140	not read.	Master's salary paid by chapel collections; and school house built by subscription.

Figures 50a-50b (see previous page): School Masters and Mistresses, 1826, from Education in Ireland: Reports from Commissioners, 1801-1826, Vol. 121. (Under UK Copyright law, a publisher's work is protected for 25 years from the end of the year in which the publication occurred. No permissions required.)

The file number of the RIC member then can be searched. The Findmypast.com version of these two and additional RIC databases allow the digitized images to be accessed next to the index.

In an immigration research strategy, the pension collection is an ideal source for tracing men in Ireland and abroad who served with the RIC. Both the Ancestry.com and Findmypast.com indexes permit a search by birthplace or a more general or keyword search, wherein the immigrant country can be inserted. For example, if a birthplace in Ireland is unknown, Australia or Canada can be the focus of the search.

This is an important genealogical topic with no shortage of information online. Primary documents can be found on The National Archives (KEW) in the United Kingdom website, which has an entire online guide to its collection "Royal Irish Constabulary." Furthermore, do not overlook the RIC historical website Royalirishconstabulary.ie.

One set of records created not about the RIC but *by* the RIC is the Outrage Papers. These are housed at the National Archives of Ireland and are a familiar source for researchers in Australia who are seeking immigrant origins. The Outrage Papers, reports, were written by the chief constables of the RIC and are short synopses of incidents in their counties. Matters are from suicides to robberies, arsons, escapes from jails (gaols), and cattle issues. They were produced before the chaos of the Famine, and so they are a valued source.

Over 18,000 Outrage Papers have survived and are part of the National Archives (KEW) collections. The details vary between RIC jurisdictions, but the basic information should include names (sometimes only surnames), sex, years born, dates of Outrages, addresses, parishes, and counties. The Findmypast.com database "Ireland, Outrage Reports 1836-1840" has both the index and digitized images. The Outrage Papers are part of the holistic approach when documenting someone who eventually was convicted in the courts and transported to one of the many British penal colonies or who was executed.

School Masters and Mistresses

The House of Commons conducted an "Irish Education Inquiry" in 1826. The purpose was to present a study on the state of education at the time. The investigation looked at instructions within the religious and district schools, and, in effect, its report created a snapshot of the teachers throughout Ireland, that is, the men and women and where they were teaching. It is an unrivaled census alternative for 1826 for that occupation.

The Inquiry noted that 11,823 schools were in Ireland. The number of Masters and Mistresses of these schools was 12,530. Of them, 3,098 were of the Established Church, 1,058 were Protestant Dissenters, 8,300 were Roman Catholics, and 74 were of religions not stated. In total, the number of children in religious schools as of autumn 1824 was 560,549 (Protestant) and 568,964 (Catholic). Some schools were operated by various societies and trusts.

The list of Masters and Mistresses teaching at the schools are indexed in the database on Ancestry.com "Ireland, School Masters and Mistresses, 1826." It includes names, counties and parishes where they taught, and the locations of the schools where they were working. In the printed version, which is digitized on Ancestry.com, whether the Masters or Mistresses were teaching at free or pay schools is noted along with their annual incomes. The schoolhouses are also described.

Of course, an ancestor employed as a schoolteacher in the immigrant country is usually proof of an education in Ireland. Often, it is assumed that the teaching career began in the immigrant country, which is not always the case.

From an immigration strategy, an ancestor's reported locality in the index does not necessarily denote the place where the man or woman was born or lived. It was where he or she taught. Yet, the location is an excellent beginning for the search.

Chapter Twelve

Petty Sessions Court Records

The records of the Petty Sessions Courts, which were kept by clerks of the courts, are fascinating. Minor and civil cases were overseen and decided by justices of the peace with no juries in attendance. The justices served without pay and often had no legal training, and so they must have been wealthier persons and perhaps land holders to have realized no incomes from their jobs. The courts were based in towns or cities, but the court districts could cross county boundaries. For example, the city of Athlone was a Petty Sessions Court jurisdiction that was almost equally divided between Counties Roscommon and Westmeath. When reading these records, the geographical factor needs to be considered to analyze findings.

Although the Petty Sessions was established as a court in 1827, most of the books began in 1851 as the government standardized and restricted the responsibilities of the justices of the peace. The justices in time were replaced by trained legal judges. Disputes presented before the judges ranged from wandering pigs or cattle to spousal abuse and public drunkenness. They did not attend to more serious offenses such as murders, which were tried before juries in the Quarter Sessions Courts held four times a year.

The Petty Sessions records are indexed and digitized through a joint effort of FamilySearch.org and Findmypast.com, and the database is on each website. The one on FamilySearch.org is "Ireland, Petty Sessions Court Registers, 1828-1912," and the Findmypast.com edition is "Ireland Petty Sessions Court Registers." It contains 5.2 million cases, but the massive collection consists of only the courts in the Republic of Ireland. The Findmypast.com website has an inventory by county and court for the years covered. Although some accounts began early, most were created from 1851 to 1913. The registers for Northern Ireland are at the PRONI. Since 1924, the Petty Sessions were called District Courts in the Republic of Ireland and Magistrates' Courts in Northern Ireland.

If a county for an ancestor has been found, noting which courts served that county and when they did so is helpful. The investigation can be limited to the county's specific courts. If a county of origin has not been discovered, an index search can display results from all counties in the Republic of Ireland.

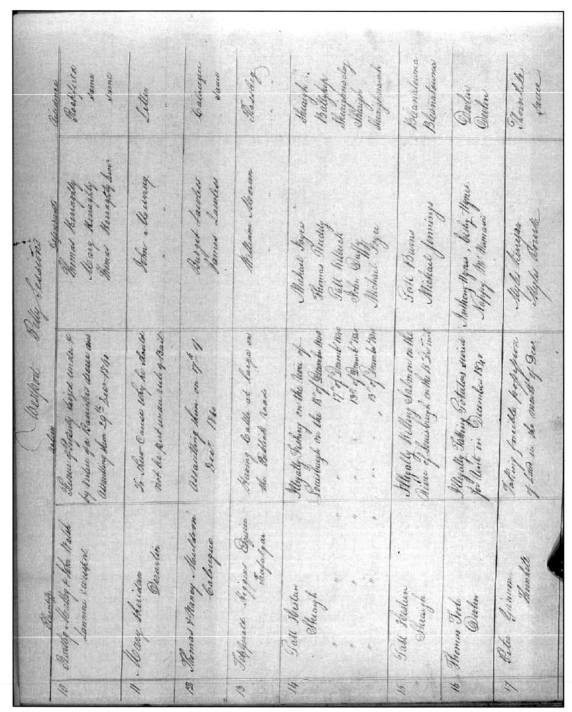

Figure 51: Petty Sessions Court Register page, December 1840, Westport, County Mayo, Ireland. (Image courtesy of FindMyPast.com. Permissions received.)

The digitized images of the manuscript books have more information than the index does. Each case lists more than one person, such as a plaintiff and a defendant. Other people may be listed as well, and they usually are indexed regardless of their participation in the case. Thus, the entire digitized copy for all columns needs to be read for the context of each person's role. The page will include names, addresses, dates in court, witnesses such as complainants (victims) or defendants (accused), the offenses, verdicts, and sentences.

The Petty Sessions Court records have the townlands where the parties resided, the accusations, and the sentences. They are boons for immigrant research if ancestors were entangled in court cases. Legal actions often involved neighbors, and in the areas where the matters occurred, since everyone knew everyone or was acquainted with someone who knew the people being accused, the Petty Sessions Courts' records also are ones about neighborhoods! Whether the charges concerned thefts, violence, or any other seedy activities, the Petty Sessions Courts can provide details found in no other places except possibly newspapers if the infractions were reported.

The digitized and indexed Petty Sessions Court reports, at least for the Republic of Ireland counties, can help with difficult immigration questions. As misdemeanors were local to defendants by their very nature, they easily could have drawn in family members. From records of immigrant countries, names of relatives already might have been ascertained. A valuable clue to the ancestral family is familiar names in one legal action.

While they were not year-by-year sources for many people, as were the dog licenses presented in the example from the register on the page following this, be aware that a certain class of people in Ireland appeared on a regular basis at the Petty Sessions Courts. When a person with multiple cases was no longer named in the records, an emigration is strongly indicated. In addition, the courts sentenced people to the local jails (gaols) or to larger prisons removed from their home counties, which can also account for the disappearances of habitual criminals. Either way, another set of papers is opened for exploration.

Dog Licenses

Perhaps one of the most peculiar sources to seek in solving an Irish genealogical problem are dog licenses. In countries where record collections have survived for long periods of time, the thought of using a dog license to delve into family history would never occur to anyone, nor would it be needed. A viable resource tool in Irish research, though, is a dog license.

Registering dogs with the courts was important, especially in agricultural areas where sheep and cattle were raised. Dog licenses are labeled as such in sections of the books of the Petty Session Courts. If people failed to register their dogs, the cases were brought before, logically, the main Petty Session Courts. The records are indexed on Findmypast.com as "Ireland Dog License Registers," but they encompass only the Republic of Ireland, as they were deposited in the National Archives of Ireland. Even though documentation started in 1865, new courts were added over time, affecting when the transcriptions began. Most courts were indexed for licenses through 1914. A chart for dog licenses designating counties and years is on the Findmypast.com website. The records for the Northern Ireland counties are on deposit at the PRONI.

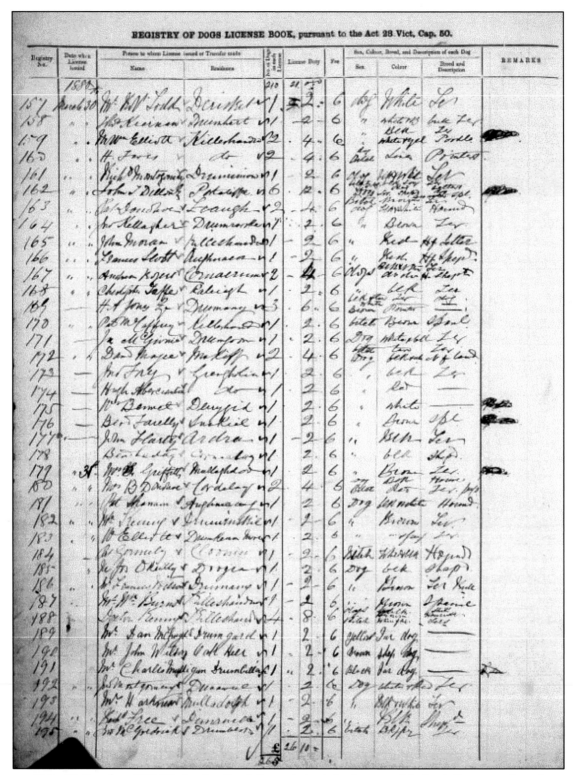

Figure 52: Page from 1880 Killeshandra, County Cavan, Ireland, dog license registry book. (Image courtesy of FindMyPast.com. Permissions received.)

The registers are by court and contain the names of the owners and their addresses, counties, and dates of licenses. The indexes do not include information about the dogs themselves, and for that reason, the registers have to be searched. The details about each dog include color, sex, name, breed, and, possibly, remarks about it.

To present the scope of this information, during 1865, the first year the licenses were issued, 353,798 were recorded. Typically, 250,000 licenses were sold each year. The Findmypast.com database consists of 7,310,994 entries with more to be added. Although it is indexed, it is helpful to locate the court if a county is already known. If a county is not known, the licenses can contribute to a surname distribution strategy or they can be viable census alternatives. Remember that many Irish ceremonies were not registered in church books, or the books had not yet been created. Records such as dog licenses also supply details about people who were born before civil registrations started in 1864 or who were never on the tax rolls because they were not heads of households. Although the licenses are odd sources, they are perfect methods for documenting people who immigrated after the Famine and before the 1901 or 1911 censuses!

Some researchers think of the dog licenses as census substitutes. If ancestors lived in locales where dogs were used for work, such as for sheep herding, the purchases of dog licenses, in essence, were annual censuses of the dog owners. The plan is similar to consulting city directories in urban areas of the world and tax rolls in rural farming districts for yearly sources. When parish registers are incomplete or nonexistent and civil registrations are not much better, all these records can fill in gaps.

Dog licenses thus prove how a peculiar source can identify an immigrant. In regions such as County Donegal where dogs were needed for the wool industry, the dog licenses can be an invaluable tactic for identifying people's birthplaces because of the large-scale emigration and especially because the Catholic registers tended to begin late. As in the rest of Ireland, names, one being John Kennedy as an example, were common. By tracking the licenses, evidence can be gathered about which John Kennedy of the many was the ancestor. If it has been determined from the records of the immigrant country that the ancestral John Kennedy immigrated in 1872, the person by that name who ceased obtaining a license that year could be the ancestor, and the John Kennedys who continued to acquire licenses each year are disqualified from the investigation.

Figure 53: December 1920. Members of the Royal Irish Constabulary Auxiliary bringing in a prisoner after a raid in Dublin. (Photo by International Newsreel Corporation. Courtesy of National Library of Ireland. International Newsreel Corporation was a US based business and therefore subject to US copyright. Corporate authors' copyright expires after 95 years from publication. No permissions required.)

Figure 54: Prison at Castlebar, County Mayo, Ireland, circa 1880. (Photographer: Thomas J. Wynne. Image courtesy of National Library of Ireland. Ireland copyrights apply for the life of the author plus 70 years. No permissions required.)

Chapter Thirteen

Prisons, Prisoners, Transported and the Executed

The methods of managing criminals and the people who were not wanted was independent in Ireland from those in England, Scotland, and Wales. Nevertheless, they resembled one another in many ways. Their complicated, horrifying histories, the subjects of countless academic books, can be divided for genealogical purposes into at least three distinct periods: 1615-1718, 1718-1776, and 1776-1945. The accounts intimately involved the Irish in every era. Before 1788, the year of the founding of Australian penal colonies, the places convicts were sent were more akin to "dumping grounds" than to penal colonies. The distinction is important because the fates of the convicted people differed from the ones in established penal colonies.

Because the handling and transportation of convicts under the government is a subject tied to genealogy and social history, online articles presenting a solid background of the practice abound. Among them is Hamish Maxwell-Stewart's "Convict Transportation from Britain and Ireland 1615-1870." His paper, which originally appeared in *History Compass* 8 (11), pp. 1221-1242, November 2010, is on the ResearchGate.net website and is an example of the many well-documented works available.

The development of the prison industrial complex in the United Kingdom and Ireland created records, especially after 1788. Before that time, evidence can be incomplete. To identify origins of the convicts, it must be stated that this documentation process, largely post-1788, often left papers with birthplaces long before most parish registers in Ireland began.

When examining prison or transportation records, keep in mind that not all the people who were sent away were criminals. Depending on the period and disregarding obvious offenses, political and religious dissidents could have been expelled. Pay attention to the crime as well. A person in Ireland during the Potato Famine could have been sent to another country for stealing bread to feed his or her family. Remember, historically, Britain and Ireland were by no means tolerant societies, and "politically correct" meant something quite different than it does today.

The 1615 to 1718 Period

Before 1718, convicts were sent abroad as laborers and auctioned on the blocks in the Caribbean and American colonies. Once sold by the ships' captains, they were properties of their new masters, who purchased them for chosen numbers of years. The practice was not institutionalized and regulated by law until 1718.

It must be stated that there is no comprehensive listing of convicts transported out of Ireland before 1788. Early records do exist, but they are scattered. Documenting Irish convicts to the American and Caribbean colonies is better undertaken from the records of those places instead of from the Irish records.

The transportation process began with sending convicts and the unwanted to the American colonies to work as servants. The English settlements in North America and the Caribbean were, in effect, dumping grounds for almost any undesirable who could be taken out of Ireland. Prisoners who could work were spared death sentences, and thus the idea of transportation was born. Although all the Caribbean and American colonies received convict labor, most of the offenders were sent to the tobacco plantations in Maryland and Virginia. Transferring convicts from Ireland to Virginia had been discussed as early as 1607, but the first ones were not shipped away until 1620. They were from the Wexford Plantation.

An example of how unexpected material can be valuable is the extractions of letters from the Irish journal *Analecta*

Hibernica, Vol. 4 (1932), pp. 157-169. A letter explaining the types of prisoners to be transported was dated 8 December 1620 and can be found in the *State Papers (Ireland)* 235 (360) 1620. Although the names of those sentenced from the Wexford Plantation were not given, an area of Ireland and a period were opened for records that may be stored in, most likely, Virginia. If ancestors are traced back to this time in Virginia, which had only a few settlements, they may have come from the Wexford Plantation. No document is in Ireland for the convicts for further research, but this one letter from 1620 demonstrates how a small piece of evidence can help identify Irish origins.

Although the Irish had been sent to the colonies from the first decades of the 1600s, the 1641 Rebellion and the rise of Oliver Cromwell and the English Civil War (1642-1651) escalated transportation of convicts and undesirables from Ireland. During this time, terms such as "Barbadosed" entered the popular language, especially in Ireland, to describe being unwillingly taken to the Caribbean and, more specifically, to Barbados. Thousands were sent to the English mainland and the Caribbean. In the Caribbean, they worked in the sugar cane plantations, and in Virginia and Maryland, on the tobacco plantations. This group of transported people should not be confused with the Irish indentured servants, who voluntarily sold themselves and who were already in those locations.

Colonial convicts were purchased as indentured servants alongside persons having no criminal histories but who had freely bound themselves to contracts because of poverty. They were on the same auction blocks as offenders from the British Isles, Africans, Native Americans, indentured servants from India (East India Indians), and others. These public sale markets were beyond any situation modern people can imagine. As researchers step into a world unfamiliar, where none of the modern standards apply, explorations become extremely convoluted and complicated. Yet, the practice changed with the Transportation Act of 1718.

The 1718 to 1776 Period

The Transportation Act, passed in 1718, defined and regulated the shipping of convicts. In effect, the practice as a legitimate form of punishment was institutionalized. Under the system, convicts continued to be carried to the North American colonies in a systematic fashion and sold as indentured servants, accomplished through contracts with the ships' masters. Subsequently, sentences were for designated numbers of years, such as seven for lesser crimes and fourteen for more serious crimes, after which times served, releases were granted.

With the Transportation Act of 1718, the English courts were more likely to relocate convicts than were the Scottish or Irish courts. From the 50,000 prisoners removed by these courts, Ireland sent about 4,000 to work as laborers. However, the practice itself came under scrutiny because jumbled up in this mess of humanity was the underground industry of kidnapping and shipping children and adults to be sold as indentured servants in the colonies. The situation caused

alarm about the management of the entire system. The residents of coastal villages throughout the British Isles lived in fear of their towns being raided next and residents being "spirited away."

In 1743, the Irish Government formed a committee to examine the process. It gathered information on 2,000 persons transported between 1735 and 1743. As a result, the Irish House of Commons tightened the rules governing the transportation of prisoners.

The findings were published as "Report of the Irish House of Commons into Enforced Emigration to America" in the *Journal of the House of Commons of the Kingdom of Ireland, Volume 7, 1796*. It was copied verbatim by Frances McDonnell for her *Emigrants from Ireland to America, 1735-1743: A Transcription of the Report of the Irish House of Commons into Enforced Emigration to America* (Baltimore, Maryland: Genealogical Publishing Co., 1992). McDonnell's is one of the few lists documenting Irish transportation to America in the 1700s. She indexed the entire committee report, and it is a database on Ancestry.com.

Generally, the list includes the names of those sentenced, counties or cities from which returns of transportation orders were obtained, dates of assizes (courts), reasons for transportations, and, occasionally, the names of ships and destinations in the colonies. Distinctions normally were made between convict felons and vagabonds.

The number of convicts transported before the American Revolution may never be known because not all of them can be

No.	NAMES.	Age.	Crimes as stated in the Committal.	When Committed.	By whom Committed.
283	Margaret Ryan	20	To Prosecute for Stealing Potatoes	March 26, 1827	Robt. Travers Esq.
284	William Mahony	24	Keeping forcible possession & Beating for Disarms	do.	Tho. Hungerford Esq.
285	Michl. Harrington	28	Stealing Potatoes	do.	Same
286	John Sweeny	40	Having Stolen Sheep in possession	do.	Revd. Wm. Stackey
287	Owen Daly	24	Same	do.	do.
288	Timothy Daly	18	Same	do.	do.
289	Daniel Deasy	23	Rape on Honora Cronin	do.	Revd. Wm. Ryan
290	Marcus Garvey	34	(Debtor)	do.	Provost of Glenakilty
291	Denis Hanlon	32	Suspicion of Assaulting & robbing Wm. Higgins the Highway	March 27th	Sr. B. Gibbs Esq.
292	Darby Hallinan	26	Sheep Stealing	do.	Same
293	Dennis Carthy	40	To Prosecute for Pig Stealing	March 28th	Robt. Travers Esq.
295	Richard Godson	26	Felony & Sheep Stealing	do.	Sir Maurice FitzGerald
296	John Goggin	18	Aiding in the Robbery of Bridget Goggin	do.	Revd. Atkins Esq.
297	Patrick Linahan	20	Being found in a Mill with Intent to Rob	do.	Same
298	Arthur Hennessy	20	Stealing twelve Shillings from John Long	March 29th	Michl. Roberts Esq.
299	Barry Leary	16	Same	do.	Same
300	Timothy Leary	18	Same	do.	Same
301	Jeremiah Lyhane	20	Stealing Clothes	March 30th	Revd. S. Travers
302	Daniel Murphy	26	Violent Assault on Johana Fitzpatrick	do.	Henry Baddel Esq.
303	David Lynch	20	Making Signals to Smugglers at night	do.	Savage French Esq.
304	John Regan	40	Taking forcible possession & Assault	March 31st	Richd. G. Adams Esq.
305	John Shea	20	Destroying a Potatoe Garden	April 1st	Revd. H. C. Harris
306	Michael Collins	50	To Prosecute for Danl. Donovan for Cutting & Wounding	do.	John Townsend Esq.
307	Cathrine Collins	40	Same	do.	do.
308	Mary Collins	20	Same	do.	do.
309	Judith Hegarty	30	Trespass	do.	C. Corker Esq.
310	William Sullivan	21	Sheep Stealing	do.	Revd. E. I. Alcock
311	Johana Casey	17	Shop lifting	April 2d	Thos. Baldwin Esq.
312	Elizabeth Sullivan	24	Robbing James Barry of Money	do.	Thos. Baldwin Esq.
313	Cornelius Casey	26	Stealing Malt	do.	do.
314	Henry Scofield	14	Plucking Wool off of Sheep	do.	Becher or Coming Esq.
315	John Hamilton	36	Stealing Potatoes	do.	Robt. Travers Esq.
316	Ellen McCarthy	14	Stealing Potatoes	do.	E. W. Hoare Esq.
317	Michl. Mahony McSwiny	40	Cow Stealing	do.	Transmitted from Co. Kerry
318	Johana Warren	25	Same	do.	Same
319	Timy. Shea on. Wise	70	Stealing Clothes	do.	Same
320	Daniel Shea on. Wise	25	Same	do.	Same
321	Margaret Sullivan	20	Same	do.	Same
322	John Riordan	40	Perjury	do.	Spring Assizes
323	Bridget Noonan	20	Vagrant	do.	Chas. B. Gande Esq.
324	John McCarthy	30	Assault on a Magistrate	April 3d	Lord Doneraile
325	Richard Lee	40	Having Stolen Mutton in possession	April 4th	C. Corker Esq.
326	Barthw. McCarthy	35	Pig Stealing	do.	Jno. Townsend Esq.
327	David Brien	20	Picking Pockets in Court	April 6th	Thos. Baldwin Esq.
328	Mary McCarthy	50	Stealing Clothes	April 7th	Earl of Kingston
329	John Deane	20	Perjury	do.	Spring Assizes
330	John Shea	20	Highway Robbery	April 9th	C. Corker Esq.

Figures 55a-55b: Irish Prison Registers, 1790-1924. Stealing cows, pigs, sheep, or money earned the convicted transport. (Image courtesy of the National Archives of Ireland. Permissions received.)

If tried, when, and before whom.	Verdict and Sentence, or other Order.	When Discharged.	By whom bailed or discharged.	If in Custody, or how disposed of.
No Bill		Spring Assizes 1827		Do.
Ignored		Do.		Do.
No Bill		Do.		Do.
Ignored		Do.		Do.
Ignored		Do.		Do.
Ignored		Do.		Do.
No Bill		Do.		Do.
		8th June 1827	Disd. by Medical Commissioner	
No Bill		Spring Assizes 1827		Do.
Spring Assizes 1827. Justice Torrens	Guilty. 7 yrs. Transportat.			Put on board Convict Hulk 7th May 1827.
No Bill		Spring Assizes 1827		Do.
Spring Assizes 1827. Justice Torrens	Guilty. 7 yrs. Transportat.			Put on board Convict Hulk 7th May 1827.
Do. Do.	Not guilty	Spring Assizes 1827		Do.
Do. Do.	Guilty. 6 Mo. hard labour			Sent to House of Correction 11th April 1827.
Do. Do.	Guilty. 7 yrs. Transportat.			Put on board Convict Hulk 7th May 1827.
Ignored		Spring Assizes 1827		Do.
Ignored		Do.		Do.
Spring Assizes 1827. Justice Torrens	Guilty. 7 yrs. Transportat.			Put on board Convict Hulk 7th May 1827.
No Bill at Mallow Sessions		April 20th 1827		Do.
Spring Assizes 1827. Justice Torrens	Guilty. one Month hard labour			Sent to House of Correction 11th April 1827.
		April 10th 1827	Bailed for Sessions before Justice Torrens	
Spring Assizes 1827. Justice Torrens	Guilty. Death Recorded			Commuted to 18 Mo. hard labour. Sent to H. Corn. 23 of 1827.
No Bill		Spring Assizes 1827		Do.
No Bill		Do.		Do.
No Bill		Do.		Do.
Convicted before the Magistrate	3 Weeks Imprist.	April 22d 1827		Do.
No Bill		Spring Assizes 1827		Do.
No Bill at Skibbereen Sessions		May 5th 1827		Do.
No Bill		Spring Assizes 1827		Do.
Spring Assizes 1827. Justice Torrens	Guilty. 6 Mo. hard labour			Sent to House of Correction 11th April 1827.
No Bill		Spring Assizes 1827		Do.
Spring Assizes 1827. Justice Torrens	Guilty. 3 Mo. hard labour			Sent to House of Correction 11th April 1827.
Do. Do.	Guilty. 7 yrs. Transportat.	May 23d 1828	Sent to Cork Penitentiary	
Do. Do.	Guilty. Transport for Life			Put on board Convict Hulk 7th May 1827.
Do. Do.	Guilty. Same			Sent to Cork Penitentiary 26th May 1827.
Do. Do.	Not guilty	Spring Assizes 1827		Do.
Do. Do.	Not guilty	Do.		Do.
Do. Do.	Guilty. 7 yrs. Transportat.			Sent to Cork Penitentiary 26th May 1827.
No Bill		Spring Assizes 1827		Do.
No Bill		Do.		Do.
Mallow Sep. Ass. 1827. Assist. Barrister	Guilty. one Mo. hard labour			Sent to House of Correction 19th April 1827
Ignored		Spring Assizes 1827		Do.
Spring Assizes 1827. Justice Torrens	Guilty. 7 yrs. Transportat.			Put on board Convict Hulk 11th May 1827.
Do. Do.	Guilty. 12 Mo. hard labour			Sent to House of Correction 11th April 1827.
Do. Do.	Guilty. 7 yrs. Transportat.			Hanged herself in Gaol 14 Apl. 1827. Inquest by Coroner.
Trial postponed	Signed Bail	Spring Assizes 1827	Bailed before Justice Torrens	
Spring Assizes 1827. Justice Torrens	Not guilty	Do.		Do.

documented. Even so, between 1718 and 1776, some figures have been established. Through the English and Scottish courts, about 37,000 were taken to the American colonies. The number of Irish people is more difficult to determine, but the estimates are 13,000, all sent mainly to Maryland and Virginia.

The transportation of convicts was never popular in the colonies. While an indentured white servant could be bought from the auction block for about a 4- or 5-year contract, a convict could be purchased for a longer period, typically 7 to 9 years and sometimes, up to 14. The only difference between the two groups in this form of temporary slavery was the duration of labor. Although the owner could have more years of labor from the convict servants, many plantation owners still hesitated to buy them. The colonies sought to ban the practice over the decades because the convicts were not welcome and were even feared.

The 1776 to 1945 Period

With the outbreak of the American Revolution, what became the United States was no longer an option for accepting prisoners. Consequently, the country that would become Australia was born in 1788. Also, another facet of the prison system was invented in the period between the two, the prison hulk ships.

Prison ships, known as hulks, were decommissioned, no longer seaworthy Navy ships. Called "floating hells" by the convicts, they housed prisoners, who worked during the days and returned to the hulks at night. Jobs were at the docks in Gibraltar and the Royal Navy

Dockyards in Bermuda, but hulks lined the coasts and rivers in the British Isles. They also quartered American prisoners of war during the Revolution. Afterward, they were the remedy for the closures of American ports to convicts until the Australian colonies were opened, lodging prisoners until they could be dispatched to Australia.

The courts in England, Ireland, Scotland, and Wales transported convicts separately. In Ireland, the system was always somewhat chaotic and resulted in convict mutinies, prison riots, and the abandonments of convicts by the captains of the ships. The great debacle of over 100 convicts who were cast off in Cape Breton (Canada) in December 1788 led to the British Home Secretary telling the Irish government that it could take convicts to New South Wales only. Transporting them to North America was then banned. However, the ship *Leinster* with 100 men and women from Dublin had already sailed to Newfoundland in July 1789. Those people were deserted by the captain. Starving and sick, they made their way to St. John's. The incident set off a political crisis, refined the laws, and completely undermined the entire Irish transportation system to North America.

The idea behind what became penal colonies, such as those in Australia, was simple: physically remove convicted men and women to a distant location, far away from the general population. If the colony was a community of convicts, it was overseen by a governor or warden who held absolute authority. The British did not invent this institution but merely perfected it on a massive scale. To understand the records being read, background is important for this topic. For example, not all penal colonies succeeded, and so they were abandoned and the convicts transferred elsewhere.

The Jails (Gaols) and Prisons

Several types of jails and prisons were set up in Ireland, among which were the Birdwell, where prisoners were put to work and awaited trial, and the Convict Depot, where prisoners were held before transportation. However, prisons and gaols across Ireland had a variety of purposes.

Many Irish can be found in the series of documents in the Findmypast.com database "England & Wales, Crime, Prisons & Punishment, 1770-1935." Within these records are birthplaces along with the courts in Ireland from which persons were convicted. Currently, it is the largest collection of British criminal records online.

Prison records for the counties now in the Republic of Ireland are at the National Archives of Ireland. They are digitized and indexed on the Findmypast.com website in the database "Irish Prison Registers 1794-1924." Many who were sentenced in counties now in Northern Ireland were documented also in prisons in the south because the main prisons drew from the entire country.

The registers for the individual prisons do vary in information presented. Typical details from them are names, ages, physical descriptions, crimes and the dates they were committed, by whom they

Figure 56: A "Plan of a Traveling Gallows, used in the Year 1798." (Henry Brocas, engraver. Image courtesy of National Library of Ireland. Irish copyrights apply for the life of the author plus 70 years. No permissions required.)

were committed, when and by whom the prisoners were tried, verdicts and sentences, dates of discharges, people who provided bails or discharges, trades, conducts, and the methods by which those convicted were disposed.

This valuable collection documents over 3 million people. Other facts in the registers are names, addresses, ages, birthplaces, occupations, educations, religions, physical descriptions, nearest relatives, details of the crimes, sentences, and dates of admissions and releases (or deaths). Findmypast.com cautions about this database that some of the prisons were nationwide, drawing inmates from throughout Ireland. Therefore, it cannot be assumed that a man or woman who was incarcerated in a particular prison was from that area. The prisons represented in this collection, adapted from the Findmypast.com guide to the database, are:

Locations of Prisons in Ireland

County	Prison	Type
Clare	Ennis Reformatory	
Cork	Bandon	Bridewell
	Charleville	Bridewell
	Clonakilty	
	Cork	
	Cunmanway	Bridewell
	Fermoy	Bridewell
	Fort Carlisle	
	Kanturk	Bridewell
	Kinsale	Bridewell
	Millstreet	Bridewell
	Mitchelstown	Bridewell
	Queenstown	Bridewell
	Skibereen	Bridewell
	Spike Island Prison	Depot
	Youghal	Bridewell
Dublin	Grangegorman Female Prison	Depot
	Kilmainham	Depot
	Mountjoy	
	Newgate	
	Richmond	Bridewell
	Smithfield	
Galway	Galway	
	Loughrea	Bridewell
Kerry	Tralee	
Kildare	Athy	
	Naas	
Kilkenny	Kilkenny	
Laois (Queen's Co.)	Maryborough	
	Queen's County	
Leitrim	Carrick-on-Shannon	
Limerick	Limerick	
Longford	Longford	
Louth	Dundalk	
Mayo	Castlebar	

Locations of Prisons in Ireland (cont.)

County	Prison	Type
Meath	Trim	
Offaly (King's Co.)	Tullamore	
Sligo	Sligo	
Tipperary	Clonmel	
	Nenagh	
Waterford	Waterford	
Wexford	New Ross	Bridewell
Wicklow	Wicklow	

Transportation to the Colonies

Each colony had its unique situation, depending on lands available, jobs required, and political situations. Because all the colonial outposts affect a research strategy, from Irish prison to convict labor or penal colony to freedom in the new country, a list of them is helpful. Research then can be adjusted to the history of that colony and its relationship to the deportations of Irish convicts, tying together the records generated at several points along the way.

When transportation shifted from the "dumping ground" concept to the institutionalized penal colonies, the British segregated convicts according to race. Only in certain colonies were the Irish sent with others from the British Isles. In other words, a soldier from the British Isles who was court-martialed in India was sent to the Australian colonies, not to the Indian penal colonies. Although all colonies were transportation spots to some degree, the list on the following page reflects some of the principle ones.

A notable database of convicts transported to the Australian colonies was produced by the National Archives of Ireland and presented as a gift to Australia for its bicentennial in 1988. "Ireland-Australia Transportation Database" covers 1788 to 1868 and can be searched on the website of the National Archives of Ireland or at the state libraries in Australia. The database was compiled from the following documents:

- Transportation Registers, 1836-1857

- Prisoners' Petitions and Cases, 1788-1857

- State Prisoners' Petitions, 1798-1799

- Convict Reference Files, 1836-1856, 1865-1868

- Free Setters' Papers, 1828-1852; Male Convict Register, 1842-1847

- Register of Convicts on Convict Ships, 1851-1853

Principal Colonies for Penal Transportation

Years	Colony	Modern Country
1614-1776	Virginia	United States
1648-1718	Barbados	Barbados
1650s-1718	Jamaica	Jamaica
1650s-1718	Montserrat	Montserrat
1650s-1718	Nevis & St. Kitts	Nevis & St. Kitts
1650s-1776	Maryland	United States
1733-1734	Savannah, Georgia	United States
1788-1840	New South Wales	Australia
1788-1855	Norfolk Island	Australian Territory
1789 (1731)	St. John's	Newfoundland, Canada
1803-1853	Van Diemen's Land	Tasmania, Australia
1823-1839	Edenglassie (Brisbane)	Queensland, Australia
1823-1863	Bermuda	British Overseas Territory
1842-1875	Gibraltar	British Oversees Territory
1850-1868	Swan River	Western Australia

Because this subject has so many facets, it has been a fascinating source for genealogists and historians alike. Although they are scattered, books, articles, and databases from which to draw background information and genealogical sources are of no shortage. Some databases online focus on convicts transported from a particular county, listing them and their destinations. Usually, the only way to access what has been published in genealogical articles is through Periodical Source Index (PerSI), the product of the Allen County Public Library in Fort Wayne, Indiana. It is on a database on Findmypast.com and is not an index to the millions of articles but, rather, an inventory of titles and subjects. The largest collections of genealogical periodicals in the world are in the United States with the main collection at the Allen County Public Library and the second, at the Family History Library in Salt Lake City.

Other convict records are available in each State Archive in Australia, particularly New South Wales, Tasmania and Western Australia, which received convicts directly from the United Kingdom and Ireland. The details about an individual are wonderful and can sometimes link back to family who remained in Ireland or emigrated elsewhere, such as North America.

Hanging and the Gallows as a Cultural Concern

Today, most people do not wonder about methods of execution. In fact, in the modern, industrialized West, people seldom think of execution at all even though it still does occur on occasions. In the United Kingdom and Ireland of the past, though, the options courts gave convicted criminals were incarcerations, banishments to the penal colonies, or the gallows. The gallows was the other half of the British justice system, making transportation preferable, if granted. The database "Britain, Executions 1606-1955" includes Ireland and is on the Findmypast.com website. Although the registers are not uniform, they can contain names, ages, birth years, years of the events, crimes or victims, dates and places of executions, methods of executions, and names of the hangmen.

A culture developed around hangings and the gallows as *events*. Acquired as well was a language that encapsulated how the common people saw this exceedingly real aspect of their lives. Just the large number of expressions associated with execution by hanging demonstrates how disturbing the subject was to them. The following terms about hanging and the gallows were drawn and adapted from the 1811 *Dictionary of the Vulgar Tongue,* which can be found in several places online.

The following glossary provides insight into the common people and their possible outlooks. In addition, it conveys their daily concerns in words that are difficult to find elsewhere. Clarifications have been added to selected definitions so that they are more comprehensible to family historians. Such terms are in nineteenth-century literature.

Beilby's Ball: He will dance at Beilby's ball where the sheriff plays the music, meaning he will be hanged.

Climb: To ascend the gallows.

Cockles: To be hanged, as in "To cry cockles." The term is thought to have come from the noise made while strangling.

Collar Day: Execution day.

Colquarron: A man's neck. His colquarron is just about to be twisted, meaning he is going to be hanged.

Crop: To be knocked down for a crop is to be condemned to be hanged. Cropped means hanged.

Dance Upon Nothing: To be hanged.

To Dangle: One meaning is to be hanged.

Deadly Nevergreen: The gallows, a reference to "Deadly Nevergreen that bears fruit all the year round." Also referred to as Three-Legged Mare.

Die Hard: To die hard is to show no signs of fear or contrition at the gallows, not to whiddle or squeak. Anxious about the honor of the gang, old comrades of felons who were going to suffer from the law frequently gave this advice.

Drop: An instrument for executing felons by means of a platform that drops from under them. Also termed the Last Drop or Morning Drop.

Frisk: To dance the Paddington frisk; to be hanged.

Frummagemmed: Choked, strangled, suffocated, or hanged.

[Die] Game: To suffer at the gallows without any signs of fear or repentance.

Gaoler's Coach: A hurdle (portable barrier or cage) usually conveyed from the gaol (jail) to the place of execution on a hurdle or sledge (vehicle drawn by draft animals).

Hempen Fever: A man who was hanged was said to have died of a hempen fever (hemp was used to make ropes).

Hempen Widow: One whose husband was hanged.

Jack Ketch: The hangman. Also called Derrick and Ketch.

Jammed: Hanged.

Ladder: To go up the ladder to rest was to be hanged.

Leaf: To go off with the fall of a leaf; to be hanged. Criminals in Dublin being

turned off from the outside of the prison by the falling of a board, which was propped up and moving on a hinge, like the leaf of a table.

Neck Verse: Formerly, the persons claiming the benefit of clergy were obliged to read a verse in a Latin manuscript psalter, which saved them from the gallows. It was Psalms 51:1.

New Drop: The scaffold used for hanging criminals (at Newgate Prison), which, dropping down, left them suspended. By this improvement, the use of a cart in the process was unnecessary.

Newman's Lift: The gallows.

Noozed: Hanged or married.

Nubbing: Hanging. The Nubbing Cheat was the gallows. The Nubbing Cove was the hangman, and the Nubbing Ken was the sessions house.

Paddington Fair Day: An execution day. To Dance the Paddington Frisk was to be hanged.

Picture Frame: The sheriff's picture frame was the gallows or pillory (stocks).

Piss: He will piss when he cannot whistle; he will be hanged.

Pit: The pit was a hole under the gallows where poor rogues unable to pay the fees were buried.

Quinsy: Choked by a hempen quinsy meant hanged.

Scapegallows: One who deserves and has narrowly escaped the gallows.

Scragged: Hanged.

Scragg'em Fair: A public execution.

Sheriff's Ball: An execution. To dance at the sheriff's ball, to loll out one's tongue at the company was to be hanged or go to rest in a horse's night cap, i.e., a halter.

Sheriff's Journeyman: The hangman.

Sheriff's Picture Frame: The gallows.

Slipgibbet: One for whom the gallows was said to grin.

Stretching: Hanging: He'll stretch for it meant he'll hang for it.

Sus Per Coll: Hanged. Persons who have been hanged were entered as such into the jailors' books.

To Swing: To be hanged. He will swing for it meant he will be hanged for it.

Topping Cheat: The gallows.

Topping Cove: The hangman.

Trine: To hang.

Trining: Hanging.

Trooper: You will die the death of a trooper's horse, which meant with your shoes on. This was a jocular method of telling anyone he would be hanged.

Tucked Up: Hanged.

Twisted: Executed, hanged.

Wry Mouth and a Pissen Pair of Breeches: Hanging.

Wry Neck Day: Hanging day.

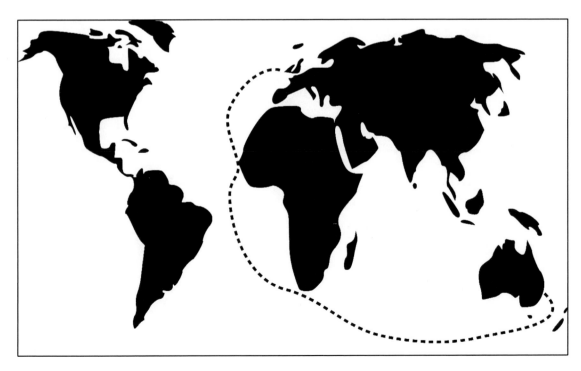

Figure 57: By 1810, this was a typical transportation route to Australia for Irish and British prisoners.

Figure 58: Prison at Cushendall, County Antrim, Ireland. (Photograph by Robert French, circa 1865-1914. Image courtesy of National Library of Ireland. Ireland copyrights apply for the life of the author plus 70 years. No permissions required.)

Chapter Fourteen

Registry of Deeds

The Irish Registry of Deeds is a sizeable and valuable archive of legal documents detailing the population's relationship with the land. The papers date from 1708 to the present day and consist of the buying and selling of lands, leases, subleases, agreements, marriage settlements, and even wills. Tenants on lands sometimes are listed as well. Because the 1922 Four Courts Fire did not affect the collection, which was always kept at the Registry of Deeds office, it became a viable alternative for many of the records destroyed. The manuscripts have been microfilmed, now digitized, and are available through FamilySearch.org as "Transcripts of Memorials of Deeds, Conveyances and Wills, 1708-1929." Until at least 1921, deeds for all of Ireland were registered in Dublin regardless of where the transactions took place.

Many, if not most, Irish ancestors were tenant farmers who leased or rented their lands directly from landowners or indirectly from middlemen. Historically, only a small percentage of people in Ireland, predominantly the Protestant gentry, owned their lands outright, and they were at the top of this pyramid-appearing system of land occupancies and ownerships in Ireland. Between the landowners and the ancestors could have been several layers of subleasing or legal arrangements. The Registry of Deeds is a complicated source, and by no means is the entire population listed in its records. If the goal is finding or confirming immigrant origins in its vast archive, a commonsense research strategy needs to be developed before approaching it. The simplest question is: Would my ancestors qualify for being mentioned in a deed?

Land-holding arrangements, such as rent agreements as opposed to lease agreements, influenced economic wellbeing, the nature of farming, inheritances, and emigration patterns. For example, to an extent because of this system, more than 200,000 Ulster-Irish immigrants flooded into Colonial America from 1718 to 1776. Most were renters without any legal recourse through registered deeds. Later migrations to other parts of the world also were impelled by the tenant problems. The opportunity of owning properties almost anywhere else in the world was a new and enticing concept to these tenant farmers who either rented or had small lease agreements.

Introduction to the Registry of Deeds
Beginning in 1708, land transactions in Ireland were submitted to the Registry of Deeds in Dublin, but because registration was not mandatory, not every land

transaction was filed. Sale and lease agreements, marriage settlements, and wills can be found at the Registry of Deeds. When a deed was taken to the Registry of Deeds, it was not stored there but was returned to the party who delivered it for registration. What was kept in the Registry of Deeds was a "memorial," a synopsis of the deed. From 1708 to 1832, 588,983 memorials of deeds were registered, and a hundred years later, more than 2,500,000.

Registering transactions was for legal purposes, generally between the gentry and the nobility, who were more or less equal in wealth. Although the practice had exceptions, at the outset, determining the social class of a family is advisable.

All parties had to be 21 years old or older, and so minors could execute deeds only through guardians. Traditionally, women did not hold property. Their rights of inheritance were through their husbands or fathers, yet scores of women are documented in the Registry of Deeds. Their listings often have their maiden names and the names of their fathers. Unmarried women and widows regularly registered deeds along with other relatives.

When studying the Registry of Deeds, remember that a deed might have been recorded years after the transaction. Often, a deed cites the earlier contracts involving the buying and selling of the property and how it reached the transaction being sought. These can help sort through the layers of owners, lessors, and sublessors. Some deeds contain only

a few townlands involved in a minor sale, while others may have hundreds. Remember that spellings of townland names are extremely variable in the deeds.

The Leasing of Land

If persons were fortunate in Ireland, they could have had legal deeds between themselves and the owners of the estates on which they lived. Lease agreements make up the bulk of the archive of the Registry of Deeds. A legal lease was preferable to its alternative, which was known as "at will," or basically, at the will of the landlord. "At will" is where most of the people found themselves for generations, having limited legal recourses if the estates wanted to clear the lands of tenants so that cattle or crops could be grown. The "mass evictions" partially defined Irish history, especially during and after the Potato Famine.

Because lands were tied up and farms were small, a system of subleasing was ordinary. A person could lease the farm and then sublet parts of it to other people so that the lessor was the landlord who also had a landlord. Even the landlord at the top of the pyramid was not necessarily the landowner but could have been the person in possession of the original lease agreement with the landowner. Griffith's Primary Valuation (1847-1864) has these successive persons on paper. By comparing the columns of who occupied the lands and who the landlords were, the pyramid of lessees, sublessees, renters, and sub-renters is obvious for entire townlands.

One common lease with great potential for genealogical information was the "lease for lives." A lease for lives stayed in effect as long as the person(s) named in the lease was living. As soon as all the named "lives" died, the lease ceased. A lease agreement for three lives was widespread and was reflected throughout the Registry of Deeds. Interestingly, one of the "lives" could be the King of England, and everyone knew when he died. Another viable "lives" scenario was to have children named, the younger the better. The theory was that the youngest children would survive and have long lives, thus ensuring the lease agreement was valid for many years.

A lease could be granted for a set number of years. Some leases were ridiculous, such as 999 years, but most were for shorter periods. A familiar arrangement was by law. From 1704 until when the Penal Laws were relaxed in 1788, Catholics were constrained by short-term leases of 31 years. Thus, during this period, far fewer Catholics registered than Protestants did, but after the Penal Laws were relaxed, the number of Catholic leases changed. Consequently, for the 1800s, the Registry of Deeds is both a Catholic and Protestant source. By around 1900, the common tenant farmers were able to purchase their farms and houses through the Lands Purchase Act, and so the Registry of Deeds for land ownerships was universal for everyone, rich or poor.

Immigration Strategy

Whether ancestors' names could be in the Registry of Deeds may be predicted by the social statuses of the families. If they immigrated in destitute conditions, they are not in the source because it is not for the poorest of the poor. For both Catholics and Protestants, poverty was the motive for emigrating. They were renters and not lease holders or landowners. However, if people immediately purchased lands in their new countries, hardship was not their reason for leaving. They might not have been rich, but they did bring enough money with them from Ireland to reestablish their lives. Such persons were of a higher social class in Ireland. Yet, small farmers who were not poor could have been involved in lease agreements and are listed in the Registry of Deeds. It was to their advantage to have had legal registered deeds of leases between themselves and the landholders.

The Registry of Deeds can assist with a search strategy for a place name. If a particular area where the family lived is in a record in the immigrant country but an official place name cannot be found, the Registry of Deeds certainly can supply it. It has a "County Index," also called the "Lands Index," that contains all the places by county mentioned in the individual deeds. It is better to know a county, but if not, the search can be limited to all county indexes for a given period, which is a manageable task. The Registry of Deeds preserves many minor place names that have been erased from history. Once the place name is found, the deed itself should narrow the place name further to a barony or a civil parish, thus solving the question of immigrant origins by identifying where the minor place name was located.

56					
Dayly	John & anr.	Way	246	28	157477
	Morgan	Adamson & anr.	229	271	150353
Dascon	Francis	OBrien	217	497	146070
	William	Duson	225	237	145908
	Do	Do	246	281	157958
	Do Eld. & yr.	Upton & anr.	250	320	163945
	Do Eld. & yr.	Do & anr.	261	9	165272
Deacon	John	Shirley	254	137	162989
	James	Harlow	265	11	167781
Deaken	Christian & ors.	Clarke & anr.	206	224	135797
	John & anr.	Do & anr.	Do	Do	Do
	Margaret & ors.	Do & anr.	Do	Do	Do
	Rutt & ors.	Do & anr.	Do	Do	Do
	Do	Astrue	261	146	166992
Deale	William	Darcy	207	383	137718
Deally	William & ors.	Walker	203	32	133696
Dean	& Chapter of ChristChurch	Lodd	199	243	132089
	Do	Fleming	201	377	133413
	Do	Esdall	200	549	134276
	Do	Talbot	203	338	135688

Figure 59: A grantor index from 1758-1768. Note that the grantees (third column) are listed by surnames only. The fourth, fifth, and sixth columns are for volume, page, and memorial/deed number, respectively. (Image courtesy of the Registry of Deeds in Dublin. Works created by an officer or employee of the Irish Government or State are copyrighted for 50 years from the end of the year in which the work is created. No permissions required.)

The grantor (seller) index in the archive is another tactic that can help if ancestors sold lands or the rights to lands before or after immigrating. Again, this applies to only the class of people who were not in poverty. If they sold their rights to lands, they were grantors (sellers) and are in the index. Until a grantee (buyer) index is fully developed, the grantors' index is all that can be studied, restricting the search capability as a result.

If an ancestor was among this class of people, a practical use of the Registry of Deeds is to look for a registered will. It is possible in general to find mentioned in the texts of the deeds, even parenthetically, deaths, inheritances, and relationships of various family members, and so the wills are important. Wills primarily were registered for prominent families and have been extracted from the pages of the deeds from 1708 to 1832 in the following three volumes:

Beryl P. Eustace. *Registry of Deeds, Dublin, Abstract of Wills.* Vol. 1 (1708-45); Vol. 2 (1746-88). Dublin: Stationery Office for the Irish Manuscript Commission, 1954-56.

Eilish Ellis and P. Beryl Eustace. *Registry of Deeds, Dublin, Abstract of Wills.* Vol. 3 (1785-1832). Dublin: Stationery Office for the Irish Manuscript Commission, 1984.

The wills noted where families lived, and if lands were involved, where those lands were located, quickly answering the issue of immigrant origins. However, be aware that the people who had wills were more affluent and Protestant. The published books, aforementioned, also have a place name index that can assist in sorting through the now defunct place names, if needed.

Other strategies can be successful by using the Registry of Deeds, but identifying an ancestor through its records, unless they were of the class involved in deeds, may not be possible. For place name identification, though, it is one of the prime sources.

Historical Land Measurements

One research area that requires clarification is land measurements in Ireland's history before the early 1830s. During this decade, they were replaced by the Ordnance Survey teams (1825-1845) in favor of the English acre. Below is a concise account of some land measurements. All of them may not be encountered in research, but some of the regional ones undoubtedly will be puzzling when they are:

Balliboe: Used in County Tyrone, similar to a Tat[h]e. Conversion: 1 Balliboe = 80 Irish acres.

Ballybetagh: A measurement comprising four quarters, totaling about 1,000 Irish acres.

Cartron: Equal to about 30 acres in Connacht and 60 acres in County Longford.

Carucate: The amount of land that an eight-oxen team could plough in a year, usually between 100 and 120 acres. It also is known as a Ploughland or Villate.

Carvagh: A measurement for acres in County Cavan.

Cunningham Acre: An Ulster measurement. It also was known as a Scottish acre. Conversion: 1 Cunningham acre = 1.3 English acres.

English Acre: The standard unit for measuring land in Ireland from the 1830s.

Great Acre: A measure equal to about 20 English acres.

Irish Acre: Common system of measuring property in Ireland from the 17th century, called a Plantation acre. Conversion: 1 Irish acre = 1.62 English acres.

Poll: A measure of land equal to about 50 or 60 acres.

Sum: A division of land in Ulster known as a collop in other parts of Ireland, considered capable of supporting a family in the eighteenth and early nineteenth centuries. The measurement was based on the land necessary for a mature animal to graze.

Tat[h]e: A measurement for acres in County Fermanagh and Monaghan. Conversion: 1 Tate = 60 Irish acres.

Towne: A local land measurement in County Antrim (also in Carlow and Offaly), equaling about 20 Great acres.

Take note that other measuring systems existed alongside the English (Statute) acres. (English acres are still used in the United States today.) They are found not only in the Registry of Deeds but also in landlord estate papers. In addition, a good portion of the Tithe Applotment is measured in Irish (Plantation) acres.

The most common land measurements are the Irish (Plantation) acres and the Cunningham (Scottish) acres. They convert to English (Statute) acres as follows:

- 1 Irish (Plantation) acres = 1.6 English acre (rounded off from 1.6198 to be exact)
- 1 Cunningham (Scottish) acre = 1.3 English acres (rounded off from 1.2913 to be exact)

Some interesting websites for old measurements include the database on "Index to Units & Systems of Units" on the website Sizes.com, which deals with weights and measurements from around the world. The Irish measurements are well represented in this database. George Gilmore of the Garvagh Historical Society (2011) has a short article worth consulting about the subject, "What Size is an Acre," posted on the website Billmacafee.com.

Indexes to the Registry of Deeds

Currently, two manuscript indexes to the Registry of Deeds have been digitized on the FamilySearch.org website, and an ongoing program is indexing the deeds online. Each index should provide the years or ranges of years, volumes, memorial numbers, and pages where the deeds were registered. Understanding the indexes is the key to accessing the trove of information in this set of records.

Surname Index. The "Surname Index," also called the "Grantor Index," has the names of the sellers (grantors) of lands. It does not list the buyers (grantees), which is a major disadvantage because Irish lands were usually a tangle of owners, lessors, and sublessors. Accessing the grantors may not identify landowners. A grantor might have been the major lease holder. A deed with many grantors is not unusual, and the names of second, third, and even fourth parties also may be indexed. The index is alphabetized by the first letters of the surnames and is arranged by periods that can be extensive or by specific years. Another limitation is that it does not identify the counties or townlands of the properties until after 1833.

Lands Index. A key index for deed research is the "Lands Index," also called the "County Index," which is arranged geographically. From 1836, there are three indexes. While a search of the Lands Index is time consuming, it is the only way to access all registered transactions for a specific place. From an immigration perspective, if a county or place in the county is not known, the

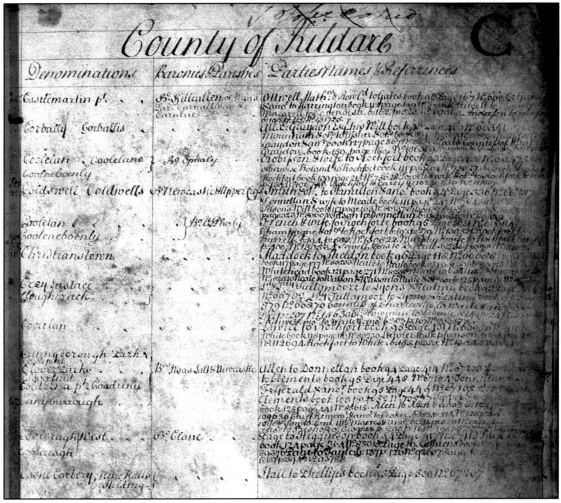

Figure 60: Page from the Lands Index for County Kildare, 1758-1786. (Image courtesy of the Registry of Deeds in Dublin. Works created by an officer or employee of the Irish Government or State are copyrighted for 50 years from the end of the year in which the work is created. No permissions required.)

index is not useful, but it works well when places have been identified or need to be verified.

Registry of Deeds Index Project Ireland: Volunteers are indexing the Registry of Deeds for the "Registry of Deeds Index Project Ireland" on the website Irishdeedsindex.net. The database is constantly growing and has the approval of the Registry of Deeds in Dublin. The project indexes all the names that appear in the memorial books, which include wills and marriage settlements. The indexers use codes to distinguish the kinds of deeds being indexed and the titles of the people involved. The index can be searched by name, grantor, family name, and memorial number but not for a place name. As this index develops, it will continue to be a foremost research tool. In addition, it is valuable in immigration research when a place in Ireland is not known. Once a person is identified in the index, the deed can be consulted on the FamilySearch.org website to obtain all the geographical locations mentioned within it.

Irish Land and Tax Dictionary

The benefits to research from the Registry of Deeds lead into those from tax lists. Both deal with properties and the conditions under which they were occupied, leased, or owned. The following "Irish Land and Tax Dictionary" was developed as a single dictionary that includes terms from the Registry of Deeds as well as from tax lists, such as the Tithe Composition Books (1823-1837) and Griffith's Primary Valuation (1847-1864). Many terms also relate to the estate records of the landlords in the forms of leases and rent books. The crossover of terms between land, tax, and estate records is noteworthy.

Glossaries have been compiled for the tax lists, but, currently, the Registry of Deeds has few. Thus, the English land law terms are the definitions for the Irish land deeds because both systems are based on English Law.

& ors*:* And others

& an(r)*:* And another. Sometimes refers to a man's wife.

Abut(ment)*:* In describing land boundaries, the shorter sides are said to abut on the adjacent plots, and the longer sides lie between them. It is seen when describing town lots.

Acre(age): In Ireland, this unit of measurement can have any number of meanings. The particular unit of measurement is mentioned in the deeds. (*See* Cunningham Acre, English Acre, Irish Acre, Plantation Acre.)

Agnomen*:* A secondary name, often given by the tax assessor to distinguish between two individuals with identical given and surnames who occupy holdings in the same townland. Father's given name, hair color, height, occupation, and similar distinguishing terms were used.

Irish Land and Tax Dictionary (cont.)

Applotment: The share of the total tax that was imposed upon each individual who was responsible for paying taxes.

Applotter: A person experienced in valuing property, both lands and buildings.

Articles of Agreement: *See* Conveyances

Assignments: *See* Conveyances

Attornment: Power of Attorney.

Balliboe: A local land measurement used in County Tyrone, equal to about 80 Irish acres. It is similar to a Tate. (*See* Tate)

Bally: The many town names beginning with "Bally" derive from the Irish baile, meaning homeplace or townland.

Ballybetagh: A land measurement comprising four quarters, totaling about 1,000 Irish acres. (*See* Irish Acre)

Barony: Based historically on original Gaelic family territories by Anglo-Norman occupiers. These administrative boundaries cross county lines. The properties mentioned in the Lands/County Index from 1828 are divided by the barony within the county and are important in genealogical research. Also called a Cantred.

Bills of Discovery: These deeds were filed when it was known that Catholics held more property than was legal. Bills of Discovery were usually filed by Protestant friends of Catholic property owners to pre-empt hostile bills.

Borough: A town granted Corporation status through a royal charter. Boroughs elected MPs to sit in the Irish House of Commons. A citizen of a borough was called a burgess.

Burgess: *See* Borough

Cantred: *See* Barony

Cartron: A local land measurement equal to about 30 acres in Connacht and 60 acres in County Longford.

Carucate: The amount of land that an eight-oxen team could plough in a year, usually between 100 and 120 acres. It is also known as a Ploughland or Villate.

Carvagh: A local unit of measurement for acres in County Cavan.

Irish Land and Tax Dictionary (cont.)

Cess*:* Tax or assessment.

Chancery*: See* Court of Chancery

Civil Parish*: See* Parish

Close*:* Enclosed piece of land, especially in contrast to the common field from which it might have been taken.

Collop*: See* Sum

Common Land*:* Land held in common by residents of a townland. This was known as the Rundale system.

Conacre*:* A system whereby land was let, not for a number of years but for a single season (eleven months), with the rent paid in labor by the occupier.

Contingent Remainder*:* A remainder limited in such a way as to depend on some event or condition which might never occur. (*See* Remainder)

Conveyances*:* The transfers to others of the rights, interests, or titles to properties. Also known as sales and assignments, they contain provisos that the grantees are to hold the properties "for ever."

Corporation Towns*: See* Borough

Cottage*:* A dwelling house of small size, such as one occupied by farm laborers, villagers, miners, etc.

Cottager*:* A peasant who occupies a cottage belonging to a farm, sometimes with a plot of land attached on which the cottager has to work at a fixed rate, when required. In Ireland, the system was known as a Cottier Tenure. The main feature of this system was the letting of the land annually in small portions directly to laborers (Cottiers), the rents being fixed not by private agreement but by public competition.

Cottier*: See* Cottager

Cottier Tenure*: See* Cottager

County*:* A major land division created for local government by the English between the Norman invasion and 1606.

County Borough*:* Towns or cities along with small surrounding areas created by medieval charters. There were eight County Boroughs: Carrickfergus, Cork, Drogheda, Dublin, Galway, Kilkenny, Limerick, and Waterford.

Irish Land and Tax Dictionary (cont.)

County Cess: A local tax levied on the occupiers of land (owners and tenants) to finance the operation of the Grand Jury.

Court of Chancery: This court served to settle disputes between parties by using rules of equity and conscience to give relief to the parties when no remedy could be found by a strict interpretation of the law in a common-law court. (*See* In Chancery)

Cunningham Acre: This unit of measurement came from Scotland to Ulster. It is designated as such in the texts of deeds. The Ordnance Survey under the Boundary Survey (1825) began replacing local measurements with English acres. It is also known as a Scottish acre. Conversion: 1 Cunningham acre = 1.3 English acres.

Demesne: Land occupied by a lord for private use.

Demise: The transfer of an estate by lease or upon the death of the owner.

Dower: The life interest of a wife in one-third of the lands and tenements that her deceased husband possessed.

Easement: A privilege without profits; e.g., a right of way the owner of a property has over an adjoining one.

English Acre: The standard unit for measuring land in Ireland from the 1830s. (*See* Cunningham Acre; Irish Acre; Plantation Acre)

Entail: An estate to be inherited according to a defined line of descent. (*See* Fee Simple)

Equity: A system of law that originated in the Court of Chancery and supplements common law by providing a remedy where none exists in the law. (*See* Court of Chancery)

Exchange: A deed of exchange is a reciprocal conveyance of property by two parties.

Fair Green: Land in a town or village set aside for activities on market day.

Fee: *See* In Fee

Fee Simple: A freehold or estate of inheritance.

Fee Tail: Estate in which the inheritance is limited.

Free: A person who holds property by the right of possession and recognizes no landlord. The tenure is called Free, which means squatter.

Freehold: A form of tenure in which land is held in fee simple, fee tail, or for a term of life.

Irish Land and Tax Dictionary (cont.)

Freeholder: A term found in tax lists that refers to the tenure of the rector or incumbent of a Church of Ireland parish in the case of the church's Glebe Lands.

Glebe Lands: Land occupied by Church of Ireland ministers.

Grange Lands: Land formerly belonging to a monastery.

Grantee: A buyer in a transaction.

Grantor: A seller in a transaction.

Great Acre: A measure equal to about 20 English acres. (*See* English Acre)

Hereditaments: Property that can be inherited.

House: A building used as a dwelling or a public building such as a house of worship, court-house, etc.

Immediate Lessor: A landowner who occupies a property or a middleman who leases from the landowner and, in turn, rents all or part of the property to another individual. The land-owner and the middleman are customarily referred to as landlords.

In Chancery: The name of the reputed proprietor of a holding in litigation in the Court of Chancery. (*See* Court of Chancery)

Indenture: A deed in which there are two or more parties.

In Fee: Owner

Irish Acre: An old, common system of measuring property in Ireland from the 17th century. The Ordnance Survey under the Boundary Survey (1825) began replacing local measurements with English acres. It was also called a Plantation acre. Conversion: 1 Irish acre = 1.62 English acre.

Laborer: See Cottager

Landlord: See Immediate Lessor

Land Measures: *See* Irish Acre

Lease: An agreement usually mentioned in the first part of a deed. This is the most common deed in Ireland. Leases are for fixed periods or for ones that extend over the lifetimes of persons alive at the time. A common lease was for three lives or for 31 years, whichever was longer. Another common lease period was 21 years. (*See* Lives)

Irish Land and Tax Dictionary (cont.)

Lease and Release: This is not an exact term, but it was used in the registration of many types of deed transactions. It can refer to deeds of sales, assignments/conveyances, rent charges, actual leases, mortgages, and even marriage settlements. The term is common in the Registry of Deeds.

Liberty: A civil unit, with authority granted by the Crown.

Lives: Leases were often given for the term of three lives, i.e, until the last of three people named was deceased. One party might have been the person transacting the lease; the other two might have been family members or friends. A common practice was to use the King's name because as a recognized person, everybody knew when he died. The lives are important in genealogy if the people are family members.

Lot: A section of land with a single physical quality.

Manse: A house occupied or formerly occupied by a minister.

Marr. Arts./ M. Arts: Marriage Articles. (*See* Marriage Settlement)

Marriage Articles: *See* Marriage Settlement

Marriage Settlement: Usually recognized as "articles of agreement" or by the mention of the marriage itself. This deed has the names, occupations, and addresses of the groom, the bride, and the bride's father. It often gave the date of the marriage. Family members were usually listed as trustees. Abbreviated as "Marr. Art" and "M. Arts." in the records.

Memorials of Deeds: The common term referencing the deeds. The memorial itself is a copy of the original deed sent to the Registry of Deeds and entered as an official document.

Middleman: An individual who leases a sizeable quantity of land from a landowner and sub-lets it to tenants, often at an excessive rent (rack rent).

Mortgages: The deeds of mortgages either say they are mortgages or that the property is conveyed with a redemption clause. Mortgage deeds are complex. The purchasing of a mortgage served the same purpose as the modern stock market.

Occupier: An individual or party who owns, leases, or rents a tenement.

Office: A building occupied by a factory, mill, store, stable, cow shed, pig sty, etc.

Orwise: Otherwise. Often used in giving a woman's maiden name in a deed.

Pale: The English Pale in Ireland encompassed Counties Dublin, Kildare, Louth, and Meath.

Irish Land and Tax Dictionary (cont.)

Palatinate: Area overseen by a lord who was granted extensive rights by the Crown. The Palatinate of Tipperary existed until 1715.

Parcel: A piece of land sometimes in a common field.

Parish: When used in a deed or tax list, a civil parish.

Partition: A deed of partition is an agreement to divide an estate.

Plantation: A section of an estate set aside by the owner for the planting and cultivation of ornamental trees and shrubbery for later planting on the manse. (*See* Manse)

Plantation acre: *See* Irish Acre

Ploughland: *See* Carucate

Poll: A measure of land equal to about 50 or 60 acres.

Poor Law Union: An administrative division created in 1834. It encompassed a market town and the surrounding area, in which taxpayers were assessed for the poor law rate.

Pound: An enclosure maintained by an authority for the detention of stray or trespassing cattle as well as for the keeping of distrained cattle or goods until redeemed.

Pound (money): Twenty shillings equal one pound of money.

Quality Lot: The part of a holding distinguished by the quality of the soil for valuation purposes.

Quit Rent: *See* Customary Tenure

Rack Rent: *See* Middleman

Recital: The preliminary statement in a deed showing the reason for its existence and explaining the operative part.

Relief of Dower: The assurance by a married woman to the purchaser of land that she relinquished her right to dower in it, generally unnecessary because the woman and her husband together made the conveyance. (*See* Dower)

Remainder: A future interest in property. An interest in a particular estate that will pass to a person at some future time, as upon the death of the current possessor. (*See* Contingent Remainder)

Irish Land and Tax Dictionary (cont.)

Rent Charge*:* A fixed sum of money paid to a person from the income of a piece of property. This was considered income for many families.

Reps of*:* An abbreviation for "representatives of," an indication that someone had died when a legal action was undertaken.

Ruin*:* Often seen in tax lists when a building is in ruins and does not have a roof.

Rundale System*: See* Common Land

Runrig*:* Another name for the Rundale System. *See* Common Land

Rural District*:* An administrative division created by the Local Government (Ireland) Act, 1898, when the Poor Law Unions were dismantled. Its boundaries were the same as the original poor law union electoral divisions.

Sales*: See* Conveyances

Scottish Acre*: See* Cunningham Acre

Severance*:* The division of an estate into independent parts.

Shilling*:* In mid-nineteenth-century Ireland, twelve pence (*d*) equaled one shilling (*s*). Twenty shillings equaled one pound.

Sum*:* A division of land in Ulster, known as a collop in other parts of Ireland. Considered capable of supporting a family in the eighteenth and early nineteenth centuries. The measurement was based on the land necessary for a mature animal to graze.

Tat[h]e: A local unit of measurement for acres in County Fermanagh and Monaghan. The Ordnance Survey under the Boundary Survey (1825) began replacing local measurements with English acres. Conversion: 1 Tate = 60 Irish acres. (*See* Irish Acre)

Tenant: An individual who rents or leases property by paying a stated rent to the middleman or owner.

Tenement*:* Any holding of land as well as a dwelling.

Tenure (Customary)*:* A tenure protected a tenant by title written in the manor court roll. Most tenures were held from the lord according to the custom of the manor. For example, certain services to the manor that were later commuted to cash payments. (*See* Quit Rents)

Tithe*:* A ten percent payment to the Established Church, required of persons of all faiths. In early periods, the tithe was paid "in kind," i.e., with produce from the fields, dairy, and farm. Under the Tithe Act of 1823, tithes could be paid by composition (i.e., money).

Irish Land and Tax Dictionary (cont.)

Title: The means by which an owner of land has the right to possess that property.

Towne: A local land measurement in County Antrim (also in Carlow and Offaly), equaling about 20 Great acres.

Townland: The smallest official government administrative division. Beginning in the 1830s, townlands had standard boundaries and names. Before this determination by the Ordnance Survey, boundaries and names were somewhat changeable. The early Registry of Deeds commonly provided alternative names as well as the most widely recognized ones.

Townreed: Township.

Trust: The estate of a person who is invested with the legal ownership of land on the condition that it is held for the benefit of another.

Villate: See Carucate

Waste: Ground under houses, yards, streets, and small gardens; land under barren cliffs, beaches, along the seashores, and small bodies of water.

Will: A probate record that deals primarily with real property (land).

Sources: Irish Land and Tax Dictionary

Cornwall, Julian. *How to Read Old Title Deeds XVI-XIX Centuries.* Shalfleet Manor, Isle of Wight: Pinhorns, 1970, pp. 39-40, 44-46.

Cornwall, Julian. *Reading Old Title Deeds,* 2nd ed. Birmingham, England: Federation of Family History Societies (Publications), Ltd., 1997, pp. 45-49.

Family History Library Staff. *Register of the Registry of Deeds Ireland With Surname and County Indexes.* Salt Lake City, Utah: Family History Library of The Church of Jesus Christ of Latter-day Saints, 2002, pp. vi-vii.

Fitzpatrick, James F., Esq. *A Practical Guide to the Valuation of Rent in Ireland.* Dublin: E. Ponsonby, 1881.

Reilly, James R. "Is there More in Griffith's Valuation Than Just Names?" *The Irish At Home and Abroad* 5, #2, 1998. pp. 58-69.

Reilly, James R. *Richard Griffith and His Valuations of Ireland.* Baltimore, Maryland: Clearfield Co., 2000, pp. 67-68.

Reilly, James R. "The Sacred Tenth: The Tithe Applotment Book as a Genealogical Resource." *The Irish At Home and Abroad* 3, #1, 1995/96, pp. 4-9.

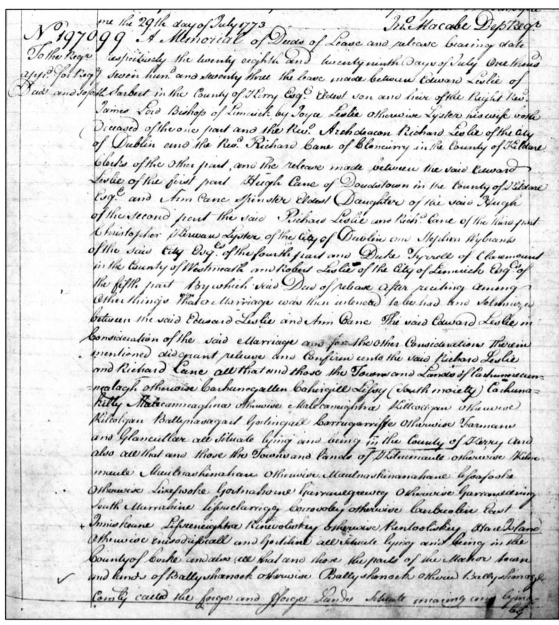

Figure 61: Land deed of Edward Leslie and Richard Leslie, dated 1773. It illustrates numerous relationships and identifies some of the people who were deceased. (Image courtesy of the Registry of Deeds in Dublin. Works created by an officer or employee of the Irish Government or State are copyrighted for 50 years from the end of the year in which the work is created. No permissions required.)

Figure 62: Sir Richard Griffith, the man behind Griffith's Primary Valuation. Image widely used across all media formats. No provenance from which to request permission is discernable.

Figure 63: Shared from Griffith's Survey Maps and Plans, 1847-1864, Townland of Aghsmear in the civil parish of Corbally, County Tipperary, Ireland. (Image courtesy of the Ordnance Survey in Dublin. Permissions received.)

Chapter Fifteen

Tax Records

Tax records, although they do not carry birthplaces, are indispensable for tracing any Irish ancestor because they position persons in exact places at specific times. The key to where an immigrant ancestor originated may be in the county, civil parish, or townland where his or her home and land were appraised and taxed. Frequently, the rest of the search for Irish origins can make sense from the locations.

To discover immigrant origins through taxes, the major ones to access are the Tithe Applotment Composition Books (1823-1837) and Griffith's Primary Valuation of Ireland (1847-1864). They, however, are not the only sources available, and if research is limited solely to them, something may be missed or the wrong family may be selected. In a holistic approach to immigrant origins, this chapter covers the following Irish tax records:

- Tithe Applotment Books (1823-1837)
- Tithe Defaulters List (1831)
- Valuation Office Books (1820s to mid-1850s)
- Griffith's Primary Valuation (1847-1864)
- Valuation Office Revision Books (1850s to present)

The presentation of the foregoing will be in chronological order to demonstrate the flow of the process. Most researchers begin with Griffith's Primary Valuation (1847-1864) and work backward and forward from that point.

Researchers refer to Irish tax rolls as "census substitutes" or "census alternatives" because the documents, especially Griffith's, can name landowners (in fee), renters, leaseholders, and even squatters (free), depending on the record group being consulted. Certainly, the definition of the tax reports explains why people consult them to locate persons. Nevertheless, they apply only to the parties paying the taxes, typically the heads of the households. Other family members were not listed, which means the rolls must be scrutinized to obtain all details that might not be immediately evident.

Ignoring tax lists because an ancestor might have emigrated before they were constructed is a mistake. The dates the records were made are precisely when they are most valuable in the search for immigrant origins. After all, it was not exceptional for family members to stay and take over the old family home and farm. A tax list from a hundred years after an ancestor left could include the old home if it had been bound to family members in a lease or rental agreement.

Immigration Strategies

Regardless of whether an ancestor emigrated before or after the tax lists were created does not matter. One tested and successful strategy commonly used among family historians is the surname distribution, which can pinpoint an ancestor's home, especially in the absence of church registers. It may be the only way to prove that an ancestor was from that townland. The evidence may not be direct, but if it is all that is left, it is considered good merely because it is the only substantiation.

The goal is to restrict the county, civil parish, and townland where the ancestors lived. Doing so is currently easier than it was in the past because of the online indexes to the tax lists. Those most used are on Ancestry.com, FamilySearch.org, and Findmypast.com. Other important ones are on Askaboutireland.ie and the website of the National Archives of Ireland.

A county already known from the records of the immigrant country is helpful in an index search. In most cases, though, the county is likely unknown, and the taxes for the entire island must be considered.

One approach is to find where the full name of the immigrant ancestor appears, which works well if the first or last name is uncommon. Even if the ancestor was gone for a long time, a given name that was not ordinary might have been passed down through another branch of the family. Ignoring the first name and placing the emphasis on a surname like Kelly or Sullivan to narrow a place of origin will not be successful unless either is attached to an unusual given name.

If a couple was married in Ireland, the wife's surname can be searched in the database for the counties or parishes in which the two surnames intersect. In the surname distribution search, if a surname is found in only three counties, the odds are that one of these is the county of origin. With two surnames, the distribution search may be more effective because it potentially shortens the list of counties even more.

The logic is straightforward when using the maiden name of a wife to limit the search. For the couple to marry in Ireland, the idea is that at some geographical point, the two families became acquainted, perhaps at a church meeting, as neighbors, or in a market town on market day. Not all marriages can be documented through the church registers, and so the surname distribution search is even more vital.

Because a tenant farmer might not have owned a horse, travel was confined to walking or riding with someone who had a wagon. If couples were in rural areas and on foot, their opportunities for encountering one another were diminished, but travel on wagons broadened the distances. An interesting scenario is how the market town as a meeting place can disrupt an immigrant research plan.

Market towns had their fairs and market days and drew people from extensive surrounding regions. A man could have been from several miles in one direction of the town and a woman from several miles in the opposite direction. When studying the tax indexes for patterns, be aware of where the market towns were located from a map and form a hypothesis about the areas from which they drew people. The indexes then will make more sense. In short, the first assumption is that a young man and woman to have met must have lived close to each other, but other options have to be considered.

In a surname distribution strategy with the surnames of the husband and wife, make sure from the records of the immigrant country that the couple was not married abroad. If records are incomplete, the principle of beginning research, although sometimes incorrect, is that the marriage took place outside Ireland if all the children were born in the immigrant country. However, take into account that the couple could have married in the immigrant country and still have been from the same Irish county.

From tax records generated in the 1800s, a standard genealogical tactic for researchers whose ancestors left in the 1700s is the surname distribution survey, to simply gain knowledge of where surnames were located. Remember, not everyone left Ireland. An ancestor's sibling or cousin might have stayed, and his or her descendants were taxed in the 1800s. They had the same surname, but they were different branches separated by a century. If relatives were not living in the same townlands and civil parishes as the ancestors had been, probably they were not far away.

Another conventional method for immigration research is to confirm or eliminate targeted people through tax lists. Never forget that names in Ireland can be common, and thus family historians cannot assume the names that are the same as those of their ancestors on tax lists are their ancestors.

If a relevant entry is found in the indexes and it is strongly suspected that this could be the ancestor, proof has to be produced. For example, several sets of tax records need to be studied for the person. If a name of interest is in Griffith's Primary Valuation records, did it disappear from the later tax lists, known as revision books? If a person continued to be taxed after the ancestor is known to have emigrated, he or she is not the ancestor. If the name is crossed off the revision books about the time the ancestor emigrated, the probability is drastically increased that this is the correct person. From that fact, some evidence has been found, but other records will need to be followed to support the supposition.

Tithe Applotment Composition Books (1823-1837)

The tithe was a tax based on how much land a person occupied, and it was paid by rural inhabitants for the support of the Church of Ireland. The established church was responsible for the well-being of the parish before the government took over specific civil responsibilities, such as road upkeep and care of the poor. The tax was applied to persons of all faiths. To say the least, it was not popular.

The tithe was not limited to one period in Ireland. The Church of Ireland, as the

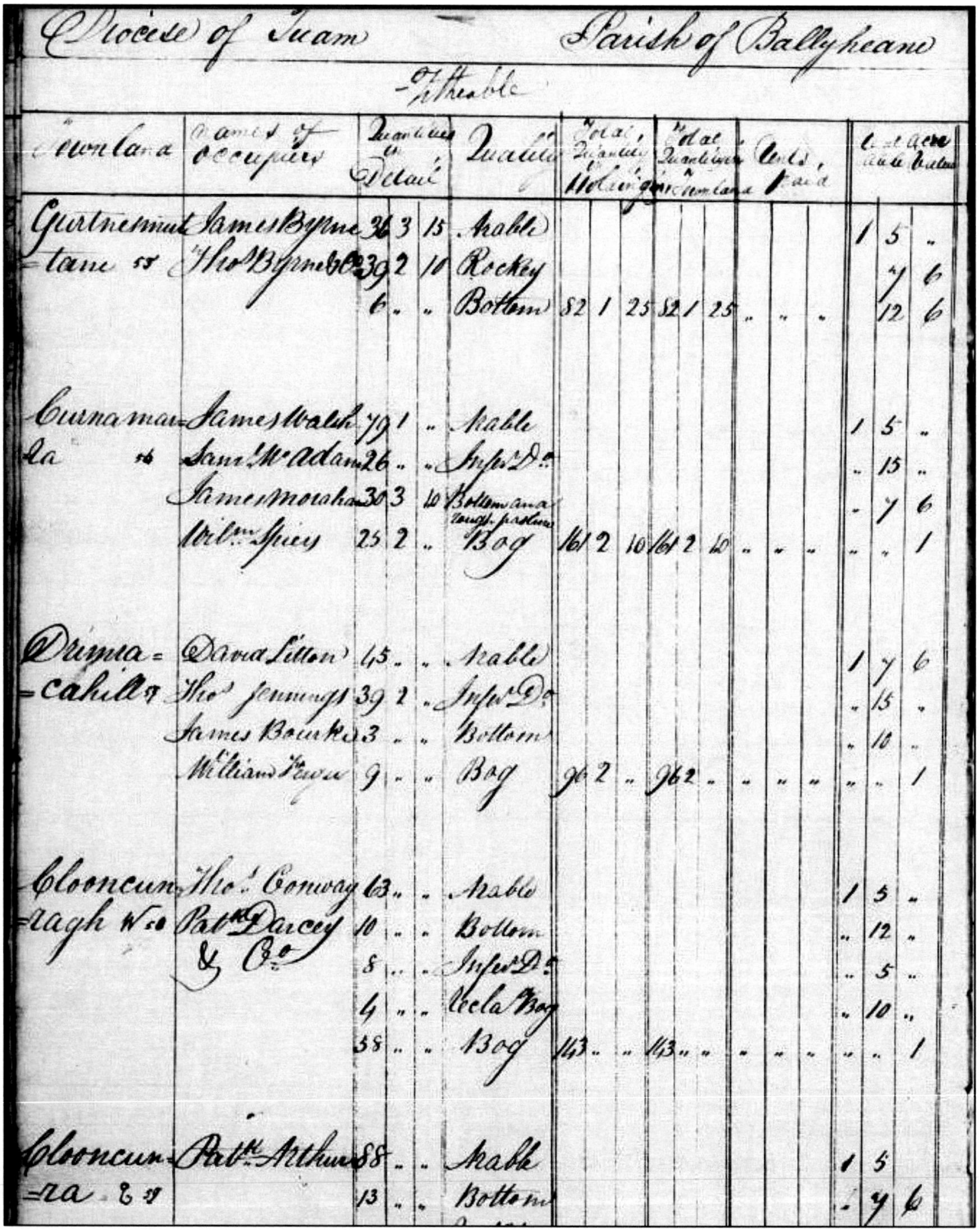
Diocese of Tuam — Parish of Ballyheane

Titheable

Townland	Names of occupiers	Quantities & Detail			Quality	Total quantity of holding	Total quantity in townland	Rate per acre
Gurtnemuntane 55	James Byrne	36	3	15	Arable			1 5 ..
	Thos. Byrne & Co.	39	2	10	Rockey			7 6
		6	..	..	Bottom	82 1 25	82 1 25	12 6
Curnamarla 46	James Walsh	79	1	..	Arable			1 5 ..
	Saml. McAdam	26	..	..	Infer. Do.			15 ..
	James Morahan	30	3	10	Bottom and rough pasture			7 6
	Willm. Spicy	25	2	..	Bog	161 2 10	161 2 10	1
Drumacahill 47	David Litton	45	..	..	Arable			1 7 6
	Thos. Jennings	39	2	..	Infer. Do.			15 ..
	James Bourke	3	..	..	Bottom			10 ..
	William Power	9	..	..	Bog	96 2 ..	96 2 ..	1
Clooncunragh W. 50	Thos. Conway	63	..	..	Arable			1 5 ..
	Patk. Darcey & Co.	10	..	..	Bottom			12 ..
		8	..	..	Infer. Do.			5 ..
		4	..	..	Reclaimed Bog			10 ..
		38	..	..	Bog	143	143	1
Clooncunra E. 57	Patk. Arthur	88	..	..	Arable			1 5
		13	..	..	Bottom			7 6

Figure 64a-64b: Tithe Applotment record from the parish of Ballyhan, County Mayo, Ireland, 1830. (Image courtesy of the National Archives of Ireland in Dublin. Permissions received.).

state religion, had levied a yearly "cess" or tax since the 1600s. The Tithe Applotment Books were compiled because the Tithe Composition Act of 1823 allowed this tax to be paid in cash rather than "in kind" (i.e., by giving a portion of crops or herds). The Tithe Applotment Books are arranged by Church of Ireland parish (the civil parish) and register the amount each person was required to pay. The Tithe Applotment Books are indexed and digitized online on the websites of the

Quantities of holding	Quantities in Grassland	Quality	Amt. of Composition for Tithe in Holding			Amt. of Composition of Tithe in Grassland			Observation
		Brought forward	130	18	2	130	18	2	Lord Lucan
..	..	L. L.	3	6	5	3	6	5	do
..	..	L. L.	6	15	..	6	15	..	Col. Browne
..	..	C. Brown	4	15	.	4	15	..	Sir Francis L. Blosse
..	..	S.F.L. Bl.	4	12	3	4	12	3	Will. Leeske

National Archives of Ireland, Ancestry.com, and FamilySearch.org.

Immigration Strategies for Using Tithe Books

The tithe is a significant source for developing an immigration strategy for seeking origins, but some of their limitations and peculiarities need to be discussed. Because it was a rural tax, a certain percentage of the heads of households in Ireland automatically were omitted, easily explaining why an ancestor does not appear in the record series.

However, it is not the only reason. Therefore, it may be as essential to understand why an ancestor did *not* appear in the tithe as why he or she did.

The rule to bear in mind is that the tithe was never meant to be a listing of all who paid. Only those responsible for paying the tithes were listed by name. One person often collected for others in each townland, resulting in an entry reading, for instance, "John Lynch & Co." The company was the unnamed people for whom funds were collected in the townland of residence. Another cause for absence of names is that some classes of occupiers, such as cottiers (occupiers who paid rent in labor) and farm servants were not listed at all.

If Irish history itself is not understood, the source can be confusing. The Ordnance Survey teams were going through Ireland during the same period that the tithe was being taken. They were surveying boundaries and standardizing townland names. At that time, they also converted the land from Irish (Plantation) acres, Cunningham (Scottish) acres, or other local measurements into English (Statute) acres. Consequently, some parishes were measured in the local units, as in the 1820s, but were measured in English acres in the 1830s. At that time also, the survey teams divided townlands, discontinued them, or changed their names. Thus, the tithe will not correspond exactly to the later Griffith's Primary Valuation, which was taken according to the new boundaries and names. The changes affect research more if the ancestor already has been found in Griffith's

Valuation, and the goal is to work backward from there.

Even though the Tithe Applotment is not a complete listing of households, the indexes to the Tithe Applotment Books remain viable sources when studying a surname distribution. The Tithe Applotment is also a pre-Famine construction, wherein an ancestor could be listed who might have been gone by the time Griffith's Primary Valuation was created, during and after the Famine. Even so, note that the tithe books do not exist for certain parishes. In some cases, one parish is titled in the books as another parish. All these inconsistencies do affect research findings but are a place to start in building a case for where an ancestor might have originated.

Tithe Defaulters (1831)

While the Tithe Applotment (1823-1837) is a standard resource in Irish genealogical research, there is a lesser known list of those who refused to pay the tithe. Appreciate that the tithe was for the support and upkeep of the state religion, which was the Protestant Church of Ireland, and all persons in rural Ireland were required to pay, regardless of religion. The situation was a source of resentment that led to the Tithe War (1831-1838).

From 1830 to 1831, an increasing number of people in particular counties refused to pay their tithes. Because of the loss of revenue of the Church of Ireland clergy, the Government set up the Clergy Relief Fund in 1831. Through it, the clergymen claimed lost income based upon persons who would not pay.

For genealogical purposes, the Tithe Defaulters' list preserves the names of the defaulters; where they lived or if they were deceased; the names of their representatives; and how much each one owed. The records include 1,061 pages, 29,027 names from 232 parishes. Defaulter statistics from counties represented are:

- Carlow (437)
- Cork (2,115)
- Kerry (20)
- Kilkenny (10,263)
- Laois/Queen's (360)
- Limerick (851)
- Louth (965)
- Meath (36)
- Offaly/Kings (23)
- Tipperary (9,346)
- Waterford (1,838)
- Wexford (2,719)

These are the only counties for which lists are available. The lists are in the database "The 1831 Tithe Defaulters" at Findmypast.com.

Even though these lists are for only a few counties, numbers of people who refused to pay are in some of them, making them perfect census alternatives if ancestors are found in one of the counties. County Kilkenny alone has 10,263 entries. Because they are indexed, they are extraordinary sources to add to the many records that can be used as part of a surname distribution search. Otherwise, they simply can complement and fill in a Tithe Applotment study. However, they are superb as a workable source for tracking immigrants if a county is already known and the county is one of the aforementioned.

Valuation Office Books (1820s-1850s)

Griffith's Primary Valuation is the widely known printed source, but the manuscript materials that led to this printed record should be consulted for more information if possible. These original materials are referred to as Valuation Office Books and comprise several different sets of records.

Richard Griffith supervised the compilation of the Townland Valuation in Ireland beginning in 1830. In the course of the work, the valuators compiled manuscript land Field Books and manuscript House Books. The former described the quality of land in each townland, and the latter described the physical dimensions of houses and construction materials. Now and then, names of occupiers were recorded in the land books. The name of each head of household occupying any house that was measured was listed in the House Books. The records can be links between the Tithe Applotment Books and Griffith's Primary Valuation, but realize that they are not universal for all places in Ireland.

These manuscripts are at the National Archives of Ireland for the Republic of Ireland and at the PRONI for the Northern Ireland counties. The National Archives of Ireland collections have been digitized and indexed on the FamilySearch.org and Findmypast.com websites. The titles are "Ireland, Valuation

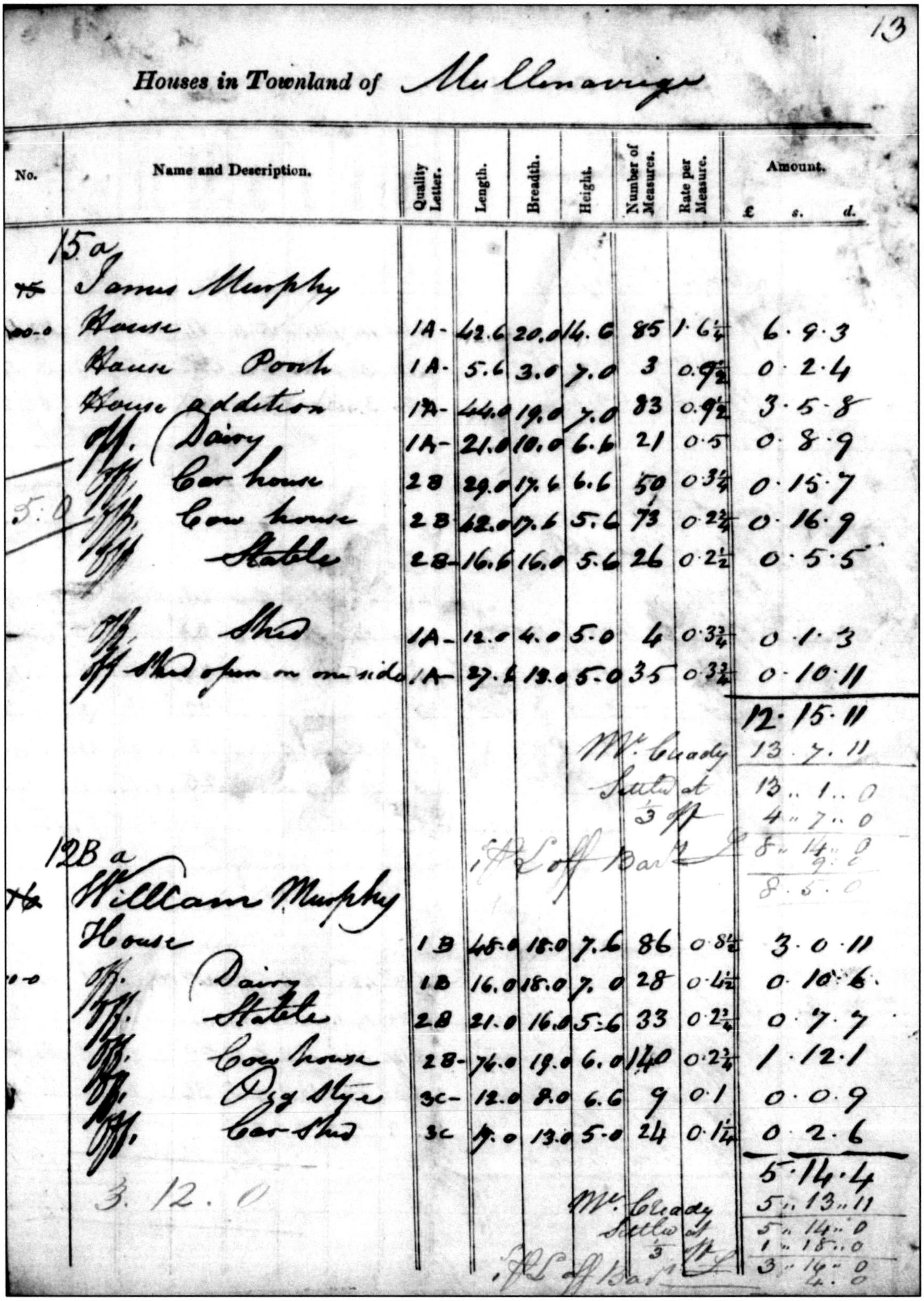

13

Houses in Townland of Mullenaveige

No.	Name and Description.	Quality Letter.	Length.	Breadth.	Height.	Number of Measures.	Rate per Measure.	Amount. £ s. d.
	15a							
	James Murphy							
	House	1A	42.6	20.0	16.6	85	1·6¼	6·9·3
	House Porch	1A	5.6	3.0	7.0	3	0·9½	0·2·4
	House addition	1A	44.0	19.0	7.0	83	0·9½	3·5·8
	Off. (Dairy	1A	21.0	10.0	6.6	21	0·5	0·8·9
	Off. Car house	2B	29.0	17.6	6.6	50	0·3¾	0·15·7
5.0	Off. Cow house	2B	62.0	17.6	5.6	73	0·2¾	0·16·9
	Off. Stable	2B	16.6	16.0	5.6	26	0·2½	0·5·5
	Off. Shed	1A	12.0	4.0	5.0	4	0·3¾	0·1·3
	Off. Shed open on one side	1A	27.6	13.0	5.0	35	0·3¾	0·10·11
								12·15·11
							Mc Cleady	13.7.11
							Settled at	13..1..0
							⅓ off	4..7..0
			1/2 L off Bar					8..14..0
								9..0
								8.5.0
	12B a							
	William Murphy							
	House	1B	48.0	18.0	7.6	86	0·8½	3·0·11
	Off. (Dairy	1B	16.0	18.0	7.0	28	0·4½	0·10·6
	Off. Stable	2B	21.0	16.0	5.6	33	0·2¾	0·7·7
	Off. Cow house	2B	76.0	19.0	6.0	140	0·2¾	1·12·1
	Off. Pig Stye	3C	12.0	8.0	6.6	9	0·1	0·0·9
	Off. Car Shed	3C	7.0	13.0	5.0	24	0·1¼	0·2·6
								5·14·4
	3.12.0						Mc Cleady	5..13..11
							Settled at	5..14..0
							⅓ off	1..18..0
			1/2 L off Bar					3..14..0
								4..0

Figure 65: House book page from the Valuation Office Books from the townland of Mullenaveige, Calary Parish, County Wicklow, Ireland, dated 1853. (Image courtesy of the National Archives of Ireland. Permissions received.)

Office Books, 1831-1856" on Family-Search.org and "Ireland Valuation Office Books" on Findmypast.com, covering 1824 through 1856. Both databases are technically the same and shared between the two websites. The search capability differs, and so accessing both is worthwhile to verify that all pertinent information has been found. The National Archives of Ireland also has its own database of these records, "Valuation Office Books 1824-1856."

If a county is already known, the search can be restricted to that county. If the goal is to find a civil parish where someone was living, the search can be limited to parishes. If the parish name appears with the names, it assures that the area was covered in the records. If nothing results, research must move on to another method. The distinct types of manuscripts can include:

- Field Books
- House Books
- Quarto Books
- Rent Books
- Survey Books
- Tenure Books

Again, the books do not all contain personal names. Some are observations about the lands in the townlands or the conditions of the houses. Some only list personal names for houses worth £5 or more. When they hold names, though, they are the perfect bridges between the Tithe and Griffiths' books. If an entry is found in the index, double-check the digitized copy of the original manuscript book to confirm the extracted date.

These books are potentially a pivotal point in immigrant research because many of the people listed in them emigrated before Griffith's Primary Valuation.

Nevertheless, the main function of these records for research is that they are indexed and can, therefore, be another source, along with the Tithe Applotment and Griffith's Valuation, in the exploration and confirmation of immigrant origins.

Griffith's Primary Valuation (1847-1864)

One of the most valuable sources for identifying Irish origins is Griffith's Primary Valuation, referred to in genealogy circles as "Griffith's" or "Griffith's Valuation." It was the original publication for values of lands and buildings. The funds collected from the taxation maintained the poorhouses. Griffith's Valuation was taken for a government tax, unlike the Tithe Applotment, which was related to the church. The records are a large archive arranged by Poor Law Union, barony, civil parish, and townland. The first step to understanding and using Griffith's Valuation is to view it from the following perspectives:

- It was published by Poor Law Unions between 1847 and 1864. Property holdings were surveyed and appraised by those administrative divisions, and accordingly, each published it by individual date. Knowing the publication date for a county is essential in emigration research.

- This valuation was a manuscript version before the published Griffith's version. It is part of the Valuation Office Books, also detailed in this chapter. The difference between the two editions can be from one to four years. Because of the delay in publishing, persons could have died or emigrated and yet have been listed as if they were still on the valued property. Consequently, dating is indispensable to developing an immigration strategy.

- This is an essential source even if family emigrated in the 1700s. Because it is indexed and readily obtainable, conducting a surname distribution survey for where in Ireland or where in a specific county a surname or group of targeted surnames resided between 1847 and 1864 is possible. Perhaps they were

relatives. Since family properties, often attached to a lease or rental agreement, were passed down to descendants for generations, the location might have been where the 1700s emigrant lived. Knowing or even suspecting a place allows access to other records about that family or property.

The following table indicates the years that Griffith's was published for the various Poor Law Unions within each county. The exact dates of publication below are from James R. Reilly's *Richard Griffith and His Valuation of Ireland* (Baltimore, Maryland: Clearfield Press, 2000), pp. 80-108. Recall that some Poor Law Unions crossed county lines, and others were published before the official completion of the project. Therefore, the dates do not always match.

Published Versions of Griffith's

County/City	Published	Completion
Antrim	1859 to 1862	1862
Armagh	1854, 1863 to 1864	1865
Belfast City	1860	---
Carlow	1852	1853
Cavan	1855 to 1857	1857
Clare	1852, 1855	1856
Cork	1850 to 1853	1853
Donegal	1857 to 1858	1858
Down	1861, 1863 to 1864	1864
Dublin (Dublin City)	1847 to 1851, 1854	1853 (County), 1854 (City)
Fermanagh	1862	1863
Galway	1855 to 1856	1856 (City), 1857 (County)
Kerry	1851 to 1853	1853
Kildare	1850 to 1853	1854
Kilkenny	1849 to 1851	---

Published Versions of Griffith's (cont.)

County/ City	Published	Completion
Leitrim	1856 to 1857	1857
Laois (Queens)	1850 to 1851	1853
Limerick	1850 to 1852	1853
Londonderry (Derry)	1858 to 1859	1859
Longford	1854	1855
Louth	1851, 1854	1855
Mayo	1855 to 1857	1857
Meath	1851, 1854	1855
Monaghan	1858, 1860 to 1861	1861
Offaly (Kings)	1851, 1853 to 1854	1855
Roscommon	1855, 1857 to 1858	1858
Sligo	1857 to 1858	1858
Tipperary	1850 to 1852	1853
Tyrone	1858 to 1860	1860
Waterford	1848 to 1851	1853
Westmeath	1854	1855
Wexford	1853	1854
Wicklow	1852 to 1854	1854

One difficulty with the online indexes to Griffith's Valuation is that often a date for the individual record being examined is not clear. The date is necessary for an immigration strategy because the ancestor has to be missing from the tax lists at some point. However, before that emigration occurred is when the targeted person must be identified in Griffith's, which, in effect, solves the question about immigrant origins.

At times, when an ancestor should have been taxed as the head of household, the family cannot be found in the Griffith's index. The most obvious explanation for the absence is that only one responsible head of household was taxed, that is, if a house was shared by two families, one head was taxed and one was not. Therefore, a segment of the population is not represented in Griffith's. In another circumstance, if an ancestor's home was owned by a large corporation, such as a mining company, the company, not the workers in the company housing, was the taxable party. This was the case in the mining districts of County Wicklow.

Indexes and Strategies for Griffith's Primary Valuation

Technology and the ability to manipulate findings in databases have revolutionized the use of Griffith's in an immigration strategy. The use of wildcards allows variants in surname spellings to be found. Indexes to Griffith's Valuation are accessible online. Major websites are Ancestry.com, Askaboutireland.ie, and Findmypast.com.

Understanding that the indexes are more than a list of names is important. They are historical snapshots of townlands, their residents, and the landlords. Yet, because each genealogy is unique, the tactics developed by family historians for approaching Griffith's should be tailored accordingly.

Perhaps the foremost principle when evaluating the indexes is not to assume a person appraised for taxes in Griffith's is the correct person because he or she has the same name as the immigrant ancestor. Both first and last names in Ireland are common. Other records in conjunction with Griffith's can prove a case. Assuming without further research can lead to a wrong conclusion.

Since names recurred often, the tax assessors had to differentiate people with the same name in the same townland. Agnomens, such as "Red," "Farmer," "Tim," or almost anything else, helped distinguish one from another. Something like John Corrigan (Patrick) was usual, Patrick most likely being John's father. If a surname is the agnomen, it may have even been the mother's maiden name of the person being assessed.

At the point when research from the records of the immigrant country has gathered more than one name with which to work, Griffith's Valuation becomes more valuable. For example, unusual surnames are easy to interpret in the indexes. If they are concentrated in a county or two or possibly in a parish or two, within reason, that was from where the emigrant came. However, Irish research is seldom that straightforward.

Even common names can be employed effectively if a wife's maiden name or her father's name is known. They assist in organizing what is viewed in the indexes. In this example, from the records of the immigrant country, if a family had close associates, also from Ireland, using their surnames in the Griffith's indexes may be worthwhile. If a pattern emerges, for instance, all surnames from the same county or a portion of the county, it might have been where they all lived, and they reunited in the immigrant country. It could have been a chain migration, one person following another who followed another over the years. They were all from the same area in Ireland but did not all leave at the same time, the opposite of a group migration.

When evaluating a surname distribution survey, the assumption is that other records, such as church records' indexes, have been searched and were of no assistance in revealing the ancestral family. Unfortunately, this is predictable. Therefore, in the search for immigrant origins, where a family originated may well rest on sources such as Griffith's. Although it perhaps is not the best proof, it may be all that is left.

In the sample research chart below, a search of the Griffith's Valuation indexes takes into account four surnames targeted from the immigrant county:

Year	County	Civil Parish	Surname #1	Surname #2	Surname #3	Surname #4

PRIMARY VALUATION OF TENEMENTS.

PARISH OF INISHLOUNAGHT.

45

No. and Letters of Reference to Map.	Townlands and Occupiers.	Immediate Lessors.	Description of Tenement.	Content of Land. A. R. P.	Net Annual Value. Land. £ s. d.	Buildings. £ s. d.	Total. £ s. d.
	INISHLOUNAGHT —continued. TOWN OF ABBEY. ABBEY—con.						
— 43	Michael Commerford,	Patrick O'Donnell,	House and yard,	—	—	0 10 0	0 10 0
— 44			House (in ruins),	—	—	—	—
— 45			House (in ruins),	—	—	—	—
— 46	Patrick Power,	Patrick O'Donnell,	House and yard,	—	—	0 11 0	0 11 0
— 47	Honoria Morrissy,	Patrick O'Donnell,	House and yard,	—	—	0 6 0	0 6 0
— 48	Mary Kelly,	Patrick O'Donnell,	House and yard,	—	—	0 6 0	0 6 0
— 49	John Neill,	Patrick O'Donnell,	House and yard,	—	—	0 5 0	0 5 0
— 50	Patrick O'Donnell,	Rev. Geo. T. Roche & L. A. B. Balmary, Esq.	Garden,	1 3 32	2 18 0	—	2 18 0
— 51			House (in ruins),	—	—	—	—
— 52			House (in ruins),	—	—	—	—
— 53	William Quinlan,	Patrick O'Donnell,	House,	—	—	0 5 0	0 5 0
— 54	Thomas Wallace,	Patrick O'Donnell,	House,	—	—	0 8 0	0 8 0
— 55	Anne Shea,	Patrick O'Donnell,	House and office,	—	—	0 10 0	0 10 0
— 56			House (in ruins),	—	—	—	—
— 57	Honoria Conway,	Patrick O'Donnell,	House, office, and yard,	—	—	0 5 0	0 5 0
— 58	John Mahony,	Patrick O'Donnell,	House and yard,	—	—	0 5 0	0 5 0
— 59			House (in ruins),	—	—	—	—
— 60	Patrick Keeffe,	Patrick O'Donnell,	House, office, and yard,	—	—	0 5 0	0 5 0
— 61	Philip Hickey,	Patrick O'Donnell,	House,	—	—	0 5 0	0 5 0
— 62			House (in ruins),	—	—	—	—
— 63	John Ryan, jun.	Rev. Geo. T. Roche & L. A. B. Balmary, Esq.	House and garden,	0 0 29	0 5 0	0 11 0	0 16 0
— 64	Ellen Byrne,	John Ryan, jun.	House and yard,	—	—	0 9 0	0 9 0
— 65	Robert Jackson and Cather. Dempsey,	John Ryan, jun.	House, office, and yard,	—	—	0 9 0	0 9 0
— 66	James Halfpenny,	Patrick O'Donnell,	House,	—	—	0 14 0	0 14 0
— 67	Patrick O'Donnell,	Rev. Geo. T. Roche & L. A. B. Balmary, Esq.	Garden,	0 2 4	0 16 0	—	0 16 0
— 68	Patrick Wallace,	Patrick O'Donnell,	House,	—	—	0 9 0	0 9 0
— 69	John Hogan,	Patrick Dunphy,	House,	—	—	0 5 0	0 5 0
— 70	Patrick Dumphy,	Patrick O'Donnell,	House,	—	—	0 5 0	0 5 0
— 71			House (in ruins),	—	—	—	—
— 72	Vacant,	John Ryan, sen.	House	—	—	0 8 0	0 8 0
— 73	John Ryan, sen.	Rev. Geo. T. Roche & L. A. B. Balmary, Esq.	House and garden,	0 0 38	0 6 0	0 7 0	0 13 0
— 74	James Keating,	John Ryan, sen.	House,	—	—	0 7 0	0 7 0
— 75	Edward Butler,	John Ryan, sen.	House,	—	—	0 15 0	0 15 0
— 76	Thomas Ryan,	Patrick O'Donnell,	House and garden,	0 0 4	0 1 0	0 5 0	0 6 0
— 77			House (in ruins),	—	—	—	—
— 78	Michael Ryan,	Patrick O'Donnell,	House and yard,	—	—	0 8 0	0 8 0
79	Patrick O'Donnell,	The Rev. Geo. T. Roche & L. A. B. Balmary, Esq.	Garden,	0 0 38	0 6 0	—	0 6 0
— 80	James Wallace,	Patrick O'Donnell,	House,	—	—	0 9 0	0 9 0
— 81	John Keeley,	Patrick O'Donnell,	House,	—	—	0 7 0	0 7 0
— 82	Vacant,	Patrick O'Donnell,	House and office,	—	—	0 13 0	0 13 0
— 83	John Maher,	Samuel Gordon, Esq.	House, office, and gar.	0 0 12	0 2 0	0 14 0	0 16 0
— 84	Catherine Maher,	Samuel Gordon, Esq.	House and garden,	0 0 11	0 2 0	0 14 0	0 16 0
— 85			House (in ruins),	—	—	—	—
— 86	John Maher,	Samuel Gordon, Esq.	Garden,	0 0 18	0 4 0	—	0 4 0
— 87			House (in ruins),	—	—	—	—
— 88	John Carroll,	Samuel Gordon, Esq.	House and garden,	0 0 12	0 2 0	0 5 0	0 7 0
— 89	John Donnell,	Samuel Gordon, Esq.	Ho., office, & sm. gar.	—	—	0 10 0	0 10 0
— 90	Michael Hogan,	Samuel Gordon, Esq.	House and garden,	0 0 8	0 1 0	0 5 0	0 6 0
— 91			House (in ruins),	—	—	—	—
— 92	John Donnell,	Samuel Gordon, Esq.	Garden,	0 0 8	0 1 0	—	0 1 0
— 93	John Donnell (Patrick),	Samuel Gordon, Esq.	House & small garden,	—	—	0 5 0	0 5 0
— 94	Edmund Talbot,	John Ryan, sen.	Ho., office, & sm. gar.	—	—	0 16 0	0 16 0
— 95	John Shea,	John Ryan, sen.	House, offices, & garden,	0 0 6	0 1 0	0 19 0	1 0 0
— 96	William Foley,	Samuel Gordon, Esq.	Ho., offices, & sm. gar.	—	—	0 11 0	0 11 0
— 97	Andrew Crawley,	Samuel Gordon, Esq.	House and small gar.	—	—	0 6 0	0 6 0
— 98	Patrick Meehan,	Samuel Gordon, Esq.	House and sm. garden,	—	—	0 16 0	0 16 0
— 99	Michael Naughten,	Samuel Gordon, Esq.	House and sm. garden,	—	—	0 16 0	0 16 0
— 100	Thomas Morrissey,	Samuel Gordon, Esq.	House and garden,	0 0 6	0 1 0	0 7 0	0 8 0
	James Rourke,	Thomas Morrissey,	House,	—	—	0 5 0	0 5 0

Figure 66: Page from Griffith's Valuation, 1847-1864, for Abbey Town, Inishlounaght Parish, County Tipperary, Ireland. (Image courtesy of Office of the General Valuation of Ireland, "General Valuation of Rateable Property in Ireland, 1847-1864." Permissions received.)

If the county is known before starting but the parish is not, the chart can be tailored by omitting the county column and adding a townland column. Adjust it also if only two surnames are being searched. If no evidence of a county of origin is in the records in the immigrant country, work first with the least conventional surnames of those chosen for the study. Once a group of parishes or counties has been identified for the uncommon surname, begin to plot the other names. If they are found geographically close to that surname, the list may have been pared down even more.

In another approach, focus on any unusual first name if an immigrant ancestor has one. It does not matter how ordinary the surname is. Given names are often passed down in separate branches of a family over generations and could be a decisive clue for isolating the immigrant ancestor's home in Ireland. Remember, the distinctive given name also might have been consigned through cousins' lines, which are not the surnames being researched. The emphasis is the first name tied to a locality. Afterward, look for familiar surnames.

Valuation Office Revision Books (1850s-Present)

The revision books created after Griffith's Valuation continued the taxation updates on each property. Occasionally, they are referred to as "cancelled books," which is not their name but is a description. When a booklet of tax updates became full, it was retired with "cancelled" written on the front page with the date. A new booklet then was started.

The updated books have no index, but the manuscript books are available for study. For Northern Ireland, they can be viewed online at FamilySearch.org or the PRONI. For the Republic of Ireland, they are mainly held in the Valuation Office in Dublin and are currently on microfilm at the Family History Library. They are cataloged on the FamilySearch.org website under the name of the county, the category of taxation, followed by the Poor Law Union, and finally, by the electoral division.

Originally, the revisions were in small booklets, and each electoral division or urban district had a series of them. This format for the Northern Ireland collection has been preserved, and the digitized version reflects it accurately. For the Republic of Ireland group, all the smaller booklets were combined and bound into larger volumes by electoral division or urban district. In the microfilm edition for the Republic of Ireland, the oldest book is typically at the end of the roll, and the most recent booklet, at the beginning.

The Northern Ireland collection on the PRONI website can be opened by the name of the townland. The one for the Republic of Ireland has to be accessed by the electoral division within the Poor Law Union. The pages themselves display when a change occurred, usually by a name scored through and the year of the change entered. These are color coded by year of update, which is reflected in the PRONI digitized versions but not preserved in the Family History Library microfilm, which is in black and white.

Even though they are not the easiest source to use, they are an essential part of further evidence for the findings of Griffith's Valuation. Usually, if a person was taxed for property years after he or she emigrated, logically, this is not the person being studied.

Sometimes, the names of people who stayed were not crossed off when they died. Names of people documented as deceased can be found in several of the tax booklets until, eventually, a line was drawn through them, resulting in the appearance that some of the persons listed must have been over a hundred years old. Evidence, such as the 1901 census or death certificates, proves that they had been deceased for years. The cases are more than simple ones of sons with their fathers' names taking over the taxes, although that also happened, but of changes not being updated. For this reason, be attentive. Listing persons during the years after they emigrated did not happen as frequently as it did for those who stayed. Always look for death certificates before deciding if the people recorded were still living.

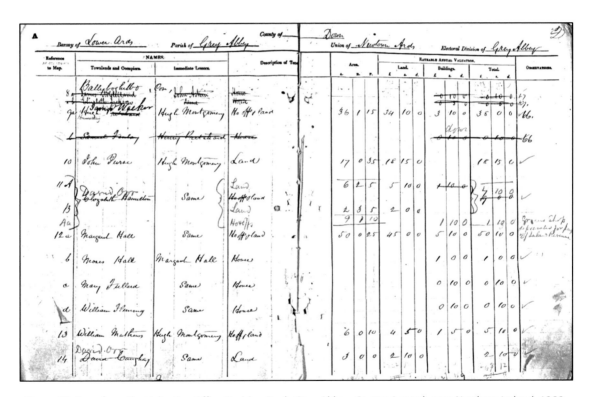

Figure 67: Page from the Valuation Office Revision Book, Grey Abbey, County Armagh, now Northern Ireland, 1866-1879. (Image courtesy of the Public Record Office of Northern Ireland. Permissions received.)

AN

ALPHABETICAL LIST

OF THE

F R E E M E N

OF THE

CITY OF DUBLIN.

Commencing January, 1774, and ending 15th January, 1824.

Name.	Date.		Corporation.	How admitted.
Andrews, William	Christmas,	1774	Weaver	B.
Alexander, Robert	Easter,	"	Merchant	B.
Ashenhurst, Richard	do.	"	Carpenter	S.
Adams, Robert	Midsummer,	1776	Weaver	B.
Appleby, Henry	Michaelmas,	"	Sheerman	S.
Appleby, John	do.	"	do.	S.
Annesley, Hon. Richard	do.	"	——	Gratis
Allen, John	Midsummer,	1777	Butcher	S.
Andrews, Samuel	Michaelmas,	"	Tailor	S.
Atkinson, Edward	do.	"	Weaver	S.
Andrews, Thomas	do.	"	Staymaker	B.
Andrews, William	Christmas,	1780	Tailor	S.
Abbott, John	do.	"	Weaver	S.
Alley, Lewis	Michaelmas,	"	Smith	G. E.
Atkinson, Andrew	Christmas,	1781	Joiner	G. E.

2

Figure 68: Page from "Freemen of Dublin City, 1774-1824." Such lists assist in finding voters during various eras. For an explanation of the abbreviations, see pp. 228-229. (Image courtesy of Rosemary ffolliott and found at FindMyPast.com. Permissions received.)

Chapter Sixteen

Voters' Records

Historically, the vote in Ireland was restricted to a class of men who were entitled to the privilege because of the values of their land holdings or their trades. The records generated through this process—arranged by county, city or borough, or barony—extend from those who met the criteria to vote (freeholders) through those who did vote (polls). Lists often were published in local newspapers or compiled into manuscript books. One class of records that is of particular interest is the freeholders' lists.

The right to vote, based upon eligibility, changed over the years depending on how the process needed to be tailored for desired results. In other words, classes of people were or were not deemed appropriate voters. Freeholders could have ranged from small farmers to the gentry, and in Ireland's past, they qualified through the value of their holdings, their trades, and being Protestant.

Records such as the ones for freeholders are indispensable for determining where people were living at specific times, and they certainly are effectual as census substitutes or for surname distribution surveys. If an ancestor is found to have been a freeholder, the Registry of Deeds should be consulted for an appropriately valued and registered lease agreement.

A freeholder was either a landowner or a man who held a "lease for lives." The most common lease was for three lives, and so the freeholder could have been one of the three lives mentioned if the value of the lease was worth the amount designated. The basic laws defining or disenfranchising voters were:

- From 1727 to 1793, freeholds were limited to Protestants who each had holdings worth 40 shillings or more.

- From 1793, every Protestant and Catholic who had a 40-shilling freehold was given the right to vote.

- From 1829, all 40-shilling freeholders lost the vote, and it was raised to £10 freeholds.

It was not until the 1872 Ballot Act that the secret vote was introduced, and no one, not even the freeholders' landlords, knew how votes were cast.

A typical freeholder record is for a certain year or number of years, and it includes the person's name, residence, and location of the freehold. The freeholder's residence might not have been in the same location as the freehold property. Also, the lessor of the freehold property could have been listed along with the conditions of the lease agreement with the lessee. The rolls are basic, but they have more than enough information to identify the people living at specific places.

Keep in mind that the voters' lists are for only a class of people, which was the Protestant one until 1793, but they are practicable sources because they are not limited to the wealthy class of Protestants. Since half of the Church of Ireland registers were destroyed in 1922 and there are few Presbyterian registers for the 1700s, freeholders' lists are ideal for pinpointing individuals who did not have christening records.

Immigration Strategy

One chief drawback to using the records for freeholders and voters, except for the Northern Ireland counties, is the current absence of a centralized database. The PRONI has indexed and digitized its collection through 1840, and so identifying in advance a county of origin is not necessary. However, a gap remains for the rest of the counties now in the Republic of Ireland.

Freeholders' lists and databases are scattered, and not one is centralized. Thus, a county has to be known ahead of time, and then the task is finding the freeholder and voting records available for that county. Often, doing so is as easy as typing "County Clare freeholders" or something similar into a search engine.

An amazing example is from County Clare, indexed in the Clare County Library

from an 1821 list of freeholders and in its database "List of Freeholders [including landlords and tenants]: County of Clare, 1821." However, this record needs further explanation, which the library website provides. The document covers a significant portion of the population for the county from 1796 to 1820 and not only includes freeholders but also tenants and the names of the landlords. It is perfect as a census alternative and as part of surname distribution searches (residences are provided) because it is from the time both Catholics and Protestants were eligible for freeholds. The records were published originally by barony.

Another example is specifically from Dublin City. Findmypast.com has a database "Freemen of Dublin City 1774-1824" that lists almost 6,000 men admitted to the Freedom of Dublin City. In this case, Freedom meant citizenship, giving these men the rights of a city subject to the laws of Dublin. Most were tradesmen and craftsmen, and, therefore, the freeholds were based upon trades, not properties. Included are the names, years, counties, occupations, how they were admitted, and the provisions of admittances. Special terms having to do with how these men were admitted also are associated with the Dublin City records, which differ from those in the County Clare lists. These designations were abbreviations and include:

- B: birth, such as the eldest surviving son of a freeman.

- S: service, such as one who served as an apprentice to a

Dublin freeman in a particular trade.

- G.E.: Grace Especial, a special request or a favor.

- Gratis: someone who was admitted through a special arrangement without payment.

The entire document is a fascinating study of trade members of Dublin City. It also opens doors to other city records for explorations. Nonetheless, as with the County Clare example, researchers previously must know that their ancestors were from County Clare or Dublin City; otherwise, targeting either one of these places is not reasonable. These are but

266]		APPENDIX TO REPORT FROM THE				
Appendix, No. 11. Valuation of Houses in Drogheda.	Description of Premises, whether House, Store, &c.	NAME of OCCUPANT and STREET.	Annual Value under Watch Applotment.	Description of Premises, whether House, Store, &c.	NAME of OCCUPANT and STREET.	Annual Value under Watch Applotment.
		West-street—continued.	£.		Peter-street—continued.	£.
	House and Ball-court.	Peter Keenan - -	40	House -	William Dawson -	30
					John Biggers - -	15
	House - -	James Kavanagh -	18		Mrs. M'Guire - -	20
		Mrs. Gilmer - -	12		Miss Byrne - -	10
	House & forge	Hugh M'Guire - -	35		Mr. Thompson - -	15
	House - -	William Owens -	10		—— Robinson - -	20
	Brewery -	Thomas Finegan -	20		Charles Farrell - -	40
	House, store, &c.	James Flood, jun. -	70		Bryan Hutton - -	20
	House - -	Miss Wootten - -	8		Thomas Curtis - -	15
		Michael Meighan -	36		Catherine Biggers -	14
		Malachi Fallon -	40			
	Two houses -	- - Thomas Beddy and Mrs. Hanlon.	50		Laurence's-street :	
	House & yard	Joseph Kelly - -	36	House -	Miss Caulfield - -	25
		Mrs. Connolly - -	30		Peter Bannon - -	20
		Bartholomew Halpin -	10		Thomas Walsh - -	20
		Mrs. Maguire - -	10		Mrs. Kelly - -	35
	Coach-office -	Thomas Simcox -	10		Edward Flanagan -	35
	Hotel - -	Thomas Simcox -	40		Philip Smith - -	15
	House, foundry, &c.	Thomas Grendon -	70		George Lacy - -	35
					John Davis - -	25
	House - -	Lewis Byrne - -	25		Charles F. Collins -	24
		John Kelly - -	20		Rev. T. Jackaberry -	10
		James Dwinin - -	30		Ditto - -	10
		John Morar - -	30		Mrs. Healey - -	15
		Miss Mathews - -	15		Pat Magrane - -	15
		Charles M'Kenna -	50		Rev. G. Needham -	160
		John Butterly - -	50		William Fairtlough -	40
		William Campbell -	50		George W. Evans -	40
		James Campbell -	40		Francis G. Fairtlough	55
		Michael Rogers -	40		Robert Pentland -	55
		Thomas North - -	65		Mrs. Smith - -	12
	House, store, &c.	George R Clark -	75		Margaret Moore -	8
	House - -	James Devlin - -	26		John Corrigan - -	40
		Mrs. Clarendon -	40		Doctor Fairtlough -	40
		Pat M'Guire - -	32		Francis W. Leland -	50
		Boyle Simpson -	40		Thomas Callaghan -	16
		Peter Verdon - -	30		James Kenny - -	20
		Patrick Kelly - -	35		Edward Kirwan - -	20
		Miss Gugerty - -	30		Richard Cavanagh -	10
		James Halligan -	15		Rev. Mr. Dardis -	6
		Samuel Crawford -	30		Patrick Darbey -	30
		—— Murphy - -	60		William Rodger -	35
		Peter-street :			Mr. M'Cullough -	40
	House - -	Henry Bagnall - -	30		Michael Walsh - -	30
		Michael Macken -	15		Michael Byrne - -	15
					John M'Auley - -	10

Figure 69: A page from the "Report of the Select Committee on Fictitious Votes, 1837-1838" for Drogheda, County Louth, Ireland. This unique source also serves as a census substitute. (Image courtesy of Tinchor and found at FindMyPast.com. Permissions received.)

two examples of information a general search engine could uncover.

No database has all freeholders and voters outside the Northern Ireland counties, and so one odd source that does encompass all of Ireland should not be ignored. Published in the *British Parliamentary Papers* was an investigation of voter fraud in Ireland. Between 1832 and 1838, voting was restricted to those who owned a set amount of property. Some votes in the Irish elections of 1832, 1835, and 1838 were challenged. The "House of Commons Select Committee on Fictitious Votes (Ireland)" investigated the disputed votes, comparing rate lists with voting lists.

The publishing of the abovementioned report by Parliament created not only a viable census substitute but also another source to add to surname distribution survey studies when counties of origins are unknown. Included in the lists were both freemen and marksmen. Marksmen were illiterate voters who signed with their marks. The report can be found on Findmypast.com in the database "Ireland, Select Committee on Fictitious Votes 1837-1838" and includes some of the following: names, counties, boroughs, residences, occupations, properties, rights to vote, and values of holdings. The Findmypast.com guide to this collection explains that it comprises 52,600 names: £10 freeholders and leaseholders, £20 leaseholders and freeholders, £50 freeholders, and those in corporation towns, cities, and boroughs who had rights to vote as freemen or paid-up members of trade guilds. The study shows that Dublin City was especially well represented with extensive facts.

The Fictitious Votes lists are printed. The information is not uniform between areas because people with dissimilar qualifications were recorded with different details gathered. Some lists are exhaustive, providing even the dates of admissions to freeholds. Others simply have tenants by street addresses for those holding tenements that were each worth under £5 and not subject to a Police Tax.

Location of Freeholders' Lists

Various inventories have been compiled for surviving freeholders' lists and their locations. An all-inclusive register of what is available does not presently exist. The closest to a complete set of records and indexes is for the Northern Ireland counties, which are on the PRONI website database. It is an impressive gathering of these records with digitized, indexed images. Scattered lists have been microfilmed and digitized or are in book form through the FamilySearch.org website. Even so, a county has to be known to work with them. Collections at the county libraries in Ireland or at the National Archives of Ireland should not be ignored, and all have websites and searchable library catalogs. Again, a county must be identified through immigrant research to use these.

The various genealogy instruction books typically include freeholders' lists in their census substitute recommendations, but none has a comprehensive catalog of all of them within each county. One noteworthy, although dated, reference article and inventory for all of Ireland is Kyle J.

Betit's "Irish Freeholders, Freemen and Voting Registers" in *The Irish At Home and Abroad* 6, #4 (4th Quarter 1999): 146-164.

8 — BARONY OF CASTLEREAGH.

No.	Name of Freeholder.	Place of Abode.	Situation of Freehold.	Name of Landlord.	Value of Freehold	Names of Lives or other Tenure.	Place & Date of Registry.
383	Mageehan, Thomas	Barnamaghery	Barnewaghery	Earl Londonderry	40s.	James Bailie,	Comber, Feb. 7, 1823.
384	Murray, Peter	same	same	same	40s.	same	same same
385	Munn, Matthew	Ballyaltikilligan	Ballyaltikilligan	Lord Baron Londonderry	40s.	Hugh Kennedy, Matthew Ford and Matthew Munn,	same same
386	Milling, James	Comber	Comber	same	40s.	James Milling,	same same
387	Moore, James	Ringeroovy	Ringereevy	Lord Viscount Castlereagh	40s.	James Moore, Edw. Ward and Thomas Kennedy,	same same
388	Miskelly, Patrick	Ravara	Ravara	James Holmes	40s.	Owen Miskelly, Catherine and Owen Miskelly,	same same
389	Miskelly, Henry	same	same	same	40s.	Henry, Owen and Mary Miskelly,	same same
390	Murray, Bernard	same	same	Bernard Murray,	40s.	Bernard Murray,	same same
391	Murdock, William	Barnemaghery	Barnemaghery	John Murdock	40s.	John Turnly and Hugh Kennedy,	same same
392	Maffot, Robert	same	same	Thos. David & Wm. Frame, and Hugh Lavey	40s.	Henry Blackwood, Alex. Turnly & Wm. Frame,	same same
393	Millan, Thomas	Ballyaltikilligan	Ballyaltikilligan	David Rea	40s.	David Rea, George and Isabella Knitlow,	same same
394	Matthews, Robert	Ballyalloly	Ballyalloly	William Brown	40s.	Pr. Augustus, Aug. Frederick & Adolphus Frederick,	N. T. Ards, June 30, 1822.
472	M'Blain, John	Scrabo Isles	Scrabo Isles	Viscount Castlereagh	40s.	The eldest Son of the Marquis of Downshire, Wm. Forde and William Young,	N. T. Ards, Feb. 6, 1822.
473	M'Clenaghan, Hugh	Ballymoney	Ballymoney	Alexander Stewart, Esq.	40s.	Pat. & Hugh M'Clenaghan & Pat. M'Clenaghan, jun.	same same
474	M'Kee, James	Newtownards	N.T Ards Corporation	Lord Baron Londonderry	40s.	James M'Kee,	same same
475	M'Cann, Samuel	Ballycullen	Ballycullen	same	40s.	Sam. M'Cann, Alex. Turnly and Robert Kennedy,	same same
476	M'Cutcheon, James	Turugardy	Turnagardy	same	40s.	Thomas Pottinger, A.J. Crawford and Wm. Baxter,	same same
477	M'Connell, Hugh	same	same	same	40s.	Thos. Pottinger, A.J.Crawford & Hugh M'Connel,	same same
478	M'Cully, James	Demesnes	N.T.Ards Corporation	Rt. Hon. Robert Stewart	40s.	Alex. Turnly, A. J. Crawford and James M'Cully,	same same
479	M'Kibben, John	Ballystockard	Ballystockard	same	40s.	Hugh Kennedy, Alex. Turnly and John M'Kibben,	Comber, 7th same
480	M'Morran, John	Ringcreevy	Ringcreevy	same	40s.	A. J. Crawford, Matthew Forde & Jn. M'Morran,	same same
481	M'Bride, John	Barnemaghery	Barnemaghery	same	40s.	John Turnly, Hugh Kennedy and Sam. M'Cleary,	same same
482	M'Greevy, Neal	same	same	Earl Londonderry	40s.	Alex. Turnly, Matthew Forde and Neal M'Greevy,	same same
483	M'Allister, Edward	Drumreagh	same	same	40s.	James Bailie,	same same
484	M'Connell, John	Ballywilliam	Ballywilliam	Alexander Stewart, Esq.	40s.	James and Mary M'Connell, and Alexander Boyd,	same same
485	M'Ilveen, William	same	same	same	40s.	same lives	same same
486	M'Mullan, John	Comber	Comber	Lord Baron Londonderry	40s	Pr. of Wales, Pr. Wm, Henry & Pr. Adol. Frederick,	same same
487	M'Connell, William	same	same	same	40s.	Prince of Wales, Agnes and John M'Connell,	same same
488	M'Mullan, Denis	Barnemaghery	Barnemaghery	James Wallace	40s.	Alexander Stewart, Esq.	same same
489	M'Kibbin, James	Comber	Comber	William Murdock	40s.	Pr. of Wales, D. of York, and Pr. William Henry,	same same
28	Nightingale, John	Carroreagh	Craigagsundlett	Lord Baron Londonderry	40s.	Alex. Kennedy, Wm. Forde and Alex. Nightingale,	N. T. Ards, Feb. 6, 1823.
133	Roddy, Samuel	Scrabo	Scrabo	Alexander Stewart, Esq.	40s.	Henry Blackwood, Alex. Turnly and John Roddy,	same same
134	Robb, Robert	same	same	same	40s.	Henry Blackwood, Alex. Turnly and John Robb,	same same
135	Roddy, John	N.T Ards Corporation	N.T Ards Corporation	Lord Baron Londonderry	40s.	Alex. Turnly, Hugh Kennedy and John Roddy,	same same
136	Robb, Alexander	Ballyskeough	Ballyskeough	same	40s.	Alexander Robb, Alex. Turnly and Alex. Kennedy,	same same
137	Robb, Thomas	same	same	same	40s.	Thos. Robb, Alex. Turnly and A. J. Crawford,	same same
138	Robb, David	same	same	same	40s.	David Robb, Hugh Kennedy and Matthew Forde,	same same
139	Robb, David	same	same	same	40s.	David Robb, Alex. Turnly and Alex. Kennedy,	same same
140	Robb, James	same	same	same	40s.	John Robb, Hugh Kennedy and Alex. Turnly,	same same
141	Robb, William	same	same	same	40s.	Hugh Robb, Alex. Turnly and Alex. Kennedy,	same same
142	Roddy, John	Comber	Comber	Rt. Hon. Robert Stewart	40s.	Pr. of Wales, Bp. of Osnaburgh & Pr. Wm. Henry,	Comber, 7th same
237	Streaton, Robert	Newtownards	Newtownards	Earl Londonderry	40s.	Pr. of Wales, D. of York & Pr. Adolphus Frederick,	N. T. Ards, Feb. 6, 1823.
238	Smith, Robert	Ballybarnes	Ballybarnes	Rt. Hon. Robert Stewart	40s.	John Turnly, Robert Kennedy and Robert Smyth,	same same

Figure 70: Freeholders' lists for those counties now in Northern Ireland, like this one for the Barony of Castlereagh, County Down, 1823, reveal names of those freeholders whose lifespans, other lessee agreements, residences, and additional information are covered. (Image courtesy of PRONI. This work is produced and copyrighted by the Crown Copyright©. Meeting Open Government License qualifications for this content, no additional permissions required.)

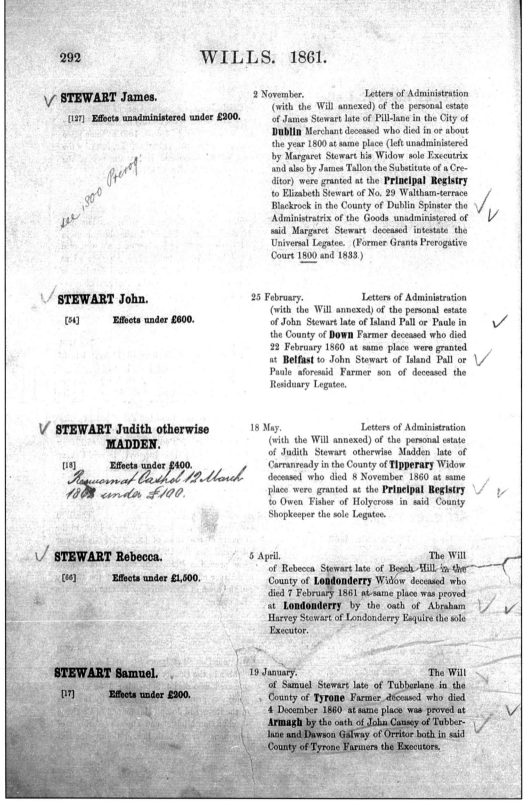

292   WILLS. 1861.

STEWART James.

[127] **Effects unadministered under £200.**

see 1800 Prerog.

2 November.   Letters of Administration (with the Will annexed) of the personal estate of James Stewart late of Pill-lane in the City of **Dublin** Merchant deceased who died in or about the year 1800 at same place (left unadministered by Margaret Stewart his Widow sole Executrix and also by James Tallon the Substitute of a Creditor) were granted at the **Principal Registry** to Elizabeth Stewart of No. 29 Waltham-terrace Blackrock in the County of Dublin Spinster the Administratrix of the Goods unadministered of said Margaret Stewart deceased intestate the Universal Legatee. (Former Grants Prerogative Court 1800 and 1833.)

STEWART John.

[54]   **Effects under £600.**

25 February.   Letters of Administration (with the Will annexed) of the personal estate of John Stewart late of Island Pall or Paule in the County of **Down** Farmer deceased who died 22 February 1860 at same place were granted at **Belfast** to John Stewart of Island Pall or Paule aforesaid Farmer son of deceased the Residuary Legatee.

STEWART Judith otherwise MADDEN.

[18]   **Effects under £400.**
Resworn at Cashel 12 March 1863 under £100.

18 May.   Letters of Administration (with the Will annexed) of the personal estate of Judith Stewart otherwise Madden late of Carranready in the County of **Tipperary** Widow deceased who died 8 November 1860 at same place were granted at the **Principal Registry** to Owen Fisher of Holycross in said County Shopkeeper the sole Legatee.

STEWART Rebecca.

[66]   **Effects under £1,500.**

5 April.   The Will of Rebecca Stewart late of Beech Hill in the County of **Londonderry** Widow deceased who died 7 February 1861 at same place was proved at **Londonderry** by the oath of Abraham Harvey Stewart of Londonderry Esquire the sole Executor.

STEWART Samuel.

[17]   **Effects under £200.**

19 January.   The Will of Samuel Stewart late of Tubberlane in the County of **Tyrone** Farmer deceased who died 4 December 1860 at same place was proved at **Armagh** by the oath of John Causey of Tubberlane and Dawson Galway of Orritor both in said County of Tyrone Farmers the Executors.

Figure 71: Calendar of Wills, 1861. (Image courtesy of the National Archives of Ireland. Permissions received.)

Chapter Seventeen

Wills and Administrations

During the search for immigrant origins, many researchers ignore the Irish wills and administrations. They assume that the family members were too poor to have wills or that the pursuit of wills is limited because the family's residence in Ireland is not known. Both suppositions can be accurate, although perhaps not entirely so. Wills should always be consulted for Protestant families or Catholics who had some means. It is not true that a location in Ireland has to be determined ahead of time. The present chapter concentrates on the roles of wills in the quest for Irish origins with instruction in the benefits of the indexes to the pre-1858 will collections that were almost entirely destroyed.

Will research in Ireland is always divided into pre-1858 and post-1858 eras. Before 1858, the Church of Ireland, as the state

religion, was responsible for the probating of estates. After 1858, it became a civil matter.

Pre-1858 Will Research

In the pre-1858 period, wills were probated through two different types of courts, the Consistorial (Consistory) Court and the Prerogative Court of Armagh. Wills proved through the Consistorial Courts were diocesan based, and in the indexes, the dioceses were noted as the basic units. Church of Ireland dioceses, which do cross county lines, are shown in the table and map found on pages 234-235.

Although the massive collection of wills was destroyed in the 1922 Four Courts Fire, the indexes were not, making them worthwhile sources to consult. If a will of interest is found, the next step is to verify whether a copy, abstract, or extract survived. Online indexes to all or part of the Consistorial Courts can be found on Ancestry.com, FamilySearch.org, Findmypast.com, and at the National Archives of Ireland website. Because of the wide coverage of the online index versions, a county does not have to be known ahead of time, and thus they are also viable sources for surname distribution survey searches for immigrant origins. When the indexes point to dioceses or residences, proper surname distribution surveys can be conducted.

The other court was the Prerogative Court of Armagh, which had jurisdiction over every estate worth more than £5 in any diocese in all of Ireland. The Church of Ireland Bishop of Armagh held the responsibility. The indexes to administrations through the Prerogative Court are available from 1595 to 1858. Naturally, wealthier people with multiple holdings in Ireland had their estates probated in the Prerogative Court. The originals for these were also consumed in the 1922 Four Courts Fire, but the indexes were not. They can be found online at Ancestry.com, FamilySearch.org, Findmypast.com, and on the National Archives of Ireland.

Although the original Prerogative Court wills were eliminated, abstracts of them were made before 1922 and are part of "Betham's Genealogical Abstracts." This important collection can be found

Pre-1858 Consistorial Court Jurisdictions for Probates

County	Diocesan Courts
Antrim	Connor, Derry, Down, Dromore
Armagh	Armagh, Dromore
Carlow	Leighlin
Cavan	Ardagh, Kilmore, Meath
Clare	Killaloe & Kilfenora, Limerick
Cork	Ardfert & Aghadoe, Cork & Ross, Cloyne
Donegal	Clogher, Derry, Raphoe
Down	Connor, Down, Dromore, Newry & Mourne
Dublin	Dublin
Fermanagh	Clogher, Kilmore
Galway	Clonfert, Elphin, Killaloe & Kilfenora, Kilmacduagh, Tuam
Kerry	Ardfert & Aghadoe
Kildare	Dublin, Kildare, Leighlin
Kilkenny	Leighlin, Ossory
Leitrim	Ardagh, Kilmore
Leix (Queen's)	Dublin, Kildare, Leighlin, Ossory
Limerick	Cashel & Emly, Killaloe & Kilfenora, Limerick
Londonderry (Derry)	Armagh, Connor, Derry
Longford	Ardagh, Meath
Louth	Armagh, Clogher, Drogheda
Mayo	Killala & Achonry, Tuam
Meath	Armagh, Kildare, Kilmore, Meath
Monaghan	Clogher
Offaly (King's)	Clonfert, Kildare, Killaloe & Kilfenora, Meath, Ossory
Roscommon	Ardagh, Clonfert, Elphin, Tuam
Sligo	Ardagh, Elphin, Killala & Achonry
Tipperary	Cashel & Emly, Killaloe & Kilfenora, Waterford & Lismore
Tyrone	Armagh, Clogher, Derry
Waterford	Waterford & Lismore
Westmeath	Ardagh, Meath
Wexford	Dublin, Ferns
Wicklow	Dublin, Ferns, Leighlin

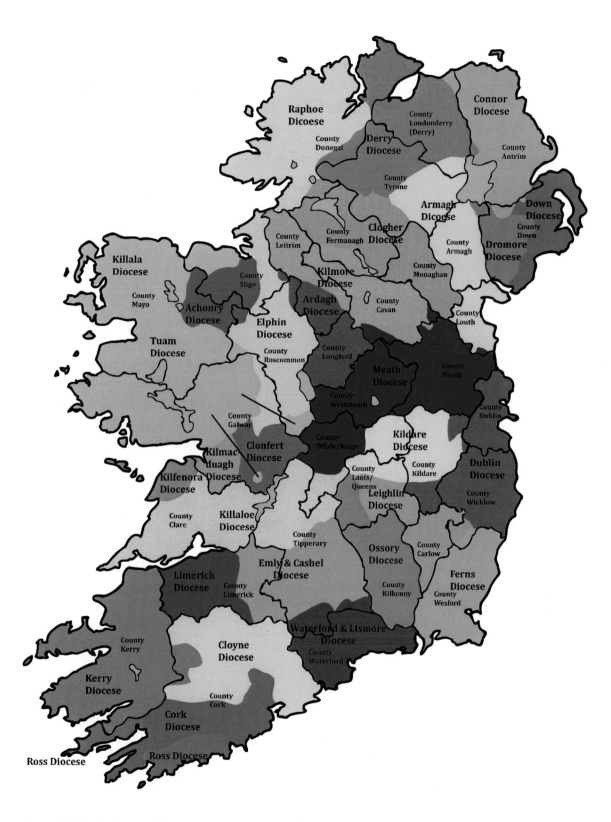

Figure 72: Church of Ireland Diocese Consistory Court jurisdictions, where estates were probated before 1858. Black borders represent county boundaries, and the color schemes denote diocese court jurisdictions.

on FamilySearch.org as "Genealogical Abstracts of Records of the Prerogative Court of Armagh," and it extends, with only a few exceptions, to 1799. The abstracts are digitized through FamilySearch.org and are at the National Archives of Ireland.

Databases often include both the Prerogative and Consistorial court indexes, such as "Ireland Diocesan and Prerogative Wills & Administrations Indexes 1595-1858" on Findmypast.com and the one by the same name on FamilySearch.org. They are from the National Archives of Ireland, which has its own database "Prerogative and Diocesan Copies of Some Wills and Indexes to Others, 1596-1858," although the indexes constitute most of it.

If a will is found in the index databases, the family's social status is indicated. In other words, it was one that was wealthy or at least had enough of an estate to warrant a will. If a will of an immigrant ancestor's family is discovered, the indexes should provide a residence. This alone solves an immigrant origins' question. If a will is noted in the indexes, indicating an estate, other records are opened, such as those in the Registry of Deeds for lease agreements or the Grand Lodge of Ireland for fraternal connections.

Because the majority of the pre-1858 wills were for Protestant families, finding one may be a clue that the family was Protestant in Ireland. Remember, religion can become confused in the immigrant country, especially as Catholics and Protestants intermarried abroad or

became irreligious, losing connections to any church loyalties in Ireland.

Appreciating that the original wills to which the indexes refer were gone in 1922 is essential. However, second copies, abstracts, and extracts might have been made before the destruction. One major index to second copies can be found on Findmypast.com in "Index to Irish Wills 1484-1858." This database pertains to the National Archives of Ireland collection, and the archives' reference numbers are given.

If some type of a second copy or abstract survived for any reference found in the various databases, it was deposited at either the PRONI or the National Archives of Ireland. Large parts of these archival documents are at the Family History Library as well.

Post-1858 Will Research

Will research conducted after 1858 is entirely different than that which is guided by pre-1858 sources and strategies. In the latter case, the originals also were burned in 1922, but second copies of most of them were in the local district registries. In addition, calendars of wills with year-by-year accounts of the estates probated and abstracts of the contents of the wills were printed. For immigrant research, perhaps the post-1858 period was most significant because it was after the Famine, when wealth was achievable. Therefore, small farmers and common people who had estates upon their deaths were numerous. The source is for both Catholics and Protestants, and mentions of relatives who had immigrated were customary. After 1858, regardless of social statuses, always look at wills. One may not be found, but it is part of the process of diligence.

In the post-1858 period, wills were registered civilly in probate district registries that did cross county lines. Also, the Principal Registry was in Dublin. The only wills that did not escape ruin, nor were second copies made of them, were those for the Principal Registry. The various counties and the registries serving them are recorded in the table below.

Because of the importance of the post-1858 collections, they are indexed in several places, and digitized copies are supplied. One site to begin searching is the

Post-1858 Probate Registry Districts

County	Probate Registry
Antrim	Belfast
Armagh	Armagh
Carlow	Kilkenny
Cavan	Cavan
Clare	Limerick
Cork	Cork
Donegal	Londonderry
Down	Belfast
Dublin	Principal Registry
Fermanagh	Armagh
Galway	Tuam
Kerry	Cork, Limerick
Kildare	Principal Registry
Kilkenny	Kilkenny
Leitrim	Ballina, Cavan
Leix (Queen's)	Kilkenny
Limerick	Limerick
Londonderry (Derry)	Londonderry
Longford	Cavan
Louth	Armagh
Mayo	Ballina
Meath	Principal Registry
Monaghan	Armagh
Offaly (King's)	Mullingar, Principal Registry
Roscommon	Tuam
Sligo	Ballina
Tipperary	Limerick, Waterford
Tyrone	Armagh, Londonderry
Waterford	Waterford
Westmeath	Mullingar
Wexford	Waterford
Wicklow	Principal Registry

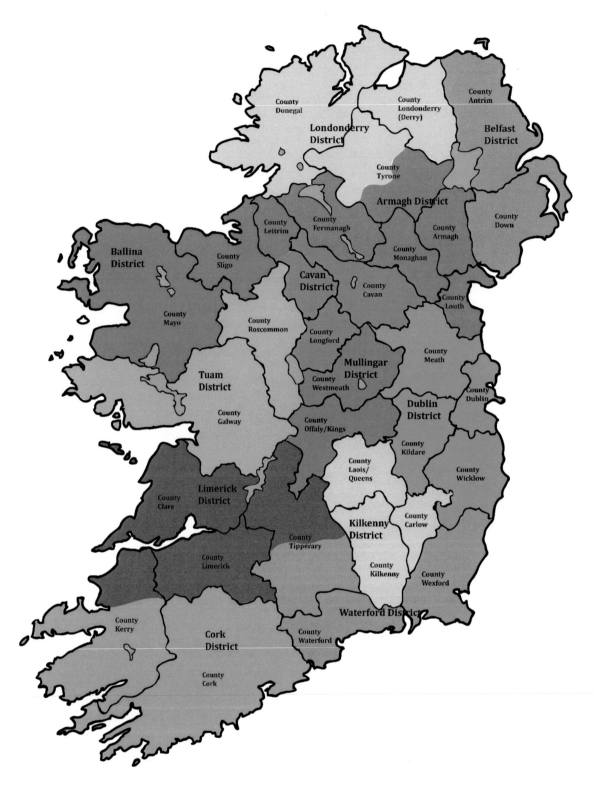

Figure 73: Probate Registry Districts for post-1858 research of probates and calendars of wills. Black borders repre-sent county boundaries, and the color schemes denote probate registry districts.

FamilySearch.org database "Ireland, Calendar of Wills and Administrations, 1858-1920." This is an index to the published calendars. If an entry of interest is found, the original published will books, which should contain more information, can be accessed in the FamilySearch Catalog under Ireland/County/Wills/Probate Records, which lists the wills by the probate registry.

These calendars are from the National Archives of Ireland. Its own database "Calendars of Wills and Administrations 1858-1920" encompasses all of Ireland through 1917, but from 1918, only the counties in the Republic of Ireland are listed. Digitized online at the National Archives of Ireland website are the wills from 1858 to 1900 for only the counties of the Republic of Ireland. Collections for the counties in Northern Ireland are at the PRONI, which has the calendars online from 1858 to 1965. The earlier records are digitized.

Super Index to Wills

An incredible but little-known resource is *Super Index: A Compilation of Available Irish Will Indexes 1270-1860* (Salt Lake City, Utah: J & J Limited, 2000), compiled by Gloria Bangerter and edited and alphabetized by Joyce Parsons and Jeanne Jensen. It is a massive alphabetical index to will indexes and usually is referred to simply as *Super Index of Wills*. The 11 volumes offer insight into the people who left wills. The index lists approximately 210,000 names, the years of the wills and the counties. It also states whether they were wills or administration bonds and whether they went through the Prerogative Court or a specific

Consistorial Court. This index can be obtained through the FamilySearch Catalog. Keep in mind that most of the wills were destroyed in the 1922 Four Courts Fire, but for several reasons, this index to all the indexes is a perfect tool for seeking Irish origins.

Although many of the facts in the *Super Index of Wills* may be on other databases for the Prerogative and Consistorial Courts, this published work is another way to check accuracy of indexing and a new manner of looking at material – on paper. Plus, it embraces all of Ireland so that the ultimate surname distribution survey can be undertaken. On the whole, it is a noteworthy source for a research design.

Wills in the Registry of Deeds

If an ancestor was in the class of people that had registered deeds, looking for a registered will in the Registry of Deeds is a practical task. Often, references to deaths, inheritances, and family relationships are in the deeds, but also registered deeds can be the texts of the wills themselves. These kinds of wills were bypassed in the 1922 Four Courts Fire, and they are indispensable. Wills were registered primarily for prominent families and have been extracted from 1708 to 1832 in the following three volumes:

Beryl P. Eustace. *Registry of Deeds, Dublin, Abstract of Wills*. Vol. 1 (1708-1745); Vol. 2 (1746-1788). Dublin: Stationery Office for the Irish Manuscript Commission, 1954-1956.

Eilish Ellis and P. Beryl Eustace. *Registry of Deeds, Dublin, Abstract of Wills*. Vol.

3 (1785-1832). Dublin: Stationery Office for the Irish Manuscript Commission, 1984.

Provided in these wills are the addresses for parties cited in the texts and the locations of any allocated lands. The personal names and place names are accessible through both indexes in the volumes. If a family member is found in the collection, the mystery of the immigrant's birthplace is solved rather quickly.

Index to Prerogative Wills of Ireland.   7

1780 **Alloway**, Sarah, Marrowbone-lane, Dubl.	1790 **Anderson**, Henry, Dunbell, co. Kilk., esq.
1766 „ William, Dublin, merchant	1799 „ Henry
1635 **Allyn**, John, *alias* **Greene**, Brehon, King's County, gent. [See ALLEN.]	1748 „ Hugh, Derrinine, King's County
	1706 „ Jas., Belfast, co. Antrim, gent.
	1763 „ James, Dublin, hosier
1793 **Alment**, John, Prussia-st., optician	1635 „ John, Dublin, gent. [**IV.** 153
1708 **Alnutt**, Thomas, par. St. Martin-in-the-Fields, Middlesex, esq. (Copy)	1696 „ John, Chester, aldn. (Copy)
	1743 „ John, Dublin, apothecary
	1762 „ John, Dublin, M.D.
1683 **Alsop**, Grace, Upper Coomb, co. Dublin	1791 „ John, Dolphin's Barn-lane, silk manufacturer
1637 „ William, Donoure, co. Dublin, yeoman	1797 „ John, lieut. in 56th regt. of foot
1805 **Alt**, John, Banagher, gent.	1805 „ John, Love-lane, co. Dublin, linen printer
1776 **Altamont**, John, earl of (Large)	1746 „ Mary, Derrinine, King's County
1781 „ Peter, earl of	1773 „ Paris, co. Tipperary, clerk
1808 **Ambrose**, Elizabeth S., inhabitant of Frankenberg	1754 „ Rachael (Copy)
1732 „ Garret, Dublin, gent. (Not proved)	1790 „ Richd, Kilternan, co. Dub., esq.
	1697 „ Robert, Glenavy, co. Antrim, farmer
1783 „ John, Erleston, Hampshire (Copy)	1751 „ Robert, Island Bridge, co. Dublin, millwright
1731 „ Michael, Dublin, brewer	1793 „ Robt., Newry, co. Down, gent.
1672 „ Thomas, Dublin, staymaker	1797 „ Robert, Ard, King's County, farmer
1715 „ William, Caledon, co. Tyrone	
1732 „ William, Ambrose Hall, co. Dublin, esq.	1758 „ Samuel
	1786 „ Samuel, city Armagh, mercht.
1679 **Amirant**, Mary, Killeniefe, co. Tipperary, spinster	1804 „ Samuel Jas. Bd., Cullinagh, Queen's County, gent.
1729 **Amory**, Elizabeth, Dublin, widow	1775 „ Sarah, Dublin, widow of Dr. John A.
1629 „ Gabriel, mariner	
1713 „ Robert, Island of Antigua, planter (Copy)	1729 „ Thomas, Cloncannon, King's County, gent.
1667 „ Thomas, Galy, co. Kerry, esq.	1676 „ William, Belfast, merchant
1728 „ Thos., Bunratty, co. Clare, esq.	1747 „ William, Stoneybatter, Dublin
1768 **Amphlet**, Thomas, Dublin, joiner	1748 „ William, Dublin, staymaker
1696 **Amye**, Anne, Edenderry, King's County, spinster	1784 „ William the elder, Mulletornan, co. Monaghan, farmer
1803 **Ancell**, Samuel, Dublin, esq.	1788 „ William, Dublin, gent.
1733 **Anderson**, Alexander, Gracedieu, co. Waterford, esq.	1808 „ William, Foxhall, co. Tipp., esq.
1805 „ Alexander, paymaster of the Tyrone militia	1723 **Andoe**, Francis, Rahallin, co. Meath, farmer
1772 „ Anne, Dublin, widow	1788 „ John, High-street, Dublin, woollen draper
1774 „ Anstace, Fethard, co. Tipperary, widow	1787 „ Mathew, Broguestown, co. Kildare, farmer
1714 „ rev. Arthur, Rower, co. Kilkenny, LL.D.	1693 **Andrew**, James, Newtown, par. St. Margaret, co. Dublin, farmer
1786 „ Catherine, Dublin city	1701 „ Jas., Manonstown, co. Meath, farmer
1762 „ Elizabeth, Dublin, spinster	
1808 „ Elizabeth, Abbey-street, Dubl., widow	1691 „ Richard, Newtown, Dunsaghly, co. Dublin, farmer
1774 „ Forster, Coote Hill, co. Cavan, apothecary	1634 **Andrewe**, Constance, widow of Hen. Andrewe, Dublin, esq.
1741 „ Francis, Dublin, gent.	1634 „ Henry, Dublin, esq.
1659 „ Geo., Dubl., mercht. [VIII. 41	1634 „ Ptk., Flemingstown, co. Meath, farmer
1729 „ Gregory, Dublin, distiller	
1784 „ Hanagh	
1772 „ Henry, Coleman, co. Tip., gent.	1710 **Andrewes**, John, Limerick, gent.

Figure 74: Page from the Prerogative Court of Armagh: "Index to Prerogative Wills in Ireland," 1536-1810. (Author Arthur Vicars. Ireland copyrights apply for the life of the author plus 70 years. No permissions required.)

Chapter Eighteen

Workhouse Records

The Poor Law records are the archives of the Boards of Guardians, the administrators of relief to the poor from 1838 through 1948. The final stops for many families and individuals in Ireland were the workhouses, whose documents may have the last listings of ancestors before they left the country. It is within the records of the workhouses that researchers may be able to reconstruct not only when families emigrated but also under what circumstances. Because the vast archive is not fully indexed, the manuscripts can be obtained with less difficulty when a county in Ireland is already known.

Workhouse records can be in various places. The PRONI and the National Archives of Ireland are predictable repositories. However, do not neglect the county libraries because some of them contain the records for workhouses operating in their counties. The Family History Library has a large collection that is digitized or on microfilm and can be accessed through the FamilySearch.org website. Findmypast.com also has many Poor Law Union records indexed and digitized. Each county has several unions serving them since the unions cross county boundaries. The records at any repository are by the Poor Law Union. (For a map of Poor Law Unions, see pages 10-11 of this publication.) An online inventory with links is on Workhouses.org.uk, which lists repositories for the United Kingdom and Ireland. This website also has histories of the poorhouses in Ireland, the residents' routines and work, the meals they were served, and emigrations from the institutions and Ireland itself. An enlightening article it carries is "Irish Workhouse Rules (1844)," a copy of the stipulations for people entering workhouses. Another excellent reproduction is on the website "The Irish Workhouse Centre" at Irishworkhousecentre.ie, based in Portumna, County Galway, at the old workhouse.

Although no composite index to all the workhouses is online, the closest is the collection on Findmypast.com. A general search can be done for the Irish records, which naturally combines all the workhouse registers into one search. Otherwise, the documents can be explored individually through their own databases of Poor Law Union records with the keywords "poor" and "workhouse" bringing up anything added to the Irish collections. The Findmypast.com catalog also can be limited to the category of "Institutes & Organizations," which is how workhouse records are cataloged for a general search.

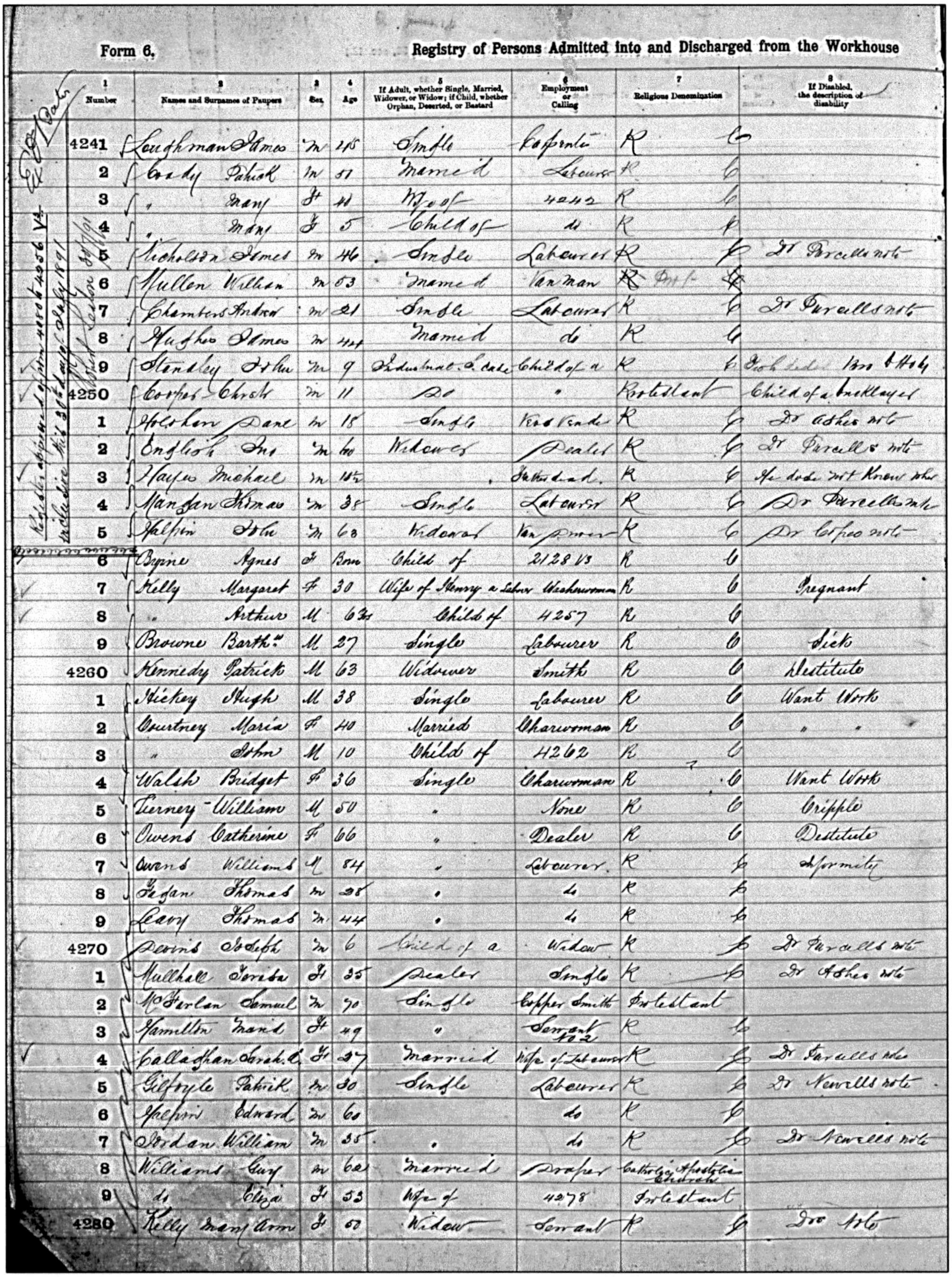

Form 6. Registry of Persons Admitted into and Discharged from the Workhouse

1 Number	2 Names and Surname of Paupers	3 Sex	4 Age	5 If Adult, whether Single, Married, Widower, or Widow; if Child, whether Orphan, Deserted, or Bastard	6 Employment or Calling	7 Religious Denomination	8 If Disabled, the description of disability
4241	Loughman James	m	28	Single	Carpenter	R	
2	Grady Patrick	m	51	Married	Labourer	R	
3	" Mary	f	44	Wife of	4242	R	
4	" Mary	f	5	Child of	do	R	
5	Nicholson James	m	46	Single	Labourer	R	Dr Purcell's note
6	Mullen William	m	53	Married	Vanman	R	
7	Chambers Andw	m	21	Single	Labourer	R	Dr Purcell's note
8	Hughes James	m	44	Married	do	R	
9	Standley John	m	9	Industrial School	Child of a	R	Scalded arms & body
4250	Corpes Chrst	m	11	do		Protestant	Child of a bricklayer
1	Holohan Dane	m	18	Single	Kes Vends	R	Dr Ashes note
2	English Jno	m	60	Widower	Dealer	R	Dr Purcell's note
3	Hayes Michael	m	18		Fatherless	R	He does not know who
4	Mangan Thomas	m	38	Single	Labourer	R	Dr Purcell's note
5	Halpin John	m	63	Widower	Vanman	R	Dr Cope's note
6	Byrne Agnes	f	Born	Child of	2128 v3	R	
7	Kelly Margaret	F	30	Wife of Henry a Labr	Washerwoman	R	Pregnant
8	" Arthur	M	6½	Child of	4257	R	
9	Browne Barthw	M	27	Single	Labourer	R	Sick
4260	Kennedy Patrick	M	63	Widower	Smith	R	Destitute
1	Hickey Hugh	M	38	Single	Labourer	R	Want Work
2	Courtney Maria	F	40	Married	Charwoman	R	
3	" John	M	10	Child of	4262	R	
4	Walsh Bridget	F	36	Single	Charwoman	R	Want Work
5	Tierney William	M	50		None	R	Cripple
6	Owens Catherine	F	66		Dealer	R	Destitute
7	Owens William	M	84		Labourer	R	Deformity
8	Logan Thomas	m	28		do	R	
9	Leary Thomas	m	44		do	R	
4270	Devins Joseph	m	6	Child of a	Widow	R	Dr Farrell's note
1	Mulhall Jorisa	f	35	Dealer	Single	R	Dr Ashes note
2	McFarlan Samuel	m	70	Single	Copper Smith	Protestant	
3	Hamilton Mary	f	49	"	Servant	R	
4	Callaghan Arch C	f	27	Married	Wife of Labourer	R	Dr Farrell's note
5	Gilfoyle Patrick	m	30	Single	Labourer	R	Dr Newell's note
6	Guerin Edward	m	60		do	R	
7	Jordan William	m	38		do	R	Dr Newell's note
8	Williams Guy	m	62	Married	Draper	Catholic Apostolic Church	
9	do Eliza	f	53	Wife of	4278	Protestant	
4280	Kelly Mary Anne	f	50	Widow	Servant	R	Dr Ashes note

Figures 75a-75b: Admission and Discharge Records (1891) of the South Dublin Union Workhouse. (Images courtesy of The National Archives of Ireland. Permissions received.)

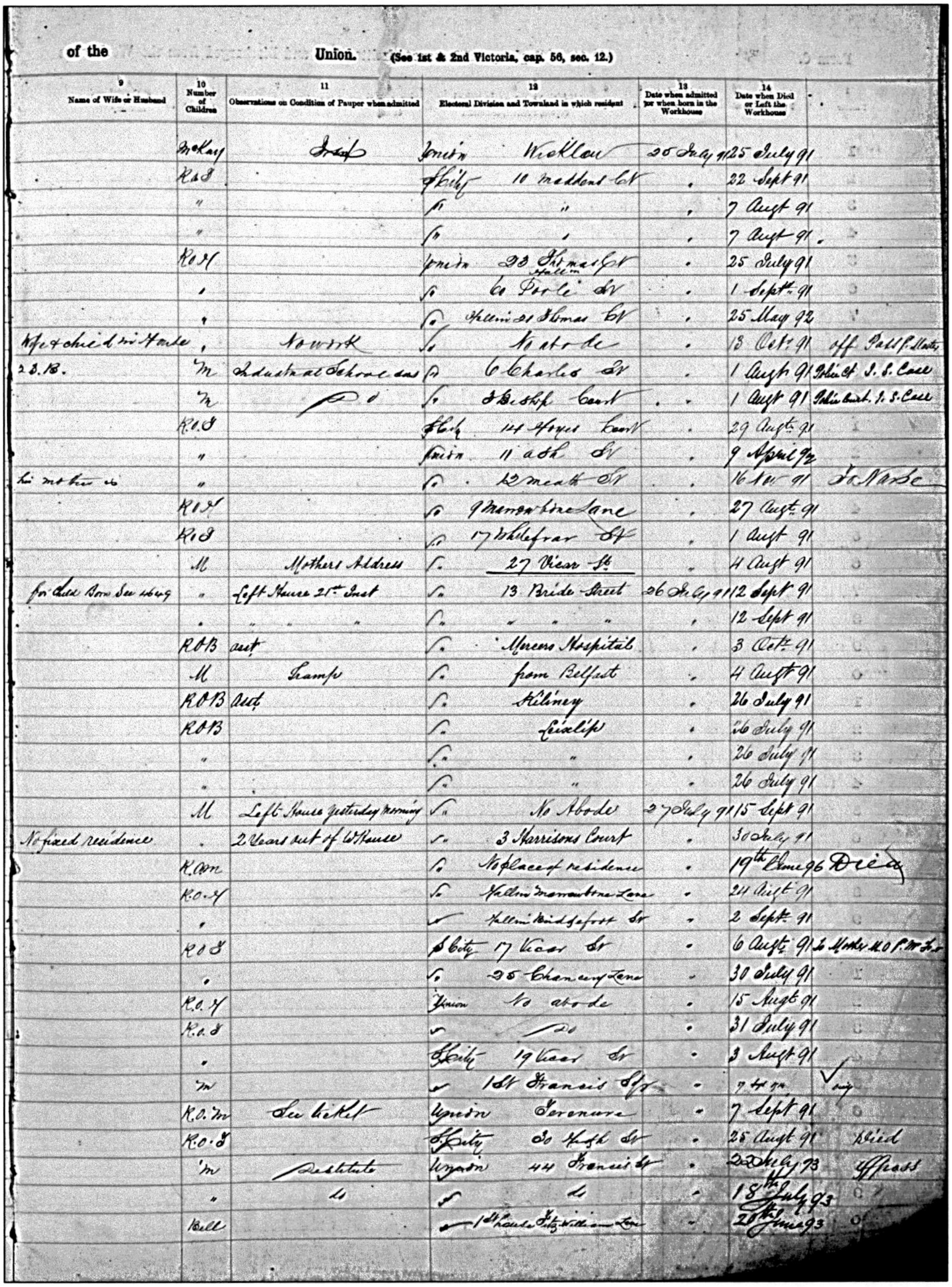

Figures 75a-75b: Admission and Discharge Records (1891) of the South Dublin Union Workhouse. (Images courtesy of The National Archives of Ireland. Permissions received.)

The Workhouse and Emigration

People entered the workhouses for several reasons. The workhouse schedules were so grueling that only those who had no other choices considered them. Hunger and unemployment might have been the main causes, but they were not the only ones. Workhouses were havens for unmarried pregnant girls, women who had been deserted by their husbands, orphaned children, and people whose relatives were too old or too poor to care for them. Sick and handicapped individuals were among the populations as well. If the members of a family entered together, they were separated into sections of the buildings by categories, such as able-bodied males and females, infants and children, and the old and infirm.

These were places of last recourses. For those who did not die in the workhouses, leaving the country might have been the only option left. For emigration purposes, the Board of Guardians' records, of which the workhouse reports are components, are important for the years of the Potato Famine (1845-1851), but they should not be neglected for the years afterward. Because of the overcrowding of the workhouses during the Famine years, the Outdoor Relief programs began in 1847 so that people could remain in their homes, work for the Poor Law Union, and be paid in food.

From the period of the 1838 Irish Poor Law Act, the Poor Law Union was authorized to spend up to one shilling of each pound of the poor rate to assist deportations of needy persons who would have been in workhouses if they remained in Ireland. Their destinations were originally the British colonies of Australia, Canada, and New Zealand. From 1848, this emigration scheme was expanded to include non-colonial countries, such as the United States.

The Poor Law Union workhouses and landlords seeking to reduce their shares of the destitute persons on their lands escalated the demand for emigrations. In response, many unmonitored and unseaworthy ships were commissioned. The term "coffin ships" was coined for them because up to twenty percent of people on some of them died during the voyages. A misperception is that these were ships sailing to America, but most American ships were regulated and monitored. The coffin ships were of British origin, and scores of them were bound for Canada.

When using workhouse records, consider the religious compositions of the geographical areas. Do not assume that workhouses were populated only by penniless Roman Catholics. This might have been true in locations where they comprised the majority of the population, but in many areas, such as in Ulster, both Catholics and Protestants lived in the workhouses. The records have the religions of the residents. Of the several types of workhouse reports, the ones most adaptable for documenting departures are the "Indoor Relief Registers" and the "Minute Books."

The Indoor Relief Registers provide information such as name, residence (townland, town, or simply the Poor Law Union), marital status (single, married, or deserted), the status of a child (bastard,

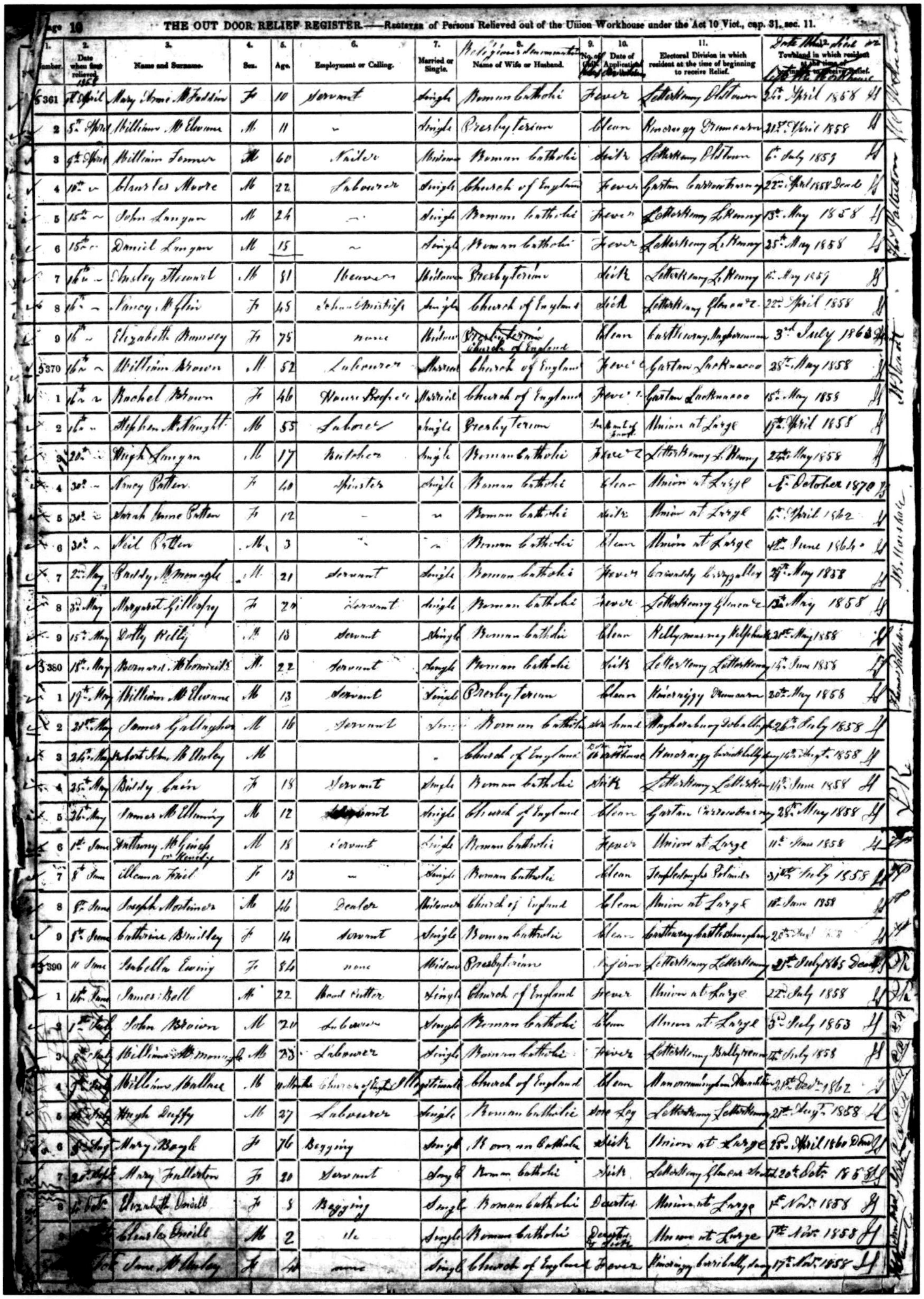

Figure 76: Outdoor Relief Register page (1858) from the Letterkenny Workhouse in County Donegal. While described as a Relief Register, it was used as an Admission and Discharge Register. (Image courtesy of Donegal County Council. Permissions received.)

orphaned, or deserted), the condition in which the person arrived (physically dirty, with clothes, and notes about physical and emotional health), religion, date arrived, and date of death or discharge. The Minute Books for the period of the Potato Famine document the people to whom the Board of Guardians gave assistance to emigrate. Details about the residents are mainly in the Indoor Relief Registers.

Another source is the Outdoor Relief Registers. The pressures of the Famine necessitated helping people but not giving them shelter in the workhouses. The Outdoor Relief Registers are less informative than are the Indoor Relief Registers.

If workhouses are the last lodgings of ancestors before their emigrations, the dates they were discharged are the closest records to departures. When dates are compared to passenger arrival lists at foreign ports, for instance, in the United States or Canada, clearer pictures will emerge, and researchers will be able to create timelines.

The workhouse is one of the many heartrending stories in Irish history. Even with its faults and horrors, it did keep people alive long enough to return to their homes or to emigrate. Many of the old workhouses still stand and deserve the attention of family historians.

Figure 77: Lismore Union Workhouse in County Waterford (1842). (Image by Robert Armstrong. Courtesy of National Library of Ireland. Ireland copyrights apply for the life of the author plus 70 years. No permissions required.)

Chapter Nineteen

Special Strategy: Names, Nicknames, and Naming Patterns

Numerous aspects of given names and surnames in Ireland's past are so uncharacteristic that sorting through them requires time. Being prepared with information can make the difference between acquiring worthwhile records from databases and completely discounting what could be unmistakable. If researchers do not know about naming patterns, name variations, and even alternative surnames, they cannot wholly comprehend what they view online or in the documents.

Naming Patterns

Novices customarily cite naming patterns as substantiations when they discover christenings in databases of Irish church records, but the method is not that simple. Not all families followed the naming customs. Moreover, consideration has to be given to the naming differences between the Irish and English, versus Scottish traditions, and inconsistencies were within each one of them. Often, children who did not live to adulthood or who emigrated had no records, absences that can ruin the naming pattern strategy. In addition, problems develop if the Ireland church records are incomplete. Most researchers start to entertain the naming archetypes as reasonable research plans as they encounter names from the immigrants' records.

For example, in the Ulster-Scots (Scots-Irish) communities, many families in the immigrant countries did pattern the names in the Scottish tradition, which thus is a viable idea to follow when exploring Ulster records. However, by the latter part of the nineteenth century, the convention began to break down.

Still, in the documents of Ireland or immigrant countries, research directed by the children's names can suffer from the same predicaments: How many children are missing from records? Did the parents practice the naming pattern? Are ages accurate in the immigrant papers?

One indication that a difficulty may arise in identifying families by naming patterns is gaps in the lists of children in census reports. Most researchers have observed a case in which the parents were married in 1840 but the first documented child in the census was born in 1845. The space of five years is obvious and most likely reflects infants or young children who died between census reports. Therefore, the arrangement of names within the family being studied, unless entire records through several generations confirm that it was the custom, cannot be an entire research approach.

In general, when an Irish emigrant family adhered to a naming sequence, it was according to religions: A Catholic family followed the Irish pattern; Anglican families, the English naming pattern; and

Irish Naming Patterns

- 1st son was named after the father's father
- 2nd son was named after the mother's father
- 3rd son was named after the father
- 4th son was named after the father's eldest brother
- 1st daughter was named after the mother's mother
- 2nd daughter was named after the father's mother
- 3rd daughter was named after the mother
- 4th daughter was named after the mother's eldest sister

English Naming Patterns

- 1st son was named after the father's father
- 2nd son was named after the mother's father
- 3rd son was named after the father
- 4th son was named after the father's eldest brother
- 1st daughter was named after the mother's mother
- 2nd daughter was named after the father's mother
- 3rd daughter was named after the mother
- 4th daughter was named after the mother's eldest sister

Scottish Naming Patterns

- 1st son was named after the father's father (variation is after the mother's father)
- 2nd son was named after the mother's father (variation is the father's father)
- 3rd son was named after the father
- 4th son was named after the father's oldest brother (variation is after the father's paternal grandfather)
- 5th son was named after the mother's oldest brother (variation is after the mother's paternal grandfather)
- 1st daughter was named after the mother's mother (variation is after the father's mother)
- 2nd daughter was named after the father's mother
- 3rd daughter was named after the mother
- 4th daughter was named after the mother's oldest sister (variation is after the mother's maternal grandmother)
- 5th daughter was named after the father's oldest sister (variation is after the father's maternal grandmother)

Presbyterians, the Scottish naming pattern. Even at this, imagine a mixed marriage in which cultures competed. An encouraging detail, though, is that in all three systems, for the most part, the first son was named after his paternal grandfather and the first daughter, after her maternal grandmother. Again, do not make assumptions based upon immigrant records unless a complete list of children in order of births is known and the church registers or censuses are extant. Naming formulas seem to be sound, but they may not relate to real families. The three naming patterns are shown in the accompanying tabs on the previous page.

The Use of *O'* and *Mc*

A general uncertainty in Irish or Irish immigration research is the incidence of the *O* and the *Mc* in Irish and Scots-Irish surnames. *Mc* or *Mac* means "son of" among the Irish and the Scots. In Ireland in the Middle Ages, naming was patronymic with the next generation having a different surname contingent on the father's first name. The practice lasted longer in Scotland. During the eleventh century, Ireland established surnames that did not change. It is interesting to note that in first Irish historical records, such as Griffith's Primary Valuation (1847-1864), the compilers did not deal with *Mc* or *Mac*. They commonly wrote *M'* and called it good enough!

The Irish *O* meant "grandson" and was applied in a fashion similar to that discussed above for the patronymic naming system, standardizing surnames in the Middle Ages.

Remember that *O* and *Mc/Mac* were prefixes of the ancient Gaelic society, and today's Anglicized versions may be two dissimilar names. O'Murphy became Murphy, which is a simple example, and genealogy records list Murphy far more often than O'Murphy. Murphy is the Anglicized form.

For genealogical research, pay attention to the presence or absence of *O* and *Mc/Mac* in a surname. Too quickly, novices discount records because *O*'s or *Mc*'s are or are not in their families' names today. Researchers sometimes tend to forget that in the past, most people were illiterate or semi-literate and were in a culture that had unpredictable enunciations. After all, in an illiterate society, people never spelled their names and never were asked to do so for records by the clerks or clergy. One of the biggest barriers for novices is assuming: "This is not my ancestor because we spell the name this way." If the uninformed conclusion is not corrected, Irish research fails before it starts. Surnames in Ireland are anything but concretized even on one page, in one document, or by one clerk or priest.

For example, the name O'Connor and Connor are identical. Retaining the *O* or dropping it (or the *Mc* in other names) makes no difference. The ancestors did not regard names as people do today, wherein everything is standardized and polished. Thinking phonetically when viewing Irish and early records in the immigrant countries is important. If it sounds like the name, it likely is the name.

A rule in Irish or Ulster-Scots research is not to give much significance to spellings, especially the oddities of the *O* and *Mc* prefixes. With phonetic pronunciations, with or without the *Mc* or *O*, the chances of finding ancestors or relatives in the many databases of Irish records are increased. Otherwise, apparent clues will be disregarded.

Variations in Surnames

A surprise for many people is that surnames, which were eventually standardized in the immigrant countries, are not what they were in Ireland. As a result, even if all Irish records were indexed, they are of little value without first addressing this hurdle. Thankfully, the situation does not present itself for every family, but it is rife enough to cause delay.

The classic work on surnames in Ireland with their principal locations is Sir Robert Edwin Matheson's *Varieties and Synonymes of Surnames and Christian Names in Ireland: for the Guidance of Registration Officers and the Public in Searching the Indexes of Births, Deaths, and Marriages* (Dublin, Ireland: Stationery Office, 1901). His book is fundamental for most, if not all, later ones on the topic. It is widely available in reprint and is digitized on FamilySearch.org.

Occasionally, the problem is not that the family "changed its name," as is the often-repeated myth, but, rather, its development was more complex. Researchers in the immigrant records have to consider that the ancestors upon leaving Ireland might have adopted a pride in being Irish. If they were living in an Irish

community, especially among Catholics, organizations related to heritage and culture might have been attached to the lives of parishes. Hence, maybe Sullivan became O'Sullivan, or surnames were standardized in a more Gaelic fashion.

Sullivan to O'Sullivan is obvious, but the opposite circumstance is true as well. If families immigrated to places hostile to the Irish, and more particularly to Irish Catholics, deemphasizing the Irish-ness of their names might have been in their best interests. Hutchinson consequently stayed Hutchinson instead of reverting to its original McCutcheon form, which was Anglicized to Hutchinson over time in Ireland. References such as Padraig Giolla-Domhanaigh's *Some Anglicised Surnames in Ireland* (Dublin, Ireland: Gael Co-operative Society, 1923) can offer insight into Irish, Scottish, and Welsh surnames that have been Anglicized. His work is digitized on FamilySearch.org.

Historic books, such as those by Matheson and Giolla-Domhanaigh, sometimes can solve a riddle. However, they just as often do not because the immigrant was not trying to develop Irish pride or hide Irish origins. He or she simply was illiterate and had an extremely thick accent. In such cases, surnames have to be thought of as spelling evolutions. Until family members became literate or semi-literate, they never wrote their names or thought in terms of proper spellings, which were merely phonetic. The families spoke their names, and the clerks muddled their way through them until educational opportunities caught up with people. At that point, the families spelled their own names, which evolved as standardized surnames. Naturally, the names were unlike those that the clerks, priests, or ministers in Ireland wrote as they listened to illiterate people, which explains most of the surname challenges. The objective of the present topic is to emphasize the point that no clerk anywhere in the world asks illiterate persons to spell.

When Surnames Were Changed

A source of untold grief among researchers is Irish ancestors who changed their surnames even though the names were not authentic and legal in the sense of modern terms. The alterations were localized and necessary for separating people with the same names, a practice to bear in mind. The first indication of it may be that certain names in one location were too familiar and so caused confusion. This occurred for several reasons:

- So many Sullivans, for example, were in a locale that a branch of the family took the surname of a female ancestor who shared the Sullivan surname. Yet, everyone in the vicinity recognized the branch of the Sullivan family by their alternate surname. How that name crept into the local records, especially church and tax registers, is a matter of concern.

- A father's given name became a surname. In the aforementioned case, five Patrick Sullivans (or any other common combination) could have been in a townland, and the only way to differentiate them was by the father's first name. Accordingly, one was Patrick Peter after his father, and another was Patrick Thomas after his father. It is important to be aware of this practice. It is frequently found in Griffith's Primary Valuation (1847-1864) but is written as Patrick Sullivan (Peter) or Patrick Sullivan (Thomas). Another variation customary in Griffith's Primary Valuation is a mother's maiden name or possibly a more distant relative's name being used. In the tax list, with Sullivan again as the illustration, it may be Patrick Sullivan (Casey). This version is called an agnomen and can afford some amazing, if not hidden, clues to the lineages in Ireland, especially if church registers did not begin early enough to document the next generations back.

- In instances in which first and last names were common, a description was the agnomen instead of a person's name. Names such as Red, Big Red, Big, and Small must have been physical observations. In the Sullivan case in point, the name thus is Patrick Sullivan (Big Red) in sources such as Griffith's Primary Valuation.

- Jr. and Sr. might have designated older and younger, not always father and son. Therefore, when Sr. was no longer taxed and more than one Patrick Sullivan was still in the townland, Jr. became Sr. and a younger

Patrick Sullivan suited Jr. They might have been father and son, but the titles could have been for more complex descriptions.

With an immigration dilemma, when trying to find the correct family in the various online databases, it is sensible to judge how common a name really is. Often, a county in Ireland already has been found from the records of the immigrant country. If the databases reveal that the name is prevalent in the county, consider alternative surnames. In some parts of rural Ireland today, agnomens are ordinary even if they are only for the postal carriers' facility in delivering mail when the addresses are townlands instead of streets.

Names and Nicknames

First names and corresponding nicknames can be obstacles in locating correct families in the many Irish indexes, especially in church, civil, and tax databases. In the immigrant countries, the first names might not have been the same as they were in Ireland. For example, if Owen Sullivan and his wife Delia Callaghan always were identified by those names abroad, it is essential to realize that alternative names in the Irish records could be Eugene Sullivan and Bridget Callaghan. Without that knowledge, a researcher easily could miss the ancestral entries in the indexes. Also, if a researcher is not aware that Jacob is Latin for James or that Guilielmus is Latin for William, the indexes for Catholic records when not cross-referenced could result in no search results or complicate the findings.

Below is a list of names, and their variants, nicknames, and, where appropriate, their Latin equivalents. Some names are instantly recognizable for each other, such as Albert and Bert, and so those are not included. However, names that are almost but not quite self-explanatory are listed. One is Aileen. Eileen and Lena are close enough to be understood for Aileen but perhaps not so at a glimpse. Irish, English, and Scottish given names are equally trying.

Only the given names that could potentially be sources of confusion are presented below. The troublesome names most often encountered are the common ones such as Bridget, Dennis, Eugene, Ellen, James, Jeremiah, Margaret, and Mary. One observation is that alternative names are more usual for Irish Catholic women than they are for Irish Catholic men. For instance, Thomas is typically Thomas, whereas Hannah can be Anna, Hanorah, Honor, Johanna, and Nora.

The chart that follows was adapted from the following sources:

Ardolina, Rosemary Muscarella. *What's in a Name?: A List of Christian Names and Their Irish Nicknames, Variants, Irish & Latin Equivalents*. Floral Park, New York: Delia Publications, 2001.

"First Names." Irish Family History Foundation, 2020, www.RootsIreland.ie.

Matheson, Sir Robert Edwin. *Varieties and Synonymes of Surnames and Christian Names in Ireland: for the Guidance of Registration Officers and the Public in*

Searching the Indexes of Births, Deaths, and Marriages. Dublin, Ireland: Stationery Office, 1901.

Wight, Judith Eccles. *A Rose by any Other Name: A Guide to Irish Christian Names*. Provo, Utah: J. E. Wight, 1985.

Name Variations and Nicknames

Common Name	Variation	Nickname	Latin
Agnes	Winifred	Nancy, Nanny, Taggy	---
Aileen/Eileen	Ellen, Evelyn	Ellen, Lena, Nellie	---
Alexander	---	Sander, Sandy	---
Alfred	---	Fred	---
Alice	Alis	Alley, Elsie, Lizzie	---
Aloysius	---	Alley, Lou, Louis	---
Amelia	---	Amy, Milly	---
Anastasia	Anstes	Annis, Atty, Eustce, Stacy	---
Andrew	---	---	Andreas
Ann		Nancy, Nanny	---
Anthony	Anton	Anthy, Owney, Tony	---
Augustine	Austin	Austey, Austin	---
Bartholomew	---	Barbel, Bart, Bartley, Batty	---
Barnard	Barnet	Barney, Bernie	---
Bridget	Bridgid, Brigit	Bedelia, Beesy, Bessie Briddy, Bridie ,Cordelia Delia, Phidelia	---
Catherine/Katherine	Catilin, Kathleen	Cassie, Cate, Caty, Kitty	---
Cecilia	Sheila	Cecil, Cecily, Cis, Sisley	---
Charles	Carl	Carroll, Cormac	Carolus
Charlotte	Carola, Carolina	Lotta	---
Christine	---	Chrissy, Tina, Xina	---
Christopher	---	Christie, Kitt	---
Cormack	Charles	Con, Corly, Mac, Mick	---
Cornelius	Con, Neil	Con, Connor, Corney, Neil	---
Daniel	Donal, Donald	Donal, Donny	---
Darby	Dermot, Jeremiah, Jerome	---	Dermicius
Dennis	Donogh, Duncan	Denny, Donat, Donough	Dionysius
Deborah	---	Debbie, Gubbie	---
Dermot	Darby, Jeremiah	---	Dermot
Dominick	Dominy	Nick	---
Donald	Donat	Donough	---
Dorothy	Doreen	Dolly, Dora, Dot	---

Name Variations and Nicknames (cont.)

Common Name	Variation	Nickname	Latin
Edmond/Edmund	Edward, Edwin	Ned, Ted	---
Eleanor	Ellen, Evelyn, Helen	Ellie, Lena, Nell, Nora	---
Elizabeth	Eliza, Isabel	Bess, Beth, Betty, Eliza, Lizzie, Sheila	---
Esther	Easter, Hester	Essie, Esty, Hessie	Esthera, Hestera
Eugene	John, Owen, Evan	Gene	Eugenus, Oenus
Eustace	---	Stacy	---
Farrell	Fergal, Fergus	Farry	---
Felix	Phelim, Philip	---	Felix
Fergus	Gustus	Fergy	---
Finbar	---	Barra, Barry	---
Frances (F)	---	Fanny, Frany	Francisca
Francis (M)	---	Frank	Franciscus
Frederick	---	Ed, Fred	---
Garrett	Gerald	Gary, Jerry	---
Giles (F)	Cecily	Giley, Jilley, Sheela	Egidia
Giles (M)	---	Giley, Gill, Jilley	Aegidius
Grace	Grizell	Gracie	Gratia
Hannah	Anna, Johanna	Anna, Honor, Norah	Ana, Honoria
Helen	Ellen, Evelyn	Lena, Nell	---
Henry	Harold	Hal, Harry	---
Herbert	Bertram, Hab, Haribert	Bert, Bertie	---
Hester	Easter, Hester	Essie, Hessy, Hetty	---
Hugh	Herbert, Hubert	Huey	Hugo, Hugonis
James	Jacob	Jamey, Jim, Shemus	Jacobus
Jane	Janet, Jane, Joan	Janet, Jeanne, Jenny	Johanna
Janet	Jane, Joan	Etta, Jan, Netty	Johanna
Jeremiah	Darby, Dermot, Darby, Dermot	Jerome	Hieremias, Jeremias
Johanna	Anna, Hannah, Joan	Anna, Hannah, Joan	---
John	Owen	Jack, Dean, Shane	Joannis, Johannes
Josephine	---	Jo, Josie, Pheny	---
Judith	Julia	Jude, Jugge	---
Laurence/Lawrence	Lantry, Larkin, Lorcan	Lantry, Law, Lorry	Lorentius
Louis	Aloysius, Lucius	Ally, Lou	Ludovicus
Louisa	---	Lou, Lula, Lulu	---

Name Variations and Nicknames (cont.)

Common Name	Variation	Nickname	Latin
Lucas	Luke	Luck, Luckett	---
Manus	Moses	Mago, Mane	---
Margaret	Marjory	Daisy, Etta, Greta, Minnie, Molly, Peg, Polly, Rita	---
Martin	---	Mertie, Murt	---
Martha	Patricia	Marta, Martle	---
Mary	---	Mae, Mamie, Maria, Marion, Maureen, Minnie, Moll, Molly, Moya	---
Matilda	Patricia	Mait, Matty, Maude, Tilda, Tilly	---
Maurice	Mortimer	Morris	Maurtius
Nancy	Anna, Hannah, Joan	Anna, Nannie	---
Nicholas	Colin	Nicol	---
Owen/Oin	Eoin, Eugene	---	Audoenus
Penelope	Fionna, Irene	Finola, Flora, Nappy, Nelly, Penny	---
Peter	Peares, Pierce	Percy	Petrus
Phelim	Felix, Philip	Phelimy	Felmeus
Philip	Felix, Phelim, Phely	Pilib, Phil, Pip	---
Philomena	---	Mena, Mina, Phil, Philly	---
Pierce	Peter	Percy, Piers	---
Raymond/Redmond	---	Mundy, Ray	---
Richard	---	Dick, Rick	---
Robert	---	Bert, Bob, Robbin, Roy	---
Roderick	Roger	Rody, Rory	Ruderius
Roger	Richard, Roderick, Rufus, Rory, Roy	Dodge, Hodge, Roddy	---
Sabina	---	Bina, Sally, Sibby	---
Samuel	---	Sorley	---
Sarah	---	Sadie, Sal, Sally	---
Susan	---	Sukey	Susanna
Sybil	---	Bel, Sibby	Sibella
Teague	Thaddeus, Timothy	Ted, Thady, Tim	Thaddeus
Terence	Turlough	Tarla, Terry, Tirlough	Terentius
Teresa/Theresa	---	Terry, Tess, Treise	---
Thaddeus	Teague	Tade	---
Timothy	Teague, Thaddeus	Tady, Teigue, Tumelty	---
Wilhelmina	---	Mena, Minny	---
William	Liam, Wilhelm, Wilkin	Will	Guilielmus
Winifred	Una	Freda, Onna, Una, Winny	---

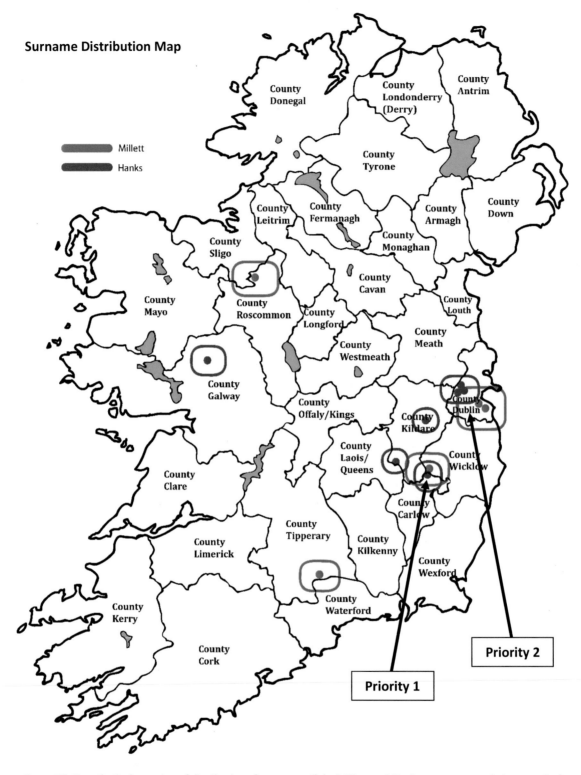

Figure 78: Hypothetical mapping of distribution of surnames. If the Millett and Hanks surnames are being searched, the primary focus can be on obvious locations. With additional surnames available for use, this triangulation strategy will be even more successful.

Chapter Twenty

Special Strategy: Surname Distribution Survey

One of the strategies for finding immigrant origins that has proved to be most successful through time and testing is the surname distribution survey. For researchers who have found their ancestors in indexes of church records or civil registrations, the present chapter will not be as interesting as it will be for those who know "Ireland" alone as the place of births.

When the location in Ireland where the ancestors lived has not been identified and all the indexes do not provide that answer, it is time to think abstractly. The plan involves inspecting a particular source or group of sources and mapping where a surname is found. This strategy also can be employed if a county has been confirmed but indexes fail to trace a town or parish. The approach has its limitations with familiar names. Kellys or Sullivans are of no shortage, and Callaghan can be spelled any number of ways. However, second names accompanying them, such as wives' birth names, assist in organizing the common names. In theory, a couple who married in Ireland probably resided in the same parish or parishes adjoining each other. Again, the tactic has its limitations, but it is one that can launch the search.

By assuming that a husband and wife lived within walking distance of each other or met at church, a viable strategy can unfold. The first question to be asked is: What records might have been made to document surnames and localities? This by itself is rather conjectural, but not everyone emigrated, leaving behind siblings, cousins, and cousins of cousins. If the people with the surnames being researched remained in Ireland, regardless of the time frame, the records are applicable. Often, a century can elapse between emigration of ancestors and the production of records from which to conduct a surname distribution survey.

Before starting a surname distribution survey, remember that although research may begin in one record source, others probably will be added along the way. When developing charts to arrange details from multiple sources, sometimes assigning numbers or abbreviations to the ones referenced simplifies proceeding with the study. The codes may be as follows:

- CCW = Consistorial Court Wills

- CRI = Irish Civil Registration Index

- GLI = Grand Lodge of Ireland

- GPV = Griffith's Primary Valuation

- ICR = Irish Church Records Database

- PCW = Prerogative Court Wills

- SWS = Spinning Wheel Survey

- TAB = Tithe Applotment Books

How the chart is set up or how the source codes are labeled cannot be right or wrong. The goal of the search is distinguishing a pattern of geographical locations of surnames.

Example Using the Ulster-Scots

Perhaps an extreme example of the survey, yet a universal one in genealogy circles, is the Scots-Irish (Ulster-Scots) who left between 1718 and 1776. More than 200,000 of them emigrated from Ulster to the American colonies. Because they departed so early and because of their social class as tenant farmers, a reasonable assessment is that finding records for them in Ireland is improbable. Generally, they remain United States research problems.

With the Ulster-Scots as an illustration, researchers have to look at the historical context that can be a constructive part of the strategy. First, they came predominantly from the Ulster counties, which are Antrim, Armagh, Cavan, Donegal, Down, Fermanagh, Londonderry (Derry), Monaghan, and Tyrone. Second, most,

but certainly not all, immigrated as Presbyterians. In other words, they were not Catholics. Third, they emigrated in groups, often following their ministers to the American colonies. The idea behind these group or congregational migrations was their safety in numbers in the hostile and treacherous frontier colonies.

Automatic limits to an initial investigation are confirmed by the three positive facets in the case of the Ulster-Scots. The geographical target for them is one province out of four and potentially one church instead of many. Also, more than one surname is obtainable with which to work because a multitude of people traveled together. Thus, the surname survey can begin.

Several sources are excellent, but all are not complete; therefore, more than one of them needs to be read. For the Ulster counties, prime records are:

- Spinning Wheel Survey (1796)

- Tithe Applotment Books (1823-1837)

- Griffith's Primary Valuation (1847-1864)

- Will indexes to the Prerogative and Consistorial courts (1270-1860)

Certainly, more than the preceding can be of assistance, but they suffice for a basic examination. The scope of the search itself can be eased by limiting it to specific records. Additional documents can be added if needed. However, the ones listed above do encompass all of

Ulster, whereas some other sources may include only one county or a few parishes.

Assume that through United States research, a total of three surnames have been identified as potentially from the same place in Ulster. For example, the United States records indicate that the three families likely came together, settled near one another, and intermarried while in the colonies. All three names, including that of the ancestor, can be searched in the four sources designated above. To sort through the findings, develop a graph similar to the form shown at the bottom of this page:

The least common surname is probably the best one with which to begin, and work around it for emerging patterns. If one is present, that is, all three surnames are found in one county or in a couple of parishes within that county, the quest may or may not be at an end.

With the theory that family members were left behind, which is what a distribution survey is, logically, they were on either the old family properties or close to them. When the search has been narrowed to a few civil parishes, it can proceed to ascertaining what sources survive for the 1700s in those exact areas. Those could include the rent books of the landlords, lease agreements in the Registry of Deeds, Grand Lodge of

Ireland membership records, or even parish histories. If no local records can be found with the ancestors' names, the surname distribution survey may be the sole, albeit indirect, proof that the emigrants were from an area—the only evidence. At that point, the lineage hunt likely is at a close.

The indication, though, about where the family may have originated is a wonderful outcome. New research strategies then can be developed to learn more about the family from that region. Although the evidence is not infallible, it is substantial in the absence of any other.

When a County is Known

The records of the immigrant county, perhaps discovered on tombstones in Catholic cemeteries or in vital records, usually supply counties of origins. However, often found after searching church records' indexes is that the records did not begin early enough to document christenings or family events were not registered by the priests or ministers. Unfortunately, the situations occurred more frequently than many researchers want to believe. In these circumstances, accept that the problem must be solved *without* the use of church registers. It is incontrovertible. Therefore, if County Limerick is all that is in records after immigration, the present strategy is imperative.

County	Civil Parish	Surname #1	Surname #2	Surname #3	Year	Source

The next part of the surname distribution survey is to identify sources with reasonable county-wide reports. The following are acceptable and can be limited to a precise county:

- Tithe Applotment (1823-1837)

- Griffith's Primary Valuation (1847-1864)

- Church Records Indexes (varies but typically indexed through 1900)

- Civil Registration Indexes (all births, marriages, deaths from 1864)

- 1901 and 1911 Irish Censuses

In the foregoing examples, if the family was not deemed to have been of the class that held leases or left behind wills for estates, the sources have to be tailored to reflect its social status, perhaps that of a poor tenant farmer. Remember, even if the ancestors were gone for decades, these sources can confine the search to a few civil parishes within the county.

Emigrations during and after the Potato Famine (1847-1851) were not necessarily in groups. Individuals left as well to join people who had already emigrated, called a chain migration, which was customary in the 1800s. In the migrations of groups, scouring the records of the immigrant country for people who came with the ancestors is the goal. In cases of chain migrations, the object is identifying the people whom the emigrants joined in the new country. Clues in the immigrant country can be numerous, among which are: with whom they associated, who witnessed their marriages, and who the godparents to their children were. Once those names are gathered, how common the surname is in the Irish county does not matter because the distribution search can indicate the area. The chart for the results could be similar to the one below at the bottom of the page and be adjusted where needed.

Once a pattern takes shape for where surnames are distributed throughout that county, the appropriate records can be searched. If a civil parish or even a townland is projected, the investigation can extend to identifying the area's landlord, whose family estate papers can be explored for any rent books. The records may list who left the estate. Even if they do not, other sources could. For example, search graveyards in the region for any "who went where" inscriptions on tombstones, which were placed either by the families who stayed or from funds of the families overseas. These memorials are traditional throughout Ireland. Engraved information about emigrants and their residences abroad is on the plaques or tombstones.

County	Civil Parish	Townland	Surname #1	Surname #2	Year	Source

When deliberating whether the ancestral place of origin has been found, perform a surname distribution search in reverse. Go to a source such as Griffith's Primary Valuation and make an inventory of the surnames in the specified townland and its surrounding townlands to test whether any of them appear with the ancestor in the immigrant country. Remember to consider a chain migration in which one or more people leave to join others, and then more join them. A chain migration can last for decades because people had firmly established destinations. This approach has been successful for researchers and can confirm the evidence from the original distribution search.

Given Name Distribution

The identical strategy can be applied to given names if they are unusual by omitting the surname or combining those given names with the surname in question. The idea is that an unusual given name derived from one of the ancestors continued to be passed down through different branches of the family regardless of the surnames. In this distribution search, a county may or may not be known, and how common the last name is does not matter because the emphasis is on the uncharacteristic first name. Certainly, Archibald is less ordinary than Patrick, and Giles is less so than Thomas.

The drawback to the procedure, depending on the record source, is that it may be mainly restricted to male given names. More men were taxable than women. More singular female names can be discovered in the indexes of church and civil records. The difficulty is whether the various databases require surnames for searches. Some websites do, and some do not. Almost all databases on Ancestry.com and FamilySearch.org are conducive to searches by first names only. In fact, for various ethnic groups throughout the world, aside from the Irish, cases are solved by the first names!

Any source can be used to isolate odd given names. If they appear in the databases, note them for special consideration. To verify a pattern, a second surname is always helpful but not always necessary in this distribution study. Correlating the findings could look similar to the sample shown at the bottom of the page.

Although the emphasis is on the unique given name, the surnames are important as well. By making a list of the surnames associated with the given name being sought, some of them may be familiar from the immigrant records. They are excellent clues about the places in Ireland requiring a researcher's special attention.

County	Civil Parish	Townland	Given Name	Surname	Year	Source

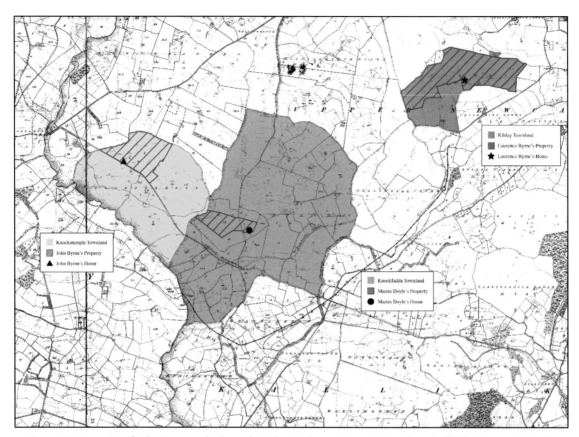

Figure 79: Homesite of John Byrne and others platted on Ordnance Survey Maps from Griffith's Primary Valuation records. (Image courtesy of Brian Barton. Permissions received.)

					Total, .	417	3	16	101	18	0	4	19	0	106	17	0
KNOCKATEMPLE. (Ord. S. 18.)																	
1	Andrew W. Byrne,	.	In fee,	. .	Houses, offices, & land,	135	2	37	50	0	0	1 15 0 / 3 5 0			} 55	0	0
2	John Byrne,	.	Andrew W. Byrne,	.	House, offices, and land,	73	2	16	25	10	0	1	15	0	27	5	0
3	George Plunkett,	.	Same,	.	House, offices, and land,	113	2	11	47	10	0	1	15	0	49	5	0
4	William Byrne,	.	Same,	.	House, offices, and land,	126	1	6	42	10	0	2	15	0	45	5	0
					Total, .	449	0	30	165	10	0	11	5	0	176	15	0
KNOCKRAHEEN. (Ord. S. 18.)																	
1	John Kelly,	.	Rev. Henry Kehoe,	.	House, offices, and land,	64	0	34	18	10	0	6	10	0	25	0	0
2	John Connolly,	.	Same,	.	House, office, and land,	2	2	0	0	15	0	0	10	0	1	5	0
3 A	Patrick Carr,	.	Same,	.	Land, . .	11	2	28	1	0	0	—			} 18 15 0		
— B					House, offices, and land,	15	2	39	4	15	0	0	10	0			
— C					Land, . .	41	1	20	12	10	0	—					
4 A	Rev. Henry Kehoe,	.	In fee,	. .	Land (p'antation),	20	0	22	5	0	0	—			} 9 10 0		
— B					Land, . .	0	3	0	0	12	0	—					
— C					Land (p'antation),	7	2	0	2	0	0	—					
— D					Land (plantation),	2	0	0	1	0	0	—					
— E					Land (bog),	4	2	38	0	5	0	—					
— F					Land (plantation),	4	1	15	0	13	0	—					
5 A	Michael Keenan,	.	Rev. Henry Kehoe,		House, offices, and land,	18	0	20	8	5	0	1	0	0	} 10 0 0		
— B					Land, . .	10	0	12	0	15	0	—					
6	Patrick Burke, .	.	Same,	.	House, offices, and land,	29	1	13	10	15	0	1	5	0	12	0	0
7 A	Walter Butler, .	.	Thomas Hugo,	.	Land, . .	27	1	8	7	0	0	—			} 35 10 0		
— B					House, offices, and land,	62	2	0	26	10	0	2	0	0			
8	Patrick Butler, .	.	Same,	.	House, offices, and land,	45	3	33	16	10	0	1	10	0	18	0	0
9	Michael Connolly,	.	Same,	.	House, offices, and land,	68	2	31	22	10	0	1	15	0	24	5	0
10	John Byrne,	.	Same,	.	House, offices, and land,	72	2	15	26	0	0	1	0	0	27	0	0

Figure 80: Griffith's Primary Valuation records of 1854 for John Byrne of Knockatemple, Calary Parish, County Wicklow, Ireland. (Image courtesy of Brian Barton. Permissions received.)

Chapter Twenty-One

Special Strategy: Finding the Ancestral Homesite

Although most of the Irish pedigrees, whether Catholic or Protestant, end in the registers of the late 1700s or early 1800s, the ultimate objectives of innumerable family historians are finding living relatives in Ireland and locating the ancestors' homesites. Many hope to discover the old houses still standing, the concrete links to their searches. Some are satisfied connecting with distant relatives worldwide through DNA, but the associations do not offer the gratification of visiting homesites, seeing what the ancestors saw, and walking where the ancestors walked.

For those ancestors who left in the 1600s or 1700s, the goal may have to be adjusted, but the basic and common questions, even if not asked consciously, are shared by many people: What did these ancestors experience? Why did they leave? How has this affected the family through the generations?

Research in the 1700s

In the 1700s, unless a family was landed or was of the class for which documents were registered, chances of finding papers for an ancestor or a homesite in Ireland and Northern Ireland are slim. Many Protestant gentry families have pedigrees on file somewhere, and their manor houses often have survived. Quaker and Moravian families also were good record keepers. Nineteenth-century Mormon immigrants are exceptions as well because after emigrating, the religion had them submit their genealogies, which can date into the 1700s. For families who were of the class to be small leaseholders, frequently for "three lives," some amazing documentation is in the Registry of Deeds. However, for the majority of tenant farmers, the situation is problematic.

Nevertheless, expectations should not be abandoned. Instead, research has to turn to "who went where," which can disclose some previously unexpected avenues for identifying homesites. For example, do the records of a man or a woman who was transported as a convict to Australia contain a birthplace? If so, the descendants of his or her siblings who might have gone to Canada, the United States, or South Africa would be intrigued with those same transportation and prison documents. In a circumstance such as transportation, historical context must be considered. When the American colonies closed as removal grounds for the prisoners and the undesirables during the American Revolutionary War (1775-1783), what is now Australia became their destination of exile beginning in 1788. Remember that the other siblings who were not convicted had the same birthplace as the one who was transported.

The transportation example is but one immigrant strategy that can help with the lack of comprehensive records from which to document most of the population in the 1700s. It does not mean a homesite can be found, but a townland of origin can certainly be identified through several approaches. The same methods can apply to any country with Irish immigrants in the 1700s. Keep in mind the history and create a plan for the family being researched.

The surname distribution survey, which is conventional in Irish research and is mentioned several times in this book, is usually the only avenue left for many research cases of the 1700s. It does require perusing records that might have been taken a century after the ancestors left, especially Griffith's Primary Valuation (1847-1864), but never forget the basic theory behind this well-trodden design. Not everyone emigrated, and thus siblings and cousins stayed behind through the generations. They might never have left the ancestral homesite. Therefore, identifying where surnames, preferably multiple surnames, occur in a pattern leads to where the ancestors originated, bringing researchers near the homesite itself. It is dependent, though, on whether a branch of the family remained in the townland after the ancestors departed in the 1700s.

A DNA match can be of assistance in the quest, but accumulating the paper trail to tie back into it may be another matter. Yet, once all other plans are exhausted, including the worldwide immigration strategy, general DNA results may be all that are left to explore.

Research in the 1800s

Research in the 1800s is quite unlike that in the 1700s because of when records began and continued. The average church, Catholic or Protestant, started registering ceremonies in the 1820s or 1830s. Tax assessment lists were compiled in earnest beginning with Tithe Applotment (1823-1837) and Griffith's Valuation (1847-1864). The Civil Registrations that documented Protestant marriages were initiated in 1845, and registrations for all births, marriages, and deaths, in 1864.

Even with the advent of record keeping, scores of inconsistencies and considerations persist, which is what much of this and other instruction books address. Perhaps the major issue is that not all church records are complete, not everyone was named in a tax list, and even though civil marriages are almost inclusive, the births and deaths are not. Consequently, a search for the homesite, even when the place is known, can be as difficult in the 1800s' research as it is in the 1700s. It is unpredictable until the records are read or the absence of records is determined.

218 .. PRIMARY VALUATION OF TENEMENTS.

PARISH OF WHITECHURCH.

No. and Letters of Reference to Map.		Names.		Description of Tenement.	Area.			Net Annual Value.		
		Townlands and Occupiers.	Immediate Lessors.					Land.	Buildings.	Total.
					A.	R.	P.	£ s. d.	£ s. d.	£ s. d.
		BALLYGAMBON, LOWER —continued.								
—	b	James Cluggers,	Arthur O'Reilly,	House and garden,	0	0	23	0 3 0	0 14 0	0 17 0
—	c	James Ryan,	Arthur O'Reilly.	House.				—	0 12 0	0 12 0
3	a	Michael Keating,	Lord Stuart De Decies.	House, office, and land,	5	3	15	5 15 0	1 5 0	7 0 0
—	b	National School,	Board of Education,	House and garden,	0	1	14	0 5 0	4 0 0	4 5 0
—	c	James Flynn,	Lord Stuart De Decies,	Teachers' house & gar.	0	0	29	0 3 0	1 17 0	2 0 0
4	a	Patrick Mangan,	John Whelan,	House, office, and land,	2	0	17	2 0 0	1 0 0	3 0 0
—	b	Thomas Dee,	Patrick Mangan,	House and garden,	0	3	13	0 12 0	0 18 0	1 10 0
5		Eleanor Roche,	John Whelan,	House, office, and land,	2	2	19	2 10 0	0 15 0	3 5 0
6	a	Michael Condon,	Lord Stuart De Decies,	House, office, and land,	11	0	29	11 5 0	1 10 0	12 15 0
—	b	Michael Walsh,	Lord Stuart De Decies,	House and land,	0	2	24	0 11 0	0 14 0	1 5 0
—	c	—— Morrissy,	Michael Walsh,	House.				—	0 8 0	0 8 0
—	d	John Colbert,	Michael Walsh,	House and garden,	0	0	27	0 3 0	0 14 0	0 17 0
7	a	John Healy,	John Whelan,	House, office, and land,	3	0	29	3 0 0	1 0 0	4 0 0
—	b	Thomas Lynch,	John Whelan,	House,				—	0 15 0	0 15 0
—		John Whelan,	Lord Stuart De Decies,	Garden,	0	0	26	0 3 0	—	0 3 0
				Total,	212	0	30	197 2 0	35 7 0	232 9 0
				Exemptions: National School-house and garden,	0	1	14	0 5 0	4 0 0	4 5 0
				Total, exclusive of Exemptions,	211	3	16	196 17 0	31 7 0	228 4 0
		BALLYGAMBON, UPPER. (Ord. S. 30.)								
1		Mrs. Catherine Quinlan,	Lord Stuart De Decies,	Land,	172	2	16	81 10 0	—	81 10 0
—	a	Johanna Stack,	Mrs. Catherine Quinlan,	House and garden,	0	2	17	0 6 0	0 8 0	0 14 0
—	b	Richard Dunne,	Mrs. Catherine Quinlan,	House and garden,	0	1	29	0 5 0	0 8 0	0 13 0
—	c	Michael Ronayne,	Mrs. Catherine Quinlan,	House,				—	0 8 0	0 8 0
—	d	Margaret Morrissy,	Mrs. Catherine Quinlan,	House and garden,	0	1	11	0 3 0	0 15 0	0 18 0
—	e	Bridget Barry,	Mrs. Catherine Quinlan,	House,				—	0 14 0	0 14 0
—	f	Thomas Costin,	Mrs. Catherine Quinlan,	House and garden,	0	2	7	0 5 0	0 10 0	0 15 0
—	g	John Cooney,	Mrs. Catherine Quinlan,	House and garden,	0	1	26	0 5 0	0 10 0	0 15 0
—	h	Michael Regan,	Mrs. Catherine Quinlan,	House and garden,	0	1	22	0 3 0	0 10 0	0 13 0
—	i	Patrick Wallace,	Mrs. Catherine Quinlan,	House and garden,	0	0	22	0 1 0	0 14 0	0 15 0
2		Garrett Meade,	Mrs. Catherine Quinlan,	House, offices, and land,	9	0	21	3 5 0	1 0 0	4 5 0
3 A — B		Richard Connell,	Mrs. Catherine Quinlan,	House, office, & land,	3 10	0 2	17 15	1 5 0 5 0 0	0 15 0	7 0 0
4		Richard Brian,	Lord Stuart De Decies,	House, office, and land,	22	3	37	10 5 0	1 0 0	11 5 0
5		Richard Brian,	Mrs. Catherine Quinlan,	Land,	3	0	5	1 15 0	—	1 15 0
—	a	John Tiernan,	Mrs. Catherine Quinlan,	House and garden,	0	3	30	0 10 0	0 10 0	1 0 0
6		John Doosey,	Lord Stuart De Decies,	House, office, and land,	28	1	37	14 15 0	1 10 0	16 5 0
7		John Hearne,	Lord Stuart De Decies,	House, office, and land,	31	0	25	12 10 0	1 5 0	13 15 0
				Total,	284	3	17	132 3 0	10 17 0	143 0 0
		BALLYHANE. (Ord. S. 22 & 30.)								
1	a	Thomas Nugent,	Beresford Power, Esq.	House, offices, orchard, and land,	133	0	33	90 10 0	7 10 0	98 0 0
—	b	Simon Shruffane,	Thomas Nugent,	House,				—	0 8 0	0 8 0
				Total,	133	0	33	90 10 0	7 18 0	98 8 0
		BALLYKENNEDY. (Ord. S. 30.)								
1	a	Edmund Scanlan,	Florence M'Carthy, Esq.	House, orchard, & land,	59	2	26	68 0 0	5 10 0	73 10 0
—	b	Bridget Molloney,	Florence M'Carthy, Esq.	House,				—	0 7 0	0 7 0
—	c	John Colbert,	Edmund Scanlan,	House,				—	0 7 0	0 7 0

Figure 81: 1854 Griffith's Primary Valuation for Michael Condon of Ballygambon Lower, Whitechurch Parish, County Waterford, Ireland. (Image courtesy of Brian Barton. Permissions received.)

In general, the chief aspiration of Irish genealogy is the identification of an ancestor or a family member in Griffith's Primary Valuation. Not only were heads of households listed but also "map reference numbers" showed the locations of the houses and properties on period maps. Roads might or might not have changed over the past 150 years, but the landscapes are similar. Correlating the old period maps with modern maps is possible so that the sites can be visited.

Steps to doing this are distinct and depend on finding the ancestor or a relative who stayed in the house appearing as a taxable in Griffith's Primary Valuation. Assuming that has been accomplished and a townland within the Poor Law Union and civil parish have been found, the following are recommendations for proceeding:

Step 1: Find the ancestor or at least the homesite as a "map reference number" in Griffith's Primary Valuation.

Step 2: Use Askaboutireland.ie to view a period Griffith's Map that accompanied the tax lists and consult modern road and satellite maps for what is there today. Askaboutireland.ie includes both the Republic of Ireland and Northern Ireland. If a researcher is fortunate, Maps.google.com will have a street view.

Step 3: To verify what became of the property between Griffith's and the modern satellite view, consult the revision books to Griffith's. When individuals were no longer responsible for the taxes, their names were crossed off and the new names and years were inserted. For Northern Ireland, the series of tax

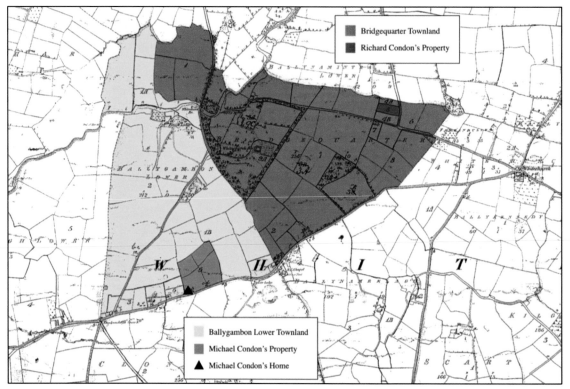

Figure 82: Platting the homesites of Michael Condon and Richard Condon based on information from Griffith's Primary Valuation (see Figure 80 on page 265 for example of Michael Condon). (Image courtesy of Brian Barton. Permissions received.)

booklets are on the PRONI website and can be accessed by townland name and then the property number within it. The collection online, digitized on the FamilySearch.org website, dates from at least 1864 through the 1930s, but the archival collection continues into 1993.

For the Republic of Ireland counties, the revision books can be read at the Valuation Office, Dublin, which accepts its share of genealogy requests for revision books and map research. Its records for research can extend into the 1990s. The revision books for the Republic of Ireland are on microfilm at the Family History Library and on the Family History Library catalog online under Ireland/County/Taxation/Poor Law Union name.

Step 4: Once a history of the property has been reconstructed, including whether the property is still in family hands, a trip can be planned with some background and insight.

The process, although ostensibly complex at first, is relatively simple once its logic is understood. While in the tax lists, whether Griffith's or the revision books, make sure to note all others with the same surname and trace them. When onsite and placing inquiries, the information collected will help arrange and locate everyone by dates.

When visiting onsite, questions are indispensable. Among them should be versions of the following:

- Where were the people who lived here in the 1800s buried? It might not have been in the parish graveyard! The old cemetery may be among some church ruins or enclosed in the middle of a cow pasture.

- Has anyone else been here asking questions about this property? If so, please share the address. Branches of the family around the world are doing the same family history, and they may know something new. The New Zealand branch of the family might have arrived at the homesite two years before.

- Who in the community could know something about the families who lived in this townland?

- If living relatives are found, always ask, Do you have pictures or old letters from the emigrants?

- The last but most significant question should be, May I take pictures?

Linking Property in Griffith's with the Tithe

When the family property is identified in Griffith's Primary Valuation (1847-1864), a worthy goal is to attempt to trace the property back in time to the Tithe

Applotment Composition Books (1823-1837). Skilled researchers are aware of the uses and limitations of the Tithe Books. The purpose is to glean the most from them, but they are not always straightforward and are frustrating when they are not.

One major obstacle is finding a family in Griffith's but not in the Tithe. At the least, it presents a demanding task. A generation or sometimes two can easily separate who was in Griffith's from who was on the family property in the Tithe. The key to understanding and linking generations between the two sources is a working knowledge of English acres and Irish acres and how the Ordnance Survey standardized townlands. Irish acres and English acres are not equal, the reason the acres in Griffith's and the Tithe are not necessarily alike.

In comparing the Tithe acres to the Griffith's acres, a few principles are essential to review:

1. Griffith's Primary Valuation was always taken in English acres, the measurement still in use in countries such as the United States. This measurement of property does not vary in the records unless land was added, deleted, or a more exacting survey was conducted in the area.

2. In Griffith's, the names of the townlands, spellings, and the amounts of acres, roods, and perches (usually seen as A-R-P) were set by the mid-1830s. These were government designations, not inevitably the

addresses the locals adapted. Differences are often reflected in church or other records in Ireland, and, therefore, do not always expect an immigrant record or even an Irish church record to correspond with the standardized Griffith's.

3. The Tithe was taken during the period when the Ordnance Survey was standardizing the names and boundaries of Irish townlands. Consequently, always check the area of a townland in both the Tithe and Griffith's. If they do not match, realize that the Tithe was given in Irish acres, and sometimes the Tithe book states Irish (Plantation) acres.

4. Townlands were divided and even discontinued by the Ordnance Survey in the 1830s, and so do not assume that a Griffith's townland is in the Tithe. If it is not, compare surnames from Griffith's to where it was in the Tithe of the civil parish. In the Tithe, it probably was in what became neighboring townlands by the years of Griffith's Primary Valuation, and thus the explanation is the creation and discontinuance of townlands between the two tax lists. Websites such as Townlands.ie and Askaboutireland.ie can aid in the scopes of the townlands from the 1830s forward.

5. The Tithe was not as complete as Griffith's in listing heads of households. The Tithe was

mostly rural, although villages and small towns were enumerated. Griffith's included all heads of households unless they were exempt, such as people living in company lodgings or working and living on landlords' immediate properties.

The key to utilizing any of the foregoing information is the conversion of Irish acres and English acres. **1 Irish acre = 1.62 English acres.** In short, an old Irish acre is just over one and one-half times bigger than an English acre. Accordingly, multiply the number of acres found in Griffith's by 1.62. It is easier to round off the total by ignoring any roods and perches. Calculations do not have to be exact because the attempt is to establish patterns and possibilities.

Once the computation has been made, ask: Where was the ancestor located in the Tithe? Or was the previous generation on the property? The answer to the latter question can extend the line another generation back, to before the advent of most parish registers.

The outcome of the effort should be rewarding. For most families, the experiences of setting their feet on their ancestors' homesites are the fulfillments of years of paperwork. They are conclusions of natural longings, as though reaching beloved homes after arduous journeys.

Figure 83: Remnants of Michael Condon's original homesite in Ballygambon Lower, Whitechurch Parish, County Waterford, Ireland. (Photograph courtesy of Dwight A. Radford. Permissions received.)

INDEX